T0159260

THE hot&spicy COOKBOOK

THE
hot&spicy
COOKBOOK

Over 325 sizzling dishes from the Caribbean, Mexico, Africa, the Middle
East, India and Thailand, shown in 1250 photographs

EDITOR: JENNI FLEETWOOD

LORENZ BOOKS

This edition is published by greene&golden, an imprint of Anness Publishing Ltd, Blaby Road, Wigston, Leicestershire LE18 4SE; info@anness.com

www.annesspublishing.com

If you like the images in this book and would like to investigate using them for publishing, promotions or advertising, please visit our website www.practicalpictures.com for more information.

Publisher: Joanna Lorenz
Project Editor: Lucy Doncaster
Editor: Joy Wotton
Consultant Editor: Jenni Fleetwood
Designer: Nigel Partridge
Production Controller: Steve Lang
Recipes contributed by: Pepita Aris, Catherine Atkinson, Alex Barker, Judy Bastyra, Angela Boggiano, Carla Capalbo, Kit Chan, Maxine Clark, Jacqueline Clarke, Trish Davies, Roz Denny, Patrizia Diemling, Matthew Drennan, Tessa Evelegh, Joanna Farrow, Rafi Fernandez, Christine France, Silvano Franco, Sarah Gates, Shirley Gill, Brian Glover, Rosamund Grant, Nicola Graimes, Deh-Ta Hsuing, Shehzad Husain, Christine Ingram, Becky Johnson, Manisha Kanani, Lucy Knox, Lesley Mackley, Sally Mansfield, Norma Miller, Jane Milton, Sallie Morris, Annie Nichols, Elisabeth Lambert Ortiz, Jennie Shapter, Marlena Spieler, Liz Trigg, Hilarie Walden, Laura Washburn, Pamela Westland, Steven Wheeler, Judy Williams, Jeni Wright

ETHICAL TRADING POLICY
Because of our ongoing ecological investment programme, you, as our customer, can have the pleasure and reassurance of knowing that a tree is being cultivated on your behalf to naturally replace the materials used to make the book you are holding. For further information about this scheme, go to www.annesspublishing.com/trees

Previously published as part of a larger volume, *Red Hot! A Cook's Encyclopedia of Fire and Spice*

NOTES

• Bracketed terms are intended for American readers.
• For all recipes, quantities are given in both metric and imperial measures and, where appropriate, in standard cups and spoons. Follow one set of measures, not a mixture, because they are not interchangeable.
• Standard spoon and cup measures are level. 1 tsp = 5ml, 1 tbsp = 15ml, 1 cup = 250ml/8fl oz.
• Australian standard tablespoons are 20ml. Australian readers should use 3 tsp in place of 1 tbsp for measuring small quantities of gelatine, flour, salt, etc.
• American pints are 16fl oz/2 cups. American readers should use 20fl oz/2.5 cups in place of 1 pint when measuring liquids.
• Electric oven temperatures in this book are for conventional ovens. When using a fan oven, the temperature will probably need to be reduced by about 10–20°C/20–40°F. Since ovens vary, you should check with your manufacturer's instruction book for guidance.
• The nutritional analysis given for each recipe is calculated per portion (i.e. serving or item), unless otherwise stated. If the recipe gives a range, such as Serves 4–6, then the nutritional analysis will be for the smaller portion size, i.e. 6 servings. Measurements for sodium do not include salt added to taste.
• Medium (US large) eggs are used unless otherwise stated.

The consultant editor would like to thank chilli grower Michael Michaud and Christine McFadden, fellow members of the Guild of Food Writers, for sharing their knowledge of and enthusiasm for chillies. Michael and Joy Michaud are market gardeners, and from July to December each year they can supply fresh chillies by mail order. Contact them at Peppers by Post, Sea Spring Farm, West Bexington, Dorchester, Dorset DT2 9DD, UK, tel: 01308 897892; http://www.peppersbypost.biz/

PUBLISHER'S NOTE

Although the advice and information in this book are believed to be accurate and true at the time of going to press, neither the authors nor the publisher can accept any legal responsibility or liability for any errors or omissions that may have been made nor for any inaccuracies nor for any loss, harm or injury that comes about from following instructions or advice in this book.

CONTENTS

INTRODUCTION

There's a ring of fire encircling the globe, and it has nothing to do with volcanic activity. This is fire we're very much in favour of: the warmth that comes from red hot chilli peppers. These powerful little pods originated in South America, but now form a very important part of many of the world's major cuisines.

India is the largest producer and exporter of chillies, with much of the crop used for local consumption. Thailand, Mexico, Japan, Turkey, Nigeria, Ethiopia, Uganda, Kenya and Tanzania are also prime producers, exporting chillies to other countries around the globe.

The word chilli is spelt in different ways. Sometimes it is chile, sometimes chili, sometimes chilli pepper. This last description is accurate insofar as it recognizes that chillies are members of the *Capsicum* family, like the sweet peppers. It also forms a link with all those spicy powders – chilli, cayenne and paprika – which are an essential part of many national dishes.

WHAT'S IN A NAME?

The great explorer Columbus was responsible for confusing chillies with peppers. When he set sail in 1492, hoping to find a sea route to the spice islands, it was a source of black pepper (*Piper nigrum*) he was seeking.

Not only did he fail to find his intended destination, discovering instead the Caribbean island of San Salvador (now Watling Island), but he also made the incorrect assumption that the hot spice flavouring the local food was black pepper. By the time it was realized that the fleshy pods of a fruit were responsible, rather than tiny black peppercorns, it was too late.

Below: Mexican chillies, clockwise from top left: small green chillies, chipotle chillies, mulato chillies, dried habanero chillies, pasilla chillies, green (bell) peppers, green jalapeño chillies, Anaheim chillies, and (centre left) Scotch bonnets, (centre right) red chillies.

Above: Chillies form an important part of many of the world's major cuisines.

The Spanish called the flavouring pimiento (pepper) and the name stuck, and it has led to confusion ever since.

It was the Aztecs who coined the name chilli. Like the Mayas and Incas, they were greatly enamoured of the brightly coloured fruit that had originated in the rainforests of South America, and used chillies both as food and for medicinal purposes. When the Spanish invaded Mexico in 1509, they found many different varieties of both fresh and dried chilli on sale at the market at Tenochtitlan and still more being cultivated in Montezuma's botanical gardens at Huaxtepec.

Mexico remains a mecca for chilli-lovers, with every region having its own special varieties. Chillies are valued for their heat and for their flavour, and accomplished Mexican cooks will often use several different types – fresh and dried – in a single dish.

A CHAIN OF CHILLIES

Columbus is credited with introducing chillies to Europe, bringing back "peppers of many kinds and colours" when he returned to Europe in 1493. Soon after this, Vasco da Gama succeeded in finding the sea route to the spice islands. By the middle of the 16th century, a two-way trade had been established. Spices such as nutmeg, cinnamon and black pepper were brought to Europe from the East, and chillies and other plants from the New World went to Asia.

The spice trade created a culinary explosion, and the chilli rapidly became an important ingredient in the food of

*Above: Chillies in all their different guises
add both flavour and heat to many
kinds of dishes. Here, they are shown
fresh and dried, preserved in oil and
ground into rich and fragrant powders.*

Below: Asian chillies

South-east Asia, India and China.
Portuguese and Arab traders introduced
it to Africa. It was enthusiastically
adopted, and when West African slaves
were taken to the Southern States of
America to work the cotton plantations,
the chillies that were part of their diet
went with them.

THE CHILLI IN EUROPE

Although parts of Europe adopted the
chilli with great enthusiasm, universal
acceptance has been relatively slow.
Spain and Portugal use chillies quite
extensively, which is not surprising,
given the influence of those early
explorers, but in France their use is
limited to a few signature dishes, like
the fiery rouille traditionally served
with bouillabaisse.

It used to be the case that the further
north you went, the less likely you
would be to encounter chilli dishes. All
this is changing, however, as Asian food
becomes increasingly popular. Don't be
surprised if you encounter chilli lollipops
(popsicles) or chilli ice cream. The
flavour of chillies can be subtle as well
as strident, and their affinity for fruit
means that, used judiciously, they can
make as valuable a contribution to fruit
salads as they do to salsas and spicy
Mexican dishes.

In response to public demand, most
supermarkets stock chillies. Chillies are
easy to grow, and many gardeners enjoy
cultivating and then cooking them.

Chillies are Good for You
An excellent source of vitamin C,
chillies also yield beta carotene,
folate, potassium and vitamin E.
They stimulate the appetite and
improve circulation, but can
irritate the stomach if eaten to
excess. Chillies are also a
powerful decongestant, and can
help to clear blocked sinuses.

THE CHILLI FAMILY

There are more than two hundred different types of chilli, all members of the nightshade *(solanaceae)* family, like tomatoes and potatoes. Most of those used for culinary purposes belong to the genus *Capsicum annuum*. These were originally thought to be annuals, which explains the name, but can be perennial when cultivated in the tropics. The plants grow to a height of 1m/1yd, and chillies of this type include jalapeños, cayennes, Anaheim chillies and poblanos, as well as the common sweet (bell) peppers.

Tabasco chillies and the very hot Punjab chillies belong to a group called *Capsicum frutescens*, while Scotch bonnets and habaneros – the fragrant hot chillies that look like tam-o'-shanters – are *Capsicum chinense*. Some of the largest chilli plants are *Capsicum baccatum*. Ajis fall into this category, as do peri-peri chillies. Finally, there is a small group called *Capsicum pubescens*. The most notable chilli in this group is the manzano. The name means "apple", and these chillies resemble crab apples in size and shape.

Unless you grow chillies or are lucky enough to live near a farmer's market that features these flavoursome ingredients, you are unlikely to encounter more than a few of the more common varieties, such as serranos, jalapeños

Below: Chillies are members of the nightshade (solanaceae) *family, like tomatoes and potatoes.*

Above: Capsicum chinense is the genus in which fragrant hot chillies such as habaneros are included.

and cayennes, and even these may not be identified as such. Supermarkets have a habit of limiting their labelling to the obvious, like "red chillies" or – one step better – "hot red chillies".

This raises another issue. How do you know whether a chilli is hot or not? Are small chillies hotter than big ones? Or red chillies hotter than green? The answer to the last two questions is no. Although some of the world's hottest chillies are tiny, there are some large varieties that are real scorchers. Colour isn't an infallible indicator either. Most chillies start out green and ripen to red, but some start yellow and become red, and yet others start yellow and stay yellow, and across the spectrum you'll find hot varieties. To confuse the issue still further, chillies on the same plant can have different degrees of heat, and in at least one type of chilli, the top of the fruit is hotter than the bottom. Fortunately for those of us who like to have some warning as to whether the contents of our shopping basket will be fragrant or fiery, there are rating systems for the heat in chillies. The best known of these grades chillies in Scoville units. Until relatively recently, the world's hottest chilli was reckoned to be the Mexican red savina habanero, which scores 557,000 on the Scoville

scale, but a new contender, the tezpur chilli, has been discovered in India. The tezpur registers a blistering 855,000 Scoville units, and is so hot that it is said to have triggered heart attacks in the unwary or novice taster. Scoville units are useful when it comes to fine comparisons such as these, but working with units measured in this way can be unwieldy. For general classification, a simpler system, which rates chillies out of ten, is more often used.

What makes one chilli hotter than another is the amount of the chemical capsaicin contained in the seeds and fibrous white lining. Apart from producing anything from a tingle to a tidal wave of heat, capsaicin also contributes to the feel-good factor by stimulating the brain to produce hormones called endorphins.

A less appealing aspect to capsaicin is that it is an irritant, and can cause severe burning to delicate parts of the face (and other parts of the anatomy) with which it comes into contact. It is therefore vital to handle chillies with care. Wear gloves while preparing them, or cut them up using a knife and fork. If you do handle chillies directly, wash your hands thoroughly in soapy water immediately afterwards (capsaicin does not dissolve in water alone) or use vegetable oil to remove any residue.

THE BURNING QUESTION

If you bite into a chilli that is unpleasantly hot, don't drink a glass of water. That will only spread the discomfort around your mouth making the burning sensation much worse. Instead, try one of these simple solutions:
• Take a large drink of creamy milk, hold it in your mouth for a minute or so, then spit it out discreetly. Repeat as necessary.
• A similar effect can be achieved with water or ice cream, as long as you do not swallow it.
• Eat a piece of fresh bread, a cooked potato or some rice. These will absorb the offending capsaicin oil.

NAMING THE CHILLI

You will find both fresh and dried chillies on sale. Dried chillies can be stored like other spices, and can be rehydrated with excellent results. Some chillies actually taste better when they have been dried. It is well worth getting to know as many different varieties as possible. Then, like a true aficionado, you can start blending several types for the ultimate in chilli pleasure.

The following descriptions of chillies are listed by their heat scale, with 10 being the hottest.

Anaheim

Heat scale 2–3: Their alternative name of "California long green" gives some idea of what these large chillies look like (they are also known as New Mexico). The pods are about 15cm/6in long and about 5cm/2in wide, making them good candidates for stuffing. The flavour is fresh and fruity, like a cross between tart apples and green (bell) peppers. Anaheim skins can be a bit tough, so these chillies are best roasted and peeled. The dried chillies are used to make a mild chilli powder.

Below: Ancho chillies

Ancho

Heat scale 3: Dried poblanos, these are larger than most other dried chillies. Open the packet and savour the wonderful fruity aroma – like dates or dried figs. After rehydration, anchos can be stuffed, and they also taste great sliced or chopped in stir-fries and similar dishes.

Guajillo

Heat scale 3: These dried chillies are about 15cm/6in long, with rough skin. The mature fresh pods are a deep reddish brown and have a smooth texture. It is thought they might be related to Anaheim chillies, as they have a similar look. They have a mild, slightly bitter flavour, suggestive of green tea. Guajillos are used in many classic salsas.

Italia

Heat scale 3: Juicy and refreshing, these dark green chillies ripen to a rich, dark red. They taste great in salads and have an affinity for tropical fruit, especially mangoes.

Below: Mulato chillies

Mulato

Heat scale 3: A dried chilli with a thin, wrinkled, dark brown skin, this is related to the ancho. The flavour is smoky and herby.

Poblano

Heat scale 3: Big and beautiful, poblanos look like sweet (bell) peppers, and are perfect for stuffing. They start off a deep green and ripen to a bright, clear red or rich, dark brown. The flavour is spicier than that of a sweet pepper, with peachy overtones. Poblanos taste wonderful with other chillies, whose flavour they appear to boost.

Below: Poblano chillies

Above: Anaheim chilli

Above: Guajillo chillies

*Below: Pasado
chillies*

Cherry Hot

Heat scale 4: Pungent, with thick walls, these chillies look like large versions of the fruit for which they are named. The skins can be tough, so they are best peeled. Cherry hot chillies have a sweetish flavour and make good pickles.

Below: Cherry hot chillies

Pasado

Heat scale 3–4: Very dark brown, skinny, dried chillies, these are generally about 10cm/4in long. When rehydrated, they taste lemony, with a hint of cucumber and apple. Pasados have an affinity for black beans, and make a fine salsa. Strips taste good on pizzas.

*Below: Cascabel
chillies*

Above: Fresno chillies

Fresno

Heat scale 5: Plump and cylindrical, with tapered ends, these fresh chillies are most often sold red, although you will sometimes find green or yellow ones in the shops. They look rather similar to jalapeños, and can be substituted for them if necessary.

Costeno Amarillo

Heat scale 4: Not to be confused with the much hotter aji amarillo, this is a pale orange dried chilli, which is ideal for use in yellow salsas and Mexican *mole* sauce. It has a citrus flavour and is often used to give depth to the flavour of soups and stews.

Pasilla

Heat scale 4: Open a packet of these deep purple dried chillies and the first thing you notice is their rich liquorice aroma. Quite large at about 15cm/6in length, pasillas have a spicy, fruity flavour that is good with shellfish, *moles* and mushrooms. Pureés made from rehydrated pasillas do not need to be sieved, as the skin is thin.

Cultivating Chillies

If you can grow tomatoes, then you'll be able to try your luck with chillies. They enjoy similar conditions, prefer higher temperatures, need watering more often and like slightly acid soils. You can grow them in tubs, hanging baskets or pots on the windowsill. Raise the plants under glass in spring, or buy them from a good plantsman. Plant out when frost is no longer a problem and the first flowers are visible. Water well in dry weather, mulch thickly and feed fortnightly with a high-potash fertilizer. Stake taller varieties. Pinch out growing tips if sideshoots are not being made and stop these once they have set fruit. During the growing season, watch for aphids, cutworms or slugs, and treat. Harvest about 12–16 weeks after planting out. Pull up plants and hang under glass in a sunny place when frost threatens to encourage the fruit to continue ripening.

Cascabel

Heat scale 4: The name translates as "little rattle", and refers to the sound the seeds make inside this round dried chilli. The woody, nutty flavour is best appreciated when the skin is removed. Soak them, then either scrape the flesh off the skin or sieve it. Cascabels are great in stews, soups and salsas.

Chilli Boost

For an instant lift, sprinkle some dried crushed chilli on your food.

*Above:
Pasilla chillies*

Above: Jalapeño chillies

Jalapeño

Heat scale 4–7: These are frequently seen in supermarkets. Plump and stubby, like fat fingers, they have shiny skins. They are sold at both the green and the red stage, although the former seem to be marginally more popular. Jalapeños have a piquant, grassy flavour, and are widely used in salsas, salads, dips and stews; they are also canned and bottled. Their fame is due to the fact that they are the best known and most commonly used chilli in Mexican food. A heat-free jalapeño has been developed in the US. Too thick-skinned to be sun-dried, jalapeños are generally smoke-dried and acquire a name change. In this form they are known as chipotle chillies.

Below: Pickled jalapeño chillies

Hungarian Wax Chillies

Heat scale 5: These really do look waxy, like novelty candles. Unlike many chillies, they start off yellow, not green. It is not necessary to peel them, and they are often used in salads and salsas.

Aji Amarillo

Heat scale 6–7: There are several different varieties of this chilli, including one that is yellow when fully ripe, and a large brown aji that is frequently dried. The chillies average about 10cm/4in in length and look rather like miniature windsocks. Red ajis originated in Peru, and were popular among the Incas.

Below: Cayenne chillies

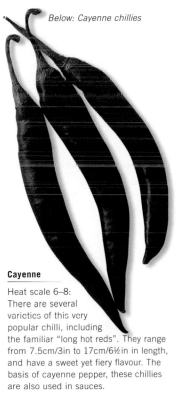

Cayenne

Heat scale 6–8: There are several varieties of this very popular chilli, including the familiar "long hot reds". They range from 7.5cm/3in to 17cm/6½in in length, and have a sweet yet fiery flavour. The basis of cayenne pepper, these chillies are also used in sauces.

Above: Chipotle chillies

Chipotle

Heat scale 6–10: This smoke-dried jalapeño has wrinkled, dark red skin and thick flesh. Chipotles need long, slow cooking to soften them and bring out their full flavour, which is hot and tasty with a deep intriguing smokiness.

Serrano

Heat scale 7: Usually sold green, these are small (about 4cm/1½in long) and quite slender. Serranos are the classic Mexican green chilli (*chiles verdes*), and are an important ingredient in guacamole. The flavour is clean and crisp, with a suggestion of citrus. Serranos are thin-skinned and do not need to be peeled. They dry well, but are seldom sold that way, although you may come across them occasionally for sale in a Mexican or Spanish market.

Above: Serrano chillies

Left: Bird's eye chillies

De Arbol

Heat scale 8: More often sold dried than fresh, these smooth cayenne-type chillies are slim and curvaceous. A warm orange-red, they are about 7.5cm/3in long. De arbols combine blistering heat with a clean, grassy flavour. Add them to soups or use to enliven vinegar or oil. Unlike most dried chillies, which must be soaked in hot water for 20–30 minutes before use, dry de arbol pods can be crumbled and added straight to stews or similar dishes. To reduce the heat, slit them and shake out the seeds first.

Above: Dried habanero chillies

reminds them of chardonnay wine; others that it is redolent of sun-warmed apricots. Don't sniff them too enthusiastically, however, and be ultra-cautious when handling habaneros, for they are excessively hot. Always wear strong gloves when preparing them, and don't stand over a food processor or blender when using them to make a paste, or the fumes may burn your face. When cooking with habaneros, a little goes a long way. They are very good with fruit and in salsas. Dried habaneros have medium-thick flesh and wrinkled skins. When rehydrated, they have a rich tropical-fruit flavour.

Bird's Eye

Heat scale 8: Small and extremely hot, these come from a highly volatile family of chillies that are found in Africa, Asia, the United States and the Caribbean, and often labelled simply as "Thai chillies". Thin-fleshed and explosively hot, they are sold green and red, often with the stems still attached. Dried, they are widely available in jars. They are called bird's eyes because they are much liked by mynah birds.

Below: Dried bird's eye chillies

Scotch Bonnets

Heat scale 10: Often confused with habaneros, which they closely resemble. Scotch bonnets are grown in Jamaica and are the principal ingredient of jerk seasoning.

Below: Scotch bonnet chillies

Above: Dried de arbol chillies

Manzano

Heat scale 9: This delicious chilli is very hot and fruity. About the size of a crab apple, it is the only chilli to have purple/black seeds.

Habanero

Heat scale 10: Don't imagine that intense heat is the only defining feature of this lantern-shaped chilli. Habaneros have a wonderful, fruity flavour, and a surprisingly delicate aroma. Some say it

Tiny Terrors

Thailand grows many different varieties of chillies.The smallest are so tiny they are popularly referred to as *prik kee noo* (mouse droppings). Use cautiously as they are fiery hot.

Use Scotch bonnets very cautiously as they are one of the hottest chillies. It is advisable to deseed them before use unless you can tolerate their intense and lingering flavour.

CHILLI PRODUCTS

Specialist shops, devoted to chillies and chilli products, are springing up all over the world. Alongside mugs, plates, bowls and aprons rioting with chilli motifs, you'll find an astonishing array of powders, pastes, sauces and oils.

POWDERS

Anything connected with chillies tends to be confusing, and chilli powder is no exception. The name suggests that this product is simply powdered chilli, but it is in fact a blend of several ingredients, designed specifically for making chilli con carne. In addition to ground hot chillies, it typically contains cumin, oregano, salt and garlic powder.

Pure powders – the whole chilli and nothing but the chilli – are less easy to come by, but are available from specialist shops and by mail order. Ancho, caribe and Anaheim (New Mexico) red powders are mild (heat scale 3). Pasilla, a rich, dark powder, registers 4 on the heat scale, while chipotle is a little hotter still.

Right: Chilli powder

Left: Ancho powder

Right: Pasilla powder

Left: Paprika

Right: Cayenne pepper

Convenient Chillies
Jars of whole chillies in white wine vinegar are handy for the home cook. Also look out for minced (ground) chillies. After opening, jars must be tightly closed, kept in the refrigerator and the contents consumed by the use-by date.

Cayenne pepper is a very fine ground powder from the *Capsicum frutescens* variety of chilli. The placenta (the fibrous white inner lining) and seeds are included, so it is very hot. Tiny amounts of cayenne are often added to cheese and egg dishes, and it is sprinkled over smoked fish and prawns (shrimp). It is also added to some curries.

Paprika is a fine, rich red powder made from mild chillies. The core and seeds are removed, but the flavour can still be quite pungent. Hungarians have adopted this as their national spice, but it is also widely used in Spanish and Portuguese cooking. Look out for *pimentón dulce*, a delicious smoked paprika from Estramadura in Spain.

Right: Crushed chilli flakes

CRUSHED CHILLIES

Dried chilli flakes are widely available. Italians call them *peperoncini* and add them to their famous arrabbiata sauce. Sprinkle them on pizzas or add to cooked dishes for a last-minute lift. Crushed dried green jalapeños are a useful pantry item, combining considerable heat with a delicious, melting sweetness.

CHILLI PASTE

It is worth keeping a few jars of ready-made chilli paste, such as harissa or *ras-el-hanout*, on your shelves. A hot chilli paste is quite easy to make at home. Simply seed fresh chillies, then purée them in a blender or food processor until smooth. Store small amounts in the refrigerator for up to 1 week, or freeze for up to 6 months. Chilli paste can also be made from dried chillies. Having rehydrated them, purée as for fresh chillies. You may have to sieve tough-skinned varieties.

Below: Hot chilli paste

Left: Red Tabasco sauce

Left: Green Tabasco sauce

CHILLI SAUCES

There are many varieties of these and the names appear to prove that chillies stimulate the imagination as well as the appetite. Some of the printable ones include Endorphin Rush, Lethal Weapon and Global Warming, along with the unforgettable Scorned Woman Hot Sauce.

The most famous chilli sauce, however, is Tabasco, developed in Louisiana by E. McIlhenny in the latter half of the 19th century. Chillies are matured in oak barrels to develop the sauce's unique flavour. Try mixing a few drops with fresh lime juice as a baste next time you grill salmon steaks, or add to sauces, soups or casseroles. Also available is Tabasco Jalapeño Sauce – often referred to as green Tabasco sauce. Milder in flavour than the red version, it is good with nachos, hamburgers or on pizza.

Chilli sauces are also widely used in Asia. Chinese chilli sauce is quite hot and spicy, with a hint of fruitiness thanks to the inclusion of apples or plums. For an even milder flavour, look out for sweet chilli sauce, which is a blend of red chillies, sugar and tamarind juice from Sichuan. There is also a thick Chinese sauce made solely from chillies and salt. This is usually sold in jars, and is much hotter than the bottled version. Vietnamese chilli sauce is very hot, while the Thai sauce tends to be thicker and more spicy. Bottled chilli sauces are used both for cooking and as a dip.

CHILLI OILS

Various types of chilli oil are on sale. Toss them with pasta, add a dash to a stir-fry, or drizzle them over pizzas.

Chilli oils also make a good basis for salad dressings. You can make your own chilli oil by heating chillies in oil, or use a ready-made mixture. Olive oil, flavoured with chipotle and de arbol chillies, with a hint of rosemary, is a particularly good blend. It can also be used for light cooking.

Chilli oil is seldom used for cooking in China and South-east Asia, but is a popular dipping sauce. Two types are widely sold. The first is a simple infusion of dried chillies, onions, garlic and salt in vegetable oil. The second, XO chilli oil, is flavoured with dried scallops and costs considerably more. Chilli oil has a pleasant smell, and a concentrated flavour, much stronger than chilli sauce. It is often drizzled over fish and shellfish just before serving. It should be used sparingly.

Below: Chilli oil

Above: Sweet chilli sauce (top) and chilli sauce

Chilli and Tomato Oil
Heating oil with chillies intensifies the rich flavour. This tastes great sprinkled over pasta.

1 Heat 150ml/¼ pint/⅔ cup olive oil in a pan. When it is very hot, but not smoking, stir in 10ml/2 tsp tomato purée (paste) and 15ml/1 tbsp dried red chilli flakes.

2 Leave to cool, then pour into an airtight jar and store in the refrigerator for up to 2 months.

CHOOSING, STORING AND EQUIPMENT

Below is some helpful advice on selecting and storing chillies and tips on equipment that will make their preparation simpler.

CHOOSING AND STORING CHILLIES

• When buying fresh chillies, apply the same criteria as when buying sweet (bell) peppers. The fruit should look bright and unblemished.
• Some chillies are naturally wrinkled when ripe, however, so a smooth skin is not essential.

Above: Chillies dried on string or canes will keep well for many months.

• Avoid any chillies that seem limp or dry, or that have bruising on the skin.
• In the supermarket, wrap your hand in a plastic bag when picking out chillies, or you may have an unpleasant surprise if you later touch your face.
• To store chillies, wrap them in kitchen paper, place in a plastic bag and keep in the salad compartment of the refrigerator for a week or more.
• Chillies can also be frozen. There is no need to blanch them if you plan to use them fairly soon.
• Frozen chillies are a huge boon to the busy cook, as they can be sliced when only partially thawed, and crushed with garlic and ginger to make a fragrant spice paste.
• To dry chillies, thread them on a string, hang them in a warm place until dry, then crush them and store in a sealed jar.

EQUIPMENT

Gloves may not seem obvious pieces of equipment, but they are invaluable for the dedicated chilli cook. The fine disposable gloves used in hospitals can be used for most chillies, but you need the heavy-duty type for really hot varieties such as habaneros. Of course, you can prepare chillies without wearing gloves, either by using a knife and fork for cutting, or by taking a chance and washing your hands in soapy water afterwards, but burns from capsaicin, the chemical found in the seeds and fibrous white lining, can be very unpleasant.

A mortar and pestle is ideal for grinding chillies and making chilli pastes, but it does involve a fair amount of hard work. Traditional Indian or Asian granite or stone sets are generally fairly large, with deep, pitted or ridged bowls. The rough surface acts like pumice, increasing the grinding effect. Porous volcanic rock is also used for the Mexican mortar – the *molcajete* – which traditionally stands on wide legs, and is very sturdy. The Mexican *tejolote* tends to be shorter than the traditional pestle, and fits neatly into the hand. *Molcajetes* must be tempered before being used. To do this, a mixture of dry rice and salt is spooned into the bowl, then ground into the surface to remove any loose sand or grit before being discarded.

A food processor is faster and easier, if less satisfying, than a mortar and pestle, especially for pastes, but must be very carefully cleaned after use. If you intend preparing chillies and spice pastes frequently, it may be worth investing in a mini food processor, and reserving it for spices.

A spice grinder, or coffee grinder kept specifically for spices, is handy when making dry spice mixtures.

Left: A smooth mortar and pestle for crushing dry ingredients.

Above: A rough mortar and pestle for making wet pastes.

Left: If you like to make your own spice mixtures, then a spice or coffee grinder kept solely for this purpose is very useful.

Left: A food processor or a blender will process chillies very efficiently, and is especially useful for large quantities.

PREPARATION AND COOKING TECHNIQUES

Every cook handling chillies has had the same experience, that unthinking moment when the hand goes to the face and the burning, tingling sensation of chilli oil is experienced, especially around the sensitive areas of the eyes, nose and mouth. It's not worth it! So be warned, be careful. Wear rubber gloves or wash your hands thoroughly in plenty of hot soapy water when handling chillies. Water alone will not remove the chemical capsaicin, and even after using soap, traces may remain. Baby oil or olive oil can be used to remove it from sensitive areas. This advice applies to dried and fresh chillies as the burning properties are equally strong for both.

Preparing Fresh Chillies

1 If the chilli is to be stuffed, and kept whole, merely slit it without separating the two halves. For all other purposes, hold the chilli firmly at the stalk end, and cut it neatly in half lengthwise with a sharp knife.

2 Cut off the stalk from both halves of the chilli, removing a thin slice containing the stalk from the top of the chilli at the same time. This will help to free the white membrane (placenta) and make it easier to scrape out the seeds to be discarded.

3 Carefully scrape out all the seeds and discard them. Remove the core with a small sharp knife.

4 Cut out any white membrane from the centre of each chilli half. Keep the knife blade close to the flesh so that all the membrane is removed. This is usually easy to do. Discard the membrane.

5 Slice each piece of chilli into thin strips. If diced chilli is needed, bunch the strips together and cut across them to produce tiny pieces.

COOK'S TIP
Much of the capsaicin, the fiery oil in chillies, is concentrated in the fibrous white section that contains the seeds. Many recipes suggest removing and discarding this, but true chilli lovers usually leave it in.

Soaking Dried Chillies

Most dried chillies must be rehydrated before being used. In some instances, a recipe will recommend toasting as a first step, to intensify the flavour. This can be done by putting the seeded chillies in a roasting pan in the oven for a few minutes, or by pressing them on to the surface of a hot, dry, heavy frying pan. Do not let them burn, or they could become bitter. Once this is done, continue as below.

1 Wipe the chillies to remove any surface dirt. If you like, you can slit them and shake out the seeds before soaking. Alternatively, just brush away any seeds you can see.

2 Put the chillies in a bowl and pour over hot water to cover. If necessary, fit a saucer in the bowl to keep the chillies submerged. Soak for 20–30 minutes (up to 1 hour if possible), until the colour is restored and the chillies have softened and swelled.

3 Drain the chillies, cut off the stalks if necessary, then slit them and scrape out the seeds. Slice or chop the flesh. If the chillies are to be puréed, process them with a little of the soaking water. Sieve the purée if necessary.

Roasting Fresh Chillies

There are several ways of roasting fresh chillies. You use the grill, roast in the oven, dry-fry as explained below, or hold them over a gas flame.

1 Put the chillies in a dry frying pan and place over the heat until the skins are charred and blistered. Alternatively, roast the chillies in a griddle pan.

2 For larger chillies that are to be stuffed, make a neat slit down the side of each one. Place in a dry frying pan over a moderate heat, turning frequently until the skins blister.

3 To roast chillies on a skewer over a flame, spear them on a long-handled metal skewer and roast them over the flame of a gas burner until the skins blister and darken.

4 Slip the roasted chillies into a strong plastic bag and tie the top to keep the steam in.

5 Set aside for 20 minutes. Take the chillies out of the bag and remove the skins, either by peeling them off, or by rubbing the chillies with a clean dishtowel. Cut off the stalks, then slit the chillies and, using a sharp knife, scrape out and discard the seeds.

Grinding Chillies

When making chilli powder, this method gives a distinctive and smoky taste.

1 Soak the chillies, if dried, pat dry and then dry fry in a heavy pan until crisp. You can also do this on a griddle. In either case, watch the chillies carefully because they can suddenly burn, and then you have to start all over again!

2 Transfer to a mortar and grind to a fine powder with a pestle. Store in an airtight container.

Making a Chilli Flower

This makes a very attractive garnish for a special dish.

1 Wearing rubber gloves and using a small pair of scissors or a slim-bladed knife, cut a chilli carefully lengthwise from the tip to within 1cm/½in of the stem end. Repeat this at regular intervals around the chilli – more cuts will produce more petals.

2 Rinse the chilli in cold water and remove all the seeds. Place in a bowl of iced water and chill for at least 4 hours. For very curly flowers, leave the chilli overnight. When ready to use, lift the chilli out and drain it on kitchen paper.

SPICE POWDERS

The name "curry powder" used to be attached to any ground spice mixture used for making hot or highly flavoured foods. It isn't an authentic term, but is a corruption of the Tamil word "karhi", which simply means a food cooked in a sauce. During the days of the Raj, British merchants and soldiers returning home were eager to continue enjoying the flavours they had encountered in India, and demand for a commercial curry powder was the result. The first of these were crude mixtures, bearing little resemblance to the sophisticated and often subtle blends that Indian cooks produced every day. These differed according to whether they were to be used for meat, poultry, fish or vegetables, and reflected the personal tastes of the maker.

Above: Ancho powder

Today, although bought curry powders have improved greatly, many individuals prefer to make their own spice mixtures in the traditional fashion, roasting and grinding whole spices and savouring the wonderful aroma that is part and parcel of the procedure.

Chillies do not feature in all spice blends, but are typical of those that originated in hot spots such as Madras, Mysore or Goa (the home of vindaloo).

Dry spice mixes – or curry powders – are popular in India, Pakistan and Sri Lanka. Each region has its own favourite blend of spices. When making your own spice powders and pastes, feel free to experiment with different types of dried or fresh chillies. Where chilli powder is listed in recipes, you can opt for the blended spice or a pure powder from a specific type of chilli.

Classic Curry Powder

This mixture can be modified to suit your own personal taste. Try not to keep it too long, or it will lose its aroma.

MAKES ABOUT 115G/4OZ/1 CUP

INGREDIENTS
6–8 dried red chillies
105ml/7 tbsp coriander seeds
60ml/4 tbsp cumin seeds
10ml/2 tsp fenugreek seeds
10ml/2 tsp black mustard seeds
10ml/2 tsp black peppercorns
15ml/1 tbsp ground turmeric
5ml/1 tsp ground ginger

1 Unless you like a fiery mixture, snap off the stalks from the dried chillies and shake out and discard most of the seeds and all the stalks.

2 Heat a heavy pan and dry-fry the chillies with the seeds and black peppercorns over a medium heat until they give off a rich aroma. Shake the pan constantly so that the spices are evenly roasted.

3 Tip the roasted spices into a mortar and grind them to a smooth powder. Alternatively, use a spice grinder or a coffee grinder reserved for spices.

4 Stir in the ground turmeric and the ginger. Use immediately or store in an airtight jar protected from strong light.

Below: Classic curry powder

Mild Curry Powder

This is a basic recipe for a mild Indian curry powder, but you can adjust the quantities to suit your taste.

MAKES ABOUT 115G/4OZ/1 CUP

INGREDIENTS
Whole spices
50g/2oz/½ cup coriander seeds
60ml/4 tbsp cumin seeds
30ml/2 tbsp fennel seeds
30ml/2 tbsp fenugreek seeds
4 dried red chillies
5 curry leaves
Ground spices
15ml/1 tbsp chilli powder
15ml/1 tbsp ground turmeric
2.5ml/½ tsp salt

1 Dry-roast the whole spices in a large heavy-based frying pan for 8–10 minutes, shaking the pan from side to side until the spices begin to darken and release a rich aroma. Allow them to cool slightly.

2 Put the spices in a spice grinder or mini food processor and process gently to achieve a fine powder.

3 Add the remaining ground spices and store in an airtight jar.

Garam Masala

Garam means "hot" and masala means "spices" so the spices used are those that "heat" the body, such as chillies, black peppercorns, cinnamon and cloves. Garam masala is added at the end of cooking and sprinkled over dishes as a garnish.

Below: Garam masala

MAKES ABOUT 50G/2OZ/½ CUP

INGREDIENTS
    10 dried red chillies
    2 × 2.5cm/1in cinnamon sticks
    2 curry leaves
    30ml/2 tbsp coriander seeds
    30ml/2 tbsp cumin seeds
    5ml/1 tsp black peppercorns
    5ml/1 tsp cloves
    5ml/1 tsp fenugreek seeds
    5ml/1 tsp black mustard seeds
    1.5ml/¼ tsp chilli powder

1 Dry-fry the chillies, cinnamon sticks and curry leaves in a large heavy frying pan for 2 minutes until you smell the spices as they roast.

2 Add the coriander and cumin seeds, peppercorns, cloves, fenugreek and mustard seeds, and dry-fry for a further 8–10 minutes, shaking the pan from side to side until the spices begin to darken and release a rich aroma.

3 Allow the mixture to cool slightly before grinding. Put the mixture into a spice grinder or electric coffee grinder, kept for spice grinding, or use a pestle and mortar. Grind to a fine powder. Add the chilli powder, mix together and store the powder in an airtight jar.

COOK'S TIP
Garam masala will keep for 2–4 months in an airtight container and the flavours will mature during storage.

> **Keep a lid on it**
> If your pan is a fairly shallow one, put a lid over it when frying the mustard seeds. When they pop, they can travel a surprising distance. Shiver the pan from side to side while the seeds are frying, so that they do not stick to the base. Fry over a gentle heat. You can use this technique for other small seeds, such as cumin.

Sambaar Powder

This blend of spices and dhal is used in South Indian cooking to flavour vegetable and lentil combinations, braised dishes and spicy broths. The powder also acts as a thickening agent.

MAKES ABOUT 105ML/7 TBSP

INGREDIENTS
    8–10 dried red chillies
    90ml/6 tbsp coriander seeds
    30ml/2 tbsp cumin seeds
    10ml/2 tsp black peppercorns
    10ml/2 tsp fenugreek seeds
    10ml/2 tsp urad dhal (white split
        gram beans)
    10ml/2 tsp channa dhal (yellow
        split peas)
    10ml/2 tsp mung dhal (yellow
        mung beans)
    25ml/1½ tbsp ground turmeric

1 Snap off the stalks from the dried chillies and shake out most of the seeds. Heat a heavy frying pan and add the first 5 ingredients.

2 Toss all the spices together over a medium heat until they give off a rich aroma, then turn into a bowl.

3 Repeat the process with the pulses, to toast them without letting them burn.

4 Mix the spices and pulses together, then grind them to a fine powder. Stir in the turmeric. Use immediately or store in an airtight jar away from strong light.

Below: Sambaar powder

Sri Lankan Curry Powder

This has totally different characteristics from Indian curry powders. The spices are roasted separately, and chilli powder is used instead of whole dried chillies. The result is a rich, dark curry powder that is ideal for fish, poultry, meat and vegetable curries.

In Sri Lanka, coriander, cumin, fennel and fenugreek seeds are roasted separately before being combined with roasted cinnamon, cloves and cardamom seeds. After grinding, chilli powder is stirred into the mixture, which is aromatic, rather than fiery. Colour and presentation are key features of Sri Lankan cuisine, and you will often find red, yellow and even black curries artistically arranged around a central bowl of rice.

MAKES ABOUT 75G/3OZ/¾ CUP

INGREDIENTS
    90ml/6 tbsp coriander seeds
    45ml/3 tbsp cumin seeds
    15ml/1 tbsp fennel seeds
    5ml/1 tsp fenugreek seeds
    5cm/2in piece cinnamon stick
    5ml/1 tsp cloves
    8 green cardamom pods
    6 dried curry leaves
    5–10ml/1–2 tsp chilli powder

1 Dry-fry or roast the coriander seeds, cumin seeds, fennel seeds and fenugreek seeds separately, because they all turn dark at different stages. Do not let the spices burn; remove them as soon as they give off a rich aroma.

2 Dry-fry the cinnamon stick, cloves and cardamom pods together for a few minutes until they give off a pungent aroma.

Above: Sri Lankan Curry powder

3 As soon as they are cool enough to handle, remove the seeds from the cardamom pods and place them in a mortar. Add the remaining dry-fried ingredients, then the curry leaves. Grind to a smooth powder. Alternatively, use a spice grinder.

4 Stir in the chilli powder. Use immediately or store in an airtight jar away from strong light.

Singapore-style Curry Powder

Chillies are a key ingredient in this curry powder for poultry and meat dishes.

MAKES ABOUT 75G/3OZ/¾ CUP

INGREDIENTS
    3–4 dried red chillies
    90ml/6 tbsp coriander seeds
    15ml/1 tbsp cumin seeds
    15ml/1 tbsp fennel seeds
    10ml/2 tsp black peppercorns
    2.5cm/1in piece cinnamon stick
    4 green cardamom pods
    6 cloves
    10ml/2 tsp ground turmeric

1 Unless you like a fiery mixture, snap off the stalks from the dried chillies and shake out most of the seeds.

2 Heat a heavy pan and add all the seeds, with the chillies, peppercorns, cinnamon stick, cardamoms and cloves. Dry-fry over a medium heat, stirring, until the spices give off a rich aroma.

Above: Singapore-style curry powder

3 When cool enough to handle, break the cinnamon stick into small pieces and remove the seeds from the cardamom pods.

4 Grind all the roasted spices to a fine powder in a mortar. Alternatively, use a spice grinder or an electric coffee grinder reserved for spices.

5 Stir in the ground turmeric. Use immediately or store in an airtight jar away from strong light.

VARIATION
To adapt Singapore-style curry powder for using with fish and shellfish, use only 2–3 chillies and 5ml/1 tsp black peppercorns, but increase the fennel seeds to 30ml/ 2 tbsp. Add 5ml/1 tsp fenugreek seeds. Leave out the cinnamon stick, cardamom pods and cloves.

Seven-seas Curry Powder

Like Sri Lankan Curry Powder, this uses chilli powder rather than whole dried chillies. Milder than some of the other mixtures, it combines the fiery taste of chilli with the warm flavours of cumin, cinnamon and cloves. It is widely used in Indonesian and Malaysian cooking.

MAKES ABOUT 90G/3½OZ/SCANT 1 CUP

INGREDIENTS
  6–8 white cardamom
    pods, bruised
  90ml/6 tbsp coriander seeds
  45ml/3 tbsp cumin seeds
  25ml/1½ tbsp celery seeds
  5cm/2in piece cinnamon stick
    or cassia
  6–8 cloves
  15ml/1 tbsp chilli powder

1 Put the cardamom pods in a heavy frying pan with all the other whole spices. Dry-fry the mixture, stirring it and shaking the pan constantly, until the spices give off a rich, heavy aroma.

2 When they are cool enough to handle, remove the cardamom seeds from the pods, then grind them finely with all the other roasted ingredients.

3 Add the chilli powder and mix. Use immediately or store in an airtight jar.

Below: Seven-seas curry powder

Malayan-Chinese Curry Powder

This is good for poultry, especially chicken, and robust fish curries. You can double or even treble the quantities, but it is better to make a smaller amount and use it fairly quickly, as curry powder will stale if stored for too long.

MAKES ABOUT 60ML/4 TBSP

INGREDIENTS
  2 dried red chillies
  6 whole cloves
  1 small cinnamon stick
  5ml/1 tsp coriander seeds
  5ml/1 tsp fennel seeds
  10ml/2 tsp Sichuan peppercorns
  2.5ml/½ tsp grated nutmeg
  2.5ml/½ tsp ground star anise
  5ml/1 tsp ground turmeric

1 Snap or cut the tops off the dried chillies and shake out most of the seeds. Use a small, sharp knife to remove any remaining seeds.

2 Put the chillies, cloves, cinnamon stick, coriander seeds and fennel seeds in a wok or heavy frying pan. Add the Sichuan peppercorns. Dry-fry over a medium heat, tossing the spices frequently, until they give off a rich, spicy aroma.

3 Tip the spices into a mortar and grind them to a smooth powder. Alternatively, use a spice grinder or an electric coffee grinder reserved for spices.

4 Stir in the grated nutmeg, star anise and turmeric. Use immediately or store in an airtight jar away from strong light to keep its flavour.

COOK'S TIPS

• When you are buying spices, always go to stores where there will be a good turnover. Indian or Asian speciality stores would be ideal. Whole spices do not have an indefinite shelf life, and you want to get the best flavour from your spice mix. Buy individual spices in small quantities and write the date of purchase on the packet if you are buying them loose and they do not have a "best before" date stamped on them. Then you can check them regularly and throw out any that have been stored for more than a couple of months.

• Although it is best to make curry powder and similar spice mixes in small quantities, a trip to a market with a fine selection of fresh spices might tempt you to make a large amount. Put some of the surplus in small jars as gifts for friends who like to cook, and store the rest in airtight tubs in the freezer.

SPICE PASTES

Unlike powdered blends, pastes are made from what are called "wet spices": lemon grass, fresh ginger, garlic, galangal, shallots, tamarind and chillies. These are traditionally ground using a mortar and pestle, but today a food processor is often used for convenience and speed. Supermarkets stock some excellent ready-made spice pastes, but making your own is simple and highly satisfying. Any surplus paste can be stored in a tub in the freezer.

Thai cooking is based on curry pastes. Thai cooks strive to create a balance between spicy hot, sweet, sour and salty tastes, and their curries reflect this. There are three principal types of curry paste – red, green and sour. Fresh ingredients such as chillies, lemon grass and shallots are given a salty tang with shrimp paste, while citrus juice and rind adds a touch of sourness. Fresh pastes can be bought from any Thai market, but most cooks prefer to make their own as needed. You will find commercial curry powder in Thailand – used in dishes such as stir-fried crab in curry sauce – but pastes are preferred.

Madrasi Masala

Masalas can be dry mixes or pastes. This one belongs to the latter category, and is a blend of dry and wet spices. The paste is cooked in oil to develop the flavours.

MAKES ABOUT 450G/1LB/2½ CUPS

INGREDIENTS
  120ml/8 tbsp coriander seeds
  60ml/4 tbsp cumin seeds
  15ml/1 tbsp black peppercorns
  15ml/1 tbsp black mustard seeds
  165ml/11 tbsp ground turmeric
  45–60ml/3–4 tbsp chilli powder
  15ml/1 tbsp salt
  8 garlic cloves, crushed
  7.5cm/3in piece fresh root ginger,
    peeled and finely grated (shredded)
  about 60ml/4 tbsp cider vinegar
  175ml/6fl oz/¾ cup sunflower oil

1 Heat a heavy frying pan and dry-fry the coriander seeds, cumin seeds and peppercorns for 1–2 minutes, stirring.

Above: Madrasi masala

2 Add the mustard seeds and toss constantly over the heat until they start to pop and the mixture gives off a rich aroma. Do not let the spices become too dark.

3 Grind the mixture to a fine powder, then add the turmeric, chilli and salt. Stir in the garlic, ginger and enough of the vinegar to make a paste.

4 Heat the oil in a large frying pan and fry the paste, stirring and turning it constantly, until the oil begins to separate from the spicy mixture.

5 Spoon the masala into a clean jar. Make sure that there is a film of oil floating on top. This will form an airtight seal and act as a preservative, ensuring that the paste keeps its colour. Store in the refrigerator for 2–3 weeks.

Thai Red Curry Paste

Some excellent versions of this classic paste are now produced commercially, but if you prefer to make your own, here's how.

MAKES ABOUT 175G/6OZ/1 CUP

INGREDIENTS
  3 lemon grass stalks
  10 fresh red chillies, seeded
    and sliced
  115g/4oz dark red onions or
    shallots, chopped
  4 garlic cloves
  1cm/½in piece fresh galangal,
    peeled, sliced and bruised
  stems from 4 fresh coriander
    (cilantro) sprigs
  15–30ml/1–2 tbsp groundnut
    (peanut) oil
  5ml/1 tsp grated (shredded) dried
    citrus rind
  1cm/½in cube of shrimp paste,
    wrapped in foil and warmed in a
    frying pan
  15ml/1 tbsp coriander seeds
  10ml/2 tsp cumin seeds
  5ml/1 tsp salt

1 Slice the tender lower portion of the lemon grass stalks and bruise them with a cleaver. Put them in a large mortar and add the chillies, onions or shallots, garlic, galangal and coriander stems.

2 Grind with a pestle, gradually adding the oil until the mixture forms a paste. Alternatively, purée the ingredients in a food processor or blender. Add the citrus rind and the shrimp paste. Mix well.

3 Dry-fry the coriander seeds and cumin seeds in a frying pan, then tip them into a large mortar and grind to a powder. Stir into the spice paste, with the salt.

4 Use the paste immediately, or scrape it into a glass jar. Cover with clear film (plastic wrap) and an airtight lid, then store in the refrigerator for 3–4 weeks.

Left: Thai red curry paste

Green Curry Paste

This medium-hot curry paste with its vivid green colour is based on chillies. It is good used with lamb, beef or chicken.

MAKES ABOUT 75G/3OZ/½ CUP

INGREDIENTS
    2 lemon grass stalks
    15 fresh hot green chillies
    3 shallots, sliced
    2 garlic cloves
    15ml/1 tbsp chopped fresh galangal
    4 kaffir lime leaves, chopped
    2.5ml/½ tsp grated (shredded) kaffir
      lime rind
    5ml/1 tsp chopped coriander
      (cilantro) root
    6 black peppercorns
    5ml/1 tsp coriander seeds, roasted
    5ml/1 tsp cumin seeds, roasted
    15ml/1 tbsp granulated sugar
    5ml/1 tsp salt
    15–30ml/1–2 tbsp groundnut
      (peanut) oil

1 Slice the tender lower portion of the lemon grass and bruise with a cleaver. Put them in a large mortar and add all the remaining ingredients except the oil. Grind to a paste. Add the oil, a little at a time, blending between each addition.

2 Use the paste immediately, or scrape it into a glass jar. Cover with clear film (plastic wrap) and an airtight lid. Store in the refrigerator for 3–4 weeks.

Below: Green curry paste

Thai Mussaman Curry Paste

Originating from the Malaysian border area, this paste can be used with beef, chicken or duck.

MAKES ABOUT 175G/6OZ/1 CUP

INGREDIENTS
    12 large dried red chillies
    1 lemon grass stalk
    60ml/4 tbsp chopped shallots
    5 garlic cloves, roughly chopped
    10ml/2 tsp chopped fresh galangal
      or fresh root ginger
    5ml/1 tsp cumin seeds
    15ml/1 tbsp coriander seeds
    2 cloves
    6 black peppercorns
    1cm/½ in cube of shrimp paste,
      wrapped in foil and warmed in a
      frying pan
    5ml/1 tsp salt
    5ml/1 tsp granulated sugar
    30ml/2 tbsp oil

1 Snap the dried chillies and shake out most of the seeds. Discard the stems. Soak the chillies in a bowl of hot water for 20–30 minutes.

2 Cut the tender lower portion of the lemon grass stalk into small pieces, using a small sharp knife. Place in a dry wok. Add the chopped shallots, roughly chopped garlic and galangal or ginger and dry-fry for a moment or two until the mixture gives off an aroma.

3 Stir in the whole cumin seeds, coriander seeds, cloves and peppercorns, and continue to dry-fry over a low heat for 5–6 minutes, stirring constantly. Spoon the mixture into a large mortar.

Above: Thai Mussaman curry paste

4 Drain the chillies and add them to the mortar. Use a pestle to grind the mixture finely, then add the prepared shrimp paste with the salt, granulated sugar and oil. Pound to form a rough paste. Use as required, then spoon any leftover paste into a jar, seal tightly and store in the refrigerator for up to 4 months.

COOK'S TIP

Shrimp paste is made from fermented shrimps. Also known as *blachan*, *terasi*, *kapi* or *ngapi*, it is widely used in the cooking of South-east Asia. It is available from Asian food stores and comes in block form, or packed in tiny tubs or jars. It smells rather vile because it is fermented, but the odour vanishes as soon as the paste is cooked. Warming it tempers the raw taste; the easiest way to do this is to wrap a small cube in foil and dry-fry it in a frying pan for about 5 minutes, turning it occasionally to heat evenly.

SAMBALS

When Westerners speak of sambals, they are usually referring to the side dishes served with curry – diced cucumber, sliced bananas and yogurt. These dishes are designed to cool the palate, but true sambals are something else entirely. They are extremely hot sauces or relishes based on chillies. Traditionally, they are served in small bowls, and used like mustard, to pep up other dishes. A sambal can also be a dish cooked with a hot chilli paste.

Chilli Sambal

This Indonesian speciality – **sambal oelek** – is a very simple mixture, made by pounding hot chillies with salt. Tamarind water is sometimes added, and Asian cooks will occasionally temper its heat by stirring ground roasted peanuts into the mixture.

MAKES 450G/1LB/2½ CUPS

INGREDIENTS
 450g/1lb fresh red chillies, seeded
 10ml/2 tsp salt

1 Cut the chillies in half and remove the stems. Using a sharp knife, scrape out and discard the seeds. Bring a pan of water to the boil, add the chillies and cook for 5–8 minutes.

2 Drain the chillies and tip them into a food processor or blender. Process to a rough paste.

3 Add the salt, process briefly to mix, then scrape the paste into a glass jar. Cover with clear film (plastic wrap) and a lid and store in the refrigerator. To serve, spoon into small dishes and offer the sambal as an accompaniment, or use it as suggested in recipes.

Sambal Blachan

Hot chillies can hold their own against strong flavours, as this sambal proves. The shrimp paste gives it a pungent quality, while the lemon or lime juice adds a welcome sharpness. Sambal blachan is frequently served with rice dishes. The rice tempers the heat.

MAKES ABOUT 30ML/2 TBSP

INGREDIENTS
 2–4 fresh red chillies, seeded
 salt
 1cm/½in cube of shrimp paste
 juice of ½ lemon or lime

1 Chop the chillies roughly and place them in a mortar. Add a little salt, then use a pestle to pound them to a paste.

2 Warm the shrimp paste, either by moulding it on to the end of a metal skewer and heating it in a gas flame until the outside begins to look dry, or by wrapping the paste in foil and heating it in a dry frying pan for about 5 minutes.

3 Add the shrimp paste to the chillies and pound to mix well. Stir in lemon or lime juice to taste.

Above: Sambal kecap

Sambal Kecap

Frequently served as a dip with chicken or beef satays, instead of the more usual peanut sauce, this is also delicious with deep-fried chicken.

MAKES ABOUT 150ML/¼ PINT/⅔ CUP

INGREDIENTS
 1 fresh red chilli, seeded and
  finely chopped
 2 garlic cloves, crushed
 60ml/4 tbsp dark soy sauce
 20ml/4 tsp lemon juice or 15ml/
  1 tbsp tamarind juice
 30ml/2 tbsp hot water
 30ml/2 tbsp deep-fried onion
  slices (optional)

1 Place the chopped chilli, crushed garlic and soy sauce in a small bowl. Stir in the lemon or tamarind juice, mix well, then thin with the hot water.

2 Stir in the deep-fried onion slices, if using. Cover and leave the sambal to stand for about 30 minutes before using.

COOK'S TIP
Deep-fried onion slices are very easy to make. Cut 2–3 onions in half, then into very thin slices. Blot these dry on kitchen paper, then add them to hot oil. Lower the heat slightly and cook until the onions have firmed up and browned. Lift out with a slotted spoon, drain on kitchen paper and leave until cold.

Above: Chilli sambal and sambal blachan (right)

Nam Prik Sauce

This is the universal Thai sauce, served solo, with rice or as a dip for fresh vegetables. The quantities can be varied.

MAKES ABOUT 275G/10OZ/1½–2 CUPS

INGREDIENTS
50g/2oz dried prawns (shrimp)
1cm/½in cube of shrimp paste, wrapped in foil and warmed in a frying pan
3–4 garlic cloves, crushed
3–4 fresh red chillies, seeded and sliced
50g/2oz peeled cooked prawns (shrimp)
a few coriander (cilantro) sprigs
8–10 tiny baby aubergines (eggplant)
45–60ml/3–4 tbsp lemon or lime juice
30ml/2 tbsp Thai fish sauce (*nam pla*) or to taste
10–15ml/2–3 tsp soft light brown sugar

1 Soak the dried prawns in water for 15 minutes. Drain and put in a mortar with the shrimp paste, garlic and chillies. Pound to a paste with a pestle, or process in a food processor. Add the cooked prawns and coriander. Pound or process again until combined.

2 Chop the aubergines roughly and gradually pound them into the sauce. Add the lemon or lime juice, fish sauce and sugar to taste.

Below: Nam prik sauce

Above: Sambal Salamat

Sambal Salamat

This hot tomato sambal is very popular in Indonesia. It has a very strong flavour and should be used sparingly.

MAKES ABOUT 120ML/4FL OZ/½ CUP

INGREDIENTS
3 ripe tomatoes
2.5ml/½ tsp salt
5ml/1 tsp chilli sauce
60ml/4 tbsp Thai fish sauce (*nam pla*)
15ml/1 tbsp chopped fresh coriander (cilantro) leaves

1 Cut a small cross in the base of each tomato. Place them in a heatproof bowl and pour over boiling water to cover. Leave the tomatoes in the water for 30 seconds.

2 Lift out the tomatoes with a slotted spoon and plunge them into a bowl of cold water. The skins will have begun to peel back from the crosses. Remove the skins completely, cut the tomatoes in half and squeeze out the seeds. Chop the flesh finely and put it in a bowl.

3 Add the salt, chilli sauce, fish sauce and coriander. Mix well. Set aside for at least 2 hours before serving, so that the flavours can blend.

VARIATION
Use a fresh red chilli instead of chilli sauce, if you prefer. Slit it, remove the seeds and then chop the flesh finely. To give the sambal a slightly smoky flavour, roast the chilli under the grill (broiler) until the skin blisters and begins to blacken, then remove the skin and seeds before chopping the flesh.

Above: Nuoc Cham

Nuoc Cham

In Vietnam, this fiery sauce is used as a condiment, and serves much the same purpose as salt and pepper does in the West. It tastes good with fried spring rolls. Chillies are widely used in Vietnamese cooking, especially in the centre of the country, where it is believed that eating them frequently keeps mosquitoes away and malaria at bay.

MAKES ABOUT 105ML/7 TBSP

INGREDIENTS
2 fresh red chillies, seeded
2 garlic cloves, crushed
15ml/1 tbsp granulated sugar
45ml/3 tbsp Thai fish sauce (*nam pla*)
juice of 1 lime or ½ lemon

1 Chop the chillies roughly, place them in a large mortar and use a pestle to pound them to a paste.

2 Scrape the paste into a bowl and add the garlic, sugar and fish sauce. Stir in lime or lemon juice to taste.

BARBECUE SPICE MIXTURES

Spice rubs and marinades are a boon to the barbecue cook, improving the appearance and flavour of cooked meats, poultry and fish while filling the air with a tantalizing aroma. Many of the mixtures are also delicious on roast chicken; just brush the bird lightly with olive oil before cooking, sprinkle the barbecue spice over it and rub in.

Basic Barbecue Spice Mix

Rub this on chops, steaks or portions of chicken. To make a marinade, add the mixture to a glass of red or white wine. Add a few slices of onion and stir in 60ml/4 tbsp of garlic-flavoured oil (or chilli oil if you are feeling adventurous).

MAKES ABOUT 60ML/4 TBSP

INGREDIENTS
    10ml/2 tsp celery seeds
    5ml/1 tsp paprika
    5ml/1 tsp grated nutmeg
    5ml/1 tsp chilli powder
    5ml/1 tsp garlic powder
    5ml/1 tsp onion salt
    10ml/2 tsp dried marjoram
    5ml/1 tsp salt
    5–10ml/1–2 tsp soft light brown sugar
    5ml/1 tsp lightly ground black pepper

1 Put the celery seeds in a mortar and grind to a powder with a pestle, or use a spice mill. Tip the powder into a bowl and stir in the remaining ingredients. Use the spice mixture immediately or store in an airtight jar.

Below: Basic barbecue spice mix

Above: Old-fashioned Philadelphia spice powder

Old-fashioned Philadelphia Spice Powder

This only has a trace of chilli, but the taste combines well with the warm, rounded flavours of the nutmeg and mace. The mixture makes a truly great seasoning for a pork joint, or can be rubbed both on steaks and chops. Do this in plenty of time before you plan to roast or cook on the barbecue, to allow the flavours to develop.

MAKES ABOUT 30–45ML/2–3 TBSP

INGREDIENTS
    8 cloves
    5ml/1 tsp chilli powder
    2.5ml/½ tsp grated nutmeg
    1.5ml/¼ tsp ground mace
    5ml/1 tsp dried basil
    5ml/1 tsp dried thyme
    2 dried bay leaves
    salt

1 Grind the cloves to a coarse powder, then add the other ingredients and continue grinding until fine.

2 Use immediately or store in an airtight container, away from strong light.

COOK'S TIP
All spices and spice mixtures start to deteriorate soon after being ground, so try to use them as soon as possible. Store in airtight and preferably tinted glass jars in a cool place, away from direct light, or keep them in the freezer.

Jamaican Jerk Paste

Give pork chops or chicken pieces a taste-lift with this delectable paste. Scotch bonnet chillies would be used in Jamaica, but they are extremely hot, so unless you are a devout chilli-head, you might prefer to substitute a milder variety, or reduce the quantity.

SUFFICIENT FOR FOUR MEAT PIECES

INGREDIENTS
    15ml/1 tbsp oil
    2 onions, finely chopped
    2 fresh red chillies, seeded and
      finely chopped
    1 garlic clove, crushed
    2.5cm/1in piece of fresh root
      ginger, grated (shredded)
    5ml/1 tsp dried thyme
    5ml/1 tsp ground allspice
    5ml/1 tsp Tabasco sauce or other
      hot pepper sauce
    30ml/2 tbsp rum
    grated (shredded) rind and juice
      of 1 lime
    salt and ground black pepper

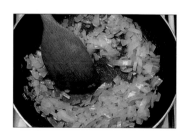

1 Heat the oil in a frying pan. Add the onions and cook for 10 minutes until soft. Stir in the chillies, garlic, ginger, thyme and allspice, and fry for 2 minutes more. Stir in the Tabasco sauce or hot pepper sauce, rum, lime rind and juice.

2 Simmer until the mixture forms a dark paste with a rich aroma. Season with salt and pepper, and leave to cool.

3 To use, rub over chops or chicken pieces, place in a shallow dish, cover and chill for 8 hours or overnight before barbecuing (grilling) or roasting.

Chermoula

This Moroccan mixture makes a very good marinade for meaty fish, but you can also use it as a cold sauce for fried fish. It is important to not use too much onion.

SUFFICIENT FOR 675G/1½LB FISH FILLETS

INGREDIENTS
    1 small red onion, finely chopped
    2 garlic cloves, crushed
    1 fresh red chilli, seeded and
      finely chopped
    30ml/2 tbsp chopped fresh
      coriander (cilantro)
    15ml/1 tbsp chopped fresh mint
    5ml/1 tsp ground cumin
    5ml/1 tsp paprika
    generous pinch of saffron threads
    60ml/4 tbsp olive oil
    juice of 1 lemon
    generous pinch of salt

1 Mix the onion, garlic, chilli, coriander, mint, cumin, paprika and saffron threads in a bowl. Add the olive oil, lemon juice and the salt. Mix well.

2 To use, add cubed fish to the bowl and toss until coated. Cover and leave in a cool place to marinate for 1 hour. Thread onto skewers and barbecue or grill (broil).

Thai Chilli and Citrus Marinade

This delectable combination of hot and sour flavours is perfect for chicken and seafood. Marinate fish or shellfish for about 1 hour; chicken for 3–4 hours.

MAKES ABOUT 175ML/6FL OZ/¾ CUP

INGREDIENTS
    2 small fresh red chillies
    15ml/1 tbsp granulated sugar
    2 garlic cloves, crushed
    white parts of 3 spring onions
      (scallions), chopped
    2.5cm/1in piece of fresh galangal or
      ginger, peeled and finely chopped
    grated (shredded) rind and juice of
      1 mandarin
    15ml/1 tbsp tamarind juice
    15ml/1 tbsp Thai fish sauce
      (*nam pla*)
    30ml/2 tbsp light soy sauce
    juice of 1 lime
    15ml/1 tbsp vegetable oil

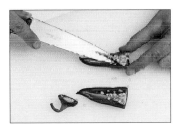

1 Slit the chillies and scrape out the seeds. Chop the flesh roughly and put it in a mortar. Add the sugar and grind to a paste with a pestle.

2 Add the crushed garlic, chopped spring onions and chopped fresh galangal or ginger. Add the grated rind of the mandarin to the mortar. Grind to a paste.

3 Scrape the paste into a bowl. Squeeze the juice from the mandarin and add it to the paste, with the tamarind juice, fish sauce and soy sauce. Stir in the lime juice and oil, mixing well. Set the marinade aside for 30 minutes, to allow the flavours to blend before using as a marinade.

Peri-peri Barbecue Marinade

Peri-peri is a hot chilli sauce that originated in Portugal, but which is now popular wherever there are large Portuguese communities. It is widely used in South Africa and Mozambique, and makes a marvellous marinade that is particularly good with shellfish.

MAKES ABOUT 75ML/5 TBSP

INGREDIENTS
    1 fresh red chilli
    2.5ml/½ tsp paprika
    2.5ml/½ tsp ground coriander
    1 garlic clove, crushed
    juice of 1 lime
    30ml/2 tbsp olive oil
    salt and ground black pepper

1 Slit the chilli using a small sharp knife and scrape out and discard the seeds. Chop the flesh finely and put it in a small bowl.

2 Stir in the paprika, ground coriander, crushed garlic and lime juice, then whisk in the olive oil, using a fork or salad dressing whisk. Season to taste with salt and pepper. This makes an excellent marinade for prawns (shrimp) and can also be used with chicken. Marinate prawns for about 30 minutes; chicken for several hours. When cooking the shellfish or chicken on the barbecue, baste it with any of the remaining marinade.

COOK'S TIP

Tamarind pods yield a sour, fruity pulp that is as widely used in South-east Asia as lemon is in the West. Buy tamarind as a compressed block, in slices or as a concentrate. To use block tamarind, pinch off the equivalent of 15ml/1 tbsp and soak this in 150ml/¼ pint/⅔ cup warm water for 10 minutes. Swirl the tamarind with your fingers to release the pulp from the seeds, then strain the liquid through a nylon sieve into a bowl. Tamarind slices must also be soaked in warm water, while the concentrate is mixed with warm water in the ratio of 15ml/1 tbsp concentrate to 75ml/5 tbsp water.

Turn up the heat with these sizzling sauces, selected to show just how versatile chillies can be in a supporting role. A spoonful of Mango and Chilli Salsa adds sweetness and spice to all sorts of dishes, from baked ham to crackers and cheese. Hot Hot Habanero Salsa stokes the fire, while Guacamole cools and comforts. Some sauces and dips are based on specific chillies, like chipotle and guajillo, while others leave the choice to you. Add chutneys, relishes, breads and nibbles, and it's easy to see why this is your passport to chilli heaven.

Scorching Salsas, Sauces, Dips, Relishes and Nibbles

SALSA VERDE

ALSO KNOWN AS GREEN FIRE, THIS IS A CLASSIC GREEN SALSA IN WHICH CAPERS PLAY AN IMPORTANT PART. MAKE IT WITH GREEN CAYENNE CHILLIES OR THE MILDER JALAPEÑOS.

SERVES FOUR

INGREDIENTS
2–4 fresh green chillies
8 spring onions (scallions)
2 garlic cloves
50g/2oz/½ cup salted capers
1 fresh tarragon sprig
bunch of fresh parsley
grated rind and juice
  of 1 lime
juice of 1 lemon
90ml/6 tbsp olive oil
15ml/1 tbsp green Tabasco sauce
ground black pepper

1 Cut the chillies in half and scrape out and discard the seeds. Trim the spring onions and cut them into short lengths. Cut the garlic in half. Mix in a food processor and pulse until chopped.

2 Use your fingertips to rub the excess salt off the capers but do not rinse them (see Cook's Tip). Add the capers, tarragon and parsley to the food processor and pulse again until they are quite finely chopped.

3 Transfer the mixture to a small bowl. Stir in the lime rind and juice, lemon juice and olive oil. Stir lightly so the citrus juice and oil do not emulsify.

4 Add green Tabasco and black pepper to taste. Chill until ready to serve but do not prepare more than 8 hours in advance.

COOK'S TIP
If you can only find capers pickled in vinegar, they must be rinsed well in cold water before using.

AVOCADO AND SWEET RED PEPPER SALSA

THIS SIMPLE SALSA IS A FIRE-AND-ICE MIXTURE THAT COMBINES HOT CHILLI WITH COOLING AVOCADO. SERVE IT WITH CORN CHIPS FOR DIPPING.

SERVES FOUR

INGREDIENTS
2 ripe avocados
1 red onion
1 sweet red (bell) pepper
4 fresh green chillies
30ml/2 tbsp chopped fresh
  coriander (cilantro)
30ml/2 tbsp sunflower oil
juice of 1 lemon
salt and ground black pepper

1 Cut the avocados in half and remove the stone (pit) from each. Scoop out the flesh and dice it. Finely chop the red onion.

2 Slice the top off the sweet red pepper and pull out the central core. Shake out any remaining seeds. Cut the pepper into thin strips, then into dice.

3 Cut the chillies in half lengthways, scrape out and discard the seeds and finely chop the flesh. Put it in a jug (pitcher) and mix in the coriander, oil, lemon juice and season with salt and pepper to taste.

4 Place the avocado, red onion and pepper in a bowl. Pour in the chilli dressing and toss well. Serve immediately.

COOK'S TIP
Serrano chillies would be a good choice, or moderate them with the milder Anaheim if you like.

CHILLI AND PESTO SALSA

USE LONG SLIM RED CHILLIES TO MAKE THIS AROMATIC SALSA, WHICH IS DELICIOUS OVER CHICKEN AND FISH OR USED TO DRESS A FRESH AVOCADO AND TOMATO SALAD. MAKE IT INTO A DIP BY MIXING IT WITH A LITTLE MAYONNAISE OR SOUR CREAM.

SERVES FOUR

INGREDIENTS
   50g/2oz/1⅓ cups fresh coriander
      (cilantro) leaves
   15g/½oz/¼ cup fresh parsley
   2 fresh red chillies
   1 garlic clove, halved
   50g/2oz/½ cup shelled pistachio nuts
   25g/1oz/⅓ cup freshly grated
      Parmesan cheese
   90ml/6 tbsp olive oil
   juice of 2 limes
   salt and ground black pepper

1 Process the coriander and parsley in a food processor until finely chopped. Cut the chillies in half, scrape out and discard seeds. Add to the herbs, with the garlic and process until finely chopped.

2 Add the pistachio nuts to the herb mixture and pulse until they are roughly chopped. Scrape the mixture into a bowl and stir in the Parmesan cheese, olive oil and lime juice.

3 Add salt and pepper to taste. Spoon the mixture into a serving bowl, cover and chill until ready to serve.

FIERY CITRUS SALSA

THIS UNUSUAL SALSA, WHICH COMBINES FRUIT WITH CHILLIES, MAKES A FANTASTIC MARINADE FOR SHELLFISH AND IS DELICIOUS DRIZZLED OVER BARBECUE-COOKED MEAT.

SERVES FOUR

INGREDIENTS
   1 orange
   1 green apple
   2 fresh red chillies
   1 garlic clove
   8 fresh mint leaves
   juice of 1 lemon
   salt and ground black pepper

1 Slice the base off the orange so that it will stand firmly on a chopping board. Using a sharp knife, remove the peel and pith in sections.

2 Holding the orange over a bowl to catch the juices, cut away the segments from the membrane, letting them fall into the bowl. Squeeze any juice from the remaining membrane into the bowl.

3 Peel, quarter and core the apple. Put it in a food processor. Cut the chillies in half and scrape out and discard the seeds. Add them to the food processor with the orange segments and juice, garlic and fresh mint.

4 Process until smooth. Then, with the motor running, pour in the lemon juice through the feeder tube. Season to taste. Pour into a bowl and serve immediately.

VARIATION
If you're feeling really daring, don't seed the chillies! They will make the salsa particularly hot and fierce.

CLASSIC MEXICAN TOMATO SALSA

THIS IS THE TRADITIONAL TOMATO-BASED SALSA THAT MOST PEOPLE ASSOCIATE WITH MEXICAN FOOD. THERE ARE INNUMERABLE RECIPES FOR IT, BUT THE BASICS OF ONION, TOMATO, CHILLI AND CORIANDER ARE COMMON TO EVERY ONE OF THEM. SERVE THIS SALSA AS A CONDIMENT WITH A WIDE VARIETY OF DISHES.

SERVES SIX AS AN ACCOMPANIMENT

INGREDIENTS
  3–6 fresh serrano chillies
  1 large white onion
  grated rind and juice of 2 limes, plus
    strips of lime rind, to garnish
  8 ripe, firm tomatoes
  a bunch of fresh coriander (cilantro)
  1.5ml/¼ tsp caster sugar
  salt

4 Remove the chillies from the bag and peel off the skins. Cut off the stalks, then slit the chillies and scrape out the seeds with a sharp knife. Chop the flesh roughly and set aside.

7 Dice the peeled tomatoes and put them in a bowl. Add the chopped onion which should have softened, together with the lime mixture. Chop the fresh coriander finely.

1 Use 3 chillies for a salsa of medium heat; up to 6 if you like it hot. To peel the chillies spear them on a long-handled metal skewer and roast them over the flame of a gas burner until the skins blister and darken. Do not let the flesh burn. Alternatively, dry fry them in a griddle pan until the skins are scorched.

2 Place the roasted chillies in a strong plastic bag and tie the top of the bag to keep the steam in. Set aside for about 20 minutes.

3 Meanwhile, chop the onion finely and put it in a bowl with the lime rind and juice. The lime juice will soften the onion.

5 Cut a small cross in the base of each tomato. Place the tomatoes in a heatproof bowl and pour over boiling water to cover.

8 Add the coriander to the salsa, with the chillies and the sugar. Mix gently until the sugar has dissolved and all the ingredients are coated in lime juice. Cover and chill for 2–3 hours to allow the flavours to blend. The salsa will keep for 3–4 days in the refrigerator. Garnish with the strips of lime rind just before serving.

VARIATIONS
Use spring onions (scallions) or mild red onions instead of white onion. For a smoky flavour, use chipotle chillies instead of fresh serrano chillies.

6 Leave the tomatoes in the water for 3 minutes, then lift them out using a slotted spoon and plunge them into a bowl of cold water. Drain. The skins will have begun to peel back from the crosses. Remove the skins completely.

ROASTED TOMATO SALSA

SLOW-ROASTING THESE TOMATOES TO A SEMI-DRIED STATE RESULTS IN A VERY RICH,
FULL-FLAVOURED SWEET SAUCE. THE COSTENO AMARILLO CHILLI IS MILD AND HAS
A FRESH LIGHT FLAVOUR, MAKING IT THE PERFECT PARTNER FOR THE RICH TOMATO
TASTE. THIS SALSA IS GREAT WITH TUNA OR SEA BASS.

SERVES SIX AS AN ACCOMPANIMENT

INGREDIENTS
   500g/1¼lb tomatoes
   8 small shallots
   5 garlic cloves
   sea salt
   1 fresh rosemary sprig
   2 costeno amarillo chillies
   grated rind and juice of ½
     small lemon
   30ml/2 tbsp extra virgin olive oil
   1.5ml/¼ tsp soft dark brown sugar

1 Preheat the oven to 160°C/325°F/
Gas 3. Cut the tomatoes into quarters
and place them on a baking tray.

2 Peel the shallots and garlic and add
them to the roasting tin. Sprinkle with
sea salt. Roast in the oven for 1¼ hours
or until the tomatoes are beginning to
dry. Do not let them burn or blacken or
they will have a bitter taste.

3 Leave the tomatoes to cool, then
peel off the skins and chop the flesh
finely. Place in a bowl. Remove the
outer layer of skin from any shallots that
have toughened.

4 Using a large, sharp knife, chop the
shallots and garlic roughly, place them
with the tomatoes in a bowl and mix.

5 Strip the rosemary leaves from the
woody stem and chop them finely. Add
half to the tomato and shallot mixture
and mix lightly.

6 Soak the chillies in hot water for about
10 minutes until soft. Drain, remove
the stalks, slit them and scrape out the
seeds with a sharp knife. Chop the flesh
finely and add it to the tomato mixture.

7 Stir in the lemon rind and juice, the
olive oil and the sugar. Mix well, taste
and add more salt if needed. Cover and
chill for at least an hour before serving,
sprinkled with the remaining rosemary.
It will keep for up to a week in the fridge.

COOK'S TIP
Use plum tomatoes or vine tomatoes,
which have more flavour than tomatoes
that have been grown for their keeping
properties rather than their flavour.

MANGO AND CHILLI SALSA

THIS HAS A FRESH, FRUITY TASTE AND IS PERFECT WITH FISH OR AS A CONTRAST TO RICH, CREAMY DISHES. THE BRIGHT COLOURS MAKE IT AN ATTRACTIVE ADDITION TO ANY TABLE.

SERVES FOUR

INGREDIENTS
  2 fresh red fresno chillies
  2 ripe mangoes
  ½ white onion
  small bunch of fresh
    coriander (cilantro)
  grated rind and juice of
    1 lime

1 To peel the chillies, spear them on a long-handled metal skewer and roast them over the flame of a gas burner, turning the chillies continually, until the skins blister and darken. Do not let the flesh burn. Alternatively, dry-fry them in a frying pan until the skins are scorched.

2 Place the roasted chillies in a strong plastic bag and tie the top. Set aside.

VARIATION
For a refreshing change, look out for juicy Italia chillies, which have a wonderful affinity for mangoes.

3 Meanwhile, put one of the mangoes on a board and cut off a thick slice close to the flat side of the stone (pit). Turn the mango round and repeat on the other side. Score the flesh on each thick slice with criss-cross lines at 1cm/½in intervals, taking care not to cut through the skin. Repeat with the second mango.

4 Fold the mango halves inside out so that the mango flesh stands proud of the skin, in neat dice. Carefully slice these off the skin and into a bowl. Cut off the flesh adhering to each stone, dice it and add it to the bowl.

5 Remove the roasted chillies from the bag and carefully peel off the skins. Cut off the stalks, then slit the chillies and scrape out the seeds with a sharp knife. Discard the seeds.

6 Chop the white onion and the coriander finely and add them to the diced mango. Chop the chilli flesh finely and add it to the mixture in the bowl, together with the lime rind and juice. Toss the ingredients in the bowl thoroughly, then cover and chill for at least 1 hour before serving. The salsa will keep for 2–3 days in the refrigerator.

ROASTED SERRANO AND TOMATO SALSA

ROASTING THE CHILLIES GIVES A GREATER DEPTH TO THE TASTE OF THIS SALSA, WHICH ALSO BENEFITS FROM THE ROUNDED FLAVOUR OF ROASTED TOMATOES.

SERVES SIX

INGREDIENTS
  500g/1¼lb tomatoes
  2 fresh serrano chillies
  1 onion
  juice of 1 lime
  large bunch of fresh
    coriander (cilantro)
  salt

1 Preheat the oven to 200°C/400°F/ Gas 6. Cut the tomatoes into quarters and place them in a roasting pan. Add the chillies. Roast for 45–60 minutes, until charred and softened.

2 Place the roasted chillies in a strong plastic bag. Tie the top to keep the steam in and set aside for 20 minutes. Leave the tomatoes to cool slightly, then remove the skins and dice the flesh.

3 Chop the onion finely, then place in a bowl and add the lime juice and the diced tomatoes.

4 Remove the chillies from the bag and peel off the skins. Cut off the stalks, then slit the chillies and scrape out the seeds with a sharp knife. Chop the chillies roughly and add them to the onion mixture. Mix well.

5 Chop the coriander and add most to the salsa. Add salt, cover and chill for at least 1 hour before serving, sprinkled with the remaining coriander. This salsa will keep in the refrigerator for 1 week.

HOT HOT HABANERO SALSA

THIS IS A VERY FIERY SALSA WITH AN INTENSE HEAT LEVEL. A DAB ON THE PLATE ALONGSIDE A MEAT OR FISH DISH ADDS A FRESH, CLEAN TASTE.

3 Put the chillies in a food processor and add a little of the soaking liquid. Purée to a fine paste. Do not lean over the processor – the fumes may burn your face. Remove the lid and scrape the mixture into a bowl.

4 Put the chopped spring onions in another bowl and add the grapefruit or orange juice, with the lime rind and juice. Roughly chop the coriander.

SERVES FOUR

INGREDIENTS
    5 dried roasted habanero chillies
    4 dried costeno amarillo chillies
    3 spring onions (scallions),
      finely chopped
    juice of ½ large grapefruit or
      1 Seville (Temple) orange
    grated rind and juice of 1 lime
    small bunch of fresh
      coriander (cilantro)
    salt

1 Soak the habanero and costeno amarillo chillies in hot water for about 20 minutes until softened. Drain, reserving the soaking water.

COOK'S TIP
Dried habanero chillies are just as hot as when fresh. Lantern shaped and deep orange in colour, they release a lovely fruity aroma when reconstituted, and go very well with the milder, citrus-flavoured costeno amarillo chillies.

2 Wear rubber gloves to handle the habaneros. Remove the stalks from all the chillies, then slit them and scrape out the seeds with a small sharp knife and discard. Chop the flesh roughly.

5 Carefully add the chopped coriander to the chilli mixture and then combine the ingredients very thoroughly. Add salt to taste. Cover the bowl and chill for at least 1 day before use. Serve this salsa very sparingly and warn your guests that it is hot.

SWEET POTATO AND JALAPEÑO SALSA

COLOURFUL AND SWEET, WITH JUST A HINT OF HEAT, THIS SALSA MAKES THE PERFECT
ACCOMPANIMENT TO HOT, SPICY MEXICAN DISHES.

SERVES FOUR

INGREDIENTS
  675g/1½lb sweet potatoes
  juice of 1 small orange
  5ml/1 tsp crushed dried
    jalapeño chillies
  4 small spring onions (scallions)
  juice of 1 small lime (optional)
  salt

COOK'S TIP
This fresh and tasty salsa is also very
good served with a simple grilled
(broiled) salmon fillet or other fish
dishes, and makes a delicious
accompaniment to veal escalopes
(scallops) or chicken breast fillets.

1 Peel the sweet potatoes and dice the
flesh finely. Bring a pan of water to
the boil. Add the sweet potato and cook
for 8–10 minutes, until just soft. Drain
off the water, cover the pan and put it
back on the stove top, having turned
off the heat.

2 Leave for 5 minutes to dry out, tip it
into a bowl and set aside.

3 Mix the orange juice and crushed
dried chillies in a bowl. Chop the spring
onions finely and add them to the juice
and chillies.

4 When the sweet potatoes are cool,
add the orange juice mixture and toss
carefully until all the pieces are coated.
Cover the bowl and chill for 2 hours.

5 Taste the salsa and season with salt.
Stir in the lime juice if you think the
mixture needs to be sharpened slightly.
The salsa will keep for 2–3 days in a
covered bowl in the refrigerator.

CACTUS PEAR SALSA

NOPALES ARE THE TENDER, FLESHY LEAVES OR "PADDLES" OF AN EDIBLE CACTUS KNOWN VARIOUSLY AS THE CACTUS PEAR AND THE PRICKLY PEAR CACTUS. THIS PLANT GROWS WILD IN MEXICO, BUT IS ALSO CULTIVATED. ALTHOUGH FRESH NOPALES ARE DIFFICULT TO TRACK DOWN OUTSIDE MEXICO, IF YOU DO LOCATE A SUPPLY, THEN LOOK FOR PADDLES THAT ARE FIRM AND SMOOTH SKINNED.

SERVES FOUR AS AN ACCOMPANIMENT

INGREDIENTS
    2 fresh red fresno chillies
    250g/9oz *nopales* (cactus paddles)
    3 spring onions (scallions)
    3 garlic cloves, peeled
    ½ red onion
    100g/3½oz fresh tomatillos
    2.5ml/½ tsp salt
    150ml/¼ pint/⅔ cup cider vinegar

1 Spear the chillies on a long-handled metal skewer and roast them over the flame of a gas burner until the skins blister and darken. Do not let the flesh burn. Alternatively, dry fry them in a griddle pan until the skins are scorched. Place the roasted chillies in a strong plastic bag and tie the top to keep the steam in. Set aside for 20 minutes.

2 Remove the chillies from the bag and peel off the skins. Cut off the stalks, then slit the chillies and scrape out the seeds. Chop the chillies roughly and set them aside.

COOK'S TIP
Fresh *nopales* are sometimes available from specialist fruit and vegetable stores. Like okra, they yield a sticky gum, and are best boiled before being used. Fresh cactus will lose about half its weight during cooking. Look out for canned *nopales* (sometimes sold as *nopalitos*) packed in water or vinegar.

3 Carefully remove the thorns from the nopales. Wearing gloves or holding each cactus paddle in turn with kitchen tongs, cut off the bumps that contain the thorns with a sharp knife.

4 Cut off and discard the thick base from each cactus paddle. Rinse the paddles well and cut them into strips then cut the strips into small pieces.

5 Bring a large pan of lightly salted water to the boil. Add the cactus paddle strips, spring onions and garlic. Boil for 10–15 minutes, until the paddle strips are just tender.

6 Drain the mixture in a colander, rinse under cold running water to remove any remaining stickiness, then drain again. Discard the spring onions and garlic.

7 Chop the red onion and the tomatillos finely. Place in a bowl and add the cactus and chillies.

8 Spoon the mixture into a large preserving jar, add the salt, pour in the vinegar and seal. Put the jar in the refrigerator for at least 1 day, turning the jar occasionally to ensure that the *nopales* are marinated. The salsa will keep in the refrigerator for up to 10 days.

PINTO BEAN SALSA

THESE BEANS HAVE A PRETTY, SPECKLED APPEARANCE. THE SMOKY FLAVOUR OF THE CHIPOTLE CHILLIES AND THE HERBY TASTE OF THE PASILLA CHILLI CONTRAST WELL WITH THE TART TOMATILLOS.

SERVES FOUR AS AN ACCOMPANIMENT

INGREDIENTS
130g/4½oz/generous ½ cup pinto
  beans, soaked overnight in water
  to cover
2 chipotle chillies
1 pasilla chilli
2 garlic cloves, peeled
½ onion
200g/7oz fresh tomatillos
salt

1 Drain the beans and put them in a large pan. Pour in water to cover and place the lid on the pan. Bring to the boil, lower the heat slightly and simmer the beans for 45–50 minutes or until tender. They should still have a little bite and should not have begun to disintegrate. Drain, rinse under cold water, then drain again and tip into a bowl. Leave the beans until cold.

COOK'S TIP
Canned tomatillos can be substituted, but to keep a clean, fresh flavour add a little lime juice.

2 Soak the chipotle and pasilla chillies in hot water for 10 minutes until softened.

3 Drain, reserving the soaking water. Remove the stalks, then slit each chilli and scrape out the seeds with a small sharp knife. Chop the flesh finely and mix it to a smooth paste with a little of the soaking water.

4 Roast the garlic in a dry frying pan over a moderate heat for a few minutes until the cloves start to turn golden. Crush them and add them to the beans.

5 Chop the onion and tomatillos and stir them into the beans. Add the chilli paste and mix well. Add salt to taste, cover and chill before serving.

BLACK BEAN SALSA

*THIS SALSA HAS A STRIKING APPEARANCE. IT IS RARE TO FIND A BLACK SPICE AND IT
PROVIDES A GOOD CONTRAST TO THE MORE COMMON REDS AND GREENS ON THE PLATE.*

SERVES FOUR

INGREDIENTS
130g/4½oz/generous ½ cup black
    beans, soaked overnight in water
1 pasado chilli
2 fresh red fresno chillies
1 red onion
grated rind and juice of 1 lime
30ml/2 tbsp Mexican
    beer (optional)
15ml/1 tbsp olive oil
small bunch of fresh coriander
    (cilantro), chopped
salt

1 Drain the beans, rinse them thoroughly
and put them in a large pan. Pour in
water to cover. Do not add salt as this
toughens the outside skin and stops the
bean cooking properly. Place the lid on
the pan and bring to the boil. Lower the
heat slightly and simmer the beans for
about 40 minutes or until tender. They
should still have a little bite and should
not have begun to disintegrate. Drain,
rinse under cold water, then drain again
and leave the beans until cold.

2 Soak the pasado chilli in hot water for
about 20 minutes until softened. Drain,
remove the stalk, then slit the chilli and,
using a small sharp knife, scrape out
the seeds and discard them. Chop the
flesh finely.

COOK'S TIP
Pasado chillies are always sold in their
dried, roasted form. Dark, almost black,
in colour, they have a subtle citrus
flavour and are only mildly hot.

3 Spear the fresno chillies on a long-
handled metal skewer and roast them
over the flame of a gas burner, turning
the chillies all the time, until the
skins blister and darken. Do not let
the flesh burn. Alternatively, dry-fry
them in a griddle pan until the skins
are scorched.

4 Place the roasted chillies in a strong
plastic bag and tie the top to keep the
steam in. Set aside for 20 minutes.

5 Meanwhile, chop the red onion finely.
Remove the chillies from the bag and
peel off the skins. Slit them, remove and
discard the seeds, and chop them finely.

6 Tip the beans into a bowl and add the
onion and both types of chilli. Stir in
the lime rind and juice, and beer, if
using, then add the oil and coriander.
Season with salt and mix well. Leave the
salsa for a day or two to allow the
flavours to develop fully. Serve chilled.

GUACAMOLE

ONE OF THE BEST-LOVED MEXICAN SALSAS, THIS BLEND OF CREAMY AVOCADO, TOMATOES, CHILLIES, CORIANDER AND LIME NOW APPEARS ON TABLES THE WORLD OVER.

SERVES SIX TO EIGHT

INGREDIENTS

4 medium tomatoes
4 ripe avocados, preferably fuerte
juice of 1 lime
½ small onion
2 garlic cloves
small bunch of fresh coriander
  (cilantro), chopped
3 fresh red fresno chillies
salt
tortilla chips, to serve

1 Cut a cross in the base of each tomato. Place the tomatoes in a heatproof bowl and pour over boiling water to cover.

2 Leave the tomatoes in the water for 30 seconds, then lift them out using a slotted spoon and plunge them into a bowl of cold water. Drain. The skins will have begun to peel back from the crosses. Remove the skins completely. Cut the tomatoes in half, remove the seeds with a teaspoon, then chop the flesh roughly and set it aside.

3 Cut the avocados in half and remove the stones (pits). Scoop the flesh into a food processor or blender. Process until almost smooth, then scrape into a bowl and stir in the lime juice.

4 Chop the onion finely, then crush the garlic. Add both to the avocado and mix well. Stir in the coriander.

5 Remove the stalks from the chillies, slit them and scrape out and discard the seeds. Chop the chillies finely and add them to the avocado mixture, with the chopped tomatoes. Mix well.

6 Check the seasoning and add salt to taste. Cover closely with clear film (plastic wrap) or a tight-fitting lid and chill for 1 hour before serving as a dip with tortilla chips. If it is well covered, guacamole will keep in the refrigerator for 2–3 days.

COOK'S TIP
Smooth-skinned fuerte avocados are native to Mexico, so would be ideal for this dip. If they are not available, use any avocados, but make sure they are ripe. To test, gently press the top of the avocado; it should give a little.

SPICY TOMATO AND CHILLI DIP

*GET YOUR TASTE BUDS TINGLING WITH THIS TANGY DIP, SPIKED WITH FRESH GREEN CHILLIES.
IT IS DELICIOUS SERVED WITH DEEP-FRIED POTATO SKINS OR HASH BROWNS.*

SERVES FOUR

INGREDIENTS
  1 shallot, halved
  2 garlic cloves, halved
  handful of fresh basil leaves,
    plus extra, to garnish
  500g/1¼lb ripe tomatoes
  30ml/2 tbsp olive oil
  2 fresh green chillies
  salt and ground black pepper

COOK'S TIP
Use green serrano or jalapeño chillies.
Anahcims are also suitable, and will
give a milder result.

1 Place the shallot and garlic in a
blender or food processor. Add the basil
leaves and process until very finely
chopped. You may need to scrape down
the sides of the bowl with a spatula.

2 Cut the tomatoes in half and add
them to the shallot mixture. Pulse until
the mixture is well blended and the
tomatoes are finely chopped.

3 With the motor still running, slowly
pour in the olive oil through the feeder
tube. Add salt and pepper to taste and
pulse briefly to mix. Spoon the mixture
into a bowl.

4 Cut the chillies lengthways and scrape
out the seeds with a sharp knife and
discard. Finely slice across the chillies,
cutting them into tiny strips and stir
them into the tomato mixture. Garnish
with a few torn basil leaves. Serve the
dip at room temperature. Refrigerated,
this will keep for 3–4 days.

SPICED CARROT DIP

THIS IS A DELICIOUS LOW-FAT DIP WITH A SWEET AND SPICY FLAVOUR. SERVE WHEAT CRACKERS OR FIERY TORTILLA CHIPS AS ACCOMPANIMENTS FOR DIPPING.

SERVES FOUR

INGREDIENTS
 1 onion
 3 carrots
 grated rind and juice of
  2 oranges
 15ml/1 tbsp hot curry paste
 150ml/¼ pint/¾ cup low-fat
  natural (plain) yogurt
 1 handful of fresh basil leaves
 15–30ml/1–2 tbsp fresh lemon
  juice, to taste
 red Tabasco sauce, to taste
 salt and ground black pepper

1 Using a sharp vegetable knife, finely chop the onion. Peel and grate the carrots. Place the onion, carrots, orange rind and juice and hot curry paste in a small pan. Bring the mixture to the boil, cover with a lid and simmer for about 10 minutes, or until tender.

2 Process in a blender or food processor until smooth and leave to cool.

3 Stir in the yogurt, then tear the basil leaves into small pieces and stir them into the carrot mixture.

4 Add lemon juice, Tabasco, salt and pepper to taste and serve.

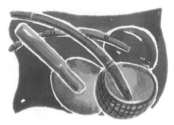

CHILLI BEAN DIP

SUBSTANTIAL ENOUGH TO SERVE FOR SUPPER ON A BAKED POTATO, THIS CREAMY BEAN DIP ALSO TASTES GREAT WITH TRIANGLES OF LIGHTLY TOASTED PITTA BREAD OR A BOWL OF CRUNCHY TORTILLA CHIPS. SERVE IT WARM TO ENJOY IT AT ITS BEST.

SERVES FOUR

INGREDIENTS

    2 fresh green chillies
    2 garlic cloves
    1 onion
    30ml/2 tbsp vegetable oil
    5–10ml/1–2 tsp hot chilli powder
    400g/14oz can kidney beans
    75g/3oz/¾ cup grated mature (sharp)
      Cheddar cheese
    1 fresh red chilli, seeded
    salt and ground black pepper

1 Slit the green chillies and use a sharp knife to scrape out the seeds. Chop the flesh finely, then crush the garlic and finely chop the onion.

2 Heat the oil in a large pan and add the garlic, onion, green chillies and chilli powder. Cook gently for 5 minutes, stirring, until the onions have softened and are transparent, but not browned.

COOK'S TIP
Fresh green chillies provide the heat in this dip. You can substitute sweet red (bell) pepper for the garnish.

3 Drain the kidney beans, reserving the liquid in which they were canned. Set aside 30ml/2 tbsp of the beans and purée the remainder in a food processor or blender.

4 Spoon the puréed beans into the pan and stir in 30–45ml/2–3 tbsp of the reserved can liquid. Heat gently, stirring to mix well.

5 Stir in the reserved whole kidney beans and the Cheddar cheese. Cook gently for 2–3 minutes, stirring regularly until the cheese melts. Add salt and pepper to taste.

6 Cut the red chilli into tiny strips. Spoon the dip into four individual serving bowls and sprinkle the chilli strips over the top. Serve warm.

CHILLI AND RED ONION RAITA

RAITA IS A TRADITIONAL INDIAN ACCOMPANIMENT, A COOLING AGENT TO SERVE WITH HOT CURRIES. IT IS ALSO DELICIOUS SERVED WITH POPPADUMS AS A DIP.

SERVES FOUR

INGREDIENTS
  5ml/1 tsp cumin seeds
  1 large red onion
  1 small garlic clove
  1 small fresh green chilli, seeded
  150ml/¼ pint/⅔ cup natural
    (plain) yogurt
  30ml/2 tbsp chopped fresh coriander
    (cilantro), plus extra, to garnish
  2.5ml/½ tsp granulated (white) sugar
  salt

1 Heat a small pan and dry-fry the cumin seeds for 1–2 minutes, until they release their aroma and begin to pop.

2 Let the seeds cool for a few minutes, then tip them into a mortar. Crush them with a pestle or flatten them with the heel of a heavy-bladed knife.

COOK'S TIPS
• For an extra tangy raita, stir in 15ml/ 1 tbsp lemon juice.
• For a thicker consistency, drain off any liquid from the yogurt before adding the ingredients.

3 Cut the red onion in half. Cut a few thin slices for the garnish and chop the rest finely. Crush the garlic, then finely chop the chilli. Stir the onion, garlic and chilli into the yogurt with the crushed cumin seeds and coriander.

4 Add sugar and salt to taste. Spoon the raita into a small bowl, cover and chill until ready to serve. Garnish with the reserved onion slices and extra coriander before serving. The dip will keep for 2 days in the refrigerator.

PUMPKIN SEED SAUCE

THE ANCESTORS OF MODERN-DAY MEXICANS DIDN'T BELIEVE IN WASTING FOOD, AS THIS TRADITIONAL RECIPE PROVES. IT IS BASED UPON PUMPKIN SEEDS AND HAS A DELICIOUS NUTTY FLAVOUR. IT IS GREAT SERVED OVER STEAMED OR BOILED NOPALES (CACTUS PADDLES) AND IS ALSO DELICIOUS WITH COOKED CHICKEN OR RACK OF LAMB.

SERVES FOUR AS AN ACCOMPANIMENT

INGREDIENTS
    130g/4½oz raw pumpkin seeds
    500g/1¼lb tomatoes
    2 garlic cloves, crushed
    300ml/½ pint/1¼ cups chicken
       stock, preferably freshly made
    15ml/1 tbsp vegetable oil
    45ml/3 tbsp red chilli sauce
    salt (optional)

1 Preheat the oven to 200°C/400°F/ Gas 6. Heat a heavy frying pan until very hot. Add the pumpkin seeds and dry fry them, stirring constantly over the heat. The seeds will start to swell and pop, but they must not be allowed to scorch (see Cook's Tip). When all the seeds have popped remove the pan from the heat.

2 Cut the tomatoes into quarters and place them on a baking tray. Roast in the hot oven for 45 minutes–1 hour, until charred and softened. Allow to cool slightly, then remove the skins using a small sharp knife.

3 Put the pumpkin seeds in a food processor and process until smooth. Add the tomatoes and process for a few minutes, then add the garlic and stock and process for 1 minute more.

COOK'S TIP
When dry frying the pumpkin seeds, don't stop stirring for a moment or they may scorch, which would make the sauce bitter. It is a good idea to stand back a little as some of the hot seeds may fly out of the pan.

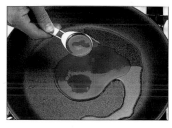

4 Heat the oil in a large frying pan. Add the red chilli sauce and cook, stirring constantly, for 2–3 minutes. Add the pumpkin seed mixture and bring to the boil, stirring all the time.

5 Simmer the sauce for 20 minutes, stirring frequently until the sauce has thickened and reduced by about half. Taste and add salt, if needed. Serve over meat or vegetables or cool and chill. The salsa will keep for up to a week in a covered bowl in the refrigerator.

SMOKY CHIPOTLE SAUCE

THE SMOKY FLAVOUR OF THIS RICH SAUCE MAKES IT IDEAL FOR BARBECUE-COOKED FOOD, AS A MARINADE OR ACCOMPANIMENT. IT IS WONDERFUL STIRRED INTO CREAM CHEESE AS A SANDWICH FILLING WITH CHICKEN. CHIPOTLE CHILLIES ARE SMOKE-DRIED JALAPEÑOS.

SERVES SIX

INGREDIENTS
500g/1¼lb tomatoes
5 chipotle chillies
3 garlic cloves, roughly chopped
150ml/¼ pint/⅔ cup red wine
5ml/1 tsp dried oregano
60ml/4 tbsp clear honey
5ml/1 tsp American mustard
2.5ml/½ tsp ground black pepper
salt

1 Preheat the oven to 200°C/400°F/ Gas 6. Cut the tomatoes into quarters and place them in a roasting pan. Roast for 45–60 minutes, until they are charred.

2 Meanwhile, soak the chillies in a bowl of cold water to cover for about 20 minutes or until soft. Remove the stalks, slit the chillies and scrape out the seeds with a small sharp knife. Discard the seeds. Chop the flesh roughly.

3 Remove the tomatoes from the oven, let them cool slightly, then remove the skins. If you prefer a smooth sauce, remove the seeds. Chop the tomatoes in a blender or food processor. Add the chillies, garlic and red wine. Process until smooth, then add the oregano, honey, mustard and black pepper. Process briefly to mix, then taste and season with salt.

4 Pour the mixture into a small pan. Bring to the boil, lower the heat and simmer the sauce for about 10 minutes, stirring occasionally, until it has reduced and thickened. Spoon into a bowl and serve hot or cold.

GUAJILLO CHILLI SAUCE

THIS SAUCE CAN BE SERVED OVER ENCHILADAS OR STEAMED VEGETABLES. IT IS ALSO GOOD EATEN HOT OR COLD WITH MEATS, AND A LITTLE MAKES A FINE SEASONING FOR SOUPS OR STEWS.

SERVES FOUR

INGREDIENTS
2 tomatoes
2 red (bell) peppers, cored, seeded and quartered
3 garlic cloves, in their skins
2 ancho chillies
2 guajillo chillies
30ml/2 tbsp tomato purée (paste)
5ml/1 tsp dried oregano
5ml/1 tsp soft dark brown sugar
300ml/½ pint/1¼ cups chicken stock

1 Preheat the oven to 200°C/400°F/ Gas 6. Cut the tomatoes into quarters and place them in a roasting pan with the peppers and whole garlic cloves. Roast for 45–60 minutes, until the tomatoes and peppers are slightly charred.

COOK'S TIP
Like chipotle chillies, guajillos are dried. They give the sauce a well-rounded, fruity flavour and do not make it too hot.

2 Put the peppers in a strong plastic bag and tie the top to keep the steam in. Set aside for 20 minutes. Remove the skin from the tomatoes. Soak the chillies in boiling water for 20 minutes.

3 Remove the peppers from the bag and rub off the skins. Cut them in half, remove the cores and seeds, then chop the flesh roughly and put it in a food processor or blender. Drain the chillies, remove the stalks, then slit them and scrape out and discard the seeds. Chop them roughly and add to the peppers.

4 Add the roasted tomatoes to the food processor. Squeeze the roasted garlic out of the skins and add to the tomato mixture, with the tomato purée, oregano, sugar and stock. Process until smooth.

5 Pour the mixture into a pan, place over a medium heat and bring to the boil. Lower the heat and simmer for 10–15 minutes until the sauce has reduced to about half. Transfer to a bowl and serve. Or leave to cool, then chill until required. The sauce will keep in the refrigerator for up to 1 week.

THAI RED CURRY SAUCE

*SERVE THIS WITH MINI SPRING ROLLS OR SPICY INDONESIAN CRACKERS, OR TOSS IT INTO
FRESHLY COOKED RICE NOODLES FOR A DELICIOUS MAIN-MEAL ACCOMPANIMENT.*

SERVES FOUR

INGREDIENTS

200ml/7fl oz/scant 1 cup
  coconut cream
10–15ml/2–3 tsp Thai red
  curry paste
4 spring onions (scallions), plus
  extra, to garnish
30ml/2 tbsp chopped fresh
  coriander (cilantro)
1 fresh red chilli, seeded and thinly
  sliced into rings
5ml/1 tsp soy sauce
juice of 1 lime
granulated (white) sugar, to taste
25g/1oz/¼ cup dry-roasted peanuts
salt and ground black pepper

1 Pour the coconut cream into a small
bowl and stir in the curry paste.

COOK'S TIP
The dip may be prepared in advance up
to the end of step 3. Cover and keep in
the refrigerator for up to 4 hours.

2 Trim the spring onions and finely
slice them on the diagonal. Stir into
the coconut cream with the chopped
fresh coriander and chilli.

3 Stir in the soy sauce and fresh lime
juice, with sugar, salt and pepper to
taste. Pour the sauce into a small
serving bowl.

4 Finely chop the dry-roasted peanuts
and sprinkle them over the sauce. Garnish
with spring onions sliced lengthways
into thin curls. Serve immediately.

VARIATION
As an alternative to spring onions (scallions),
try using 1–2 baby leeks. They can be
prepared in the same way.

MEXICAN VINEGAR SEASONING

ADOBO MEANS VINEGAR SAUCE, AND THIS ONE IS A PASTE MADE FROM DRIED CHILLIES,
USED FOR MARINATING PORK CHOPS OR STEAKS. ADOBOS ARE USED IN MEXICAN COOKING.

MAKES ENOUGH TO MARINATE
SIX CHOPS OR STEAKS

INGREDIENTS
   1 small head of garlic
   5 ancho chillies
   2 pasilla chillies
   15ml/1 tbsp dried oregano
   5ml/1 tsp cumin seeds
   6 cloves
   5ml/1 tsp coriander seeds
   10cm/4in piece of cinnamon stick
   10ml/2 tsp salt
   120ml/4fl oz/½ cup white
     wine vinegar

1 Preheat the oven to 180°C/350°F/
Gas 4. Cut a thin slice off the top of the
head of garlic, so that the inside of each
clove is exposed. Wrap the head of
garlic in foil. Roast for 45–60 minutes
or until the garlic is soft.

2 Meanwhile, slit the chillies and shake
out most of the seeds. Break up the
dried chillies a little and put them in a
food processor, spice mill or mortar.
Add the oregano, cumin seeds, cloves,
coriander seeds, cinnamon stick and
salt. Process or grind to a fine powder.

3 Remove the garlic from the oven.
When it is cool enough to handle,
squeeze the pulp out of each clove.

4 Add the garlic and white wine vinegar
to the spice mixture and process or
grind to a smooth paste. Scrape into a
bowl and leave to stand for 1 hour, to
allow the flavours to blend. Spread over
pork chops or steaks as a marinade,
before cooking.

COOK'S TIP
You can buy wild Mexican oregano from
Mexican food stores or by mail order.

CHILLI RELISH

FOR INSTANT HEAT, KEEP A POT OF THIS SPICY RELISH. IT TASTES GREAT WITH SAUSAGES,
BURGERS AND CHEESE. IT WILL KEEP IN THE REFRIGERATOR FOR UP TO TWO WEEKS.

SERVES EIGHT

INGREDIENTS
6 tomatoes
1 onion
1 sweet red (bell) pepper, seeded
2 garlic cloves
30ml/2 tbsp olive oil
5ml/1 tsp ground cinnamon
5ml/1 tsp dried chilli flakes
5ml/1 tsp ground ginger
5ml/1 tsp salt
2.5ml/½ tsp ground black pepper
75g/3oz/scant ⅔ cup light muscovado
 (brown) sugar
75ml/5 tbsp cider vinegar
handful of fresh basil leaves

COOK'S TIP
This relish thickens slightly on cooling,
so do not worry if the mixture seems a
little sloppy when it is first made.

1 Skewer each of the tomatoes in turn
on a metal fork and hold in a gas flame
for 1–2 minutes, turning until the skin
splits and wrinkles. Place the tomatoes
on a chopping board, slip off the skins,
then roughly chop.

2 Roughly chop the onion, red pepper
and garlic. Gently heat the oil in a pan.
Tip in the onion, red pepper and garlic,
stirring lightly.

3 Cook gently for 5–8 minutes, until the
pepper has softened. Add the chopped
tomatoes, cover and cook for 5 minutes.

4 Stir in the cinnamon, chilli flakes,
ginger, salt, pepper, sugar and vinegar.
Bring gently to the boil, stirring until the
sugar dissolves.

5 Simmer, uncovered, for 20 minutes,
until the mixture is pulpy. Stir in the
basil leaves and check the seasoning.

6 Allow to cool completely, then spoon
into a glass jar or a plastic tub with a
tightly fitting lid. Store, covered, in
the refrigerator. This relish will keep
in the refrigerator for up to a fortnight.
Stir before using.

SPICY CORN RELISH

*A TOUCH OF HEAT TEMPERS THE SWEETNESS OF THIS DELICIOUS RELISH. TRY IT WITH
CRISP ONION BHAJIS OR SLICES OF HONEY-ROAST HAM FOR A SPICY SNACK.*

SERVES FOUR

INGREDIENTS
1 large onion
1 fresh red chilli, seeded
2 garlic cloves
30ml/2 tbsp vegetable oil
5ml/1 tsp black mustard seeds
10ml/2 tsp hot curry powder
320g/11¼oz can corn
grated rind and juice of 1 lime
45ml/3 tbsp chopped fresh
   coriander (cilantro)
salt and ground black pepper

1 Chop the onion, chilli and garlic. Heat
the vegetable oil in a large frying pan
and cook the onion, chilli and garlic
over a high heat for 5 minutes, until
the onions are just beginning to brown.

2 Stir in the mustard seeds and curry
powder. Cook for a further 2 minutes,
stirring, until all the seeds start to
splutter and the onions have browned.

COOK'S TIP
Opt for canned rather than frozen corn if
possible, as the kernels are plump, moist
and ready to eat.

3 Remove the fried onion mixture from
the heat and allow to cool. Place in a
glass bowl. Drain the corn and stir it
into the onion mixture.

4 Add the lime rind and juice, coriander
and salt and pepper to taste. Cover and
refrigerate until needed. The relish is
best served at room temperature.

RED ONION, GARLIC AND CHILLI RELISH

THIS POWERFUL RELISH IS FLAVOURED WITH NORTH AFRICAN SPICES AND PUNCHY PRESERVED LEMONS, AVAILABLE FROM DELICATESSENS AND LARGER SUPERMARKETS.

2 Add the garlic cloves and coriander seeds. Cover and cook gently for another 5–8 minutes, stirring occasionally to prevent the onions from browning, until the garlic is beginning to soften.

3 Add a pinch of salt, lots of pepper and the sugar, and cook, uncovered, for 5 minutes. Meanwhile, soak the saffron in the warm water for 5 minutes. Then add the saffron mixture (including the saffron threads) to the onions. Add the cinnamon, chillies and bay leaves. Stir in 30ml/2 tbsp of the sherry vinegar and the orange juice.

SERVES SIX

INGREDIENTS
    45ml/3 tbsp olive oil
    3 large red onions, sliced
    2 heads of garlic, separated into
      cloves and peeled
    10ml/2 tsp coriander seeds, crushed
      but not finely ground
    10ml/2 tsp light muscovado (brown)
      sugar, plus a little extra
    pinch of saffron threads
    45ml/3 tbsp warm water
    10cm/2in piece of cinnamon stick
    2–3 small whole dried red chillies
    2 fresh bay leaves
    30–45ml/2–3 tbsp sherry vinegar
    juice of ½ small orange
    30ml/2 tbsp chopped
      preserved lemon
    salt and ground black pepper

1 Heat the oil in a heavy pan. Add the onions and stir, then cover and reduce the heat to the lowest setting. Cook for 10–15 minutes, stirring occasionally, until the onions are very soft but not browned.

4 Cook gently, uncovered, until the onions are very soft and most of the liquid has evaporated. Stir in the preserved lemon and cook gently for 5 minutes. Taste and adjust the seasoning, adding sugar and/or vinegar to balance the flavours. You may not need to add more salt, since the lemons are preserved in it.

5 Serve warm or at room temperature, but not hot or chilled. The relish tastes best the day after it is made. Remove the cinnamon stick before serving.

PIQUANT PINEAPPLE RELISH

THIS FRUITY SWEET AND SOUR RELISH IS REALLY EXCELLENT WHEN IT IS SERVED WITH GRILLED CHICKEN OR BACON SLICES.

SERVES FOUR

INGREDIENTS

400g/14oz can crushed pineapple
   in natural juice
30ml/2 tbsp light muscovado
   (brown) sugar
30ml/2 tbsp wine vinegar
1 garlic clove
4 spring onions (scallions)
2 red chillies
10 fresh basil leaves
salt and ground black pepper

1 Drain the crushed pineapple pieces thoroughly and reserve about 60ml/ 4 tbsp of the juice.

2 Place the pineapple juice in a small pan with the muscovado sugar and wine vinegar, then heat gently, stirring, until the sugar dissolves. Remove the pan from the heat and add salt and pepper to taste.

3 Finely chop the garlic and spring onions. Halve the chillies, remove the seeds and finely chop the flesh. Finely shred the basil.

4 Place the pineapple, garlic, spring onions and chillies in a bowl. Mix well and pour in the sauce. Leave to cool for 5 minutes, then stir in the basil.

COOK'S TIP
This relish tastes extra special when made with fresh pineapple – substitute the juice of a freshly squeezed orange for the canned juice.

CHILLI STRIPS WITH LIME

THIS FRESH RELISH IS IDEAL FOR SERVING WITH STEWS, RICE DISHES OR BEAN DISHES. THE OREGANO ADDS A SWEET NOTE WHILE THE ABSENCE OF SUGAR OR OIL MAKES THIS A VERY HEALTHY CHOICE.

MAKES ABOUT 60ML/4 TBSP

INGREDIENTS
10 fresh green chillies
½ white onion
4 limes
2.5ml/½ tsp dried oregano
salt

COOK'S TIP
This method of roasting chillies is ideal if you need more than one or two, or if you do not have a gas burner. To roast over a burner, spear the chillies, four or five at a time, on a long-handled metal skewer and hold them over the flame, turning them round frequently, until the skins blister.

1 Roast the chillies in a griddle pan over a medium heat until the skins are charred and blistered but not blackened, as this might make the salsa bitter. Place the roasted chillies in a strong plastic bag and tie the top to keep the steam in. Set aside for 20 minutes.

2 Meanwhile, slice the onion very thinly and put it in a large bowl. Squeeze the limes and add the juice to the bowl, with any pulp that gathers in the strainer. The lime juice will have the effect of softening the onion. Stir in the oregano.

3 Remove the chillies from the bag and peel off the skins. Slit them, then scrape out and discard all the seeds. Cut the chillies into long strips using a sharp knife. These are called "rajas".

4 Add the chilli strips to the onion mixture and season lightly with salt. Cover the bowl and chill for at least 1 day before serving, to allow the flavours to blend. Taste the salsa and add more salt at this stage if necessary. The salsa will keep for up to 2 weeks in a covered bowl in the refrigerator.

VARIATION
White onions have a mild sweet flavour, as do red onions, which could equally well be used in their place. The colour combination of red and green would look particularly good with rice dishes.

HOT THAI PICKLED SHALLOTS WITH CHILLIES

THAI PINK SHALLOTS REQUIRE LENGTHY PREPARATION, BUT THEY LOOK EXQUISITE WITH
WHOLE CHILLIES IN THIS SPICED PICKLE. SERVE THEM FINELY SLICED.

MAKES TWO TO THREE JARS

INGREDIENTS
  5–6 small red or green bird's
    eye chillies
  500g/1¼lb Thai pink shallots, peeled
  2 large garlic cloves, halved

For the vinegar
  600ml/1 pint/2½ cups cider vinegar
  45ml/3 tbsp granulated (white) sugar
  10ml/2 tsp salt
  5cm/2in piece fresh root
    ginger, sliced
  15ml/1 tbsp coriander seeds
  2 lemon grass stalks, trimmed and
    cut in half lengthways
  4 kaffir lime leaves or strips of lime rind
  15ml/1 tbsp chopped fresh
    coriander (cilantro)

1 Prick the chillies several times with a cocktail stick (toothpick). Bring a large pan of water to the boil. Blanch the chillies, shallots and garlic for 1–2 minutes, then drain. Rinse all the vegetables under cold water, then drain again thoroughly in a colander.

2 To prepare the vinegar, put the cider vinegar, sugar, salt, ginger, coriander seeds, lemon grass and lime leaves or lime rind in a pan and bring to the boil. Reduce the heat and simmer for 3–4 minutes, then leave to cool.

3 Scoop out the ginger, then bring the vinegar back to the boil. Add the fresh coriander, garlic and chillies (leave the shallots in the colander) and cook for 1 minute.

4 Pack the shallots into sterilized jars, distributing the lemon grass, lime leaves, chillies and garlic between them. Pour over the hot vinegar. Cool, then seal and leave in a dark place for 2 months before eating.

COOK'S TIPS
• When making pickles, see that bowls and pans used for the vinegar are not chemically affected by the acid of the vinegar. China and glass bowls and stainless steel pans are suitable.
• Ensure that metal lids do not come in contact with the pickle. The acid in the vinegar would corrode the metal. Use plastic-coated lids or glass lids with rubber rings. Or, when using metal lids, cover the top of each jar with a circle of waxed paper to prevent direct contact.
• Let hot jars cool slightly after sterilizing. But do not let them cool completely, or they might crack when the hot vinegar is poured in.

COCONUT CHUTNEY WITH ONION AND CHILLI

SERVE THIS REFRESHING COCONUT CHUTNEY AS AN ACCOMPANIMENT TO INDIAN-STYLE
DISHES OR AT THE START OF A MEAL, WITH POPPADUMS, A RAITA AND OTHER CHUTNEYS.

SERVES FOUR TO SIX

INGREDIENTS
    200g/7oz fresh coconut, grated
    3–4 fresh green chillies, seeded
      and chopped
    60ml/4 tbsp chopped fresh
      coriander (cilantro)
    30ml/2 tbsp chopped fresh mint
    30–45ml/2–3 tbsp lime juice
    about 2.5ml/½ tsp salt
    2.5ml/½ tsp granulated (white) sugar
    15–30ml/1–2 tbsp coconut milk
    30ml/2 tbsp groundnut
      (peanut) oil
    5ml/1 tsp kalonji (nigella seeds)
    1 small onion, very finely chopped
    fresh coriander (cilantro) sprigs,
      to garnish

1 Place the coconut, chillies, coriander
and mint in a food processor. Add
30ml/2 tbsp of the lime juice, then
process until thoroughly chopped.

2 Scrape the mixture into a bowl. Stir in
more lime juice to taste, with the salt,
sugar and coconut milk.

3 Heat the oil in a small pan and fry the
kalonji until they begin to pop. Reduce
the heat and add the onion. Fry, stirring
frequently, until the onion is soft.

4 Stir the spiced onions into the
coconut mixture and cool. Garnish with
coriander sprigs before serving.

ONION, MANGO AND CHILLI RELISH

CHAATS ARE SPICED RELISHES OF VEGETABLES AND NUTS SERVED WITH INDIAN MEALS. USE GREEN
JALAPEÑOS OR SERRANOS FOR MEDIUM HEAT, OR GREEN CAYENNE CHILLIES IF YOU WANT IT HOT.

SERVES FOUR

INGREDIENTS
    15ml/1 tbsp groundnut (peanut) oil
    90g/3½oz/1 cup unsalted peanuts
    1 onion, chopped
    10cm/4in piece cucumber, seeded
      and cut into 5mm/¼in dice
    1 mango, peeled, stoned (pitted)
      and diced
    1–2 fresh green chillies, seeded and
      finely chopped
    30ml/2 tbsp chopped fresh
      coriander (cilantro)
    15ml/1 tbsp chopped fresh mint
    15ml/1 tbsp lime juice
    a pinch of granulated (white) sugar

For the chaat masala
    10ml/2 tsp ground toasted cumin seeds
    2.5ml/½ tsp cayenne pepper
    5ml/1 tsp mango powder (amchoor)
    2.5ml/½ tsp garam masala
    salt and ground black pepper

1 To make the chaat masala, grind all
the spices together, then season with
2.5ml/½ tsp each of salt and pepper.

2 Heat the oil in a small pan and fry
the peanuts until lightly browned, then
drain on kitchen paper and set aside
until cool.

COOK'S TIP
Mango powder (amchoor) is made by
grinding sun-dried mango slices and
mixing the powder with a little turmeric.

3 Mix the onion, cucumber, mango,
chilli, fresh coriander and mint. Sprinkle
in 5ml/1 tsp of the chaat masala. Stir in
the peanuts and then add the lime juice
and sugar to taste. Set the mixture
aside for 20–30 minutes for the flavours
to mature.

4 Spoon the mixture into a serving bowl,
sprinkle another 5ml/1 tsp of the chaat
masala over and serve. Any remaining
chaat masala will keep in a sealed jar
for 4–6 weeks.

MIXED VEGETABLE PICKLE

*FRESH TURMERIC WILL MAKES A GREAT DIFFERENCE TO THE COLOUR OF ACAR CAMPUR. YOU CAN USE
ALMOST ANY VEGETABLE, SO LONG AS YOU HAVE A BALANCE OF TEXTURES, FLAVOURS AND COLOURS.*

MAKES TWO OR THREE 300G/11OZ JARS

INGREDIENTS
    1 fresh red chilli, seeded and sliced
    1 onion, quartered
    2 garlic cloves, crushed
    1cm/½ in cube shrimp paste
    4 macadamia nuts or 8 almonds
    2.5cm/1in fresh turmeric,
      peeled and sliced, or 5ml/1 tsp
      ground turmeric
    50ml/2fl oz/¼ cup sunflower oil
    475ml/16fl oz/2 cups white vinegar
    250ml/8fl oz/1 cup water
    25–50g/1–2oz sugar
    3 carrots
    225g/8oz/1½ cups green beans
    1 small cauliflower
    1 cucumber
    225g/8oz white cabbage
    115g/4oz/1 cup dry-roasted peanuts,
      coarsely crushed
    salt

1 Place the chilli, onion, garlic, shrimp
paste, nuts and turmeric in a food
processor and blend to a paste,
or pound in a mortar with a pestle.

2 Heat the oil and stir-fry the paste to
release the aroma. Add the vinegar,
water, sugar and salt. Bring to the boil.
Simmer for 10 minutes.

3 Cut the carrots into flower shapes.
Cut the green beans into short, neat
lengths. Separate the cauliflower into
neat, bitesize florets. Peel and seed the
cucumber and cut the flesh in neat,
bitesize pieces. Cut the cabbage in
neat, bitesize pieces.

4 Blanch each vegetable separately,
in a large pan of boiling water, for 1
minute. Transfer to a colander and rinse
with cold water, to halt the cooking.
Drain well.

5 Add the vegetables to the sauce.
Gradually bring to the boil and cook for
5–10 minutes. Do not overcook – the
vegetables should still be quite crunchy.

COOK'S TIP
This pickle is even better if you make it
a few days ahead.

6 Add the peanuts and cool. Spoon into
clean jars with lids.

SPICY FRIED DUMPLINGS

These little dumplings are easy to make. In the Caribbean, they are often served with saltfish or fried fish, but they can be eaten simply with butter and jam or cheese.

MAKES ABOUT TEN

INGREDIENTS

450g/1lb/4 cups self-raising
   (self-rising) flour
10ml/2 tsp sugar
2.5ml/½ tsp ground cinnamon
pinch of ground nutmeg
2.5ml/½ tsp salt
300ml/½ pint/1¼ cups milk
oil, for frying

3 Heat a little oil in a non-stick frying pan until moderately hot. Place half the dumplings in the pan, reduce the heat to low and cook for about 15 minutes until they are golden brown, turning once.

4 Stand the dumplings on their sides for a few minutes to brown the edges, before removing them and draining on kitchen paper. Serve warm.

1 Sift the dry ingredients together into a large bowl, add the milk and mix and knead until smooth.

2 Divide the dough into ten balls, kneading each ball with floured hands. Press the balls gently to flatten into 7.5cm/3in rounds.

CHICKPEA BREADS

THESE FLAVOUR-PACKED UNLEAVENED BREADS ARE POPULAR IN NORTHERN INDIA. THEY ARE MADE WITH GRAM FLOUR, WHICH IS MILLED FROM CHANA DHAL, A TYPE OF CHICKPEA.

2 Mix in enough water to make a pliable, soft dough. Place the dough on a lightly floured surface and knead it until smooth, then place it in a lightly oiled bowl, cover with lightly oiled clear film (plastic wrap) and rest for 1 hour.

3 Transfer the dough to a lightly floured surface. Divide into four equal pieces and shape into balls. Roll out each ball of dough into a thick round, about 15–18cm/6–7in in diameter. Heat a griddle or heavy frying pan over a medium heat for a few minutes until it is hot.

4 Brush both sides of one roti with a little of the remaining oil or melted butter. Add it to the griddle or frying pan and cook for about 2 minutes, turning after 1 minute. Brush the cooked roti lightly with oil or melted butter again, slide it on to a plate and keep warm in a preheated low oven while cooking the remaining rotis in the same way. Serve warm.

VARIATION
Use 1.5–2.5ml/¼– ½ tsp chilli powder instead of the fresh chilli.

MAKES FOUR

INGREDIENTS
  115g/4oz/1 cup gram flour
  115g/4oz/1 cup wholemeal
    (whole-wheat) flour
  1 fresh green chilli, seeded
    and chopped
  ½ onion, finely chopped
  15ml/1 tbsp chopped fresh
    coriander (cilantro)
  2.5ml/½ tsp ground turmeric
  2.5ml/½ tsp salt
  45ml/3 tbsp oil or melted butter
  120–150ml/4–5fl oz/½– ⅔ cup
    lukewarm water

1 Mix the gram and wholemeal flours, chopped chilli, onion and coriander, ground turmeric and salt well together in a large bowl. Stir in 15ml/1 tbsp of the oil or melted butter.

CHILLI POORI PUFFS

THESE SMALL DISCS OF DOUGH PUFF UP INTO LIGHT AIRY BREADS WHEN FRIED. LIGHTLY STUDDED WITH PIECES OF CHILLI, THEY MELT IN YOUR MOUTH AND LEAVE YOU WITH A WARM GLOW.

MAKES TWELVE

INGREDIENTS

   115g/4oz/1 cup unbleached plain
     (all-purpose) flour
   115g/4oz/1 cup wholemeal
     (whole-wheat) flour
   2.5ml/½ tsp salt
   2.5ml/½ tsp mild chilli powder
   30ml/2 tbsp vegetable oil
   1 fresh red chilli, seeded and finely
     chopped (optional)
   100–120ml/3½–4fl oz/
     scant ½ cup–½ cup water
   oil, for frying

VARIATION
To make spinach-flavoured pooris, omit the fresh chilli. Thaw 50g/2oz/¼ cup frozen chopped spinach, drain and add to the dough with 5ml/1 tsp grated fresh ginger and 2.5ml/½ tsp ground cumin.

1 Sift the flours, salt and chilli powder into a large bowl. Add the vegetable oil then mix in enough water to make a dough. Turn the dough out on a lightly floured surface and knead for 8–10 minutes until it is smooth, elastic and springy.

2 Place in a lightly oiled bowl and cover with lightly oiled clear film (plastic wrap). Leave to rest for 30 minutes.

3 Turn out on to a lightly floured surface. Knead in the chopped fresh chilli, if using, then divide the dough into 12 equal pieces. Keeping the rest of the dough covered, roll one piece into a 13cm/5in round. Repeat with the remaining dough. Stack the pooris, layered between clear film.

4 Pour oil into a deep pan to a depth of 2.5cm/1in. Heat it to 180°C/350°F or until a cube of day-old bread, added to the oil, browns in about 45 seconds. Using a spatula, lift one poori and slide it into the oil; it will sink but will rise and begin to sizzle. Press the poori into the oil. It will puff up. Turn it over after a few seconds and cook for 20–30 seconds. Remove the poori from the pan and drain on kitchen paper. Keep warm in a preheated low oven while cooking the remaining pooris. Serve warm.

MIXED SPICED NUTS

SPICE UP YOUR VERY OWN HAPPY HOUR WITH THESE SUPERB NUTTY SNACKS.

SERVES FOUR TO SIX

INGREDIENTS
  75g/3oz/1 cup dried unsweetened
    coconut flakes
  75ml/5 tbsp groundnut (peanut) oil
  2.5ml/½ tsp hot chilli powder
  5ml/1 tsp paprika
  5ml/1 tsp tomato purée (paste)
  225g/8oz/2 cups unsalted
    cashew nuts
  225g/8oz/2 cups whole
    blanched almonds
  60ml/4 tbsp granulated (white) sugar
  5ml/1 tsp ground cumin
  2.5ml/½ tsp salt
  ground black pepper
  fresh herbs, to garnish

1 Heat a wok, add the coconut flakes
and dry-fry until golden. Tip out on to a
plate and leave to cool.

COOK'S TIP
The nuts can be stored separately for
up to 1 month in an airtight tub.

2 Heat the wok again and add 45ml/
3 tbsp of the oil. When it is hot, add the
chilli powder, paprika and tomato purée.
Stir well, add the cashew nuts and
gently stir-fry until well coated. Drain,
season with pepper and leave to cool.

3 Wipe out the wok with kitchen paper,
heat it, then add the remaining oil.
When the oil is hot, add the almonds
and sprinkle in the sugar. Stir-fry gently
until the almonds are golden brown and
the sugar has caramelized. Place the
cumin and salt in a bowl. Add the hot
almonds, toss well, then leave to cool.

4 Either mix the cashew nuts, almonds
and coconut flakes together or serve
them in separate bowls. Garnish with
sprigs of fresh herbs such as parsley
and coriander.

RED-HOT ROOTS

*COLOURFUL AND CRISP CHIPS, MADE FROM A SELECTION OF ROOT VEGETABLES, TASTE DELICIOUS WITH
A LIGHT DUSTING OF CHILLI POWDER AND SEA SALT.*

SERVES FOUR TO SIX

INGREDIENTS
  1 carrot
  2 parsnips
  2 raw beetroot (beets)
  1 sweet potato
  groundnut (peanut) oil, for
    deep-frying
  1.5ml/¼ tsp hot chilli powder
  5ml/1 tsp sea salt flakes

1 Peel all the vegetables, then slice
the carrot and parsnips into long, thin
ribbons and the beetroot and sweet
potato into thin rounds. Pat dry all
the vegetable ribbons and rounds on
kitchen paper.

2 Half-fill a wok with oil. Heat it to
180°C/350°F or until a cube of day-old
bread, added to the oil, browns in about
45 seconds. Add the vegetable slices in
batches and deep-fry for 2–3 minutes
until golden and crisp. Remove and
drain on kitchen paper.

3 Place the chilli powder and sea salt in
a mortar and grind with a pestle to a
coarse powder. Pile up the vegetable
chips on a serving plate, sprinkle over
the spiced salt and serve immediately.

COOK'S TIP
To save time, you can slice the
vegetables using a mandoline or a food
processor fitted with a thin slicing disc.

CHILLI-SPICED PLANTAIN CHIPS

THIS SNACK HAS A LOVELY SWEET TASTE, WHICH IS BALANCED BY THE HEAT FROM THE
CHILLI POWDER AND SAUCE. COOK THE CHIPS JUST BEFORE YOU INTEND TO SERVE THEM.

SERVES FOUR

INGREDIENTS
2 large plantains with very
  dark skins
groundnut (peanut) oil, for
  shallow-frying
2.5ml/½ tsp hot chilli powder
5ml/1 tsp ground cinnamon
hot chilli sauce, to serve

1 Peel the plantains. Cut off and throw
away the ends, then slice the fruit
diagonally into rounds; do not make
them too thin.

2 Pour the oil for frying into a small
frying pan, to a depth of about
1cm/½in. Heat the oil until it is very
hot, watching it closely all the time. Test
by carefully adding a slice of plantain;
it should float and the oil should
immediately bubble up around it.

3 Fry the plantain slices in small
batches or the temperature of the oil
will drop. When they are golden brown,
remove from the oil with a slotted spoon
and drain on kitchen paper.

4 Mix the chilli powder with the
cinnamon. Put the plantain chips on a
serving plate, sprinkle them with the
chilli and cinnamon mixture and serve
immediately, with a small bowl of hot
chilli sauce for dipping.

COOK'S TIP
Plantains are more starchy than the
bananas to which they are related, and
must be cooked before being eaten. When
ready to eat, the skin is almost black.

POPCORN WITH LIME AND CHILLI

IF THE ONLY POPCORN YOU'VE HAD CAME OUT OF A CARTON AT THE CINEMA, TRY THIS
MEXICAN SPECIALITY. THE LIME JUICE AND CHILLI POWDER ARE INSPIRED ADDITIONS,
AND THE SNACK IS QUITE A HEALTHY CHOICE TO SERVE WITH DRINKS.

MAKES ONE LARGE BOWL

INGREDIENTS
30ml/2 tbsp vegetable oil
225g/8oz/1¼ cups corn kernels
  for popcorn
10ml/2 tsp mild or hot chilli powder
juice of 2 limes

1 Heat the oil in a large, heavy frying
pan until it is very hot. Add the popcorn
and immediately cover the pan with a
lid and reduce the heat.

2 After a few minutes, the corn should
start to pop. Resist the temptation to
lift the lid to check. Shake the pan
occasionally so that all the corn will
be cooked and lightly browned.

3 When the sound of popping corn has
stopped, quickly remove the pan from
the heat and allow to cool slightly. Take
off the lid and use a spoon to lift out
and discard any corn kernels that have
not popped. Any uncooked corn will
have fallen to the base of the pan and
will be inedible.

4 Add the chilli powder to the pan.
Replace the lid firmly and shake the
pan repeatedly to make sure that all of
the corn is covered with a colourful
dusting of chilli powder.

5 Tip the popcorn into a large bowl
and keep warm. Sprinkle over the juice
of the limes immediately prior to serving
the popcorn.

TORTILLA CHIPS

THESE ARE KNOWN AS TOTOPOS *IN MEXICO, AND THE TERM REFERS TO BOTH THE FRIED TORTILLA STRIPS USED TO GARNISH SOUPS AND THE TRIANGLES USED FOR SCOOPING DIPS. USE TORTILLAS THAT ARE A FEW DAYS OLD; FRESH ONES WILL NOT CRISP UP SO WELL.*

SERVES FOUR

INGREDIENTS
    4–8 corn tortillas
    oil, for frying
    salt

VARIATION
When fried, wheat flour tortillas do not crisp up as well as corn tortillas, but they make a delicious sweet treat when sprinkled with ground cinnamon and sugar. Serve them hot with a little whipped cream.

1 Cut each tortilla into six triangular wedges. Pour oil into a large frying pan to a depth of 1cm/½in, place the pan over a moderate heat and heat until very hot (see Cook's Tip).

COOK'S TIP
The oil needs to be very hot for cooking the tortillas – test it by carefully adding one of the wedges. It should float and begin to bubble in the oil immediately.

2 Fry the tortilla wedges in the hot oil in small batches until they turn golden and are crisp. This will only take a few moments. Remove with a slotted spoon and drain on kitchen paper. Sprinkle with salt.

3 *Totopos* should be served warm. They can be cooled completely and stored in an airtight container for a few days, but will need to be reheated in a microwave or a warm oven before being served.

HOT PUMPKIN SEEDS

THESE LITTLE SNACKS ARE IRRESISTIBLE, ESPECIALLY IF YOU INCLUDE CHIPOTLE CHILLIES. THEIR SMOKY FLAVOUR IS THE PERFECT FOIL FOR THE NUTTY TASTE OF THE PUMPKIN SEEDS AND THE SWEETNESS CONTRIBUTED BY THE SUGAR. SERVE THEM WITH PRE-DINNER DRINKS.

SERVES FOUR

INGREDIENTS
    130g/4½oz/1 cup pumpkin seeds
    4 garlic cloves, crushed
    1.5ml/¼ tsp salt
    10ml/2 tsp crushed dried chillies
    5ml/1 tsp caster (superfine) sugar
    a wedge of lime

COOK'S TIP
It is important to keep the pumpkin seeds moving as they cook. Watch them carefully and do not let them burn, or they will taste bitter.

1 Heat a small, heavy frying pan, add the pumpkin seeds and dry-fry for a few minutes, stirring constantly as they swell to prevent them from burning.

2 When all the seeds have swollen, add the garlic and cook for a few minutes more, stirring all the time. Add the salt and the crushed chillies and stir to mix. Turn off the heat, but keep the pan on the stove. Sprinkle sugar over the seeds and shake the pan to ensure that they are all coated.

3 Tip the *pepitas* into a bowl and serve with the wedge of lime for squeezing over the seeds. If the lime is omitted, the seeds can be cooled and stored in an airtight container for reheating later, but they are best served fresh.

Dips and snacks may whet the appetite, but it's the

first course that really determines whether a meal will

go with a swing. Play safe with a humdrum soup,

and you set the scene for a staid and sensible evening;

introduce chillies and there's no telling what could

happen! Whether you select a Warming Spinach and

Rice Soup with a teasing heat that will keep everyone

guessing as to its source, or make a more blatant

statement with classic Chicken Pepper Soup, the

conversation – and compliments – will flow like wine.

Spicy Soups

HOT AND SOUR SOUP

ONE OF CHINA'S MOST POPULAR SOUPS, THIS IS FAMED FOR ITS BALANCE OF FLAVOURS. THE "HOT" COMES FROM PEPPER; THE "SOUR" FROM VINEGAR. SIMILAR SOUPS ARE FOUND THROUGHOUT ASIA.

SERVES SIX

INGREDIENTS
4–6 Chinese dried mushrooms
2–3 small pieces of wood ear
  and a few golden needles (lily
  buds) (optional)
115g/4oz pork fillet (tenderloin),
  cut into fine strips
45ml/3 tbsp cornflour (cornstarch)
150ml/¼ pint/⅔ cup water
15–30ml/1–2 tbsp sunflower oil
1 small onion, finely chopped
1.5 litres/2½ pints/6¼ cups good
  quality beef or chicken stock, or
  2 × 300g/11oz cans consommé
  made up to the full quantity
  with water
150g/5oz drained fresh firm
  tofu, diced
60ml/4 tbsp rice vinegar
15ml/1 tbsp light soy sauce
1 egg, beaten
5 ml/1 tsp sesame oil
salt and ground white or black pepper
2–3 spring onions (scallions), finely
  chopped, to garnish

1 Place the dried mushrooms in a bowl, with the pieces of wood ear and the golden needles (lily buds), if using. Add sufficient warm water to cover and leave to soak for about 30 minutes. Drain the mushrooms, reserving the soaking water. Cut off and discard the mushroom stems and slice the caps finely. Trim away any tough stem from the wood ears, then chop them finely. Using kitchen string, tie the golden needles into a bundle.

2 Lightly dust the strips of pork fillet with some of the cornflour; mix the remaining cornflour to a smooth paste with the measured water.

3 Heat the oil in a wok or pan and fry the onion until soft. Increase the heat and fry the pork until it changes colour. Add the stock or consommé, mushrooms, soaking water, and wood ears and golden needles, if using. Bring to the boil, then simmer for 15 minutes.

4 Discard the golden needles, lower the heat and stir in the cornflour paste to thicken. Add the tofu, vinegar, soy sauce, and salt and pepper.

5 Bring the soup to just below boiling point, then drizzle in the beaten egg by letting it drop from a whisk (or to be authentic, the fingertips) so that it forms threads in the soup. Stir in the sesame oil and serve immediately, garnished with spring onion.

WARMING SPINACH <u>AND</u> RICE SOUP

THE CHILLI ADDS JUST A FLICKER OF FIRE TO THIS LIGHT AND FRESH-TASTING SOUP,
MADE USING VERY YOUNG SPINACH LEAVES AND RISOTTO RICE.

SERVES FOUR

INGREDIENTS

- 675g/1½lb fresh spinach, washed
- 45ml/3 tbsp extra virgin olive oil
- 1 small onion, finely chopped
- 2 garlic cloves, finely chopped
- 1 small fresh red chilli, seeded and finely chopped
- 115g/4oz/generous ½ cup risotto rice
- 1.2 litres/2 pints/5 cups vegetable stock
- 60ml/4 tbsp grated Pecorino cheese
- salt and ground black pepper

1 Place the spinach in a large pan with just the water that clings to its leaves. Add a pinch of salt. Heat until the spinach has wilted, then remove from the heat and drain, reserving any liquid.

2 Either chop the spinach finely using a large knife or place in a food processor and process briefly to achieve a fairly coarse purée.

3 Heat the oil in a large pan and gently cook the onion, garlic and chilli for 4–5 minutes until softened but not browned. Stir in the risotto rice until well coated with the mixture.

4 Pour in the stock and reserved spinach liquid. Bring to the boil, reduce the heat and simmer for 10 minutes.

5 Add the spinach, with salt and pepper to taste. Cook for 5–7 minutes more, until the rice is tender. Check the seasoning and serve in heated soup plates or bowls, with the Pecorino cheese sprinkled over.

HOT <u>AND</u> SWEET VEGETABLE <u>AND</u> TOFU SOUP

AN INTERESTING COMBINATION OF HOT, SWEET AND SOUR FLAVOURS THAT MAKES FOR A SOOTHING, NUTRITIOUS SOUP THAT TAKES ONLY MINUTES TO MAKE.

SERVES FOUR

INGREDIENTS

1.2 litres/2 pints/5 cups
  vegetable stock
5–10ml/1–2 tsp Thai red
  curry paste
2 kaffir lime leaves, torn
40g/1½oz/3 tbsp palm sugar (jaggery)
  or light muscovado (brown) sugar
30ml/2 tbsp soy sauce
juice of 1 lime
1 carrot, cut into thin batons
50g/2oz baby spinach leaves, any
  coarse stalks removed
225g/8oz block silken tofu, diced

1 Heat the stock in a large pan, then add the red curry paste. Stir constantly over a medium heat until the paste has dissolved. Add the lime leaves, sugar and soy sauce and bring to the boil.

2 Add the lime juice and carrot to the pan. Reduce the heat and simmer for 5–10 minutes. Place the spinach and tofu in four individual serving bowls and pour the hot stock on top to serve.

HOT AND SPICY MISO BROTH WITH TOFU

THE JAPANESE EAT MISO BROTH, A SIMPLE BUT HIGHLY NUTRITIOUS SOUP, ALMOST EVERY DAY — IT IS STANDARD BREAKFAST FARE AND IS EATEN WITH RICE OR NOODLES LATER ON.

SERVES FOUR

INGREDIENTS
  1 bunch of spring onions (scallions)
    or 5 baby leeks
  15g/½oz/⅓ cup fresh
    coriander (cilantro)
  3 thin slices fresh root ginger
  2 star anise
  1 small dried red chilli
  1.2 litres/2 pints/5 cups dashi stock
    or vegetable stock
  225g/8oz pak choi (bok choy) or
    other Asian greens, thickly sliced
  200g/7oz firm tofu, cut into
    2.5cm/1in squares
  45–60ml/3–4 tbsp red miso
  30–45ml/2–3 tbsp Japanese soy
    sauce (shoyu)
  1 fresh red chilli, seeded
    and finely chopped

1 Cut the coarse green tops off half of the spring onions or leeks and place in a pan with the coriander stalks, ginger, star anise and dried chilli. Pour in the dashi or vegetable stock. Heat gently until boiling, then simmer for 10 minutes. Strain, return to the pan and reheat until simmering.

2 Slice the remaining spring onions or leeks finely on the diagonal and add the green portion to the soup with the pak choi or greens and squares of tofu. Cook for 2 minutes.

3 Mix 45ml/3 tbsp of the miso with a little of the hot soup in a bowl, then stir it into the soup. Taste the soup and add more miso with soy sauce to taste.

4 Coarsely chop the coriander leaves and stir most of them into the soup with the white part of the spring onions or leeks. Cook for 1 minute, then ladle the soup into heated serving bowls. Sprinkle with the remaining chopped coriander and the chopped fresh red chilli and serve immediately.

COOK'S TIPS
• Dashi powder is available in most Asian and Chinese stores. Alternatively, make your own by gently simmering 10 15cm/4–6in kombu seaweed in 1.2 litres/2 pints/5 cups water for 10 minutes. Do not boil the stock vigorously as this would make the dashi bitter. Remove the kombu, then add 15g/½oz dried bonito flakes and bring to the boil. Strain through a fine sieve (strainer).
• Kombu seaweed is usually dried, pickled or shaved thinly in dry sheets. Wash dried Kombu before using.
• Red miso is a paste made from fermented beans and grains. Buy it from Asian food stores. It will keep almost indefinitely in an airtight container in the refrigerator.

COCONUT AND PUMPKIN SOUP

THE NATURAL SWEETNESS OF THE PUMPKIN IS HEIGHTENED BY THE ADDITION OF A LITTLE SUGAR IN THIS SOUP, BUT THIS IS BALANCED BY THE CHILLIES, SHRIMP PASTE AND DRIED SHRIMP.

SERVES FOUR TO SIX

INGREDIENTS
  450g/1lb pumpkin
  2 garlic cloves, crushed
  4 shallots, finely chopped
  2.5ml/½ tsp shrimp paste
  1 lemon grass stalk, chopped
  2 fresh green chillies, seeded
  15ml/1 tbsp dried shrimp soaked
    for 10 minutes in warm water
    to cover
  600ml/1 pint/2½ cups chicken stock
  600ml/1 pint/2½ cups
    coconut cream
  30ml/2 tbsp Thai fish sauce
  5ml/1 tsp granulated (white) sugar
  115g/4oz small cooked shelled
    prawns (shrimp)
  salt and ground black pepper

To garnish
  2 fresh red chillies, seeded and
    thinly sliced
  10–12 fresh basil leaves

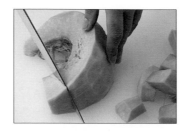

1 Peel the pumpkin and cut it into quarters with a sharp knife. Scoop out the seeds with a teaspoon and discard. Cut the flesh into chunks about 2cm/¾in thick and set aside.

2 Put the garlic, shallots, shrimp paste, lemon grass, green chillies and salt to taste in a mortar. Drain the dried shrimp, discarding the soaking liquid, and add them, then use a pestle to grind the mixture into a paste. Alternatively, place all the ingredients in a food processor and process to a paste.

3 Bring the chicken stock to the boil in a large pan. Add the ground paste and stir well to dissolve.

4 Add the pumpkin chunks and bring to a simmer. Simmer for 10–15 minutes, or until the pumpkin is tender.

5 Stir in the coconut cream, then bring the soup back to simmering point. Do not let it boil. Add the fish sauce, sugar and ground black pepper to taste.

6 Add the prawns to the pan and cook for a further 2–3 minutes, until they are heated through. Serve in warm soup bowls, garnished with chillies and basil leaves.

COOK'S TIP
Shrimp paste is made from ground shrimp fermented in brine.

SPICED RED LENTIL AND COCONUT SOUP

HOT, SPICY AND RICHLY FLAVOURED, THIS SUBSTANTIAL SOUP IS A MEAL IN ITSELF. IF YOU ARE REALLY HUNGRY, SERVE IT WITH CHUNKS OF WARMED NAAN BREAD OR THICK SLICES OF TOAST.

SERVES FOUR

INGREDIENTS

30ml/2 tbsp sunflower oil
2 red onions, finely chopped
1 bird's eye chilli, seeded and
 finely sliced
2 garlic cloves, chopped
1 lemon grass stalk, outer layers
 removed and inside finely sliced
200g/7oz/scant 1 cup red lentils,
 rinsed and drained
5ml/1 tsp ground coriander
5ml/1 tsp paprika
400ml/14fl oz/1⅔ cups
 coconut milk
900ml/1½ pints/3¾ cups water
juice of 1 lime
3 spring onions (scallions), chopped
20g/¾oz/½ cup fresh coriander
 (cilantro), finely chopped
salt and ground black pepper

1 Heat the oil in a large pan and add the onions, chilli, garlic and lemon grass. Cook for 5 minutes or until the onions have softened but not browned, stirring occasionally.

COOK'S TIP
Bird's eye chillies may look insubstantial, but they pack quite a punch. Don't be tempted to add more unless you are a real chilli head!

2 Add the lentils and spices. Pour in the coconut milk and water, and stir. Bring to the boil, stir, then reduce the heat and simmer for 40–45 minutes or until the lentils are soft and mushy.

3 Stir in the lime juice and add the spring onions and fresh coriander, reserving a little of each for the garnish. Season, then ladle into heated bowls. Top with the reserved garnishes.

SPICY BEAN SOUP

THIS DELICIOUS SEPHARDI ISRAELI SOUP, OF BLACK-EYED BEANS AND TURMERIC-TINTED TOMATO BROTH, IS FLAVOURED WITH TANGY LEMON AND SPECKLED WITH CHOPPED FRESH CORIANDER.

SERVES FOUR

INGREDIENTS

175g/6oz/1 cup black-eyed
  beans (peas)
15ml/1 tbsp olive oil
2 onions, chopped
4 garlic cloves, chopped
1 medium-hot or 2–3 mild fresh
  chillies, chopped
5ml/1 tsp ground cumin
5ml/1 tsp ground turmeric
250g/9oz fresh or canned
  tomatoes, diced
600ml/1 pint/2½ cups chicken,
  beef or vegetable stock
25g/1oz fresh coriander (cilantro)
  leaves, roughly chopped
juice of ½ lemon
pitta bread, to serve

1 Put the beans in a pan, cover with cold water, bring to the boil, then cook for 5 minutes. Remove from the heat, cover and leave to stand for 2 hours.

2 Heat the oil in a pan, add the onions, garlic and chilli and cook for 5 minutes, or until the onion is soft. Stir in the cumin, turmeric, tomatoes, stock, half the coriander and the beans and simmer for 20–30 minutes. Stir in the lemon juice and remaining coriander and serve immediately with pitta bread.

GAZPACHO WITH AVOCADO SALSA

CHILLIES IN A CHILLED SOUP MAKE AN UNUSUAL COMBINATION. GAZPACHO TASTES DELICIOUS WITH THE ADDITION OF CHILLI AND TABASCO. THE FLAVOURS ARE ECHOED IN THE SALSA.

SERVES FOUR

INGREDIENTS
  2 slices day-old bread
  600ml/1 pint/2½ cups chilled water
  1kg/2¼lb tomatoes
  1 cucumber
  1 red (bell) pepper, seeded
    and chopped
  1 fresh green chilli, seeded
    and chopped
  2 garlic cloves, chopped
  30ml/2 tbsp extra virgin olive oil
  juice of 1 lime and 1 lemon
  a few drops Tabasco sauce
  salt and ground black pepper
  8 ice cubes, to serve
  a handful of basil leaves, to garnish

For the croûtons
  2 slices day-old bread, crusts removed
  1 garlic clove, halved
  15ml/1 tbsp olive oil

For the avocado salsa
  1 ripe avocado
  5ml/1 tsp lemon juice
  2.5cm/1in piece cucumber, diced
  ½ fresh red chilli, seeded and
    finely chopped

1 Soak the bread in 150ml/¼ pint/⅔ cup of the chilled water for 5 minutes. Place the tomatoes in a bowl and cover with boiling water. Leave for 30 seconds, then peel, seed and chop the flesh.

2 Thinly peel the cucumber, then cut it in half lengthways and scoop out the seeds with a teaspoon. Discard the seeds and chop the flesh.

3 Place the bread (with any free liquid) in a food processor or blender. Add the tomatoes, cucumber, red pepper, chilli, garlic, olive oil, citrus juices and Tabasco then pour in the remaining 450ml/¾ pint/scant 2 cups chilled water. Blend until well combined but still chunky. Season to taste, pour into a bowl and chill in the refrigerator for 2–3 hours.

4 To make the croûtons, rub the slices of bread with the garlic clove. Cut the bread into cubes and place in a plastic bag with the olive oil. Seal the bag and shake until the bread cubes are evenly coated. Heat a large non-stick frying pan and fry the croûtons over a medium heat until crisp and golden.

5 Just before serving, make the salsa. Cut the avocado in half, remove the stone (pit), then peel and dice the flesh. Put it in a small bowl. Add the lemon juice, toss to prevent browning, then mix with the cucumber and chilli.

6 Ladle the soup into chilled bowls, add the ice cubes, and top each portion with a spoonful of the avocado salsa. Garnish with the basil and hand round the croûtons separately.

SPICY YOGURT SOUP

THIS DELCIOUS AND ENERGIZING SOUP IS IDEAL FOR A COLD DAY AS IT IS BOTH WARMING AND NUTRITIOUS. YOU CAN ADJUST THE AMOUNT OF CHILLI USED ACCORDING TO YOUR PREFERENCE.

SERVES FOUR TO SIX

INGREDIENTS
- 450ml/¾ pint/scant 2 cups natural (plain) yogurt, beaten
- 60ml/4 tbsp gram flour
- 2.5ml/½ tsp chilli powder
- 2.5ml/½ tsp ground turmeric
- 2–3 green chillies, finely chopped
- 60ml/4 tbsp vegetable oil
- 4 whole dried red chillies
- 5ml/1 tsp cumin seeds
- 3–4 curry leaves
- 3 garlic cloves, crushed
- 5cm/2in piece of fresh root ginger, crushed
- salt
- fresh coriander (cilantro) leaves, chopped, to garnish

1 Mix together the yogurt, gram flour, chilli powder, turmeric and salt and strain them into a pan. Add the green chillies and cook gently for about 10 minutes, stirring occasionally. Be careful not to let the soup boil over.

2 Heat the oil in a frying pan and fry the remaining spices, crushed garlic and fresh ginger until the dried chillies turn black.

3 Pour the oil and the spices over the yogurt soup, remove the pan from the heat, cover and leave to rest for 5 minutes. Mix well and gently reheat for a further 5 minutes. Serve hot, garnished with the coriander leaves.

VARIATION
Sugar can be added to this soup to bring out the full flavour. For an extra creamy soup, use Greek (US strained plain) yogurt instead of natural (plain) yogurt. Adjust the amount of chillies according to how hot you want the soup to be.

TAMARIND SOUP WITH PEANUTS AND VEGETABLES

SAYUR ASAM IS A COLOURFUL AND REFRESHING SOUP FROM JAKARTA, RICH IN VEGETABLES
AND WITH MORE THAN A HINT OF SHARPNESS.

SERVES FOUR OR EIGHT

INGREDIENTS
For the spice paste
   5 shallots or 1 medium red
     onion, sliced
   3 garlic cloves, crushed
   2.5cm/1in galangal, peeled
     and sliced
   1–2 fresh red chillies, seeded and sliced
   25g/1oz/¼ cup raw peanuts
   1cm/½in cube shrimp
     paste, prepared
   1.2 litres/2 pints/5 cups stock
   50–75g/2–3oz/½–¾ cup salted
     peanuts, lightly crushed
   15–30ml/1–2 tbsp soft dark
     brown sugar
   5ml/1 tsp tamarind pulp, soaked in
     75ml/5 tbsp warm water for
     15 minutes
   salt

For the vegetables
   1 chayote, thinly peeled, seeds
     removed, flesh finely sliced
   115g/4oz/¾ cup green beans,
     trimmed and finely sliced
   50g/2oz/⅓ cup corn kernels (optional)
   handful green leaves, such as
     watercress, rocket (arugula) or
     Chinese leaves (Chinese cabbage),
     finely shredded
   1 fresh green chilli, sliced,
     to garnish

1 Prepare the spice paste by grinding
the shallots or onion, garlic, galangal,
chillies, raw peanuts and shrimp paste
to a paste in a food processor or with a
mortar and pestle.

2 Pour in some of the stock to moisten
and then pour this mixture into a pan or
wok, adding the rest of the stock. Cook
for 15 minutes with the lightly crushed
peanuts and sugar.

3 Strain the tamarind, discarding the
seeds, and reserve the juice.

4 About 5 minutes before serving, add
the chayote slices, beans and corn,
if using, to the soup and cook fairly
rapidly. At the last minute, add the
green leaves and salt to taste.

5 Add the tamarind juice and taste for
seasoning. Serve, garnished with slices
of green chilli.

PLANTAIN SOUP WITH CORN AND CHILLI

THE AMOUNT OF CHILLI CAN BE VARIED ACCORDING TO TASTE; ADD MORE FOR A FIERY HOT SOUP.

SERVES FOUR

INGREDIENTS
  25g/1oz/2 tbsp butter or margarine
  1 onion, finely chopped
  1 garlic clove, crushed
  275g/10oz yellow plantains, peeled
    and sliced
  1 large tomato, peeled and chopped
  175g/6oz/1 cup corn kernels
  5ml/1 tsp dried tarragon, crushed
  900ml/1½ pints/3¾ cups vegetable or
    chicken stock
  1 green chilli, seeded and chopped
  pinch of grated nutmeg
  salt and ground black pepper

1 Melt the butter or margarine in a large pan over a medium heat, add the onion and garlic and cook for a few minutes until the onion is soft. Add the plantain, tomato and corn and cook for 5 minutes.

2 Add the tarragon, vegetable stock, chilli and salt and pepper and simmer for 10 minutes, or until the plantain is tender. Stir in the nutmeg and serve the soup immediately.

SPICY GROUNDNUT SOUP

THIS SOUP IS WIDELY EATEN IN AFRICA. GROUNDNUTS (OR PEANUTS) ARE SPICED WITH A MIXTURE OF FRESH GINGER AND CHILLI POWDER.

SERVES FOUR

INGREDIENTS
  45ml/3 tbsp pure groundnut (peanut)
    paste or peanut butter
  1.5 litres/2½ pints/6¼ cups stock
    or water
  30ml/2 tbsp tomato purée (paste)
  1 onion, chopped
  2 slices fresh root ginger
  1.5ml/½ tsp dried thyme
  1 bay leaf
  salt and chilli powder
  225g/8oz white yam, diced
  10 small okra, trimmed

1 Place the groundnut paste or peanut butter in a bowl, add 300ml/½ pint/1¼ cups of the stock or water and the tomato purée and blend together to make a smooth paste.

2 Spoon the nut mixture into a pan and add the onion, ginger, thyme, bay leaf, salt, chilli and the remaining stock.

COOK'S TIP
Use crunchy peanut butter for an excitingly different soup, or smooth peanut butter for a combination that will combine beautifully with the sticky juice produced by the okra.

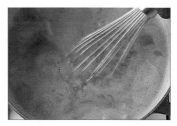

3 Simmer for 1 hour, stirring occasionally. Add the yam and cook for 10 minutes.

4 Add the okra, and simmer until tender. Serve immediately.

SPICY PEPPER SOUP

THIS IS A SOOTHING BROTH FOR WINTER EVENINGS, ALSO KNOWN AS MULLA-GA-TANI. SERVE WITH THE WHOLE SPICES, OR STRAIN AND REHEAT IF YOU LIKE. THE LEMON JUICE MAY BE ADJUSTED TO TASTE.

SERVES FOUR TO SIX

INGREDIENTS
30ml/2 tbsp vegetable oil
2.5ml/½ tsp ground black pepper
5ml/1 tsp cumin seeds
2.5ml/½ tsp mustard seeds
1.5ml/¼ tsp asafoetida
2 whole dried red chillies
4–6 curry leaves
2.5ml/½ tsp ground turmeric
2 garlic cloves, crushed
300ml/½ pint/1¼ cups tomato juice
juice of 2 lemons
120ml/4fl oz/½ cup water
salt, to taste
coriander (cilantro) leaves, chopped,
  to garnish

2 Lower the heat and add the tomato juice, lemon juice, water and salt. Bring the soup to the boil, then simmer gently for about 10 minutes. Pour the soup into bowls, garnish with the chopped coriander and serve.

VARIATION
If you prefer, use lime juice instead of lemon juice. Add 5ml/1 tsp tamarind paste for extra sourness.

1 In a large pan, heat the oil and fry the pepper, cumin and mustard seeds, asafoetida, red chillies, curry leaves, turmeric and garlic until the chillies are nearly black and the garlic is golden brown.

COOK'S TIP
Dried red chillies may look withered and insubstantial, but they pack quite a punch. Don't be tempted to add more chillies to a dish unless you are a real chilli enthusiast.

PROVENÇAL FISH SOUP <u>WITH</u> ROUILLE

*AN AUTHENTIC CHILLI-SPIKED ROUILLE LIFTS THIS EXCELLENT SOUP INTO THE REALMS OF
THE SUBLIME. A GOOD SOUP FOR A PARTY BECAUSE YOU CAN PREPARE IT ALL IN ADVANCE.*

SERVES FOUR TO SIX

INGREDIENTS
30ml/2 tbsp olive oil
1 leek, sliced
2 celery sticks, chopped
1 onion, chopped
2 garlic cloves, chopped
4 ripe tomatoes, chopped
15ml/1 tbsp tomato purée (paste)
150ml/¼ pint/⅔ cup dry white wine
1 bay leaf
5ml/1 tsp saffron threads
fish trimmings, bones and heads
1kg/2¼lb mixed fish fillets and
    prepared shellfish
salt and ground black pepper
croûtons and grated Gruyère cheese,
    to serve

For the rouille
1 slice of white bread, crusts removed
1 red (bell) pepper, cored, seeded
    and quartered
1–2 fresh red chillies, seeded
    and chopped
2 garlic cloves, roughly chopped
olive oil (optional)

1 Make the rouille. Soak the bread in 30–45ml/2–3 tbsp cold water for 10 minutes. Meanwhile, grill (broil) the red pepper, skin side up, until the skin is charred and blistered. Put into a plastic bag and tie the top to keep the steam in. Leave until cool enough to handle. Peel off the skin. Drain the bread and squeeze out excess water.

2 Roughly chop the pepper quarters and place in a blender or food processor with the bread, chillies and garlic. Process to a fairly coarse paste, adding a little olive oil, if necessary. Scrape the rouille into a small bowl and set it aside.

COOK'S TIP
If you are preparing this soup in advance, cook it for the time stated then cool and chill as rapidly as possible. A fish soup should not be left simmering on top of the stove.

3 Heat the olive oil in a large pan. Add the leek, celery, onion and garlic. Cook gently for 10 minutes until soft. Add the tomatoes, tomato purée, wine, bay leaf, saffron and the fish trimmings. Bring to the boil, reduce the heat, cover and simmer for 30 minutes.

4 Strain through a colander into a clean pan, pressing out all the liquid. Cut the fish fillets into large chunks and add to the liquid, with the shellfish. Cover and simmer for 5–10 minutes until cooked.

5 Strain through a sieve (strainer) into a clean pan. Put half the cooked fish into a blender or food processor with about 300ml/½ pint/1¼ cups of the soup. Process for just long enough to blend, while retaining some texture.

6 Stir the processed mixture back into the remaining soup, then add the fish and shellfish from the sieve, with salt and pepper to taste. Reheat gently. Serve the soup with the rouille, croûtons and cheese.

SPICED MUSSEL SOUP

CHUNKY AND COLOURFUL, THIS FISH SOUP HAS THE CONSISTENCY OF A CHOWDER. THE CHILLI FLAVOUR COMES FROM HARISSA, A SPICY SAUCE THAT IS POPULAR IN NORTH AFRICAN COOKING.

SERVES SIX

INGREDIENTS

1.6kg/3½lb live mussels
150ml/¼ pint/⅔ cup white wine
3 tomatoes
30ml/2 tbsp olive oil
1 onion, finely chopped
2 garlic cloves, crushed
2 celery sticks, thinly sliced
bunch of spring onions (scallions),
  thinly sliced
1 potato, diced
7.5ml/1½ tsp harissa
45ml/3 tbsp chopped fresh parsley
ground black pepper
thick yogurt, to serve (optional)

1 Scrub the mussels and remove the beards, discarding any mussels that are damaged or that fail to close when tapped with a knife.

2 Bring the wine to the boil in a large pan. Add the mussels and cover tightly with a lid. Cook for 4–5 minutes until the mussels have opened. Drain the mussels, reserving the cooking liquid. Discard any mussels that remain closed. Reserve a few mussels in their shells for the garnish. Shell the rest.

3 Cut a small cross in the base of each tomato. Put them in a heatproof bowl and pour over boiling water. Leave for 30 seconds, then lift out and plunge into cold water. Drain, peel off the skins and dice the flesh. Heat the oil in a pan and fry the onion, garlic, celery and spring onions for 5 minutes.

COOK'S TIP
Harissa can be bought in tubes or jars. Stir it into salads or cooked vegetable dishes to give them a spicy lift.

4 Add the shelled mussels, reserved liquid, potato, harissa and tomatoes. Bring just to the boil, reduce the heat and cover. Simmer gently for about 25 minutes, or until the potatoes are beginning to break up.

5 Stir in the parsley and pepper, and add the reserved mussels, in their shells. Heat through for 1 minute. Serve with a spoonful of yogurt if you like.

HOT AND SPICY SHELLFISH SOUP

FOR A SPECIAL OCCASION SERVE CREAMY RICE NOODLES IN A SPICY COCONUT-FLAVOURED
SOUP, TOPPED WITH SHELLFISH. YOU CAN MAKE THE SOUP BASE AHEAD, IF YOU LIKE.

SERVES FOUR

INGREDIENTS
  4 red chillies, seeded and
    roughly chopped
  1 onion, coarsely chopped
  1 small piece shrimp paste
  1 lemon grass stalk, chopped
  1 small piece fresh root ginger,
    coarsely chopped
  6 macadamia nuts or almonds
  60ml/4 tbsp vegetable oil
  5ml/1 tsp paprika
  5ml/1 tsp ground turmeric
  475ml/16fl oz/2 cups stock or water
  600ml/1 pint/2½ cups coconut milk
  Thai fish sauce (see method)
  12 king prawns (jumbo shrimp),
    peeled and deveined
  8 scallops
  225g/8oz prepared squid, cut
    into rings
  350g/12oz rice vermicelli or rice
    noodles, soaked in warm water
    until soft
  salt and ground black pepper
  lime halves, to serve

For the garnish
  ¼ cucumber, cut into sticks
  2 red chillies, seeded and
    finely sliced
  30ml/2 tbsp fresh mint leaves
  30ml/2 tbsp fried shallots
    or onions

1 In a blender or food processor,
process the chillies, onion, shrimp
paste, lemon grass, ginger and nuts
until smooth in texture.

2 Heat 45ml/3 tbsp of the oil in a large
pan. Add the chilli paste and cook
for 6 minutes. Stir in the paprika
and turmeric and cook for about
2 minutes more.

COOK'S TIP
Dried shrimp paste is sold in small
blocks and you will find it in Asian
stores and supermarkets.

3 Add the stock or water and the
coconut milk to the pan. Bring to
the boil, reduce the heat and simmer
gently for 15–20 minutes. Season the
soup to taste with Thai fish sauce.

4 Season the seafood. Heat the
remaining oil in a frying pan, add
the seafood and cook quickly for
2–3 minutes until tender.

5 Add the noodles to the soup and
heat through. Divide among individual
serving bowls. Place the seafood on
top, then garnish with the cucumber,
chillies, mint and fried shallots or
onions. Serve with the lime halves.

COCONUT AND SHELLFISH SOUP

*THE LONG LIST OF INGREDIENTS COULD MISLEAD YOU INTO THINKING THAT THIS SOUP IS
COMPLICATED AND VERY TIME-CONSUMING TO PREPARE. IN FACT, IT IS EXTREMELY EASY TO
PUT TOGETHER AND THE MARRIAGE OF FLAVOURS WORKS BEAUTIFULLY.*

SERVES FOUR

INGREDIENTS
    600ml/1 pint/2½ cups fish stock
    5 thin slices fresh galangal or fresh
      root ginger
    2 lemon grass stalks, chopped
    3 kaffir lime leaves, shredded
    bunch garlic chives, about 25g/1oz
    small bunch fresh coriander
      (cilantro), about 15g/½oz
    15ml/1 tbsp vegetable oil
    4 shallots, chopped
    400ml/14fl oz can coconut milk
    30–45ml/2–3 tbsp Thai fish sauce
    45–60ml/3–4 tbsp Thai green
      curry paste
    450g/1lb raw large prawns (shrimp),
      peeled and deveined
    450g/1lb prepared squid
    a little fresh lime juice (optional)
    salt and ground black pepper
    60ml/4 tbsp crisp fried shallot
      slices, to serve

1 Pour the fish stock into a large pan
and add the slices of galangal or ginger,
the lemon grass and half the shredded
kaffir lime leaves.

VARIATIONS
• Instead of squid, you could add 400g/
14oz firm white fish, such as monkfish,
cut into small pieces.
• You could also replace the squid with
mussels. Steam 675g/1½lb live mussels
in a tightly covered pan for 3–4 minutes,
or until they have opened. Discard any
that remain shut, then remove them from
their shells and add to the soup.

2 Reserve a few garlic chives for the
garnish, then chop the remainder. Add
half the chopped garlic chives to the
pan. Strip the coriander leaves from
the stalks and set the leaves aside. Add
the stalks to the pan. Bring to the boil,
reduce the heat to low and cover the
pan, then simmer gently for 20 minutes.
Strain the stock into a bowl.

3 Rinse and dry the pan. Add the oil
and shallots. Cook over a medium heat
for 5–10 minutes, until the shallots are
just beginning to brown.

4 Stir in the strained stock, coconut
milk, the remaining kaffir lime leaves
and 30ml/2 tbsp of the fish sauce. Heat
gently until simmering and cook over a
low heat for 5–10 minutes.

5 Stir in the curry paste and prawns,
then cook for 3 minutes. Add the squid
and cook for a further 2 minutes. Add
the lime juice, if using, and season,
adding more fish sauce to taste. Stir in
the remaining chives and the reserved
coriander leaves. Serve in bowls and
sprinkle each portion with fried shallots
and whole garlic chives.

CHILLI SQUASH AND SHELLFISH SOUP

THIS HEARTY SHELLFISH, SQUASH AND GREEN BEAN SOUP COMES FROM NORTHERN THAILAND.
FULL OF CHUNKY VEGETABLES, IT IS SOMETHING OF A CROSS BETWEEN A SOUP AND A STEW.
THE BANANA FLOWER ISN'T ESSENTIAL, BUT IT DOES ADD A UNIQUE AND AUTHENTIC FLAVOUR.

SERVES FOUR

INGREDIENTS
1 butternut squash, about 300g/11oz
1 litre/1¾ pints/4 cups stock
90g/3½ oz/scant 1 cup green beans,
    cut into 2.5cm/1in pieces
45g/1¾ oz dried banana
    flower (optional)
15ml/1 tbsp Thai fish sauce
225g/8oz raw prawns (shrimp)
small bunch fresh basil
cooked rice, to serve

For the chilli paste
115g/4oz shallots, sliced
10 drained bottled green peppercorns
1 small fresh green chilli, seeded and
    finely chopped
2.5ml/½ tsp shrimp paste

1 Peel the butternut squash and cut it in half. Scoop out the seeds, then cut the flesh into neat cubes. Set aside.

2 Make the chilli paste by pounding the shallots, peppercorns, chilli and shrimp paste together using a mortar and pestle or puréeing them in a spice blender or a food processor.

3 Heat the stock gently in a large pan, then stir in the chilli paste. Add the squash, beans and banana flower, if using. Bring to the boil and cook for 15 minutes.

4 Add the fish sauce, prawns and basil. Bring to simmering point, then simmer for 3 minutes. Serve in warmed bowls, accompanied by rice.

MALAYSIAN PRAWN SOUP

This spicy soup is not a dish you can throw together in 20 minutes, but it is good party food. Guests spoon noodles into wide soup bowls, add accompaniments of their choice, top up with soup and then take a few prawn crackers to nibble.

SERVES SIX

INGREDIENTS

675g/1½ lb small clams
2 × 400ml/14fl oz cans coconut milk
50g/2oz ikan bilis (dried anchovies)
900ml/1½ pints/3¾ cups water
115g/4oz shallots, finely chopped
4 garlic cloves, chopped
6 macadamia nuts or blanched
  almonds, chopped
3 lemon grass stalks, root trimmed
90ml/6 tbsp sunflower oil
1cm/½in cube shrimp paste (blachan)
25g/1oz/¼ cup mild curry powder
a few curry leaves
2–3 aubergines (eggplants), total
  weight about 675g/1¼lb, trimmed
675g/1½lb raw peeled prawns (shrimp)
10ml/2 tsp sugar
1 head Chinese leaves (Chinese
  cabbage), sliced
115g/4oz/2 cups beansprouts, rinsed
2 spring onions (scallions), chopped
50g/2oz crispy fried onions
115g/4oz fried tofu
675g/1½lb mixed noodles (laksa,
  mee and behoon) or one type only
prawn crackers, to serve

2 Meanwhile, put the shallots, garlic and nuts into a mortar. Cut off the lower 5cm/2in of two of the lemon grass stalks, chop finely and add to the mortar. Pound the mixture to a paste.

3 Heat the oil in a large heavy pan, add the shallot paste and fry until the mixture gives off a rich aroma. Bruise the remaining lemon grass stalk and add to the pan. Toss over the heat to release its flavour. Mix the shrimp paste (blachan) and curry powder to a paste with a little of the coconut milk, add to the pan and toss the mixture over the heat for 1 minute, stirring all the time, and keeping the heat low. Stir in the remaining coconut milk. Add the curry leaves and leave the mixture to simmer while you prepare the accompaniments.

1 Scrub the clams and then put in a large pan with 1cm/½in water. Bring to the boil, cover and steam for 3–4 minutes until all the clams have opened. Drain. Make up the coconut milk to 1.2 litres/2 pints/5 cups with water. Put the ikan bilis (dried anchovies) in a pan and add the water. Bring to the boil and simmer for 20 minutes.

4 Strain the stock into a pan. Discard the ikan bilis, bring to the boil, then add the aubergines; cook for about 10 minutes or until tender and the skins can be peeled off easily. Lift out of the stock, peel and cut into thick strips.

5 Arrange the aubergines on a serving platter. Sprinkle the prawns with sugar, add to the stock and cook for 2–4 minutes until they turn pink. Remove and place next to the aubergines. Add the Chinese leaves, beansprouts, spring onions and crispy fried onions to the platter, along with the clams.

6 Gradually stir the remaining ikan bilis stock into the pan of soup and bring to the boil. Rinse the fried tofu in boiling water, cool slightly and squeeze to remove excess oil. Cut each piece in half and add to the soup. Lower the heat to a very gentle simmer.

7 Cook the noodles according to the instructions, drain and pile in a dish. Remove the curry leaves and lemon grass from the soup. Place the noodles, soup and the platter of seafood and vegetables on the table, along with a bowl of prawn crackers. Guests can then help themselves.

VARIATION
You could substitute mussels for clams if preferred. Scrub them thoroughly, removing any beards, and cook them in lightly salted water until they open. Like clams, discard any that remain closed.

COOK'S TIP
Dried shrimp or prawn paste, also called blachan, is sold in small blocks and is available from Asian supermarkets.

THAI CHICKEN AND CHILLI SOUP

*THIS AROMATIC SOUP IS RICH WITH COCONUT MILK AND INTENSELY FLAVOURED WITH
GALANGAL, WHICH IS MILDLY PEPPERY AND GINGERY, LEMON GRASS AND KAFFIR LIME LEAVES.*

SERVES FOUR TO SIX

INGREDIENTS

    4 lemon grass stalks, trimmed and
        outer leaves discarded
    2 × 400ml/14fl oz/1⅔ cup cans
        coconut milk
    475ml/16fl oz/2 cups chicken stock
    2.5cm/1in piece galangal
    2 fresh red chillies
    10 black peppercorns, crushed
    10 kaffir lime leaves, torn
    300g/11oz skinless chicken breast
        fillets, cut into strips
    115g/4oz/1½ cups button
        (white) mushrooms
    50g/2oz/½ cup baby corn cobs,
        quartered lengthways
    60ml/4 tbsp lime juice
    45ml/3 tbsp Thai fish sauce
    chopped spring onions (scallions)
        and fresh coriander (cilantro)
        leaves, to garnish

1 Cut off the lower 5cm/2in from each lemon grass stalk and chop it finely. Bruise the remaining pieces of stalk. Bring the coconut milk and chicken stock to the boil in a large pan. Peel and thinly slice the galangal. Seed and finely chop the chillies. Add all the lemon grass, the galangal and half the chopped chillies, then stir in the peppercorns and half the lime leaves, lower the heat and simmer gently for 10 minutes. Strain into a clean pan.

2 Return the soup to the heat, then add the chicken, mushrooms and the quartered baby corn cobs. Bring to the boil, then lower the heat and simmer for 5–7 minutes or until the chicken is cooked.

3 Stir in the lime juice and fish sauce, then add the remaining lime leaves. Serve hot, garnished with the remaining chopped chillies and the spring onions and coriander.

HOT-AND-SOUR SHELLFISH SOUP

*THIS IS A CLASSIC THAI SHELLFISH SOUP — TOM YAM KUNG. THE BALANCE OF FLAVOURS IS
WHAT COUNTS, SO YOU MAY WANT TO START WITH HALF THE CHILLIES AND ADD MORE TO TASTE.*

SERVES FOUR TO SIX

INGREDIENTS

    450g/1lb raw king prawns (jumbo
        shrimp), thawed if frozen
    1 litre/1¾ pints/4 cups chicken
        stock or water
    3 lemon grass stalks, trimmed
    10 kaffir lime leaves, torn in half
    225g/8oz can straw mushrooms
    45ml/3 tbsp Thai fish sauce
    60ml/4 tbsp lime juice
    30ml/2 tbsp chopped spring
        onion (scallion)
    15ml/1 tbsp fresh coriander
        (cilantro) leaves
    4 fresh red chillies, seeded and
        thinly sliced
    salt and ground black pepper

1 Shell the prawns, putting the shells in a colander. Devein the prawns and set them aside. Rinse the shells under cold water, drain, then put in a large pan with the stock or water. Bring to the boil.

2 Bruise the lemon grass stalks and add them to the stock with half the lime leaves. Simmer gently for 5–6 minutes.

3 Strain the stock, return it to the clean pan and reheat. Drain the straw mushrooms and add them with the prawns. Cook until the prawns turn pink. Stir in the fish sauce, lime juice, spring onion, coriander, chillies and the remaining lime leaves. Taste and adjust the seasoning. The soup should be sour, salty, spicy and hot.

MULLIGATAWNY SOUP

MULLIGATAWNY (WHICH MEANS "PEPPER WATER") WAS INTRODUCED INTO ENGLAND IN THE 18TH CENTURY BY MEMBERS OF THE BRITISH ARMY AND COLONIAL SERVICE RETURNING HOME FROM INDIA.

SERVES FOUR

INGREDIENTS

50g/2oz/4 tbsp butter or
  60ml/4 tbsp oil
2 large chicken fillets, about
  350g/12oz each
1 onion, chopped
1 carrot, chopped
1 small turnip, chopped
about 15ml/1 tbsp curry powder,
  to taste
4 cloves
6 black peppercorns,
  lightly crushed
50g/2oz/¼ cup lentils
900ml/1½ pints/3¾ cups
  chicken stock
40g/1½ oz/¼ cup sultanas
  (golden raisins)
salt and ground black pepper

1 Melt the butter or heat the oil in a large pan, then brown the chicken over a brisk heat. Transfer the chicken to a plate.

2 Add the chopped onion, carrot and turnip to the pan and cook, stirring occasionally, until they are lightly coloured. Stir in the curry powder, cloves and black peppercorns and cook for 1–2 minutes more before adding the lentils.

3 Pour the stock into the pan, bring to the boil, then add the sultanas and chicken and any juices from the plate. Cover and simmer gently for about 1¼ hours.

4 Remove the chicken from the pan and discard the skin and bones. Chop the flesh, return to the soup and reheat. Check the seasoning before serving the soup piping hot.

COOK'S TIP
Choose red split lentils for the best colour, although either green or brown lentils could also be used.

CHICKEN PEPPER SOUP

*THIS NUTRITIOUS SOUP IS MADE USING STOCK MADE FROM A WHOLE CHICKEN, TO WHICH AROMATIC
AND FIERY SPICES ARE ADDED BEFORE THE COOKED CHICKEN MEAT IS RETURNED TO THE PAN.*

SERVES FOUR TO SIX

INGREDIENTS

900g/2lb chicken, boned
  and skinned
600ml/1 pint/2½ cups water
6 green cardamom pods
5cm/2in piece of cinnamon stick
4–6 curry leaves
15ml/1 tbsp ground coriander
5ml/1 tsp ground cumin
2.5ml/½ tsp ground turmeric
3 garlic cloves, crushed
12 whole peppercorns
4 cloves
1 onion, finely chopped
115g/4oz coconut cream
juice of 2 lemons
salt
deep-fried onions and coriander
  (cilantro) leaves, chopped,
  to garnish

1 Cut the chicken into pieces, then
place it in a large pan with the water
and cook for about 30 minutes, until
the chicken is tender.

2 Skim the surface, then strain,
reserving the stock and keeping the
chicken pieces warm.

3 Return the chicken stock to the pan
and reheat.

4 Add the cardamom pods, cinnamon
stick, curry leaves, ground coriander,
cumin and turmeric, crushed garlic,
peppercorns, cloves, finely chopped
onion, coconut cream, lemon juice
and salt to the pan.

5 Simmer the soup for 10–15 minutes,
then strain the stock to remove the
whole spices and return the chicken
to the soup.

6 Reheat the soup and divide between
individual bowls. Garnish each bowl
with deep-fried onions and chopped
coriander and serve.

COOK'S TIP
For a fast version of this soup, use
ready-cooked chicken. Remove any skin
and bone and chop into cubes. Add to
the soup just before serving, then reheat.

RICE PORRIDGE

ORIGINATING IN CHINA, THIS DISH HAS NOW SPREAD THROUGHOUT THE WHOLE OF SOUTH-EAST ASIA AND IS LOVED FOR ITS COMFORTING BLANDNESS. IT IS INVARIABLY SERVED WITH A FEW STRONGLY FLAVOURED ACCOMPANIMENTS.

SERVES TWO

INGREDIENTS
    900ml/1½ pints/3¾ cups
        vegetable stock
    200g/7oz/1¾ cups cooked rice
    225g/8oz minced (ground) pork
    15ml/1 tbsp Thai fish sauce
    2 heads pickled garlic, finely chopped
    1 celery stick, finely diced
    salt and ground black pepper

To garnish
    30ml/2 tbsp groundnut (peanut) oil
    4 garlic cloves, thinly sliced
    4 small red shallots, finely sliced

1 Make the garnishes by heating the groundnut oil in a frying pan and cooking the garlic and shallots over a low heat until brown. Drain on kitchen paper and reserve for the soup.

2 Pour the stock into a large pan. Bring to the boil and add the rice. Season the minced pork. Add it by taking small teaspoons and tapping the spoon on the side of the pan so that the meat falls into the soup in small lumps.

3 Stir in the fish sauce and pickled garlic and simmer for 10 minutes, until the pork is cooked. Stir in the celery.

4 Serve the rice porridge in individual warmed bowls. Sprinkle the prepared garlic and shallots on top and season with plenty of ground pepper.

COOK'S TIP
Pickled garlic has a distinctive flavour and is available from Asian food stores.

THAI CHICKEN AND NOODLE SOUP

NOWADAYS A SIGNATURE DISH OF THE CITY OF CHIANG MAI, THIS DELICIOUS NOODLE SOUP ORIGINATED IN BURMA, NOW CALLED MYANMAR, WHICH LIES ONLY A LITTLE TO THE NORTH. IT IS ALSO THE THAI EQUIVALENT OF THE FAMOUS MALAYSIAN "LAKSA".

SERVES FOUR TO SIX

INGREDIENTS
  600ml/1 pint/2½ cups coconut milk
  30ml/2 tbsp Thai red curry paste
  5ml/1 tsp ground turmeric
  450g/1lb chicken thighs, boned and
    cut into bitesize chunks
  600ml/1 pint/2½ cups chicken stock
  60ml/4 tbsp Thai fish sauce
  15ml/1 tbsp dark soy sauce
  juice of ½–1 lime
  450g/1lb fresh egg noodles, blanched
    briefly in boiling water
  salt and ground black pepper

To garnish
  3 spring onions (scallions), chopped
  4 fresh red chillies, chopped
  4 shallots, chopped
  60ml/4 tbsp sliced pickled mustard
    leaves, rinsed
  30ml/2 tbsp fried sliced garlic
  coriander (cilantro) leaves
  4–6 fried noodle nests (optional)

1 Pour about one-third of the coconut milk into a large, heavy pan or wok. Bring to the boil over a medium heat, stirring frequently with a wooden spoon until the milk separates.

2 Add the curry paste and ground turmeric, stir to mix completely and cook until the mixture is fragrant.

3 Add the chunks of chicken and toss over the heat for about 2 minutes, making sure that all the chunks are thoroughly coated with the paste.

4 Add the remaining coconut milk, the chicken stock, fish sauce and soy sauce. Season with salt and pepper to taste. Bring to simmering point, stirring frequently, then lower the heat and cook gently for 7–10 minutes. Remove from the heat and stir in lime juice to taste.

5 Reheat the fresh egg noodles in boiling water, drain and divide among four to six warmed bowls. Divide the chunks of chicken among the bowls and ladle in the hot soup. Top each serving with spring onions, chillies, shallots, pickled mustard leaves, fried garlic, coriander leaves and a fried noodle nest, if using. Serve immediately.

SPICED LAMB SOUP

PACKED WITH BEANS, PUMPKIN AND BANANA AS WELL AS CHUNKS OF DELCIOUS, TENDER LAMB, THIS
LIGHTLY SPICED SOUP MAKES A WARMING MEAL WHEN SERVED WITH FRESH BREAD.

4 Cover and simmer over a medium
heat for 1 hour, until tender.

5 Add the onion, pumpkin, cardamoms,
turmeric, coriander, caraway, chilli and
seasoning and stir. Bring back to a
simmer and then cook, uncovered, for
15 minutes, until the pumpkin is tender,
stirring occasionally.

6 When the beans are cool, spoon into a
blender or food processor with their
liquid and blend to a smooth purée.

7 Cut the bananas into medium slices
and the carrot into thin slices. Stir into
the soup with the beans and cook for
10–12 minutes, until the vegetables are
tender. Adjust the seasoning and serve.

SERVES FOUR

INGREDIENTS
  115g/4oz/⅔ cup split black-eyed
    beans (peas), soaked for 1–2 hours,
    or overnight
  675g/1½ lb neck (US shoulder) of
    lamb, cut into medium chunks
  5ml/1 tsp chopped fresh thyme,
    or 2.5ml/½ tsp dried
  2 bay leaves
  1.2 litres/2 pints/5 cups stock
    or water
  1 onion, sliced
  225g/8oz pumpkin, diced
  2 black cardamom pods
  7.5ml/1½ tsp ground turmeric
  15ml/1 tbsp chopped coriander
    (cilantro)
  2.5ml/½ tsp caraway seeds
  1 fresh green chilli, seeded and chopped
  2 green bananas
  1 carrot
  salt and ground black pepper

1 Drain the beans, place them in a pan
and cover with fresh cold water.

2 Bring the beans to the boil, boil
rapidly for 10 minutes and then reduce
the heat and simmer, covered for
40–50 minutes, until tender, adding
more water if necessary. Remove from
the heat and set aside to cool.

3 Meanwhile, put the lamb in a large
pan, add the thyme, bay leaves and
stock or water and bring to the boil.

BEEF AND TURMERIC SOUP

THE ADDITION OF TURMERIC AND SAFFRON COLOURS THIS SATISFYING SOUP A DEEP, VIBRANT
YELLOW. IT IS A POPULAR DISH IN IRAN.

SERVES SIX

INGREDIENTS

2 large onions
30ml/2 tbsp oil
15ml/1 tbsp ground turmeric
100g/3½ oz/½ cup yellow
  split peas
1.2 litres/2 pints/5 cups water
225g/8oz/2 cups minced
  (ground) beef
200g/7oz/1 cup rice
45ml/3 tbsp each fresh chopped
  parsley, coriander (cilantro)
  and chives
15g/½ oz/1 tbsp butter
1 large garlic clove, finely chopped
60ml/4 tbsp chopped fresh mint
2–3 saffron threads dissolved
  in 15ml/1 tbsp boiling
  water (optional)
salt and ground black pepper
yogurt and naan bread, to serve

1 Chop one of the onions, then heat the oil in a large pan and cook the onion until golden brown. Add the turmeric, split peas and water, bring to the boil, then reduce the heat and simmer for 20 minutes.

COOK'S TIP
Fresh spinach is also delicious in this soup. Add 50g/2oz/⅔ cup finely chopped spinach leaves to the soup with the parsley, coriander (cilantro) and chives.

2 Grate the other onion into a bowl, add the minced beef and seasoning and mix well. Using your hands, form the mixture into small balls, about the size of walnuts. Carefully add to the pan and simmer for 10 minutes.

3 Add the rice, then stir in the parsley, coriander, and chives and simmer for about 30 minutes, until the rice is tender, stirring frequently.

4 Melt the butter in a small pan and gently cook the garlic for 2–3 minutes, ensuring that it does not burn. Add the mint, stir briefly and sprinkle over the soup with the saffron, if using. Spoon the soup into warmed serving dishes and serve with yogurt and naan bread.

Red hot appetizers and snacks offer lots of highly spiced,

mouth-watering morsels and searingly hot bites. Potato

Skins with Cajun Dip will set the taste buds tingling,

while Chilli Spiced Onion Koftas and Fried Dough

Balls with Fiery Salsa are perfect to hand round at a

drinks party for a quick spicy appetizer. Start off a

meal in lively style with Peri-peri Prawns with Aioli or

enjoy an easy-to-prepare supper with Chicken Tortillas

with Fresno Chilli Salsa.

Red Hot
Appetizers
and Snacks

SPICY PEANUT BALLS

TASTY RICE BALLS, ROLLED IN CHOPPED PEANUTS AND DEEP-FRIED, MAKE A DELICIOUS SNACK. SERVE THEM AS THEY ARE OR WITH A CHILLI SAUCE FOR DIPPING.

2 Add three-quarters of the cooked rice to the paste in the food processor, and process until smooth and sticky. Scrape into a mixing bowl and stir in the remainder of the rice. Wet your hands and shape the mixture into small balls.

3 Roll the balls, a few at a time, in the chopped peanuts, making sure they are evenly coated.

4 Heat the oil for deep-frying to 180–190°C/350–375°F or until a cube of day-old bread browns in about 45 seconds. Deep-fry the peanut balls until crisp. Drain on kitchen paper, then pile on to a platter. Serve hot with lime wedges and a chilli dipping sauce, if you like.

MAKES SIXTEEN

INGREDIENTS
    1 garlic clove, crushed
    1cm/½ in piece of fresh root ginger,
      peeled and finely chopped
    1 small fresh red chilli, seeded and
      roughly chopped
    1.5ml/¼ tsp ground turmeric
    5ml/1 tsp granulated (white) sugar
    2.5ml/½ tsp salt
    5ml/1 tsp chilli sauce
    10ml/2 tsp soy sauce
    30ml/2 tbsp chopped fresh
      coriander (cilantro)
    juice of ½ lime
    225g/8oz/2 cups cooked white long
      grain rice
    115g/4oz/1 cup peanuts, chopped
    vegetable oil, for deep-frying
    lime wedges and chilli dipping sauce,
      to serve (optional)

1 Put the crushed garlic, ginger and chilli in a food processor. Add the turmeric and process to a paste. Add the granulated sugar, salt, chilli sauce and soy sauce, with the chopped coriander and lime juice. Process briefly to mix.

COOK'S TIP
Coat the balls in the peanuts and then chill for 30 minutes before deep-frying.

LITTLE ONIONS COOKED WITH CHILLIES

WHOLE DRIED CHILLIES GIVE THIS SIMPLE DISH AN UNDERLYING WARMTH THAT ADDS TO ITS APPEAL. FOR A SMOKY FLAVOUR, USE CHIPOTLE CHILLIES, OR AN ANAHEIM RED CHILLI.

SERVES SIX

INGREDIENTS

   105ml/7 tbsp olive oil
   675g/1½lb small onions
   150ml/¼ pint/⅔ cup dry white wine
   2 bay leaves
   2 garlic cloves, bruised
   1 2 small dried red chillies
   15ml/1 tbsp coriander seeds, toasted
     and lightly crushed
   2.5ml/½ tsp granulated (white) sugar
   a few fresh thyme sprigs
   30ml/2 tbsp currants
   10ml/2 tsp chopped fresh oregano
   5ml/1 tsp grated lemon rind
   15ml/1 tbsp chopped fresh flat
     leaf parsley
   30–45ml/2–3 tbsp pine
     nuts, toasted
   salt and ground black pepper

1 Spoon 30ml/2 tbsp of the olive oil into a wide pan. Add the onions, place the pan over a medium heat and cook gently for about 5 minutes, or until the onions begin to colour. Use a slotted spoon to remove the onions from the pan and set them aside.

2 Add the remaining oil to the pan, with the wine, bay leaves, garlic, chillies, coriander seeds, sugar and thyme. Bring to the boil and cook for 5 minutes.

3 Return the onions to the pan. Add the currants, reduce the heat and cook gently for 15–20 minutes, or until the onions are tender but not falling apart. Use a slotted spoon to transfer the onions to a serving dish.

4 Boil the liquid vigorously until it reduces considerably. Taste and adjust the seasoning, if necessary, then pour it over the onions. Sprinkle the chopped fresh oregano over the cooked onions, cool, cover and then chill them for several hours.

VARIATION
The same method can be used for courgettes (zucchini), celery, small mushrooms, fennel and baby leeks. Cut the larger vegetables in 2.5cm/1in pieces and cook as for small onions.

5 Just before serving, stir in the grated lemon rind, chopped parsley and toasted pine nuts.

CHILLI SPICED ONION KOFTAS

THESE DELICIOUS DEEP-FRIED INDIAN ONION FRITTERS ARE PEPPED UP WITH GREEN CHILLIES.
SERVE THEM WITH A YOGURT DIP, TO DAMP DOWN THEIR FIRE.

SERVES FOUR TO FIVE

INGREDIENTS
  675g/1½lb onions, halved and sliced
  5ml/1 tsp salt
  5ml/1 tsp ground coriander
  5ml/1 tsp ground cumin
  2.5ml/½ tsp ground turmeric
  1–2 fresh green chillies, seeded and
    finely chopped
  45ml/3 tbsp chopped fresh
    coriander (cilantro)
  90g/3½oz/¾ cup chickpea flour
  2.5ml/½ tsp baking powder
  vegetable oil, for deep-frying

To serve
  lemon wedges
  fresh coriander (cilantro) sprigs
  yogurt and herb dip (see Cook's Tips)

1 Put the onion slices in a colander, add the salt and toss well. Stand the colander on a plate or bowl and leave for 45 minutes, tossing once or twice with a fork. Rinse the onions, then squeeze out the excess moisture. Tip the onions into a bowl. Add the ground coriander, cumin, turmeric, chillies and fresh coriander. Mix well.

COOK'S TIPS
• Chickpea flour, available from supermarkets and Indian food stores, is sometimes labelled gram flour or *besan*.
• To make a yogurt and herb dip, stir 30ml/2 tbsp each of chopped fresh coriander (cilantro) and mint into 250ml/8fl oz/1 cup thick yogurt. Add salt, ground toasted cumin seeds and a pinch of sugar. Top with a chopped chilli.

2 Add the chickpea flour and baking powder, then use your hand to mix all the ingredients thoroughly.

3 Shape the mixture by hand into 12–15 koftas. They should be about the size of golf balls.

4 Heat the oil for deep-frying to 180–190°C/350–375°F or until a cube of day-old bread browns in about 45 seconds.

5 Fry the koftas, 4–5 at a time, until deep golden brown all over. Drain each batch on kitchen paper and keep warm until all the koftas are cooked. Serve with lemon wedges, coriander sprigs and a yogurt and herb dip.

CHILLI YOGURT CHEESE IN OLIVE OIL

YOGURT, HUNG IN MUSLIN TO DRAIN OFF THE WHEY, MAKES A SUPERB SOFT CHEESE. HERE IT IS BOTTLED IN OLIVE OIL WITH CHILLI AND HERBS, READY FOR SERVING ON TOAST.

FILLS TWO 450G/1LB JARS

INGREDIENTS
  800g/1¾lb/about 4 cups Greek
    (US strained, plain) yogurt
  2.5ml/½ tsp salt
  10ml/2 tsp crushed dried chillies or
    chilli powder
  15ml/1 tbsp chopped fresh rosemary
  15ml/1 tbsp chopped fresh thyme
    or oregano
  about 300ml/½ pint/1¼ cups olive
    oil, preferably garlic-flavoured
  lightly toasted country bread, to serve

1 Sterilize a 30cm/12in square of muslin (cheesecloth) by steeping it in boiling water. Drain and lay over a large plate. Mix the yogurt with the salt and tip on to the centre of the cloth. Bring up the sides of the cloth and tie firmly.

2 Hang the bag from a kitchen cabinet handle or in any convenient, cool position that allows a bowl to be placed underneath to catch the whey. Leave for 2–3 days until the yogurt stops dripping.

3 Sterilize two 450g/1lb clean glass preserving or jam jars by heating them in the oven at 150°C/300°F/Gas 2 for 15 minutes.

4 Mix the dried chillies and herbs in a bowl. Take teaspoonfuls of the cheese and roll into balls between the palms of your hands. Lower into jars, sprinkling each layer with the herb mixture.

5 Pour the oil over the cheese until the balls are completely covered. Close the jars tightly and store in the refrigerator for up to 3 weeks.

6 To serve the cheese, spoon out of the jars with a little of the flavoured olive oil and spread on to lightly toasted bread.

SPICED FETA WITH CHILLI SEEDS AND OLIVES

CHILLI SEEDS FLAVOUR MARINATED CUBES OF FETA CHEESE SPIKED WITH SPICES AND OLIVES. SPOON THE CUBES OVER GREEN LEAVES AND SERVE WITH WARM BREAD AS AN APPETIZER.

MAKES FOUR TO FIVE SMALL JARS

INGREDIENTS
  500g/1¼lb feta cheese
  50g/2oz/½ cup stuffed olives
  10ml/2 tsp coriander seeds
  10ml/2 tsp whole peppercorns
  5ml/1 tsp chilli seeds
  few sprigs fresh rosemary or thyme
  750ml/1¼ pint/3 cups virgin olive oil

1 Drain the feta cheese, dice it and put it in a bowl. Slice the olives. Using a pestle, crush the coriander seeds and peppercorns in a mortar and add them to the cheese, with the olives, chilli seeds and rosemary or thyme leaves. Toss lightly.

2 Sterilize 4–5 small, clean, glass jars by heating them in the oven at 150°C/300°F/Gas 2 for 15 minutes.

3 Spoon the cheese into the warm, dry sterilized jars and top up with olive oil, making sure that the cheese is well covered by the oil. Close the jars tightly and store them in the refrigerator for up to 3 weeks.

COOK'S TIP
Seal the jars with screw-topped or clip-down lids. The jars need to be totally airtight to keep the cheese fresh.

COURGETTE FRITTERS WITH CHILLI JAM

CHILLI JAM IS HOT, SWEET AND STICKY — RATHER LIKE A THICK CHUTNEY. IT ADDS A PIQUANCY TO THESE FRITTERS BUT IS ALSO DELICIOUS WITH PIES OR CHEESE.

MAKES TWELVE

INGREDIENTS
    450g/1lb/3½ cups coarsely grated
        courgettes (zucchini)
    50g/2oz/⅔ cup freshly grated
        Parmesan cheese
    2 eggs, beaten
    60ml/4 tbsp unbleached plain
        (all-purpose) flour
    vegetable oil, for frying
    salt and ground black pepper

For the chilli jam
    75ml/5 tbsp olive oil
    4 large onions, diced
    4 garlic cloves, chopped
    1–2 fresh Thai chillies, seeded
        and sliced
    25g/1oz/2 tbsp soft dark brown sugar

1 First make the chilli jam. Heat the oil in a frying pan until hot, then add the onions and garlic. Reduce the heat to low, then cook for 20 minutes, stirring frequently, until the onions are very soft.

VARIATION
Substitute Pecorino Romano for Parmesan cheese. It is good for grating.

2 Leave the onion mixture to cool, then scrape into a food processor or blender. Add the chillies and sugar, and blend until smooth, then return the mixture to the pan. Cook for 10 minutes, stirring frequently, until the liquid evaporates and the mixture has the consistency of jam. Cool slightly.

3 To make the fritters, squeeze the courgettes in a dishtowel to remove any excess water, then tip them into a bowl. Add the Parmesan, eggs and flour. Mix well, then season with salt and pepper.

4 Heat enough oil to cover the base of a large frying pan. Add 30ml/2 tbsp of the mixture for each fritter and cook 3 fritters at a time. Cook them for 2–3 minutes on each side until golden, then remove from the pan and keep hot while you cook the remaining fritters. Drain on kitchen paper and serve warm with a large spoonful of the chilli jam.

COOK'S TIP
Any leftover chilli jam can be kept in an airtight jar in the refrigerator for up to 1 week.

SAMOSAS

*A SELECTION OF HIGHLY SPICED VEGETABLES IN A PASTRY CASING MAKES THESE SAMOSAS
A DELICIOUS SNACK AT ANY TIME OF THE DAY.*

MAKES THIRTY

INGREDIENTS
  1 packet spring roll pastry, thawed
    and wrapped in a damp towel
  vegetable oil, for deep-frying

For the filling
  3 large potatoes, boiled and
    coarsely mashed
  75g/3oz/¾ cup frozen peas, thawed
  50g/2oz/⅓ cup canned corn, drained
  5ml/1 tsp ground coriander
  5ml/1 tsp ground cumin
  5ml/1 tsp amchur (dry mango powder)
  1 small onion, finely chopped
  2 green chillies, finely chopped
  30ml/2 tbsp coriander (cilantro)
    leaves, chopped
  30ml/2 tbsp mint leaves, chopped
  juice of 1 lemon
  salt, to taste
  chilli sauce, to serve

1 Toss all the filling ingredients together
in a large mixing bowl until they are all
well blended. Adjust the seasoning with
salt and lemon juice, if necessary.

2 Using one strip of pastry at a time,
place 15ml/1 tbsp of the filling
mixture at one end of the strip and
diagonally fold the pastry up to form
a triangle shape.

3 Heat enough oil for deep-frying and
fry the samosas in small batches until
they are golden brown. Keep them hot
while frying the rest. Serve hot with
chilli sauce.

THAI TEMPEH CAKES WITH CHILLI SAUCE

MADE FROM SOYA BEANS, TEMPEH IS SIMILAR TO TOFU BUT HAS A NUTTIER TASTE. HERE, IT IS COMBINED WITH CHILLIES, LEMON GRASS AND GINGER AND FORMED INTO SMALL PATTIES.

MAKES EIGHT

INGREDIENTS
2 chillies, seeded and finely chopped
1 lemon grass stalk, trimmed
2 garlic cloves, chopped
2 spring onions (scallions),
  finely chopped
2 shallots, finely chopped
2.5cm/1in piece fresh root ginger,
  finely chopped
60ml/4 tbsp chopped fresh coriander
  (cilantro), plus extra to garnish
250g/9oz tempeh, thawed if
  frozen, sliced
15ml/1 tbsp lime juice
5ml/1 tsp granulated (white) sugar
45ml/3 tbsp plain (all-purpose) flour
1 large (US extra large) egg, beaten
vegetable oil, for frying
salt and ground black pepper

For the dipping sauce
45ml/3 tbsp mirin or dry sherry
45ml/3 tbsp white wine vinegar
2 spring onions (scallions),
  thinly sliced
15ml/1 tbsp granulated (white) sugar
2 fresh red chillies, finely chopped
30ml/2 tbsp chopped fresh
  coriander (cilantro)

1 To make the dipping sauce, mix the mirin, vinegar, spring onions, sugar, chillies, coriander and a large pinch of salt in a small bowl and set aside.

COOK'S TIP
Chill the tempeh cakes for 30 minutes in the refrigerator before frying. It will prevent them from breaking.

2 Place the chopped chillies in a food processor or blender. Cut off the lower 5cm/2in piece of the lemon grass stalk and chop it roughly. Add it to the processor or blender, with the garlic, spring onions, shallots, ginger and coriander. Process to a coarse paste; the mixture should not be too smooth at this stage.

3 Add the tempeh, lime juice and sugar, then process again until combined. Add the flour and egg, with salt and pepper to taste, and process again until the mixture forms a coarse, sticky paste.

4 Wet your hands, then take a generous spoonful of the tempeh mixture and form it into a round between your palms. Repeat with the remaining mixture, wetting your hands slightly each time.

5 Heat enough oil to cover the base of a large frying pan. Fry the tempeh cakes, in batches if necessary, for 5–6 minutes, turning once, until golden. Drain on kitchen paper. Pile on to plates and garnish with the extra coriander. Serve warm, with the dipping sauce.

POTATO SKINS WITH CAJUN DIP

DIVINELY CRISP AND NAUGHTY, THESE POTATO SKINS TASTE GREAT WITH THE PIQUANT CHILLI DIP AND MAKE AN IDEAL SNACK TO ACCOMPANY PRE-DINNER DRINKS.

SERVES TWO

INGREDIENTS
  2 large baking potatoes, about
    275g/10oz each
  vegetable oil, for frying

For the dip
  120ml/4fl oz/½ cup natural
    (plain) yogurt
  1 garlic clove, crushed
  5ml/1 tsp tomato purée (paste)
  2.5ml/½ tsp green chilli purée
  1.5ml/¼ tsp celery salt
  salt and ground black pepper

COOK'S TIP
If you prefer, you can microwave the potatoes to save time. This will take about 10 minutes.

1 Preheat the oven to 180°C/350°F/ Gas 4. Bake the potatoes for about 1 hour, until tender. Cut them in half and scoop out the flesh, leaving a thin layer on the skins. Keep the flesh for another meal.

2 To make the piquant chilli dip, mix all the ingredients in a bowl. Chill until ready to serve.

3 Heat a 1cm/½in layer of oil in a large, shallow pan. Cut each potato skin in half again, then fry them until crisp and golden on both sides. Drain on kitchen paper, sprinkle with salt and black pepper and spoon a dollop of piquant chilli dip into each skin. Serve the remaining dip separately so that people can help themselves.

SPICY POTATO WEDGES WITH CHILLI DIP

THESE DRY-ROASTED POTATO WEDGES WITH CRISP SPICY CRUSTS ARE DELICIOUS AS AN APPETIZER OR SNACK SERVED WITH A SPICY TOMATO AND CHILLI DIP .

SERVES TWO

INGREDIENTS
   2 baking potatoes, about 225g/
     8oz each
   30ml/2 tbsp olive oil
   2 garlic cloves, crushed
   5ml/1 tsp ground allspice
   5ml/1 tsp ground coriander
   15ml/1 tbsp paprika
   salt and ground black pepper

For the dip
   15ml/1 tbsp olive oil
   1 small onion, finely chopped
   1 garlic clove, crushed
   200g/7oz can chopped tomatoes
   1 fresh red chilli, seeded and chopped
   15ml/1 tbsp balsamic vinegar
   15ml/1 tbsp chopped fresh coriander
   (cilantro), plus extra to garnish

1 Preheat the oven to 200ºC/400ºF/ Gas 6. Cut the potatoes in half, then into 8 wedges.

2 Add the wedges to a pan of cold water. Bring to the boil, then reduce the heat and simmer gently for 10 minutes or until the wedges have softened slightly but the flesh has not started to disintegrate. Drain well and pat dry on kitchen paper.

COOK'S TIP
To save time, par-boil the potatoes and toss them with the spices in advance, but make sure that the potato wedges are perfectly dry and completely covered in the spice mixture before roasting.

3 Mix the olive oil, garlic, allspice, coriander and paprika in a roasting pan. Add salt and pepper to taste. Add the potatoes to the pan and shake to coat them thoroughly. Roast for 20 minutes, until the wedges are browned, crisp and fully cooked. Turn the potato wedges occasionally during the roasting time.

4 Meanwhile, make the chilli dip. Heat the oil in a small pan, add the onion and garlic, and cook for 5–10 minutes until soft.

5 Tip in the chopped tomatoes, with any juice. Stir in the chilli and vinegar. Cook gently for 10 minutes until the mixture has reduced and thickened, then taste and check the seasoning. Stir in the chopped fresh coriander.

6 Pile the spicy potato wedges on a plate, garnish with the extra coriander and serve with the chilli dip.

VARIATION
Instead of balsamic vinegar, try brown rice vinegar, which has a mellow flavour.

SPICY POTATOES

SPICY POTATOES, PATATAS PICANTES, ARE AMONG THE MOST POPULAR TAPAS DISHES IN
SPAIN, WHERE THEY ARE SOMETIMES DESCRIBED AS PATATAS BRAVAS (WILD POTATOES).

SERVES TWO TO FOUR

INGREDIENTS
225g/8oz small new potatoes
15ml/1 tbsp olive oil
5ml/1 tsp paprika
5ml/1 tsp chilli powder
2.5ml/½ tsp ground cumin
2.5ml/½ tsp salt
flat leaf parsley, to garnish

1 Preheat the oven to 200°C/400°F/
Gas 6. Prick the skin of each potato in
several places with a fork, then place
them in a bowl.

2 Add the olive oil, paprika, chilli,
cumin and salt and toss well.

3 Transfer the potatoes to a roasting
pan and bake for 40 minutes.

4 During cooking, remove the potatoes
from the oven and turn occasionally,
until tender. Serve hot, garnished
with parsley.

FRIED DOUGH BALLS WITH FIERY SALSA

THESE CRUNCHY DOUGH BALLS ARE ACCOMPANIED BY A HOT AND SPICY TOMATO SALSA.
SERVE THEM WITH A JUICY TOMATO SALAD, IF YOU PREFER.

SERVES TEN

INGREDIENTS
   450g/1lb/4 cups strong white
      bread flour
   5ml/1 tsp easy-blend (rapid-rise)
      dried yeast
   5ml/1 tsp salt
   30ml/2 tbsp chopped fresh parsley
   2 garlic cloves, finely chopped
   30ml/2 tbsp olive oil, plus extra
      for greasing
   vegetable oil, for frying

For the salsa
   6 hot red chillies, seeded and
      coarsely chopped
   1 onion, coarsely chopped
   2 garlic cloves, quartered
   2.5cm/1in piece of root ginger,
      coarsely chopped
   450g/1lb tomatoes, coarsely
      chopped
   30ml/2 tbsp olive oil
   pinch of sugar
   salt and ground black pepper

1 Sift the flour into a large bowl. Stir in the yeast and salt and make a well in the centre. Add the parsley, garlic, olive oil and enough warm water to make a firm dough.

2 Gather the dough in the bowl together, then tip out on to a lightly floured surface or board. Knead for about 10 minutes, until the dough feels very smooth and elastic.

3 Rub a little oil into the surface of the dough. Return it to the clean bowl, cover with clear film (plastic wrap) or a clean dishtowel and leave in a warm place to rise for about 1 hour, or until doubled in bulk.

4 Meanwhile, make the salsa. Combine the chillies, onion, garlic and ginger in a food processor and process together until very finely chopped. Add the tomatoes and olive oil and process until smooth.

5 Sieve the mixture into a pan. Add sugar, salt and pepper to taste and simmer gently for 15 minutes. Do not allow the salsa to boil.

6 Roll the dough into about 40 balls. Shallow fry in batches in hot oil for 4–5 minutes, until crisp and golden. Drain on kitchen paper and serve hot, with the fiery salsa for dipping.

COOK'S TIP
These dough balls can be deep-fried for 3–4 minutes or baked at 200°C/ 400°F/Gas 6 for 15–20 minutes.

STUFFED CHILLIES <u>WITH</u> CHEESE

STUFFED CHILLIES ARE POPULAR ALL OVER MEXICO. THE TYPE OF CHILLI USED DIFFERS FROM REGION TO REGION, BUT LARGER CHILLIES ARE EASIER TO STUFF THAN SMALLER ONES.

MAKES SIX

INGREDIENTS

  6 fresh poblano or Anaheim chillies
  2 potatoes, total weight about
    400g/14oz
  200g/7oz/scant 1 cup cream cheese
  200g/7oz/1¾ cups grated mature
    (sharp) Cheddar cheese
  5ml/1 tsp salt
  2.5ml/½ tsp ground black pepper
  2 eggs, separated
  115g/4oz/1 cup plain
    (all-purpose) flour
  2.5ml/½ tsp white pepper
  oil, for frying
  dried chilli flakes, to garnish (optional)

1 Make a neat slit down one side of each chilli. Place them in a dry frying pan over a medium heat, turning them frequently until the skins blister.

2 Place the chillies in a strong plastic bag and tie the top to keep the steam in. Set aside for 20 minutes, then carefully peel off the skins and remove the seeds through the slits, keeping the chillies whole. Dry the chillies with kitchen paper and set them aside.

COOK'S TIP
Take care when making the filling; mix gently, in order to avoid breaking up the diced potato.

VARIATION
Whole ancho (dried poblano) chillies can be used instead of fresh chillies, but will need to be reconstituted in water before they can be seeded and stuffed.

3 Scrub or peel the potatoes and cut them into 1cm/½in dice. Bring a large pan of water to the boil, add the potatoes and let the water return to boiling point. Lower the heat and simmer for 5 minutes or until the potatoes are just tender. Do not overcook. Drain them thoroughly.

4 Put the cream cheese in a bowl and stir in the grated Cheddar cheese, with 2.5ml/½ tsp of the salt and all the black pepper. Add the par-cooked potato and mix gently.

5 Spoon some of the potato filling into each chilli. Put them on a plate, cover with clear film (plastic wrap) and chill for 1 hour so the filling becomes firm.

6 Put the egg whites in a clean, grease-free bowl and whisk them to firm, dry peaks. In a separate bowl, beat the yolks until pale, then carefully fold in the whites. Scrape the mixture into a large, shallow dish. Spread out the plain flour in another large shallow dish and season it with the remaining salt and the white pepper.

7 Heat the oil for frying to 190°C/ 375°F. Coat a few chillies first in seasoned flour and then in egg before adding carefully to the hot oil.

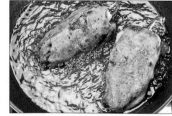

8 Fry the chillies in batches until golden and crisp. Drain on kitchen paper and serve hot, garnished with a sprinkle of chilli flakes, if you like.

PEPPERS WITH CHEESE AND CHILLI FILLING

SWEET PEPPERS AND CHILLIES ARE NATURAL COMPANIONS, SO IT ISN'T SURPRISING THAT THEY WORK SO WELL TOGETHER IN THIS TRADITIONAL BULGARIAN APPETIZER.

3 Using a sharp knife, carefully peel away the skin from the peppers.

4 Beat together all the ingredients for the filling in a bowl. Divide evenly among the 4 peppers.

5 Reshape the peppers to look whole. Dip them into the seasoned flour, then in the egg and then the flour again.

SERVES TWO TO FOUR

INGREDIENTS
    4 red, yellow or green sweet peppers,
      either bell peppers or long peppers
    50g/2oz/½ cup plain (all-purpose)
      flour, seasoned
    1 egg, beaten
    olive oil, for shallow frying
    cucumber and tomato salad, to serve

For the filling
    1 egg
    90g/3½oz/generous ½ cup finely
      crumbled feta cheese
    30ml/2 tbsp chopped fresh parsley
    1 small fresh red or green chilli,
      seeded and finely chopped

1 Preheat the grill (broiler). Slit open the peppers lengthways on one side only, enabling you to scoop out the seeds and remove the cores, but leaving them in one piece.

2 Place the peppers in a grill (broiling) pan. Cook under medium heat until the skin is charred and blackened. Place the peppers in a plastic bag, tie the top to keep the steam in and set aside for 20 minutes.

COOK'S TIP
Feta cheese should have a bland, salt-edged taste. If kept in brine for some time it will be saltier and may need to be first soaked in water.

6 Heat the olive oil for shallow frying in a large pan and fry the peeled peppers gently for 6–8 minutes, turning once with a spatula, until they are golden brown and the filling is set. Drain the peppers thoroughly on kitchen paper before serving with a cucumber and tomato salad.

COURGETTES WITH CHEESE AND GREEN CHILLIES

THIS IS A VERY TASTY WAY TO SERVE COURGETTES, OFTEN A RATHER BLAND VEGETABLE, AND IT LOOKS GOOD TOO WITH TOMATOES AND FRESH OREGANO ADDING COLOUR.

SERVES SIX

INGREDIENTS

    30ml/2 tbsp vegetable oil
    ½ onion, thinly sliced
    2 garlic cloves, crushed
    5ml/1 tsp dried oregano
    2 tomatoes
    50g/2oz/⅓ cup drained pickled
      jalapeño chilli slices, chopped
    500g/1¼lb courgettes (zucchini)
    115g/4oz/½ cup cream
      cheese, cubed
    salt and ground black pepper
    fresh oregano sprigs, to garnish

1 Heat the oil in a frying pan. Add the onion, garlic and dried oregano. Fry for 3–4 minutes, until the onion is soft and translucent.

2 Cut a cross in the base of each tomato with a sharp knife. Place in a heatproof bowl and cover with boiling water. Leave in the water for 3 minutes, then lift out on a slotted spoon and plunge into a bowl of cold water. Drain. The skins will have begun to peel back from the crosses.

3 Remove the skins and cut the tomatoes in half and squeeze out the seeds. Chop the flesh into strips.

4 Top and tail the courgettes, then cut them lengthways into 1cm/½in wide strips. Slice the strips into matchsticks.

5 Stir the courgettes into the onion mixture and fry for 10 minutes, stirring occasionally, until just tender. Add the tomatoes and chopped jalapeños and cook for 2–3 minutes more.

6 Add the cream cheese. Reduce the heat to the lowest setting. As the cheese melts, stir gently to coat the courgettes.

7 Season to taste with salt, pile into a heated dish and serve, garnished with fresh oregano.

TOASTED CHEESE TORTILLAS

FILLED WITH CHEESE AND CHILLIES, THESE ARE THE MEXICAN EQUIVALENT OF TOASTED SANDWICHES. SERVE THEM AS SOON AS THEY ARE COOKED, OR THEY WILL BECOME CHEWY.

SERVES FOUR

INGREDIENTS
    200g/7oz mozzarella, Monterey Jack
      or mild Cheddar cheese
    1 fresh fresno chilli
    8 wheat flour tortillas, about
      15cm/6in across
    onion relish or classic tomato salsa,
      to serve

VARIATIONS
Try spreading a thin layer of your favourite Mexican salsa on the tortilla before adding the cheese, or adding a few pieces of cooked chicken before folding the tortilla in half.

2 Spear the chilli on a long-handled metal skewer and roast it over the flame of a gas burner until the skin blisters and darkens. Do not let the flesh burn. Alternatively, dry-fry it in a griddle pan until the skin is scorched. Place the roasted chilli in a strong plastic bag and tie the top to keep the steam in. Set aside for 20 minutes.

3 Remove the chilli from the bag and peel off the skin. Cut off the stalk, then slit the chilli and scrape out the seeds. Cut the flesh into eight thin strips.

4 Warm a large frying pan or griddle. Place 1 wheat tortilla on the pan or griddle at a time, sprinkle about one-eighth of the cheese on to one half and add a strip of chilli. Fold the tortilla over the cheese and press the edges gently together. Cook the tortilla for 1 minute, then turn over and cook the other side for 1 minute. You can prepare these in advance but cook only when needed.

1 If using mozzarella cheese, place it in the freezer for 30 minutes to make it easier to slice. Drain it thoroughly and pat it dry, then slice it into thin strips. Monterey Jack and Cheddar cheese should both be coarsely grated, as finely grated cheese will melt and ooze away when cooking. Set the cheese aside in a bowl.

5 Remove the filled tortilla from the pan or griddle, cut it into three triangles or four strips and serve immediately, with the onion relish or tomato salsa.

PIMIENTO TARTLETS

KNOWN AS TARTALITAS DE PIMIENTO IN SPAIN, THESE PRETTY LITTLE TARTLETS ARE FILLED WITH STRIPS OF ROASTED SWEET PEPPERS AND A DELICIOUSLY CREAMY, CHEESY CUSTARD.

SERVES FOUR

INGREDIENTS
1 red (bell) pepper
1 yellow (bell) pepper
175g/6oz/1½ cups plain
   (all-purpose) flour
75g/3oz/6 tbsp chilled butter, diced
30 45ml/2 3 tbsp cold water
60ml/4 tbsp double (heavy) cream
1 egg
15ml/1 tbsp grated fresh
   Parmesan cheese
salt and ground black pepper

VARIATION
Use strips of grilled aubergine (eggplant) mixed with sun-dried tomatoes in place of the roasted peppers.

1 Preheat the oven to 200°C/400°F/ Gas 6, and heat the grill (broiler). Place the peppers on a baking sheet and grill for 10 minutes, turning occasionally, until blackened. Cover with a dishtowel and leave for 5 minutes. Peel away the skin, then discard the seeds and cut the flesh into very thin strips.

2 Sift the flour and a pinch of salt into a bowl. Add the butter and rub it in until the mixture resembles fine breadcrumbs. Stir in enough of the water to make a firm, not sticky, dough.

3 Roll the dough out thinly on a lightly floured surface and line 12 individual moulds or a 12-hole tartlet tin (muffin pan). Prick the bases with a fork and fill the pastry cases with crumpled foil. Bake for 10 minutes.

4 Remove the foil from the pastry cases and divide the pepper strips among the pastry cases.

5 Whisk the cream and egg in a bowl. Season well and pour over the peppers. Sprinkle each tartlet with Parmesan cheese and bake for 15–20 minutes until firm.

6 Cool for 2 minutes, then remove from the moulds and transfer to a wire rack. Serve warm or cold.

DESERT NACHOS

TORTILLA CHIPS ARE LIVENED UP WITH JALAPEÑOS IN THIS QUICK-AND-EASY SNACK.

SERVES TWO

INGREDIENTS
  450g/1lb tortilla chips
  45ml/3 tbsp chopped pickled jalapeño
    chillies, according to taste
  12 black olives, sliced
  225g/8oz/2 cups grated Cheddar cheese
  Guacamole, tomato salsa and sour
    cream, to serve

1 Preheat the oven to 180°C/350°F/
Gas 4. Put the tortilla chips in a
23 × 33cm/9 × 13in ovenproof dish
and spread them out evenly. Sprinkle
the jalapeños, olives and cheese evenly
over the tortilla chips.

2 Place the prepared tortilla chips in
the top of the oven and bake for
10–15 minutes, until the cheese melts.
Serve the nachos immediately, with the
guacamole, tomato salsa and sour
cream for dipping.

TORTILLAS ᵂᴵᵀᴴ ENCHILADA SAUCE

SERVED WITH A SPICY MEXICAN DIP, THIS ALWAYS PROVES TO BE A POPULAR DISH.

SERVES FOUR

INGREDIENTS
  450g/1lb can refried beans
  300ml/½ pint/1¼ cups enchilada sauce
  oil, for frying
  4 corn tortillas
  4 eggs
  150g/5oz/1½ cups grated
    Cheddar cheese
  salt and ground black pepper

1 Heat the refried beans in a pan.
Cover and set aside.

2 Heat the enchilada sauce in a small
pan. Cover and set aside.

COOK'S TIP
For a simple enchilada sauce, blend a
can of tomatoes with 3 garlic cloves,
1 chopped onion, 45ml/3 tbsp chilli
powder, 5ml/ 1 tsp each cayenne and
cumin, and 2.5ml/½ tsp each dried
oregano and salt.

3 Preheat the oven to 110°C/225°F/
Gas ¼. Put a 5mm/¼in layer of oil in a
small non-stick frying pan and heat .
When the oil is hot, add the tortillas,
one at a time, and fry for about 30
seconds on each side, until just crisp.
Remove and drain the tortillas on
kitchen paper and keep them warm
on a baking sheet in the oven.

4 Discard the oil used for frying. Let
the pan cool slightly, then wipe it with
kitchen paper to remove all but a film
of oil.

5 Heat the frying pan over a low heat.
Break in two eggs and cook until the
whites are just set. Season with salt and
pepper, then transfer to the oven to
keep warm. Repeat to cook the
remaining eggs.

6 To serve, place a warm tortilla on
each of four serving plates. Spread a
layer of refried beans over each tortilla,
then top each with a fried egg. Spoon
over the warm enchilada sauce, then
sprinkle with the grated Cheddar
cheese. Serve hot.

PERI-PERI PRAWNS WITH AIOLI

THE NAME PERI-PERI REFERS TO THE SMALL, EXTREMELY HOT ANGOLAN CHILLIES FROM WHICH THIS PORTUGUESE DISH IS TRADITIONALLY MADE.

SERVES FOUR

INGREDIENTS
    1 fresh red chilli, finely chopped
    2.5ml/½ tsp paprika
    2.5ml/½ tsp ground coriander
    1 garlic clove, crushed
    juice of ½ lime
    30ml/2 tbsp olive oil
    20 large raw prawns (shrimp) in shells
    salt and ground black pepper
    whole chillies, to garnish (optional)

For the aioli (quick method)
    150ml/¼ pint/⅔ cup mayonnaise
    2 garlic cloves, crushed
    5ml/1 tsp Dijon mustard

For the aioli (classic method)
    2 egg yolks
    2 crushed garlic cloves
    5ml/1 tsp granulated (white) sugar
    5ml/1 tsp Dijon mustard
    10ml/2 tsp lemon juice
    250ml/8fl oz/1 cup mixed olive oil
      and sunflower oil

1 To make the aioli by the quick method, mix the mayonnaise, garlic and mustard in a small bowl and set aside. For the classic method, put the egg yolks in a blender or food processor and add the garlic, sugar, mustard and lemon juice. Process until mixed, then, with the motor running, add the oil through the hole in the lid or feeder tube, drip by drip at first, then in a steady stream, until all the oil has been added and the aioli is smooth.

2 Devein the prawns and remove their heads, but leave the shells on.

3 Make a peri-peri marinade by mixing the chilli, paprika, coriander, garlic, lime juice and olive oil in a non-metallic bowl. Add salt and pepper to taste. Pour over the prawns and mix well. Cover and leave in a cool place to marinate for 30 minutes, turning the prawns in the mixture from time to time.

4 Thread the prawns on to metal skewers and cook under the grill (broiler) or on the barbecue, basting and turning frequently, for 6–8 minutes until pink. Serve with the aioli, garnished with extra chillies, if you like.

FIENDISH FRITTERS

THESE DELECTABLE FRITTERS COME FROM THE PHILIPPINES. UNUSUALLY, THEY ARE FIRST SHALLOW FRIED, THEN DEEP-FRIED. EAT THEM FRESH FROM THE PAN, DIPPED IN THE PIQUANT SAUCE.

SERVES TWO TO FOUR

INGREDIENTS
  16 raw prawns (shrimp),
    in the shell
  225g/8oz/2 cups plain
    (all-purpose) flour
  5ml/1 tsp baking powder
  2.5ml/½ tsp salt
  1 egg, beaten
  1 small sweet potato
  1 garlic clove, crushed
  115g/4oz/2 cups beansprouts,
    soaked in cold water for
    10 minutes and well drained
  vegetable oil, for shallow and
    deep-frying
  4 spring onions
    (scallions), chopped

For the dipping sauce
  1 jumbo garlic clove, sliced
  45ml/3 tbsp rice or wine vinegar
  15–30ml/1–2 tbsp water
  salt, to taste
  6–8 small fresh red chillies

1 Mix together all the ingredients for the dipping sauce and divide between two to four small bowls. The garlic slices and whole chillies will float on top.

2 Put the prawns in a pan with cold water to cover. Bring to the boil, reduce the heat and then simmer for about 4–5 minutes or until the prawns are pink and tender when pierced with the tip of a sharp knife. Lift them out with a slotted spoon and drain well. Discard the heads and the body shell, but leave the tails on. Strain and reserve the cooking liquid. Set aside and leave to cool.

VARIATIONS
• Use cooked tiger prawns (jumbo shrimp) if you prefer. In this case, make the batter using ready-made fish stock or chicken stock.
• You could substitute 15ml/1 tbsp very finely sliced fresh ginger for the garlic in the dipping sauce, if you like.

3 Sift the flour, baking powder and salt into a bowl. Add the beaten egg and about 300ml/½ pint/1¼ cups of the reserved prawn stock and beat to make a batter that has the consistency of double (heavy) cream.

4 Peel the sweet potato and grate it coarsely. Add it to the batter, then stir in the crushed garlic. Pat the beansprouts dry in kitchen paper and add to the batter.

5 Pour the oil for shallow frying into a large frying pan. It should be about 5mm/¼in deep. Pour more oil into a wok for deep-frying. Heat the oil in the frying pan. Taking a generous spoonful of the batter, drop it carefully into the frying pan so that it spreads out to a fritter about 10cm/4in across.

6 Add more batter to the pan but do not let the fritters touch. As soon as the fritters have set, top each one with a single prawn and a few pieces of chopped spring onion. Continue to cook over a medium heat for 1 minute, then remove with a spatula.

7 Heat the oil in the wok to 190°C/375°F and deep-fry the fritters in batches until they are crisp and golden brown. Drain on kitchen paper and then arrange on a serving plate or platter. Serve with the dipping sauce.

PAN-STEAMED CHILLI MUSSELS

IF YOU CAN TAKE THE HEAT, USE BIRD'S EYE CHILLIES FOR THIS SIMPLE DISH, OR SUBSTITUTE ONE RED CAYENNE OR TWO RED FRESNO CHILLIES. LEMON GRASS ADDS A REFRESHING TANG.

2 Cut off the lower 5cm/2in of each lemon grass stalk and chop finely. Add to the pan, with the shallots, kaffir lime leaves, chillies, Thai fish sauce and lime juice.

3 Cover the pan with a lid and place it over medium-high heat. Steam for 5–7 minutes, shaking the pan occasionally, until the mussels open. Discard any of the mussels that have not opened.

SERVES FOUR TO SIX

INGREDIENTS
  1kg/2¼lb live mussels
  2 lemon grass stalks
  4 shallots, chopped
  4 kaffir lime leaves,
    roughly torn
  1–2 fresh red chillies, seeded
    and sliced
  15ml/1 tbsp Thai fish sauce
  30ml/2 tbsp lime juice
  2 spring onions (scallions), chopped,
    to garnish
  coriander (cilantro) leaves,
    to garnish

1 Scrub the mussels and remove the beards, discarding any mussels that are damaged or that fail to close when tapped with a knife. Place in a large heavy pan.

4 Using a slotted spoon, transfer the cooked mussels to a serving dish, along with any liquid that has been produced. Garnish with chopped spring onions and coriander leaves. Serve immediately.

SPICY SHELLFISH WONTONS

THESE TASTY WONTONS LOOK A BIT LIKE TORTELLINI BUT THE TASTE IS MORE THAI THAN TRIESTE. WATER CHESTNUTS ADD A LIGHT CRUNCH TO THE CRAB AND CHILLI FILLING.

SERVES FOUR

INGREDIENTS
225g/8oz raw prawns (shrimp),
  peeled and deveined
115g/4oz white crab meat,
  picked over
4 drained canned water chestnuts,
  finely diced
1 spring onion (scallion), chopped
1 small fresh green chilli,
  seeded and finely chopped
1.5ml/¼ tsp grated fresh root ginger
1 egg, separated
20–24 wonton wrappers
salt and ground black pepper
coriander (cilantro) leaves, to garnish

For the dressing
30ml/2 tbsp rice vinegar
15ml/1 tbsp chopped
  pickled ginger
90ml/6 tbsp olive oil
15ml/1 tbsp soy sauce
45ml/3 tbsp chopped
  coriander (cilantro)
30ml/2 tbsp diced red (bell) pepper

1 Finely dice the prawns and place them in a bowl. Stir in the next 5 ingredients and the egg white. Season with salt and pepper and mix well.

2 Place a wonton wrapper on a board. Put about 5ml/1 tsp of the filling just above the centre of the wrapper. With a pastry brush, moisten the edges of the wrapper with a little of the egg yolk. Bring the bottom of the wrapper up over the filling. Press gently to expel any air, then seal neatly in a triangle.

3 For a more elaborate shape, bring the 2 side points up over the filling, overlap the points and pinch the ends firmly together. Space the filled wontons on a large baking sheet lined with some greaseproof (waxed) paper, so that they do not stick together.

4 Half-fill a large pan with water. Bring to simmering point. Add the filled wontons, a few at a time, and simmer for 2–3 minutes. The wontons will float to the surface and when they are cooked and ready to remove, the wrappers will be translucent and the filling cooked. Remove the wontons with a large slotted spoon, drain them briefly, then spread them on trays. Keep warm while cooking the remaining wontons.

5 Make the dressing by whisking all the ingredients together in a bowl. Divide the warm wontons among four serving dishes, drizzle with the spicy dressing and serve garnished with a handful of coriander leaves.

CEVICHE OF FISH WITH CITRUS FRUITS

FRESH FISH IS "COOKED" BY BEING MARINATED IN A MIXTURE OF MANGO, LIME JUICE AND CHILLIES. THE RESULT IS AN APPETIZER WITH A WONDERFULLY FRESH FLAVOUR.

SERVES SIX

INGREDIENTS
    350g/12oz medium cooked
      prawns (shrimp)
    350g/12oz scallops, removed from
      their shells, with corals intact
    2 tomatoes, about 175g/6oz
    1 red onion, finely chopped
    1 small mango
    350g/12oz salmon fillet
    1 fresh red chilli
    12 limes
    30ml/2 tbsp caster (superfine) sugar
    2 pink grapefruit
    3 oranges
    salt and ground black pepper
    lime slices, to garnish (optional)

3 Skin the salmon, if necessary, then cut it into small pieces.Slit the chilli and scrape out and discard the seeds. Dice the flesh. Add the tomatoes, mango, salmon, chilli and onion to the shellfish in the bowl.

4 Squeeze 8 of the limes and add the juice to the bowl, with the sugar and seasoning. Stir, cover and leave the ceviche to marinate for 3 hours in the refrigerator.

5 Segment the grapefruit, oranges and remaining limes. Drain off as much excess lime juice as possible from the marinated fish and gently fold in the fruit segments. Season to taste and arrange on a platter. Garnish with lime slices, if you like. Serve immediately.

COOK'S TIP
Take very special care in choosing the fish for this dish; it must be very fresh and served on the day it is prepared.

1 Peel the prawns and place them in a large bowl. Cut the scallop meat into 1cm/½in dice. Add it to the bowl.

2 Dice the tomatoes. Peel the mango and cut off a thick slice close to the flat side of the stone (pit). Repeat on the other side. Score the flesh with criss-cross lines, then fold the slices inside out so the dice stand proud of the skin. Slice these off the skin and into a bowl.

THAI-STYLE MARINATED SALMON

*THIS IS A WONDERFUL WAY OF PREPARING SALMON, SIMILAR TO THE SCANDINAVIAN SPECIALITY,
GRAVLAX. START THE PREPARATION TWO TO FIVE DAYS BEFORE YOU INTEND TO EAT IT.*

SERVES FOUR TO SIX

INGREDIENTS

tail piece of 1 salmon, about
    675g/1½lb, cleaned and prepared
    (see below)
20ml/4 tsp coarse sea salt
20ml/4 tsp granulated (white) sugar
2.5cm/1in piece fresh root
    ginger, grated
2 lemon grass stalks
4 kaffir lime leaves, finely chopped
    or shredded
grated rind of 1 kaffir lime
1 fresh red chilli, seeded
    and chopped
5ml/1 tsp black peppercorns,
    coarsely crushed
30ml/2 tbsp chopped fresh coriander
    (cilantro), plus sprigs to garnish
wedges of kaffir lime, to garnish

For the dressing
150ml/¼ pint/⅔ cup mayonnaise
juice of ½ lime
10ml/2 tsp chopped fresh
    coriander (cilantro)

1 Ask your fishmonger to scale the fish
and remove the skin, splitting the
fish lengthways to remove it from
the backbone in 2 matching fillets.
Use tweezers to remove all the bones
from the salmon.

2 In a bowl, mix together the salt, sugar
and ginger. Remove the outer leaves
from the lemon grass and slice the
inner portion finely. Add to the bowl,
with the lime leaves, lime rind, chilli,
peppercorns and coriander.

3 Place one-quarter of the spice mixture
in a shallow dish. Place one salmon
fillet, skin-side down, on top of the
spices. Spread two-thirds of the
remaining mixture over the flesh then
place the remaining fillet on top, flesh-
side down. Arrange the rest of the spice
mixture over the fish.

COOK'S TIP

Kaffir lime leaves and the rind of the
fruit are very aromatic and a distinctive
feature of Thai cooking. They should be
available from Asian food stores. If not,
substitute ordinary limes.

4 Cover the fish with foil, then place
a board on top. Add some weights,
such as clean cans of food. Chill for
2–5 days, turning the fish each day
in the spicy marinade to ensure that the
flavour permeates all parts of the fish.

5 Make the dressing by mixing the
mayonnaise, lime juice and chopped
coriander in a bowl.

6 Scrape the spices off the fish. Slice it
as thinly as possible. Serve with the
lime dressing, garnished with fresh
coriander and wedges of kaffir lime.

SINGAPORE CRABS

*EAT THESE CRABS WITH THE FINGERS. GIVE GUESTS CRAB CRACKERS FOR THE CLAWS AND
HAVE SOME FINGER BOWLS OR HOT TOWELS TO HAND AS THE MEAL WILL BE MESSY!*

SERVES FOUR

INGREDIENTS

2 cooked crabs, each about
    675g/1½lb
90ml/6 tbsp sunflower oil
2.5cm/1in piece fresh root ginger,
    peeled and chopped
2–3 garlic cloves, crushed
1–2 fresh red chillies, seeded and
    pounded to a paste
175ml/6fl oz/¾ cup tomato ketchup
30ml/2 tbsp soft light brown sugar
15ml/1 tbsp light soy sauce
120ml/4fl oz/½ cup boiling water
salt
hot toast and cucumber chunks,
    to serve

1 Prepare each crab in turn. Twist off
the large claws, then turn the crab on
its back with its mouth and eyes facing
away from you. Using both of your
thumbs, push the body, with the small
legs attached, upwards from beneath
the flap, separating the body from the
main shell in the process. Discard the
stomach sac and grey spongy lungs.

2 Using a teaspoon, scrape the brown
creamy meat from the large shell into a
small bowl. Twist the legs from the body.
Cut the body section in half. Pick out
the white meat and add it to the bowl.
Pick out the meat from the legs, or
leave it for guests to remove at the table.

3 Heat the oil in a wok and gently fry
the ginger, garlic and fresh chilli paste
for 1–2 minutes without browning. Stir
in the ketchup, sugar and soy sauce,
with salt to taste and heat gently.

4 Stir in all the crab meat. Pour in the
boiling water, stir well and heat through
over a high heat. Pile on serving plates.
If the crab claws were left intact, add
them to the plate, with the cucumber.
Serve immediately, with pieces of toast.

PORK SATAY STICKS

*THERE ARE FEW DISHES AS DELICIOUS AS SATAY. THE SKEWERS OF SPICED MEAT CAN BE SERVED
AS SNACKS, AS PART OF A BARBECUE OR AS A LIGHT MEAL.*

SERVES EIGHT TO TWELVE

INGREDIENTS

450g/1lb pork fillet (tenderloin)
15ml/1 tbsp soft light brown sugar
1cm/½in cube shrimp paste
1–2 lemon grass stalks, trimmed
30ml/2 tbsp coriander seeds,
    dry-fried
6 macadamia nuts or blanched almonds
2 onions, roughly chopped
3–6 fresh red chillies, seeded and
    roughly chopped
2.5ml/½ tsp ground turmeric
300ml/½ pint/1¼ cups canned
    coconut milk
30ml/2 tbsp groundnut (peanut) oil
    or sunflower oil
salt

COOK'S TIP
How many chillies you use for the
marinade depends on their strength.

1 Soak eight to twelve bamboo skewers
in water for at least 1 hour to prevent
them from scorching when they are
placed under the grill (broiler).

2 Cut the pork into small chunks, then
spread it out in a single layer in a
shallow dish. Sprinkle with the sugar
to help release the juices. Wrap the
shrimp paste in foil and heat it briefly in
a dry frying pan or warm it on a skewer
held over a gas flame.

3 Cut off the lower 5cm/2in of the
lemon grass stalks and chop finely.
Process the dry-fried coriander seeds to
a powder in a food processor. Add the
nuts and chopped lemon grass, process
briefly, then add the onions, chillies,
shrimp paste, turmeric and a little salt;
process to a fine paste. Pour in the
coconut milk and oil. Switch the
machine on very briefly to mix.

4 Pour the mixture over the pork, stir
well, cover and leave to marinate for
1–2 hours.

5 Preheat the grill or prepare the
barbecue. Drain the bamboo skewers
and thread 3–4 pieces of marinated
pork on each. Cook the skewered meat
for 8–10 minutes, turning often until
tender and basting frequently with the
remaining marinade. Serve as soon as
they are cooked.

SAN FRANCISCO CHICKEN WINGS

THESE AROMATIC WINGS ARE COATED IN A FLAVOURSOME SWEET, SOUR AND HOT SAUCE MADE FROM ORANGE JUICE, GINGER, SOY SAUCE AND CHILLI SAUCE BEFORE BEING BAKED IN THE OVEN.

SERVES FOUR

INGREDIENTS

   75ml/5 tbsp soy sauce
   15ml/1 tbsp soft light brown sugar
   15ml/1 tbsp rice vinegar
   30ml/2 tbsp dry sherry
   juice of 1 orange
   5cm/2in strip of orange rind
   1 star anise
   5ml/1 tsp cornflour (cornstarch)
   50ml/2fl oz/¼ cup water
   15ml/1 tbsp chopped fresh
     root ginger
   5ml/1 tsp chilli-garlic sauce, to taste
   1.5kg/3½lb chicken wings,
     tips removed

1 Preheat the oven to 200°C/400°F/ Gas 6. Mix the soy sauce, soft light brown sugar, vinegar, sherry, orange juice and rind and the star anise in a medium pan. Heat over a medium heat until it is boiling.

2 Combine the cornflour and water in a small bowl and stir until blended. Add to the boiling soy sauce mixture, stirring well until it has dissolved. Boil for another minute, stirring constantly.

3 Remove the soy sauce mixture from the heat and stir in the ginger and chilli-garlic sauce.

4 Arrange the chicken wings, in one layer, in a large ovenproof dish. Pour over the soy sauce mixture and stir to coat the wings evenly.

5 Bake in the centre of the oven for 30–40 minutes, until the chicken wings are tender and browned, basting occasionally. Serve the chicken wings either hot or warm.

CHICKEN SATAY

CONCERTINAS OF TENDER CHICKEN, SERVED WITH A CHILLI-FLAVOURED PEANUT SAUCE,
ARE IRRESISTIBLE. GARNISH WITH SLICED FRESH RED CHILLIES FOR EXTRA FIRE.

SERVES FOUR

INGREDIENTS
    4 skinless chicken fillets
    10ml/2 tsp soft light brown sugar

For the marinade
    5ml/1 tsp cumin seeds
    5ml/1 tsp fennel seeds
    7.5ml/1½ tsp coriander seeds
    6 small onions, chopped
    1 garlic clove, crushed
    1 lemon grass stalk, trimmed
    3 macadamia nuts or 6 cashew nuts
    2.5ml/½ tsp ground turmeric

For the peanut sauce
    4 small onions, sliced
    2 garlic cloves, crushed
    1cm/½in cube shrimp paste
    6 cashew nuts or almonds
    2 lemon grass stalks, trimmed
    45ml/3 tbsp sunflower oil, plus extra
    5–10ml/1–2 tsp chilli powder
    400ml/14fl oz can coconut milk
    60–75ml/4–5 tbsp tamarind water or
        30ml/2 tbsp tamarind concentrate
        mixed with 45ml/3 tbsp water
    15ml/1 tbsp soft light brown sugar
    175g/6oz/½ cup crunchy peanut butter

1 Cut the chicken into 16 thin strips, sprinkle with the sugar and set aside.

2 Make the marinade. Dry-fry the spices, then grind to a powder in a food processor. Set aside. Add the onions and garlic to the processor. Chop the lower 5cm/2in of the lemon grass and add with the nuts, spices and turmeric. Grind to a paste; scrape into a bowl.

3 Add the chicken and stir well until coated. Cover loosely with clear film (plastic wrap) and leave to marinate for at least 4 hours. Soak 16 bamboo skewers for 1 hour in a bowl of warm water before use to prevent scorching.

4 Prepare the sauce. Pound or process the onions with the garlic and shrimp paste. Slice the lower parts of the lemon grass stalks and add with the nuts. Process to a fine purée. Heat the oil in a wok and fry the purée for 2–3 minutes. Add the chilli powder and cook for 2 minutes more.

5 Stir in the coconut milk and bring slowly to the boil. Reduce the heat and stir in the tamarind water and brown sugar. Add the peanut butter and cook over a low heat, stirring gently, until fairly thick. Keep warm. Prepare the barbecue or preheat the grill (broiler).

6 Thread the chicken on to the bamboo skewers. Cook on the barbecue or under the grill for about 5 minutes or until golden and tender, brushing with oil occasionally. Serve with the hot peanut sauce handed around in a separate bowl.

CHICKEN TORTILLAS <u>WITH</u> FRESNO SALSA

CRISP FRIED TORTILLAS WITH A CHICKEN AND CHEESE FILLING MAKE A DELICIOUS LIGHT MEAL, ESPECIALLY WHEN SERVED WITH A SPICY TOMATO SALSA.

MAKES TWELVE

INGREDIENTS
  2 skinless chicken breast fillets
  15ml/1 tbsp vegetable oil
  1 onion, chopped
  2 garlic cloves, crushed
  90g/3½oz/generous ½ cup crumbled
    feta cheese
  12 corn tortillas
  oil, for frying
  salt and ground black pepper

For the salsa
  3 tomatoes, peeled seeded
    and chopped
  juice of ½ lime
  small bunch of fresh coriander
    (cilantro), chopped
  ½ small onion, finely chopped
  3 fresh green fresno chillies,
    seeded and chopped

1 Start by making the salsa. Mix the chopped tomatoes, lime juice, chopped coriander, onion and chillies in a bowl. Season with salt to taste, cover and chill until needed.

2 Put the chicken portions in a large pan, add water to cover and bring to the boil. Reduce the heat and simmer for 15–20 minutes or until the chicken is cooked. Remove the chicken from the pan and let it cool a little. Using two forks, shred the chicken into small pieces. Set it aside.

3 Heat the oil in a frying pan and fry the onion and garlic over a low heat for about 5 minutes, or until the onion has softened but not coloured. Add the shredded chicken, with salt and pepper to taste. Mix well, remove from the heat and stir in the feta.

4 Before attempting to roll the tortillas, soften 3 or 4 at a time by steaming them on a plate over boiling water. Alternatively, wrap them in microwave-safe clear film (plastic wrap) and then heat them in a microwave oven on full power for about 30 seconds.

5 Place a teaspoonful of the chicken filling on one of the tortillas. Roll the tortilla tightly around the filling to make a neat cylinder. Secure with a cocktail stick (toothpick). Immediately cover the roll with clear film to prevent the tortilla from drying out and splitting. Fill and roll the remaining tortillas in exactly the same way, covering them each time with clear film.

6 Pour oil into a frying pan to a depth of 2.5cm/1in. Heat it until a small cube of day-old bread, added to the oil, rises to the surface and bubbles at the edges before turning golden. Remove the cocktail sticks or toothpicks, then add the flutes to the pan, a few at a time.

7 Fry the flutes for 2–3 minutes until golden, turning frequently. Drain on kitchen paper and serve immediately, with the spicy tomato salsa.

COOK'S TIP
You might find it easier to keep the cocktail sticks (toothpicks) in place until after the flutes have been fried. Remove them before serving.

CHICKEN NAAN POCKETS

THIS QUICK-AND-EASY DISH IS IDEAL FOR A SNACK LUNCH OR SUPPER.

SERVES FOUR

INGREDIENTS
  4 naan
  45ml/3 tbsp natural (plain) yogurt
  7.5ml/1½ tsp garam masala
  5ml/1 tsp chilli powder
  5ml/1 tsp salt
  45ml/3 tbsp lemon juice
  15ml/1 tbsp chopped fresh
    coriander (cilantro)
  1 fresh green chilli, chopped
  450g/1lb chicken, skinned, boned
    and cubed
  15ml/1 tbsp vegetable oil
  8 onion rings
  2 tomatoes, quartered
  ½ white cabbage, shredded
  lemon wedges, 2 small tomatoes,
    halved, mixed salad leaves and
    fresh coriander, to garnish

1 Using a small, sharp knife, carefully cut into the middle of each naan to make a pocket, then set them aside until needed.

2 In a bowl, mix together the natural yogurt, garam masala, chilli powder, salt, lemon juice, fresh coriander and chopped fresh green chilli. Pour this marinade over the chicken pieces and leave to marinate for about 1 hour.

3 After 1 hour preheat the grill (broiler) to very hot, then lower the heat to medium. Place the marinated chicken pieces in a flameproof dish and grill (broil) for about 15–20 minutes, until they are tender and cooked through, turning the chicken pieces at least twice. Baste with the vegetable oil occasionally while cooking.

4 Remove the dish from the heat and fill each naan with the chicken and then with the onion rings, tomatoes and shredded cabbage. Serve garnished with lemon, tomatoes, salad leaves and coriander.

CHICKEN TIKKA

GINGER, GARLIC AND CHILLI POWDER ADD A CHARACTERISTIC SPICY TASTE TO THIS POPULAR INDIAN APPETIZER, WHICH IS QUICK AND EASY TO COOK.

SERVES SIX

INGREDIENTS
  450g/1lb chicken, skinned, boned
    and cubed
  5ml/1 tsp ginger pulp
  5ml/1 tsp garlic pulp
  5ml/1 tsp chilli powder
  1.5ml/¼ tsp ground turmeric
  5ml/1 tsp salt
  150ml/¼ pint/⅔ cup natural
    (plain) yogurt
  60ml/4 tbsp lemon juice
  15ml/1 tbsp chopped fresh
    coriander (cilantro)
  15ml/1 tbsp vegetable oil
  1 small onion, cut into rings, lime
    wedges, mixed salad and fresh
    coriander, to garnish

1 In a medium mixing bowl, combine the chicken pieces, ginger and garlic pulp, chilli powder, turmeric, salt, yogurt, lemon juice and fresh coriander and leave to marinate for at least 2 hours.

2 Place the marinated chicken on a grill (broiler) tray or in a flameproof dish lined with foil and baste with the vegetable oil.

3 Preheat the grill to medium. Grill (broil) the chicken for 15–20 minutes, until cooked, turning and basting 2–3 times. Serve garnished with onion, lime, salad and coriander.

COOK'S TIP
Chicken tikka can be served with naan or chapatis, pickles and salad as a main dish for four people.

STUFFED ROLLS <u>WITH</u> SPICY SALSA

MEXICAN STREET TRADERS SELL THIS TASTY SNACK WITH A CHUNKY SALSA, SPIKED WITH CHILLIES.

<u>SERVES FOUR</u>

INGREDIENTS
  4 crusty finger rolls
  50g/2oz/¼ cup butter, softened
  225g/8oz/1⅓ cups canned
    refried beans
  30ml/2 tbsp chopped bottled pickled
    jalapeño chillies
  150g/5oz/1¼ cups grated medium
    Cheddar cheese
  green salad leaves, to garnish
  120ml/4fl oz/½ cup tomato salsa,
    to serve

1 Preheat the grill (broiler). Cut the rolls in half, then take a sliver off the base so that they lie flat. Remove a little of the crumb. Spread them lightly with butter.

2 Arrange the rolls on a baking sheet and grill (broil) for about 5 minutes, or until they are crisp and golden.

3 Meanwhile, heat the refried beans over a low heat in a small pan, stirring occasionally to avoid them sticking. Add the pickled jalapeño chillies.

4 Scoop the beans on to the rolls, then sprinkle over the cheese. Place them under the grill until the cheese melts.

5 Garnish with salad leaves and serve with the tomato salsa. If the salsa is not very spicy, add a seeded and finely chopped chilli to enhance the flavour.

EGGS <u>WITH</u> TORTILLAS <u>AND</u> BEANS

A TASTY AND FILLING SNACK, TORTILLAS ARE TOPPED WITH BEANS, FRIED EGG AND HOT CHILLI SAUCES.

<u>SERVES FOUR</u>

INGREDIENTS
  225g/8oz/generous 1 cup black
    beans, soaked overnight in water
  1 small onion, finely chopped
  2 garlic cloves, crushed
  small bunch of fresh coriander
    (cilantro), chopped
  150g/5oz/1 cup frozen peas
  4 corn tortillas
  30ml/2 tbsp oil
  4 eggs
  150g/5oz cooked ham, diced
  60ml/4 tbsp hot chilli sauce
  75g/3oz/generous ½ cup feta
    cheese, crumbled
  salt and ground black pepper
  tomato salsa, to serve

1 Drain the beans, rinse them under cold water and drain again. Put them in a pan, add the onion and garlic with water to cover. Bring to the boil, then simmer for 40 minutes. Stir in the coriander, season to taste, and keep hot.

2 Cook the peas in a small pan of boiling water until they are just tender. Drain and set aside. Heat the tortillas, following the instructions on the packet.

3 Heat the oil in a frying pan and fry the eggs until the whites are set. Lift them on to a plate and keep them warm while you quickly heat the ham and peas in the oil remaining in the pan.

COOK'S TIP
When frying eggs, crack them into a saucer first, to avoid breaking the yolk. Then slide into the pan.

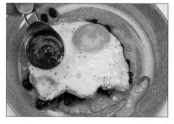

4 Place the tortillas on warmed plates and top each one with some beans. Place an egg on each tortilla, spoon over 15ml/1 tbsp hot chilli sauce, then surround each egg with some peas and ham. Sprinkle feta over the peas and serve immediately, with salsa on the side.

VARIATIONS
Tortillas with a foundation of black beans and feta cheese can be covered with a variety of toppings. Try them with a dab of salsa and sliced radishes. Or try courgettes (zucchini), guacamole and spring onions (scallions).

ROLLS WITH REFRIED BEANS AND CHILLI

FILLED ROLLS WITH A DIFFERENCE, TORTAS ARE LIKE EDIBLE TREASURE CHESTS, WITH MEAT, CHEESE, CHILLIES AND TOMATOES PILED ON TOP OF REFRIED BEANS.

SERVES TWO

INGREDIENTS
2 fresh jalapeño chillies
juice of ½ lime
2 French bread rolls or 2 pieces of
   French bread
115g/4oz/⅔ cup home-made or
   canned refried beans
150g/5oz roast pork
2 small tomatoes, sliced
115g/4oz Cheddar cheese, sliced
small bunch of fresh
   coriander (cilantro)
30ml/2 tbsp crème fraîche

VARIATIONS
The essential ingredients of a *torta* are
refried beans and chillies. Everything
else is subject to change. Ham, chicken
or turkey could all be used instead of
pork, or another kind of cheese, and
lettuce is often added.

1 Cut the chillies in half, scrape out the
seeds, then cut the flesh into thin
strips. Put it in a bowl, pour over the
lime juice and leave to stand.

2 If using rolls, slice them in half and
remove some of the crumb so that they
are slightly hollowed. If using French
bread, slice each piece in half
lengthways and hollow likewise. Set
the tops aside and spread the bottom
halves with the refried beans.

3 Cut the pork into thin shreds and put
these on top of the refried beans. Top
with the tomato slices. Drain the
jalapeño strips and put them on top of
the tomato slices. Add the cheese and
sprinkle with coriander leaves.

4 Turn the top halves of the bread or
rolls over, so that the cut sides are
uppermost, and spread these with
crème fraîche. Sandwich back together
again and serve.

SPRING ROLLS WITH FIERY CHILLI SAUCE

THIS POPULAR SNACK COMES FROM SOUTH-EAST ASIA. THE SAUCE IS TRADITIONALLY MADE WITH HOT CHILLIES, BUT SUBSTITUTE MILDER ONES, IF YOU PREFER.

MAKES FIFTEEN

INGREDIENTS

25g/1oz cellophane noodles soaked
  for 10 minutes in hot water
  to cover
6–8 dried wood ears, soaked for
  30 minutes in warm water to cover
225g/8oz minced (ground) pork
225g/8oz fresh or canned crab meat
4 spring onions (scallions), chopped
5ml/1 tsp Thai fish sauce
250g/9oz packet spring roll wrappers
flour and water paste, to seal
vegetable oil, for deep-frying
salt and ground black pepper

For the sauce

2 fresh red chillies, seeded
2 garlic cloves, chopped
15ml/1 tbsp granulated (white) sugar
45ml/3 tbsp Thai fish sauce
juice of 1 lime or ½ lemon

2 Mix the noodles and the wood ears with the pork and set aside. Remove any cartilage from the crab meat and add to the pork mixture with the spring onions and Thai fish sauce. Season to taste, mixing well.

3 Place a spring roll wrapper in front of you, diamond-fashion. Spoon some mixture just below the centre, across the width, fold over the nearest point and roll once.

4 Fold in the sides to enclose the mixture, then brush the edges with flour paste and roll up to seal. Repeat with the remaining spring roll wrappers and filling mixture.

5 Heat the oil in a wok or deep-fryer to 190°C/375°F. Deep-fry the rolls in batches for 8–10 minutes or until they are cooked through. Drain them well on kitchen paper and serve hot. To eat, dip the rolls in the fiery chilli sauce.

1 Make the sauce by pounding the chillies and garlic to a paste. Scrape into a bowl and mix in the sugar and fish sauce, with citrus juice to taste. Drain the noodles and snip them into 2.5cm/1in lengths. Drain the wood ears, trim away any rough stems and slice the caps finely. Mix with the noodles.

COOK'S TIPS

• Wood ears (Chinese black fungus) is a gelatinous species collected and cultivated in China.

• Serve the rolls Vietnamese-style by wrapping each one in a lettuce leaf with a few sprigs of fresh mint and coriander (cilantro) and a stick of cucumber.

FIRECRACKERS

IT'S EASY TO SEE HOW THESE PASTRY-WRAPPED PRAWN SNACKS GOT THEIR NAME (KRATHAK IN THAI) — AS WELL AS RESEMBLING FIREWORKS, THEIR CONTENTS EXPLODE WITH FLAVOUR.

MAKES SIXTEEN

INGREDIENTS

16 large, raw king prawns (jumbo shrimp), heads and shells removed but tails left on
5ml/1 tsp red curry paste
15ml/1 tbsp Thai fish sauce
16 small wonton wrappers, about 8cm/3¼ in square, thawed if frozen
16 fine egg noodles, soaked (see Cook's Tip)
oil, for deep-frying

1 Place the prawns on their sides and cut two slits through the underbelly of each, one about 1cm/½ in from the head end and the other about 1cm/½ in from the first cut, cutting across the prawn. This will prevent the prawns from curling when they are cooked.

2 Mix the curry paste with the fish sauce in a shallow dish. Add the prawns and turn them in the mixture until they are well coated. Cover and leave to marinate for 10 minutes.

3 Place a wonton wrapper on the work surface at an angle so that it forms a diamond shape, then fold the top corner over so that the point is in the centre. Place a prawn, slits down, on the wrapper, with the tail projecting from the folded end, then fold the bottom corner over the other end of the prawn.

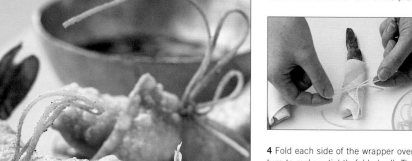

4 Fold each side of the wrapper over in turn to make a tightly folded roll. Tie a noodle in a bow around the roll and set it aside. Repeat with the remaining prawns and wrappers.

5 Heat the oil in a deep-fryer or wok to 190°C/375°F or until a cube of bread, added to the oil, browns in 45 seconds. Fry the prawns, a few at a time, for 5–8 minutes, until golden brown and cooked through. Drain well on kitchen paper and keep hot while you cook the remaining batches.

COOK'S TIP
Soak the fine egg noodles used as ties for the prawn rolls in a bowl of boiling water for 2–3 minutes, until softened, then drain, refresh under cold running water and drain well again.

CHILLI CRAB CLAWS

CRAB CLAWS ARE READILY AVAILABLE FROM THE FREEZER CABINET OF MANY ASIAN STORES AND SUPERMARKETS. THAW THEM THOROUGHLY AND DRY ON KITCHEN PAPER BEFORE COATING THEM.

SERVES FOUR

INGREDIENTS
  50g/2oz/⅓ cup rice flour
  15ml/1 tbsp cornflour (cornstarch)
  2.5ml/½ tsp granulated (white) sugar
  1 egg
  60ml/4 tbsp cold water
  1 lemon grass stalk, root trimmed
  2 garlic cloves, finely chopped
  15ml/1 tbsp chopped fresh
    coriander (cilantro)
  1–2 fresh red chillies, seeded and
    finely chopped
  5ml/1 tsp Thai fish sauce
  vegetable oil, for deep-frying
  12 half-shelled crab claws
  ground black pepper

For the chilli vinegar dip
  45ml/3 tbsp granulated (white) sugar
  120ml/4fl oz/½ cup water
  120ml/4fl oz/½ cup red
    wine vinegar
  15ml/1 tbsp Thai fish sauce
  2–4 fresh red chillies, seeded
    and chopped

1 First make the chilli vinegar dip. Mix the sugar and water in a pan. Heat gently, stirring until the sugar has dissolved, then bring to the boil. Lower the heat and simmer for 5–7 minutes. Stir in the rest of the ingredients, pour into a serving bowl and set aside.

2 Combine the rice flour, cornflour and sugar in a bowl. Beat the egg with the cold water, then stir the egg and water mixture into the flour mixture and beat well until it forms a light batter.

3 Cut off the lower 5cm/2in of the lemon grass stalk and chop it finely. Add the lemon grass to the batter, with the garlic, coriander, red chillies and fish sauce. Stir in pepper to taste.

4 Heat the oil in a deep-fryer or wok to 190°C/375°F or until a cube of bread browns in 45 seconds. Dip the crab claws into the batter, then fry, in batches, until golden. Serve with the dip.

Fresh fish is popular all over the world so fire up your fish with red hot chillies or chilli paste, pickle it with jalapeño chillies or turn it into a curry with aromatic warm spices. Although chillies have a reputation for robust flavour, they can also be surprisingly subtle, a fact that creative cooks have capitalized on for centuries. If it's fiery fish you're after, try Cajun Blackened Fish with Papaya Salsa or Balinese Fish Curry. Or step into calmer waters to savour Salmon with Tequila Cream Sauce or Seared Tuna with Red Onion Salsa.

Fiery Fish
and Shellfish

SALT AND PEPPER PRAWNS

*THIS SPICY DISH FLAVOURED WITH CHILLIES, GINGER AND FRIED SALT AND PEPPERCORNS
MAKES A DELICIOUS SUPPERTIME TREAT. SERVE WITH CRUSTY WARM BREAD.*

2 Carefully remove and discard the heads and legs from the raw prawns. Leave the body shells and the tails in place. Pat the prepared prawns dry with kitchen paper.

3 Heat the oil for deep-frying to 190°C/375°F or until a cube of day-old bread, added to the oil, browns in 30–45 seconds. Fry the prawns for 1 minute, then lift them out and drain thoroughly on kitchen paper. Spoon 30ml/2 tbsp of the hot oil into a large frying pan, leaving the rest of the oil to one side to cool.

4 Heat the oil in the frying pan. Add the fried salt, with the finely chopped onion, garlic, ginger, chillies and sugar. Toss together for 1 minute, then add the prawns and toss them over the heat for 1 minute more until they are coated and the shells are impregnated with the seasonings. Serve immediately, garnished with the spring onions.

SERVES THREE TO FOUR

INGREDIENTS
  15–18 large raw prawns (shrimp),
    in the shell, about 450g/1lb
  vegetable oil, for deep-frying
  1 small onion, finely chopped
  2 garlic cloves, crushed
  1cm/½in piece fresh root ginger,
    peeled and very finely grated
  2 fresh red chillies, seeded and sliced
  2.5ml/½ tsp granulated (white) sugar
  3–4 spring onions (scallions), sliced,
    to garnish

For the fried salt
  10ml/2 tsp salt
  5ml/1 tsp Sichuan peppercorns

1 Make the fried salt by dry-frying the salt and peppercorns in a heavy frying pan over a medium heat until the peppercorns begin to release their aroma. Cool the mixture, then tip into a mortar and crush with a pestle or process in a blender.

COOK'S TIPS
• These succulent prawns (shrimp) beg to be eaten with the fingers, so provide finger bowls or hot cloths for your guests.
• "Fried salt" is also known as "Cantonese salt" or simply "salt and pepper mix". It is widely used as a table condiment or as a dip for deep-fried or roasted food, but can also be an ingredient, as here. It is best when freshly prepared.
• Black or white peppercorns can be substituted for the Sichuan peppercorns.

SPICY PRAWNS WITH OKRA

OKRA ARE A CLASSIC INDIAN VEGETABLE, AND THEY PARTNER VERY WELL WITH SWEET, SUCCULENT KING PRAWNS AND A SIMPLE COMBINATION OF FLAVOURSOME SPICES.

SERVES FOUR TO SIX

INGREDIENTS

60–90ml/4–6 tbsp oil
225g/8oz okra, washed, dried and
    left whole
4 garlic cloves, crushed
5cm/2in piece of fresh root
    ginger, chopped
4–6 green chillies, cut diagonally
2.5ml/½ tsp ground turmeric
4–6 curry leaves
5ml/1 tsp cumin seeds
450g/1lb raw king prawns (jumbo
    shrimp), peeled and deveined
10ml/2 tsp soft light brown sugar
juice of 2 lemons
salt, to taste

1 Heat the oil in a frying pan and cook the okra on a fairly high heat until they are slightly crisp and browned on all sides. Remove from the oil and keep aside on a piece of kitchen paper.

2 In the same oil, gently cook the garlic, ginger, chillies, turmeric, curry leaves and cumin seeds for 2–3 minutes. Add the prawns and mix well. Cook until the prawns are tender.

3 Add the salt, sugar, lemon juice and cooked okra. Increase the heat and quickly cook for a further 5 minutes, stirring gently to prevent the okra from breaking. Adjust the seasoning, if necessary. Serve hot.

COOK'S TIP
Okra should be cooked rapidly to prevent the pods from breaking up and releasing their distinctive thick, sticky liquid. Try to buy firm brightly coloured pods – larger pods may be tough or fibrous.

STIR-FRIED PRAWNS with TAMARIND

THE SOUR, TANGY FLAVOUR THAT IS CHARACTERISTIC OF MANY THAI DISHES COMES FROM TAMARIND.
THAIS GENERALLY USE COMPRESSED BLOCKS OF TAMARIND PASTE RATHER THAN FRESH PODS.

SERVES FOUR TO SIX

INGREDIENTS
    50g/2oz tamarind paste
    150ml/¼ pint/⅔ cup boiling water
    30ml/2 tbsp vegetable oil
    30ml/2 tbsp chopped onion
    30ml/2 tbsp palm sugar (jaggery)
    30ml/2 tbsp chicken stock or water
    15ml/1 tbsp fish sauce
    6 dried red chillies, fried
    450g/1lb raw shelled
      prawns (shrimp)
    15ml/1 tbsp fried chopped garlic
    30ml/2 tbsp fried sliced shallots
    2 spring onions (scallions), chopped,
      to garnish

1 Put the tamarind paste in a small bowl, pour over the boiling water and stir well to break up any lumps. Leave to stand for 30 minutes. Strain, pushing as much of the juice through as possible. Measure 90ml/6 tbsp of the tamarind juice, the amount needed, and store the remainder in the refrigerator. Heat the oil in a wok. Add the chopped onion and cook until golden brown.

2 Add the sugar, stock, fish sauce, dried chillies and the tamarind juice, stirring well until the sugar dissolves. Bring to the boil.

3 Add the prawns, garlic and shallots. Stir-fry until the prawns are cooked, about 3–4 minutes. Garnish with the spring onions.

SPICY PRAWNS WITH CORNMEAL

THESE CRISPY FRIED PRAWNS WITH A CORNMEAL COATING AND A CHEESE TOPPING ARE
DELICIOUS WHEN SERVED WITH A SPICY TOMATO SALSA AND LIME WEDGES TO EASE THE HEAT.

SERVES FOUR

INGREDIENTS

115g/4oz/¾ cup cornmeal
5–10ml/1–2 tsp
  cayenne pepper
2.5ml/½ tsp ground cumin
5ml/1 tsp salt
30ml/2 tbsp chopped
  fresh coriander (cilantro)
  or parsley
900g/2lb large raw prawns (shrimp),
  peeled and deveined
flour, for dredging
¼ cup vegetable oil
115g/4oz/1 cup grated
  Cheddar cheese
lime wedges and tomato salsa,
  to serve

2 Coat the prawns lightly in flour, then dip them in water and roll them in the cornmeal mixture to coat.

3 Heat the oil in a non-stick frying pan. When hot, add the prawns, in batches if necessary. Cook them until they are opaque throughout, for about 2–3 minutes on each side. Drain on kitchen paper.

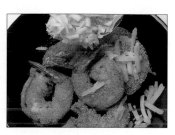

4 Place the prawns in a large ovenproof dish, or in individual dishes. Sprinkle the cheese evenly over the top. Grill (broil) about 8cm/3in from the heat until the cheese melts, for about 2–3 minutes. Serve immediately, with lime wedges and tomato salsa.

1 Preheat the grill (broiler). In a mixing bowl, combine the cornmeal, cayenne, cumin, salt and coriander or parsley.

COOK'S TIP
Fresh prawns (shrimp) should be eaten as soon as possible after purchase. All fresh raw prawns should have crisp, firm shells and a fresh smell. Do not buy them if they smell of ammonia.

CHILLI CRABS

THERE ARE VARIATIONS ON THIS RECIPE ALL OVER ASIA, BUT ALL ARE HOT AND SPICY. THIS DELICIOUS DISH OWES ITS SPICINESS AND FLAVOUR TO CHILLIES, GINGER AND SHRIMP PASTE.

SERVES FOUR

INGREDIENTS
  2 cooked crabs, about
    675g/1½ lb
  1cm/½ in cube shrimp paste
  2 garlic cloves
  2 fresh red chillies, seeded,
    or 5ml/1 tsp chopped chilli
    from a jar
  1cm/½ in fresh root ginger,
    peeled and sliced
  60ml/4 tbsp sunflower oil
  300ml/½ pint/1¼ cups
    tomato ketchup
  15ml/1 tbsp soft dark brown sugar
  150ml/¼ pint/⅔ cup
    warm water
  4 spring onions (scallions),
    chopped, to garnish
  cucumber chunks and hot toast,
    to serve (optional)

1 Remove the large claws of one crab and turn on to its back, with the head facing away from you. Use your thumbs to push the body up from the main shell. Discard the stomach sac and "dead men's fingers", i.e. lungs and any green matter. Leave the creamy brown meat in the shell and cut the shell in half, with a cleaver or strong knife. Cut the body section in half and crack the claws with a sharp blow from a hammer or cleaver. Avoid splintering the claws. Repeat with the other crab.

2 Grind the shrimp paste, garlic, chillies and root ginger to a rough paste with a mortar and pestle.

3 Heat a work and add the oil. Fry the spice paste, stirring it all the time, without browning.

4 Stir in the tomato ketchup, sugar and water and mix the sauce well. When just boiling, add all the crab pieces and toss in the sauce until well-coated and hot. Serve in a large bowl, sprinkled with the spring onions. Place in the centre of the table for everyone to help themselves.

5 Accompany this dish with cool cucumber chunks and hot toast for mopping up the sauce, if you like.

CARIBBEAN CHILLI CRAB CAKES

CRAB MEAT MAKES WONDERFUL FISH CAKES, AS EVIDENCED WITH THESE GUTSY MORSELS.
THE RICH, SPICY TOMATO DIP IS DELICIOUS, AND YOU CAN SUBSTITUTE FRESH TOMATOES.

MAKES ABOUT FIFTEEN

INGREDIENTS
  225g/8oz white crab meat (fresh,
    frozen or canned)
  115g/4oz cooked floury
    potatoes, mashed
  30ml/2 tbsp fresh herb seasoning
  2.5ml/½ tsp mild mustard
  2.5ml/½ tsp ground black pepper
  ½ fresh hot chilli, seeded and
    finely chopped
  5ml/1 tsp chopped fresh oregano
  1 egg, beaten
  plain (all-purpose) flour, for dredging
  vegetable oil, for frying
  lime wedges, coriander (cilantro)
    sprigs and fresh whole chillies,
    to garnish

For the tomato dip
  15g/½oz/1 tbsp butter
  ½ onion, finely chopped
  2 drained canned plum
    tomatoes, chopped
  1 garlic clove, crushed
  150ml/¼ pint/⅔ cup water
  5–10ml/1–2 tsp malt vinegar
  15ml/1 tbsp chopped fresh
    coriander (cilantro)
  ½ fresh chilli, seeded and chopped

1 To make the crab cakes, mix the crab meat, potatoes, herb seasoning, mustard, pepper, chilli, oregano and egg in a large bowl. Chill the mixture in the bowl for at least 30 minutes.

COOK'S TIP
Use French Dijon mustard for this dish as it is not as overpowering as English.

2 Meanwhile, make the tomato dip. Melt the butter in a small pan and sauté the onion, tomatoes and garlic for about 5 minutes until the onion is tender. Add the water, vinegar, coriander and fresh chilli. Bring to the boil, then reduce the heat and simmer for 10 minutes.

3 Pour the mixture into a blender or food processor and blend to a smooth purée. Scrape into a pan or bowl. Keep warm or chill.

4 Preheat the oven. Using a spoon, shape the crab mixture into rounds and dredge with flour, shaking off the excess. Heat a little oil in a frying pan and fry, a few at a time, for 2–3 minutes on each side. Drain the crab cakes on kitchen paper and keep warm in a low oven while cooking the remainder.

5 Garnish with lime wedges, coriander sprigs and whole chillies. Serve with the tomato dip.

FLASH-FRIED SQUID WITH PAPRIKA AND GARLIC

THESE QUICK-FRIED SQUID ARE GOOD SERVED WITH A DRY SHERRY AS AN APPETIZER OR AS PART OF MIXED TAPAS. SERVE THEM ON A BED OF SALAD LEAVES.

SERVES FOUR TO SIX

INGREDIENTS
 500g/1¼lb very small squid, cleaned
 90ml/6 tbsp olive oil
 1 fresh red chilli, seeded and
  finely chopped
 10ml/2 tsp Spanish mild smoked
  paprika (*pimentón dulce*)
 30ml/2 tbsp plain (all-purpose) flour
 2 garlic cloves, finely chopped
 15ml/1 tbsp sherry vinegar
 5ml/1 tsp grated lemon rind
 30–45ml/2–3 tbsp finely chopped
  fresh parsley
 salt and ground black pepper
 salad leaves, to serve (optional)

1 Choose small squid that are no longer than 10cm/4in. Cut the body sacs into rings and cut the tentacles into bitesize pieces.

2 Place the squid in a bowl and add 30ml/2 tbsp of the oil, half the chilli and the paprika. Season with a little salt and some pepper, cover and marinate for 2–4 hours in the refrigerator.

COOK'S TIPS
• Make sure the wok or pan is very hot, as the squid should cook for only 1–2 minutes: any longer and it will begin to toughen.
• Smoked paprika, known as *pimentón dulce* in Spain, has a wonderful smoky flavour. If you cannot find it, use mild paprika, which should be described as such on the packet.

3 Heat the remaining oil in a preheated wok or fairly deep frying pan over a high heat until very hot. Toss the squid in the flour and divide it into two batches. Add the first batch of squid to the wok or frying pan and stir-fry quickly, turning the squid constantly for 1–2 minutes, or until the squid rings become opaque and the tentacles have curled.

4 Sprinkle in half the garlic. Stir to mix then turn out on to a plate and keep warm. Repeat the stir-frying with the second batch of squid and garlic.

5 Sprinkle the sherry vinegar, lemon rind, remaining chilli and parsley over the squid. Taste for seasoning and serve hot or cool, on a bed of salad leaves, if you like.

FIVE-SPICE SQUID WITH CHILLI AND BLACK BEAN SAUCE

SQUID IS PERFECT FOR STIR-FRYING AS IT BENEFITS FROM FAST COOKING. THE SPICY SAUCE MAKES THE IDEAL ACCOMPANIMENT AND CAN BE MADE VERY QUICKLY.

SERVES SIX

INGREDIENTS
  450g/1lb small prepared squid
  45ml/3 tbsp oil
  2.5cm/1in piece fresh root
    ginger, grated
  1 garlic clove, crushed
  8 spring onions (scallions), cut
    diagonally into 2.5cm/1in lengths
  1 red (bell) pepper, seeded and cut
    into strips
  1 fresh green chilli, seeded and
    thinly sliced
  6 mushrooms, sliced
  5ml/1 tsp five-spice powder
  30ml/2 tbsp black bean sauce
  30ml/2 tbsp soy sauce
  5ml/1 tsp granulated (white) sugar
  15ml/1 tbsp rice wine or dry sherry

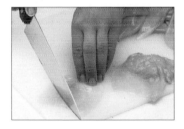

1 Rinse the squid and pull away the outer skin. Dry on kitchen paper. Make a lengthways slit down the body of each squid, then open out the body flat. Score the outside of the bodies in a criss-cross pattern with the tip of a sharp knife. Cut the squid into strips.

2 Heat a wok briefly and add the oil. When it is hot, stir-fry the squid quickly. Remove the squid strips from the wok with a slotted spoon and set aside. Add the ginger, garlic, spring onions, red pepper, chilli and mushrooms to the oil in the wok and stir-fry for 2 minutes.

3 Return the partially cooked squid to the wok and stir in the five-spice powder. Stir in the black bean sauce, soy sauce, sugar and rice wine or sherry. Bring to the boil and cook, stirring, for 1 minute. Serve immediately in warmed bowls.

SPICED SCALLOPS IN THEIR SHELLS

SCALLOPS ARE EXCELLENT STEAMED. WHEN SERVED WITH THIS SPICY GINGER AND CHILLI SAUCE, THEY MAKE A DELICIOUS APPETIZER.

SERVES FOUR

INGREDIENTS
    8 scallops, shelled (ask the fishmonger
      to reserve the cupped side of 4 shells)
    2 slices fresh root ginger, grated
    1 garlic clove, grated
    2 spring onions (scallions), green
      parts only, shredded
    salt and ground black pepper

For the sauce
    1 garlic clove, crushed
    15ml/1 tbsp grated fresh
      root ginger
    2 spring onions (scallions), white
      parts only, chopped
    1–2 fresh green chillies, seeded and
      finely chopped
    15ml/1 tbsp light soy sauce
    15ml/1 tbsp dark soy sauce
    10ml/2 tsp sesame oil

1 Remove the dark beard-like fringe and tough muscle from the scallops. Leave the corals attached.

COOK'S TIPS
• When the fishmonger is preparing the scallops, ask for the gills and mantle to use in soup or stock.
• If you do not have a bamboo steamer, you can use a flat-based stainless steel steamer or flour sifter.

2 Place 2 scallops in each shell. Season lightly with salt and pepper, then sprinkle the ginger, garlic and spring onion green on top. Place the shells in a bamboo steamer and steam for about 6 minutes until the scallops look opaque (you may do this in batches).

3 Meanwhile, make the sauce. Mix the garlic and ginger in a bowl and stir in the white parts of the spring onions. Add the chillies, both soy sauces and the sesame oil. Stir well and set aside.

4 Carefully remove each shell from the steamer, taking care not to spill the juices, and arrange them on a serving plate with the sauce bowl in the centre. Serve immediately.

MUSSELS <u>IN</u> CHILLI <u>AND</u> BLACK BEAN SAUCE

THE LARGE GREEN-SHELLED MUSSELS FROM NEW ZEALAND ARE PERFECT FOR THIS DELICIOUS DISH. BUY THE COOKED MUSSELS ON THE HALF-SHELL.

2 Remove the sauce from the heat and stir in the sesame oil and soy sauce. Mix thoroughly.

3 Have ready a bamboo steamer or a pan holding 5cm/2in of simmering water, and fitted with a metal trivet. Place the mussels in a single layer on a heatproof plate that will fit inside the steamer or pan. Spoon over the sauce.

SERVES FOUR

INGREDIENTS

15ml/1 tbsp vegetable oil
2.5cm/1in piece of fresh root ginger, finely chopped
2 garlic clove, finely chopped
1 fresh red chilli, seeded and chopped
15ml/1 tbsp black bean sauce
15ml/1 tbsp dry sherry
5ml/1 tsp granulated (white) sugar
5ml/1 tsp sesame oil
10ml/2 tsp dark soy sauce
20 cooked New Zealand green-shelled mussels
2 spring onions (scallions), 1 shredded and 1 cut into fine rings

1 Heat the vegetable oil in a pan or wok. Fry the ginger, garlic and chilli with the black bean sauce for a few seconds, then add the sherry and sugar and cook for 30 seconds more, stirring with cooking chopsticks or a wooden spoon to ensure the sugar is dissolved.

4 Sprinkle all the spring onions over the mussels. Place in the steamer or cover the plate tightly with foil and place it on the trivet in the pan. It should be just above the level of the water. Cover and steam over a high heat for about 10 minutes or until the mussels have heated through. Serve immediately.

THREE-COLOUR FISH KEBABS

FOR FOOD TO BE APPETIZING, IT NEEDS TO LOOK AS WELL AS TASTE GOOD, AND THIS DISH, WITH ITS SWEET TOMATO AND CHILLI SALSA, SCORES ON BOTH COUNTS.

SERVES FOUR

INGREDIENTS
120ml/4fl oz/½ cup olive oil
finely grated rind and juice of
  1 large lemon
5ml/1 tsp crushed chilli flakes
350g/12oz monkfish fillet, cubed
350g/12oz swordfish fillet, cubed
350g/12oz thick salmon fillet or
  steak, cubed
2 red, yellow or orange (bell)
  peppers, cored, seeded and cut
  into squares
30ml/2 tbsp finely chopped fresh flat
  leaf parsley
salt and ground black pepper

For the salsa
2 ripe tomatoes, finely chopped
1 garlic clove, crushed
1 fresh red chilli, seeded and chopped
45ml/3 tbsp extra virgin olive oil
15ml/1 tbsp lemon juice
15ml/1 tbsp finely chopped fresh flat
  leaf parsley
pinch of granulated (white) sugar

1 Put the oil in a shallow glass or china bowl and add the lemon rind and juice, the chilli flakes and pepper to taste. Whisk to combine, then add the fish chunks. Turn to coat evenly.

2 Add the pepper squares, stir, then cover and marinate in a cool place for 1 hour, turning occasionally. Preheat the grill (broiler) or prepare the barbecue.

COOK'S TIP
Don't let the fish marinate for more than an hour. The lemon juice will start to break down the fibres of the fish after this time and it will be quickly overcooked.

3 Drain the fish and peppers, reserving the marinade, then thread them on to 8 oiled metal skewers. Barbecue or grill (broil) the skewered fish for 5–8 minutes, turning once to ensure even cooking.

4 Meanwhile, make the salsa by mixing all the ingredients in a bowl, seasoning to taste with salt and pepper. Heat the reserved marinade in a small pan, remove from the heat and stir in the parsley, with salt and pepper to taste. Serve the fish kebabs hot, with the marinade spooned over, accompanied by the tomato and chilli salsa.

SEARED TUNA WITH RED ONION SALSA

A FRUITY CHILLI SUCH AS ITALIA WOULD BE GOOD IN THIS SALSA, AS WOULD A PEACHY POBLANO CHILLI. THE SALSA MAKES A FINE ACCOMPANIMENT FOR THE TUNA.

SERVES FOUR

INGREDIENTS
    4 tuna loin steaks, each weighing
        about 175–200g/6–7oz
    5ml/1 tsp cumin seeds, toasted
        and crushed
    pinch of dried red chilli flakes
    grated rind and juice of 1 lime
    45–60ml/3–4 tbsp extra virgin
        olive oil
    salt and ground black pepper
    lime wedges and coriander (cilantro)
        sprigs, to garnish

For the salsa
    1 small red onion,
        finely chopped
    6 red or yellow cherry tomatoes,
        roughly chopped
    1 avocado, peeled, stoned (pitted)
        and chopped
    2 kiwi fruit, peeled and chopped
    1 fresh red or green chilli, seeded
        and finely chopped
    60ml/4 tbsp chopped fresh
        coriander (cilantro)
    leaves from 6 fresh mint sprigs,
        finely chopped
    5–10ml/1–2 tsp Thai fish sauce
    about 5ml/1 tsp muscovado
        (molasses) sugar

1 Wash the tuna steaks and pat them dry with kitchen paper. Sprinkle with half the crushed cumin seeds, the dried chilli flakes, a little salt and freshly ground black pepper and half the lime rind and juice. Rub in 30ml/ 2 tbsp of the olive oil and set aside in a glass or china dish for 30 minutes.

2 Meanwhile, make the salsa: mix the onion, tomatoes, avocado, kiwi fruit, fresh chilli, chopped coriander and mint in a bowl. Add the remaining crushed cumin, the rest of the lime rind and half the remaining lime juice. Add Thai fish sauce and sugar to taste. Set aside for 15–20 minutes for the flavours to develop, then add a further seasoning of Thai fish sauce, lime juice and extra virgin olive oil to taste.

3 Heat a ridged, cast-iron grill (broiling) pan for at least 5 minutes. Cook the tuna, allowing about 3 minutes on each side if you like it rare or a little longer for a medium result.

4 Serve the tuna steaks immediately, garnished with lime wedges and coriander sprigs. Serve the salsa separately or spoon some or all of it on the plates with the tuna.

BAKED <small>OR</small> GRILLED SPICED WHOLE FISH

MOST MEATY FISH CAN BE PREPARED IN THIS WAY, MAKING IT AN IDEAL RECIPE FOR A FISHING TRIP.

SERVES SIX

INGREDIENTS
   1kg/2¼lb bream, carp or pomfret,
      cleaned and scaled if necessary
   1 fresh red chilli, seeded and ground,
      or 5ml/1 tsp chopped chilli
      from a jar
   4 garlic cloves, crushed
   2.5cm/1in fresh root ginger, peeled
      and sliced
   4 spring onions (scallions), chopped
   juice of ½ lemon
   30ml/2 tbsp sunflower oil
   salt
   boiled rice, to serve

1 Rinse the fish and dry it well inside and out with absorbent kitchen paper. Slash two or three times through the fleshy part on each side of the fish.

2 Place the chilli, garlic, ginger and spring onions in a food processor and blend to a paste, or grind the mixture together with a mortar and pestle. Add the lemon juice and salt, then stir in the oil.

COOK'S TIP
Almost any kind of firm fish can be used for this recipe.

3 Spoon a little of the mixture inside the fish and pour the rest over the top. Turn the fish to coat it completely in the spice mixture and leave to marinate for at least 1 hour.

4 Preheat the grill (broiler). Place a long strip of double foil under the fish to support it and to make turning it over easier. Put on a rack in a grill pan and cook under the hot grill for 5 minutes on one side and 8 minutes on the second side, basting with the marinade during cooking. Serve immediately with boiled rice.

VINEGAR CHILLI FISH

IT IS BEST TO USE OILY FISH FOR THIS RECIPE, AS THE ROBUST FLAVOUR STANDS UP TO THE CHILLI.

SERVES TWO TO THREE

INGREDIENTS
   2–3 mackerel, filleted
   2–3 fresh red chillies, seeded
   4 macadamia nuts or 8 almonds
   1 red onion, quartered
   2 garlic cloves, crushed
   1cm/½in fresh root ginger, peeled
      and sliced
   5ml/1 tsp ground turmeric
   45ml/3 tbsp coconut or vegetable oil
   45ml/3 tbsp wine vinegar
   150ml/¼ pint/⅔ cup water
   salt
   deep-fried onions, to garnish
   finely chopped fresh chilli, to garnish

1 Rinse the fish and then dry them well on kitchen paper. Set aside.

2 Grind the chillies, nuts, onion, garlic, ginger, turmeric and 15ml/1 tbsp of the oil to a paste in a food processor or with a mortar and pestle. Heat the remaining oil in a frying pan and cook the paste for 1–2 minutes, without browning. Stir in the vinegar and water. Add salt to taste. Bring to the boil, then reduce to a simmer.

3 Place the fish fillets in the sauce. Cover and cook for 6–8 minutes, or until the fish is tender.

4 Lift the fish on to a plate and keep warm. Reduce the sauce by boiling rapidly for 1 minute. Pour over the fish and serve. Garnish with deep-fried onions and chopped chilli.

MEXICAN SPICY FISH

THIS IS A TYPICAL MEXICAN SUPPER DISH, POPULAR AS IT CAN BE LEFT TO MARINATE.

SERVES SIX

INGREDIENTS
 1.5kg/3–3½ lb striped bass or any
   non-oily white fish, cut into 6 steaks
 120ml/4fl oz/½ cup corn oil
 1 large onion, thinly sliced
 2 garlic cloves, chopped
 350g/12oz tomatoes, sliced
 2 drained canned jalapeño chillies,
   rinsed and sliced

For the marinade
 4 garlic cloves, crushed
 5ml/1 tsp black peppercorns
 5ml/1 tsp dried oregano
 2.5ml/½ tsp ground cumin
 5ml/1 tsp ground annatto
 2.5ml/½ tsp ground cinnamon
 120ml/4fl oz/½ cup mild white vinegar
 salt
 flat leaf parsley, to garnish

1 Arrange the fish steaks in a single layer in a shallow dish. Make the marinade. Using a pestle, grind the garlic and black peppercorns in a mortar. Add the dried oregano, cumin, annatto and cinnamon and mix to a paste with the vinegar. Add salt to taste and spread the marinade on both sides of each of the fish steaks. Cover with clear film (plastic wrap) and leave in a cool place for 1 hour.

2 Select a flameproof dish large enough to hold the fish in a single layer and pour in enough of the oil to coat the base. Arrange the fish in the dish with any remaining marinade.

3 Top the fish with the onion, garlic, tomatoes and chillies and pour the rest of the oil over the top.

4 Cover the dish and cook over a low heat on top of the stove for 15–20 minutes, or until the fish is no longer translucent. Serve immediately garnished with flat leaf parsley.

CITRUS FISH WITH CHILLIES

THIS REFRESHING, PALATE-CLEANSING DISH IS IDEAL FOR A LIGHT SUMMER SUPPER PARTY.

SERVES FOUR

INGREDIENTS
4 halibut or cod steaks, 175g/6oz each
juice of 1 lemon
5ml/1 tsp garlic granules
5ml/1 tsp paprika
5ml/1 tsp ground cumin
4ml/¾ tsp dried tarragon
about 60ml/4 tbsp olive oil
flour, for dusting
300ml/½ pint/1¼ cups fish stock
2 red chillies, seeded and chopped
30ml/2 tbsp chopped fresh
  coriander (cilantro)
1 red onion, cut into rings
salt and ground black pepper

1 Place the fish in a shallow bowl and mix together the lemon juice, garlic, paprika, cumin, tarragon and a little salt and pepper. Spoon over the lemon mixture, cover loosely with clear film (plastic wrap) and marinate for a few hours or overnight in the refrigerator.

2 Gently heat all of the oil in a large non-stick frying pan, dust the fish with flour and then fry the fish for a few minutes each side, until golden brown all over.

3 Pour the fish stock around the fish, and simmer, covered for about 5 minutes, until the fish is thoroughly cooked through.

4 Add the chopped red chillies and 15ml/1 tbsp of the coriander to the pan. Simmer for 5 minutes.

5 Transfer the fish and sauce to a serving plate and keep warm.

6 Wipe the pan, heat some olive oil and stir-fry the onion rings until speckled brown. Sprinkle over the fish with the remaining chopped coriander and serve immediately.

SAFFRON FISH

SAFFRON HAS A DELICATE YET DISTINCTIVE FLAVOUR THAT PARTNERS BEAUTIFULLY WITH FRESH FISH.

SERVES FOUR

INGREDIENTS
  2–3 saffron threads
  2 egg yolks
  1 garlic clove, crushed
  4 salmon trout steaks
  oil, for deep-frying
  salt and ground black pepper
  green salad, to serve

1 Soak the saffron in 15ml/1 tbsp boiling water and then beat the mixture into the egg yolks. Season to taste with garlic, salt and pepper.

VARIATION
Any type of fish can be used in this recipe. Try a combination of plain and smoked for a change, such as smoked and unsmoked cod or haddock.

2 Place the fish steaks in a shallow dish and coat with the egg mixture. Cover with clear film (plastic wrap). and marinate for up to 1 hour.

3 Heat the oil in a deep-fryer until it is very hot, then fry the fish, one steak at a time, for about 10 minutes, until golden brown. Drain each steak on kitchen paper. Serve with a green salad.

PAN-FRIED SPICY SARDINES

THIS DELICIOUS FISH RECIPE IS A FAVOURITE IN MANY ARAB COUNTRIES.

SERVES FOUR

INGREDIENTS
  10g/¼oz fresh parsley
  3–4 garlic cloves, crushed
  8–12 sardines, prepared
  30ml/2 tbsp lemon juice
  50g/2oz/½ cup plain
    (all-purpose) flour
  2.5ml/½ tsp ground cumin
  60ml/4 tbsp vegetable oil
  salt and ground black pepper
  naan bread and salad, to serve

1 Finely chop the parsley and mix in a small bowl with the garlic.

2 Pat the parsley and garlic mixture all over the outsides and insides of the sardines. Sprinkle them with the lemon juice and set aside, covered, in a cool place for about 2 hours to absorb the flavours.

COOK'S TIP
If you don't have a garlic crusher, then crush the garlic using the flat side of a large knife blade instead.

3 Place the flour on a large plate and season with cumin, salt and pepper. Roll the sardines in the flour, taking care to coat each fish throughly.

4 Heat the oil in a large frying pan and fry the fish, in batches, for 5 minutes on each side, until crisp. Keep warm in the oven while cooking the remaining fish and then serve with naan bread and salad.

SPICED FISH <u>WITH</u> CHILLIES, LEMON <u>AND</u> RED ONIONS

SOMETIMES IT'S THE SIMPLEST DISHES THAT MAKE THE MOST IMPACT. THIS DISH NOT ONLY LOOKS PRETTY, IT ALSO TASTES GOOD, WITH PAPRIKA AND FRESH RED CHILLIES.

SERVES FOUR

INGREDIENTS

    4 halibut or cod steaks or cutlets,
       about 175g/6oz each
    juice of 1 lemon
    5ml/1 tsp crushed garlic
    5ml/1 tsp paprika
    5ml/1 tsp ground cumin
    4ml/¾ tsp dried tarragon
    about 60ml/4 tbsp olive oil, plus
       extra for frying the onion
    flour, for dusting
    300ml/½ pint/1¼ cups fish stock
    2 fresh red chillies, seeded and
       finely chopped
    30ml/2 tbsp chopped fresh
       coriander (cilantro)
    1 red onion, cut into rings
    salt and ground black pepper

1 Place the fish in a single layer in a shallow dish. Mix together the lemon juice, garlic, paprika, cumin, tarragon and a little salt and pepper. Spoon over the fish, cover loosely with clear film (plastic wrap) and marinate for a few hours or overnight in the refrigerator. The longer the fish is left to marinate, the stronger the flavour will be.

2 Gently heat the olive oil in a large non-stick frying pan. Drain the fish, dust the pieces with flour, then fry for a few minutes on each side, until golden brown all over.

3 Pour the fish stock around the fish, and simmer, covered, for about 5 minutes until the fish is thoroughly cooked through.

4 Add the chopped red chillies and 15ml/1 tbsp of the coriander to the pan. Simmer for 5 minutes.

5 Transfer the fish and sauce to a serving plate and keep warm.

6 Wipe the pan, heat some extra olive oil and stir-fry the onion rings until speckled brown. Arrange them over the fish, with the remaining chopped coriander and serve immediately.

RED SNAPPER WITH CHILLI, GIN AND GINGER SAUCE

CHILLIES, GINGER AND GIN ADD SPICE AND PIQUANCY TO A COLOURFUL OVEN-BAKED DISH THAT TASTES EVERY BIT AS GOOD AS IT LOOKS.

SERVES FOUR

INGREDIENTS

1 red snapper, about
   1.6kg/3½lb, cleaned
30ml/2 tbsp sunflower oil
1 onion, chopped
2 garlic cloves, crushed
50g/2oz/½ cup sliced button
   (white) mushrooms
5ml/1 tsp ground coriander
15ml/1 tbsp chopped fresh parsley
30ml/2 tbsp grated fresh root ginger
2 fresh red chillies, seeded
   and sliced
15ml/1 tbsp cornflour (cornstarch)
45ml/3 tbsp gin
300ml/½ pint/1¼ cups chicken or
   vegetable stock
salt and ground black pepper

For the garnish
15ml/1 tbsp sunflower oil
6 garlic cloves, sliced
1 lettuce heart, finely shredded
1 bunch fresh coriander (cilantro),
   tied with red raffia

1 Preheat the oven to 190°C/375°F/
Gas 5. Grease a flameproof dish that is
large enough to hold the fish. Make
several diagonal cuts on one side of
the fish.

2 Heat the oil in a frying pan and
gently fry the onion, garlic and sliced
mushrooms for 2–3 minutes. Stir in
the ground coriander and the chopped
parsley. Season with salt and pepper
to taste.

3 Spoon the filling into the cavity of the
fish, then lift the snapper into the dish.
Pour in enough cold water to cover the
base of the dish. Sprinkle the ginger
and chillies over, then cover and bake
for 30–40 minutes, basting from time to
time. Remove the cover for the last
10 minutes.

4 Carefully lift the snapper on to a
serving dish, cover with foil and keep
hot. Tip the cooking juices from the
dish into a pan.

5 Mix the cornflour and gin in a cup
and stir into the cooking juices. Pour in
the stock. Bring to the boil and cook
gently for 3–4 minutes or until thickened,
stirring. Taste for seasoning, then pour
into a bowl.

6 Make the garnish. Heat the oil in a
small pan and stir-fry the garlic and
lettuce over a high heat until crisp.
Spoon alongside the snapper. Place the
coriander bouquet on the other side.
Serve with the sauce.

WHOLE FISH WITH SWEET AND SOUR SAUCE

CRISP FRIED FISH SERVED WITH AN AROMATIC SPICED SAUCE AND PLENTY OF BOILED RICE MAKES AN APPETIZING AND IMPRESSIVE MAIN COURSE DISH. ENSURE THE FISH IS VERY FRESH.

SERVES FOUR

INGREDIENTS
1 whole fish, such as red snapper
  or carp, about 1kg/2½lb
30–45ml/2–3 tbsp
  cornflour (cornstarch)
oil, for frying
salt and ground black pepper
boiled rice, to serve

For the spice paste
2 garlic cloves
2 lemon grass stalks
2.5cm/1in fresh galangal, peeled
2.5cm/1in fresh root ginger
2cm/¾in fresh turmeric or 2.5ml/
  ½ tsp ground turmeric
5 macadamia nuts or 10 almonds

For the sauce
15ml/1 tbsp brown sugar
45ml/3 tbsp cider vinegar
about 350ml/12fl oz/1½ cups water
2 lime leaves, torn
4 shallots, quartered
3 tomatoes, peeled and cut in wedges
3 spring onions (scallions), shredded
1 fresh red chilli, seeded and grated

1 Ask the fishmonger to clean and scale the fish, leaving on the head and tail, or you may do this yourself. Wash and dry the fish thoroughly and then sprinkle it inside and out with salt. Set aside for 15 minutes, while preparing the other recipe ingredients.

2 Peel and crush the garlic cloves. Use only the lower white part of the lemon grass stalks and slice thinly. Peel and slice the fresh galangal, the fresh root ginger and fresh turmeric and grind to a fine paste in a food processor or with a mortar and pestle. Scrape the paste into a bowl.

3 To make the sauce, add the brown sugar, vinegar, seasoning to taste, the water and the lime leaves to the paste.

4 Dust the fish with the cornflour and fry on both sides in hot oil for about 8–9 minutes, or until almost cooked through. Drain on kitchen paper and transfer to a serving dish. Keep warm.

5 Pour off most of the oil. Pour in the sauce and bring to the boil. Reduce the heat and cook for 3–4 minutes. Add the shallots and tomatoes, followed a minute later by the spring onions and chilli. Taste and adjust the seasoning.

6 Pour the sauce over the fish. Serve immediately, with plenty of rice.

TURKISH COLD FISH

GREEN CHILLI, GARLIC AND PAPRIKA ADD SUBTLE SPICING TO THIS DELICIOUS FISH DISH.
COLD FISH IS ENJOYED IN MANY PARTS OF THE MIDDLE EAST.

SERVES FOUR

INGREDIENTS
60ml/4 tbsp olive oil
900g/2lb red mullet or snapper
2 onions, sliced
1 green chilli, seeded and chopped
1 each red and green (bell)
   pepper, sliced
3 garlic cloves, crushed
15ml/1 tbsp tomato purée (paste)
50ml/2fl oz/¼ cup fish stock
6 6 tomatoes, peeled and sliced or
   400g/14oz can tomatoes
30ml/2 tbsp chopped fresh parsley
30ml/2 tbsp lemon juice
5ml/1 tsp paprika
15–20 green and black olives
salt and ground black pepper
bread and salad, to serve

COOK'S TIP
One large fish looks spectacular, but it is
tricky to cook and serve. Instead, buy 4
smaller fish and cook for a shorter time,
until tender but not overdone.

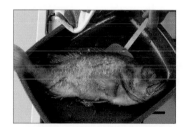

1 Heat 30ml/2 tbsp of the oil in a large
roasting pan or frying pan and cook the
fish on both sides until golden brown.
Remove from the pan, and keep warm.

2 Heat the remaining oil in the pan and
cook the onions for 2–3 minutes, until
slightly softened. Add the chilli and red
and green peppers and continue
cooking for 3–4 minutes, stirring
occasionally, then add the garlic and
stir-fry for a further minute.

3 Blend the tomato purée with the
fish stock and stir into the pan with
the tomatoes, parsley, lemon juice,
paprika and seasoning. Simmer
gently without boiling for 15 minutes,
stirring occasionally.

4 Return the fish to the pan and
cover with the sauce. Cook for 10
minutes, then add the olives and cook
for a further 5 minutes, or until just
cooked through.

5 Transfer the fish to a serving dish
and pour the sauce over the top.
Leave to cool, then cover and chill
until completely cold. Serve cold with
bread and salad.

CAJUN BLACKENED FISH WITH PAPAYA SALSA

THIS IS AN EXCELLENT WAY OF COOKING FILLETS OF SNAPPER OR COD, LEAVING IT MOIST IN THE MIDDLE AND CRISP AND SPICY ON THE OUTSIDE.

SERVES FOUR

INGREDIENTS
  5ml/1 tsp black peppercorns
  5ml/1 tsp cumin seeds
  5ml/1 tsp white mustard seeds
  10ml/2 tsp paprika
  5ml/1 tsp chilli powder
  5ml/1 tsp dried oregano
  10ml/2 tsp dried thyme
  4 skinned fish fillets, 225g/8oz each
  50g/2oz/¼ cup butter, melted
  salt
  lime wedges and coriander (cilantro)
    sprigs, to garnish

For the papaya salsa
  1 papaya
  1 fresh red chilli
  ½ small red onion, diced
  45ml/3 tbsp chopped fresh
    coriander (cilantro)
  grated rind and juice of 1 lime

1 Start by making the salsa. Cut the papaya in half and scoop out the seeds. Remove the skin, cut the flesh into small dice and place it in a bowl. Slit the chilli, remove and discard the seeds and finely chop the flesh.

2 Add the onion, chilli, coriander, lime rind and juice to the papaya. Season with salt to taste. Mix well and set aside.

3 Dry-fry the peppercorns, cumin and mustard seeds in a pan, then grind them to a fine powder. Add the paprika, chilli powder, oregano, thyme and 5ml/ 1 tsp salt. Grind again and spread on a plate.

4 Preheat a heavy frying pan over a medium heat for about 10 minutes. Brush the fish fillets with the melted butter then dip them in the spices until well coated.

5 Place the fish in the hot pan and cook for 1–2 minutes on each side until blackened. Garnish with lime and coriander, and serve with the salsa.

COOK'S TIP
Cooking fish in this way can be a smoky affair, so make sure the kitchen is well ventilated or use an extractor fan.

CARIBBEAN FISH STEAKS

THIS QUICK AND EASY RECIPE IS A GOOD EXAMPLE OF HOW CHILLIES, CAYENNE AND ALLSPICE CAN ADD AN EXOTIC ACCENT TO A TOMATO SAUCE FOR FISH.

SERVES FOUR

INGREDIENTS
  4 cod steaks
  5ml/1 tsp muscovado (molasses) sugar
  10ml/2 tsp angostura bitters
  salt
  steamed okra or green beans,
    to serve

For the tomato sauce
  45ml/3 tbsp oil
  6 shallots, finely chopped
  1 garlic clove, crushed
  1 fresh green chilli, seeded and
    finely chopped
  400g/14oz can chopped tomatoes
  2 bay leaves
  1.5ml/¼ tsp cayenne pepper
  5ml/1 tsp crushed allspice
  juice of 2 limes

1 First make the tomato sauce. Heat the oil in a frying pan and fry the shallots, until soft. Add the garlic and chilli, and cook for 2 minutes. Stir in tomatoes, bay, cayenne, allspice and lime juice, with salt to taste.

VARIATION
Almost any robust fish steaks or fillets can be cooked in this way.

2 Cook gently for 15 minutes, then add the cod steaks and baste with the tomato sauce. Cover and cook for 10 minutes or until the cod steaks are cooked. Keep hot in a warmed dish.

3 Stir the sugar and angostura bitters into the sauce, simmer for 2 minutes, then pour it over the fish. Serve with steamed okra or green beans.

COCONUT SALMON

CHILLIES AND COCONUT MILK HAVE A SPECIAL AFFINITY, THE FORMER PROVIDING HEAT AND COLOUR WHILE THE LATTER IS COOL, CREAMY AND PALE.

SERVES FOUR

INGREDIENTS

    10ml/2 tsp ground cumin
    10ml/2 tsp chilli powder
    2.5ml/½ tsp ground turmeric
    30ml/2 tbsp white wine vinegar
    1.5ml/¼ tsp salt
    4 salmon steaks, about
      175g/6oz each
    45ml/3 tbsp oil
    1 onion, chopped
    2 fresh green chillies, seeded
      and chopped
    2 garlic cloves, crushed
    2.5cm/1in piece root ginger, grated
    5ml/1 tsp ground coriander
    175ml/6fl oz/¾ cup coconut milk
    spring onion (scallion) rice,
      to serve
    fresh coriander (cilantro) sprigs,
      to garnish

1 In a small bowl, mix half the cumin with the chilli powder, turmeric, vinegar and salt. Place the salmon in a single layer in a non-metallic dish and rub all over with the paste. Cover and leave to marinate for 15 minutes.

COOK'S TIP

Make coconut milk by dissolving grated creamed coconut (coconut cream) in boiling water, then strain.

2 Heat the oil in a wide, deep-sided frying pan and fry the onion, chillies, garlic and ginger for 5–6 minutes. Scrape the mixture into a food processor or blender and process to a paste. Use a hand-held blender if you prefer.

3 Return the paste to the pan. Add the coriander and remaining cumin, then pour in the coconut milk, stirring constantly. Bring to the boil, then simmer for 5 minutes.

4 Add the salmon steaks and spoon the sauce over them. Cover and cook for 15 minutes until the fish is tender. Serve with spring onion rice and garnish with coriander sprigs.

SALMON WITH TEQUILA CREAM SAUCE

ROASTED JALAPEÑO CHILLIES AND LIGHTLY AGED REPOSADA TEQUILA ARE A WINNING
COMBINATION IN THIS EXCITING AND UNUSUAL DINNER-PARTY FISH DISH.

SERVES FOUR

INGREDIENTS

   3 fresh green jalapeño chillies
   45ml/3 tbsp olive oil
   1 small onion, finely chopped
   150ml/¼ pint/⅔ cup fish stock
   grated rind and juice of 1 lime
   120ml/4fl oz/½ cup single
    (light) cream
   30ml/2 tbsp reposada tequila
   1 firm avocado
   4 salmon fillets
   salt and ground white pepper
   strips of green (bell) pepper
    and fresh flat leaf parsley,
    to garnish

1 Roast the chillies in a frying pan until the skins are blistered but not burnt. Put them in a strong plastic bag and tie the top to keep the steam in. Set aside.

2 Heat 15ml/1 tbsp of the oil in a pan. Add the onion and fry for 3–4 minutes, then pour in the stock with the lime rind and juice. Cook for 10 minutes, until the stock starts to reduce. Remove the chillies from the bag. Peel them, then slit and scrape out the seeds.

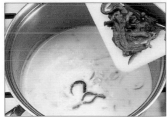

3 Stir the cream into the onion and stock mixture. Slice the chilli flesh into strips and add to the pan. Cook over a gentle heat, stirring constantly, for 2–3 minutes. Season to taste with salt and white pepper.

4 Stir the tequila into the onion and chilli mixture. Leave the pan over a very low heat. Peel the avocado, remove the stone (pit) and slice the flesh. Brush the salmon fillets on one side with a little of the remaining oil.

5 Heat a frying pan or ridged griddle pan until very hot and add the salmon, oiled side down. Cook for 2–3 minutes, until the underside is golden, then brush the top with oil, turn each fillet over and cook the other side until the fish is cooked and flakes easily when tested with the tip of a sharp knife.

6 Serve on a pool of sauce, with the avocado slices. Garnish with strips of green pepper and fresh parsley. This dish is good with fried potatoes.

SALMON PARCELS WITH SPICED LEEKS

COOKING THE FISH "EN PAPILLOTE" MAKES A LOT OF SENSE, ENSURING THAT IT RETAINS ITS FLAVOUR WHILE IT COOKS IN ITS STEAMY PARCEL WITH LEEKS, FENNEL AND CHILLI.

SERVES SIX

INGREDIENTS

25ml/5 tsp groundnut
  (peanut) oil
2 yellow (bell) peppers, seeded
  and thinly sliced
4cm/1½in fresh root ginger, peeled
  and finely grated
1 large fennel bulb, finely sliced,
  feathery tops chopped
  and reserved
1 fresh green chilli, seeded and
  finely chopped
2 large leeks, cut into 10cm/4in
  lengths and shredded lengthways
30ml/2 tbsp chopped chives
10ml/2 tsp light soy sauce
6 portions salmon fillet, each
  weighing 150–175g/5–6oz, skinned
10ml/2 tsp toasted sesame oil
salt and ground black pepper

1 Heat the oil in a large non-stick frying pan and cook the peppers, ginger and fennel for 5–6 minutes, until they have softened but not browned. Add the chilli and leeks, and cook for 2–3 minutes. Stir in half the chives and the soy sauce with seasoning to taste. Set aside.

2 Preheat the oven to 190°C/375°F/Gas 5. Cut six 35cm/14in circles of baking parchment or foil. Divide the vegetable mixture among the circles of paper or foil and place a portion of salmon on each pile of vegetables. Drizzle with sesame oil and sprinkle with the remaining chives and the chopped fennel tops. Season with salt and pepper to taste.

3 Fold the baking parchment or foil over to enclose the fish and vegetable mixture, rolling and twisting the edges together to seal the parcels.

4 Place the parcels on a baking sheet and bake for 15–20 minutes, until the parcels are puffed up and, if made with paper, lightly browned. Transfer the parcels to warmed individual plates and serve immediately.

TROUT WITH TAMARIND AND CHILLI SAUCE

SOMETIMES TROUT CAN TASTE RATHER BLAND, BUT THIS SPICY SAUCE REALLY GIVES IT A ZING. IF YOU LIKE YOUR FOOD VERY SPICY, ADD AN EXTRA CHILLI.

SERVES FOUR

INGREDIENTS

   4 trout, cleaned
   6 spring onions (scallions), sliced
   60ml/4 tbsp soy sauce
   15ml/1 tbsp vegetable oil
   30ml/2 tbsp fresh coriander (cilantro)
    and fresh red chilli, to garnish

For the sauce

   50g/2oz tamarind pulp
   105ml/7 tbsp boiling water
   2 shallots, coarsely chopped
   1 fresh red chilli, seeded and chopped
   1cm/½in piece fresh root ginger,
    peeled and chopped
   5ml/1 tsp soft light brown sugar
   45ml/3 tbsp Thai fish sauce

3 Make the sauce. Put the tamarind pulp in a small bowl and pour on the boiling water. Mash well with a fork until softened. Tip the tamarind mixture into a food processor or blender, and add the shallots, fresh chilli, ginger, sugar and fish sauce. Process to a coarse pulp. Scrape into a bowl.

4 Heat the oil in a large frying pan or wok and cook the trout, one at a time if necessary, for about 5 minutes on each side, until the skin is crisp and browned and the flesh cooked. Put on warmed plates and spoon over some of the sauce. Chop the coriander and chilli and serve with the remaining sauce.

1 Slash the trout diagonally four or five times on each side. Place them in a shallow dish that is large enough to hold them all in a single layer.

2 Fill the cavities with spring onions and douse each fish with soy sauce. Carefully turn the fish over to coat both sides with the sauce. Sprinkle any remaining spring onions over the top.

SWORDFISH TACOS

*COOKED CORRECTLY, SWORDFISH IS MOIST AND MEATY, AND SUFFICIENTLY ROBUST
TO MORE THAN HOLD ITS OWN WHEN MIXED WITH CHILLIES.*

<u>SERVES SIX</u>

INGREDIENTS
3 swordfish steaks
30ml/2 tbsp vegetable oil
2 garlic cloves, crushed
1 small onion, chopped
3 fresh green chillies, seeded
   and chopped
3 tomatoes
small bunch of fresh coriander
   (cilantro), chopped
6 fresh corn tortillas
½ iceberg lettuce, shredded
salt and ground black pepper
lemon wedges, to serve (optional)

1 Preheat the grill (broiler). Put the swordfish on an oiled rack over a grill (broiling) pan and grill (broil) for no longer than 2–3 minutes on each side. When cool, remove the skin and flake the fish into a bowl.

2 Heat the oil in a pan and gently fry the crushed garlic, and chopped onion and chillies for 5 minutes or until the onion is soft.

3 Cut a cross in the base of each tomato. Put them in a heatproof bowl and pour over boiling water. After 30 seconds, plunge into cold water. Drain and remove the skins. Cut them in half and squeeze out the seeds and dice the flesh.

4 Add the tomatoes and swordfish to the onion mixture. Cook for 5 minutes over a low heat. Add the coriander and cook for 1–2 minutes. Season to taste with salt and pepper.

5 Wrap the tortillas in foil and steam on a plate over boiling water until pliable. Place some shredded lettuce and fish mixture on each tortilla. Fold in half and serve immediately, with lemon wedges if you like.

SWORDFISH WITH CHILLI AND LIME SAUCE

*SWORDFISH IS A PRIME CANDIDATE FOR THE BARBECUE, AS LONG AS IT IS NOT OVERCOOKED.
IT TASTES WONDERFUL WITH A SPICY SAUCE WHOSE FIRE IS TEMPERED WITH CRÈME FRAÎCHE.*

<u>SERVES FOUR</u>

INGREDIENTS
2 fresh serrano chillies
4 tomatoes
45ml/3 tbsp olive oil
grated rind and juice of 1 lime
4 swordfish steaks
2.5ml/½ tsp salt
2.5ml/½ tsp ground black pepper
175ml/6fl oz/¾ cup crème fraîche
fresh flat leaf parsley,
   to garnish

1 Roast the chillies in a dry griddle pan until the skins are blistered. Put in a plastic bag and tie the top. Set aside for 20 minutes, then peel off the skins. Cut off the stalks, then slit the chillies, scrape out the seeds and slice the flesh.

2 Cut a cross in the base of each tomato. Place them in a heatproof bowl and pour over boiling water to cover. After 30 seconds, lift the tomatoes out on a slotted spoon and plunge them into a bowl of cold water. Drain. The skins will have begun to peel back from the crosses. Remove the skin from the tomatoes, then cut them in half and squeeze out the seeds. Chop the flesh into 1cm/½in pieces.

3 Heat 15ml/1 tbsp of the oil in a small pan and add the strips of chilli, with the lime rind and juice. Cook for 2–3 minutes, then stir in the tomatoes. Cook for 10 minutes, stirring the mixture occasionally, until the tomato is pulpy. Preheat the grill (broiler) or prepare the barbecue.

4 Brush the swordfish steaks with olive oil and season. Barbecue or grill (broil) for 3–4 minutes or until just cooked, turning once. Meanwhile, stir the crème fraîche into the sauce and heat it through gently. Pour over the swordfish steaks. Serve garnished with fresh parsley. This is delicious served with chargrilled vegetables.

FIERY FISH STEW

CHILLI POWDER AND FRESH CHILLIES ARE USED IN THIS SPICY DISH, SO THERE'S DOUBLE
DELIGHT FOR ANYONE WHO LIKES THEIR FOOD GOOD AND HOT.

2 Stir in the salt, ground cumin, ground coriander and chilli powder, and cook for 3–4 minutes.

3 Add the tomatoes and potatoes, then stir in the fish stock. Bring to the boil, then reduce the heat and simmer for 10 minutes.

4 Add the fish, then cover and simmer for 10 minutes, or until the fish is tender. Serve with the chapatis.

SERVES FOUR

INGREDIENTS
    30ml/2 tbsp oil
    5ml/1 tsp cumin seeds
    1 onion, chopped
    1 red (bell) pepper, thinly sliced
    1 garlic clove, crushed
    2 fresh red chillies, finely chopped
    2 bay leaves
    2.5ml/½ tsp salt
    5ml/1 tsp ground cumin
    5ml/1 tsp ground coriander
    5ml/1 tsp chilli powder
    400g/14oz can chopped tomatoes
    2 large potatoes, cut into 2.5cm/
      1in chunks
    300ml/½ pint/1¼ cups fish stock
    4 cod fillets
    chapatis, to serve

1 Heat the oil in a large, deep-sided frying pan and fry the cumin seeds for 2 minutes until they begin to splutter. (You may need to cover the pan at this stage to prevent the seeds from leaping out, but do not let them burn.) Add the onion, pepper, garlic, chillies and bay leaves, and fry for 5–7 minutes until the onions have browned.

COOK'S TIP
The potatoes will help to moderate the heat of this curry, but if you prefer a milder flavour, use half the amount of fresh chillies and a mild chilli powder.

CREOLE FISH STEW

HERE'S YOUR CHANCE TO EXPERIMENT WITH A HABANERO CHILLI — IF YOU DARE. HABANEROS HAVE A WONDERFUL FLAVOUR, SO IF YOU FEAR THEIR FIRE, START WITH HALF OF ONE.

SERVES FOUR TO SIX

INGREDIENTS

  2 whole red bream or large snapper, prepared and cut into 2.5cm/1in thick slices
  30ml/2 tbsp Creole or Cajun spice seasoning
  30ml/2 tbsp malt vinegar
  flour, for dusting
  oil, for frying
  fresh herb sprigs, to garnish

For the sauce
  30ml/2 tbsp vegetable oil
  15g/½oz/1 tbsp butter
  1 onion, finely chopped
  3 fresh tomatoes, peeled and finely chopped
  2 garlic cloves, crushed
  2 fresh thyme sprigs
  600ml/1 pint/2½ cups fish stock or water
  2.5ml/½ tsp ground cinnamon
  1 fresh hot chilli, chopped
  1 red (bell) pepper, seeded and chopped
  1 green (bell) pepper, seeded and finely chopped
  salt

1 Spread out the fish slices in a large non-metallic dish and sprinkle with the spice seasoning and vinegar, turning to coat. Cover and set aside to marinate for 2 hours or overnight in the refrigerator.

COOK'S TIP
Handle all chillies with care, especially habaneros. Wear gloves and wash all utensils in hot soapy water when preparation is complete.

2 Make the sauce. Heat the oil and butter in a large frying pan and sauté the onion for 5 minutes. Add the tomatoes, garlic and thyme, stir well and simmer for 5 minutes more. Stir in the stock or water, cinnamon and chilli. Leave over a low heat while you cook the fish.

3 When ready to cook, place a little flour on a large plate. Coat the fish pieces, shaking off any excess flour.

4 Heat a little oil in a large frying pan and fry the fish pieces, in batches if necessary, for about 5 minutes until golden brown.

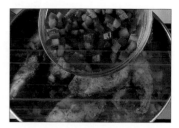

5 Add the fish pieces and the chopped red and green peppers to the sauce and simmer until the fish is cooked through, and the sauce is thick and flavoursome. Adjust the seasoning with salt to taste. Garnish with fresh herb sprigs and serve hot.

CURRIED SHELLFISH WITH COCONUT MILK

THIS CURRY IS BASED ON A THAI CLASSIC. THE LOVELY GREEN COLOUR IS IMPARTED BY THE FINELY CHOPPED CHILLI AND FRESH HERBS.

SERVES FOUR

INGREDIENTS
225g/8oz small ready-prepared squid
225g/8oz raw tiger prawns
  (jumbo shrimp)
400ml/14fl oz/1⅔ cups coconut milk
2 kaffir lime leaves, finely shredded
30ml/2 tbsp Thai fish sauce
450g/1lb firm white fish fillets,
  skinned, boned and cut into chunks
2 fresh green chillies, seeded and
  finely chopped
30ml/2 tbsp torn fresh basil or
  coriander (cilantro) leaves
squeeze of fresh lime juice
cooked Thai jasmine rice, to serve

For the curry paste
6 spring onions (scallions),
  coarsely chopped
4 fresh coriander (cilantro) stems,
  coarsely chopped, plus 45ml/3 tbsp
  chopped fresh coriander (cilantro)
4 kaffir lime leaves, shredded
8 fresh green chillies, seeded and
  coarsely chopped
1 lemon grass stalk,
  coarsely chopped
2.5cm/1in piece fresh root ginger,
  peeled and coarsely chopped
45ml/3 tbsp chopped fresh basil
15ml/1 tbsp vegetable oil

1 Make the curry paste. Put all the ingredients, except the oil, in a food processor and process to a paste. Alternatively, pound together in a mortar with a pestle. Stir in the oil.

2 Rinse the squid and pat dry with kitchen paper. Cut the bodies into rings and halve the tentacles, if necessary.

3 Heat a wok until hot, add the prawns and stir-fry, without any oil, for about 4 minutes, until they turn pink.

4 Remove the prawns from the wok and leave to cool slightly, then peel off the shells, saving a few with shells on for the garnish. Make a slit along the back of each one and remove the black vein.

5 Pour the coconut milk into the wok, then bring to the boil over a medium heat, stirring constantly. Add 30ml/ 2 tbsp of curry paste, the shredded lime leaves and fish sauce and stir well to mix. Reduce the heat to low and simmer gently for about 10 minutes.

6 Add the squid, prawns and chunks of fish and cook for about 2 minutes, until the shellfish is tender. Take care not to overcook the squid as it will become tough very quickly.

7 Just before serving, stir in the chillies and basil or coriander. Taste and adjust the flavour with a squeeze of lime juice. Garnish with prawns in their shells, and serve with Thai jasmine rice.

VARIATIONS
• You can use any firm-fleshed white fish for this curry, such as monkfish, cod, haddock or John Dory.
• If you prefer, you could substitute shelled scallops for the squid. Slice them in half horizontally and add them with the prawns (shrimp). As with the squid, be careful not to overcook them.

COCONUT FISH CURRY

*THIS IS A VERY POPULAR SOUTH-EAST ASIAN FISH CURRY IN A COCONUT SAUCE. CHOOSE A
FIRM-TEXTURED FISH SO THAT THE PIECES STAY INTACT DURING THE BRIEF COOKING PROCESS.*

SERVES FOUR

INGREDIENTS
  500g/1¼lb firm-textured fish fillets,
    skinned and cut into 2.5cm/
    1in cubes
  2.5ml/½ tsp salt
  50g/2oz/⅔ cup desiccated (dry
    unsweetened shredded) coconut
  6 shallots or small onions,
    roughly chopped
  6 blanched almonds
  2–3 garlic cloves, roughly chopped
  2.5cm/1in piece fresh root ginger,
    peeled and sliced
  2 lemon grass stalks, trimmed
  10ml/2 tsp ground turmeric
  45ml/3 tbsp vegetable oil
  2 × 400ml/14fl oz cans coconut milk
  1–3 fresh red or green chillies,
    seeded and sliced
  salt and ground black pepper
  fresh chives, to garnish
  boiled long grain rice, to serve

1 Spread out the pieces of fish in a
shallow dish and sprinkle them with the
salt. Dry-fry the coconut in a wok over
medium to low heat, turning all the time
until it is crisp and golden (see Cook's
Tip below).

2 Tip the dry-fried coconut into a
food processor and process until you
have an oily paste. Scrape into a bowl
and reserve.

3 Add the shallots or onions, almonds,
garlic and ginger to the food processor.
Cut off the lower 5cm/2in of the lemon
grass stalks, chop them roughly and
add to the other ingredients in the
processor. Process the mixture to a
paste. Bruise the remaining lemon grass
and set the stalks aside.

4 Add the ground turmeric to the
mixture in the processor and process
briefly to mix.

5 Heat the oil in the clean wok. Add
the onion mixture and cook for a few
minutes without browning. Stir in the
coconut milk and bring to the boil,
stirring constantly to prevent the
mixture from curdling.

6 Add the cubes of fish, most of the
sliced chillies and the bruised lemon
grass stalks. Cook for 3–4 minutes. Stir
in the coconut paste (moistened with
some of the sauce if necessary) and
cook for a further 2–3 minutes only. Do
not overcook the fish. Taste and adjust
the seasoning.

7 Remove the lemon grass stalks.
Spoon the moolie on to a hot serving
dish and sprinkle with the remaining
slices of chilli. Garnish with chopped
and whole chives and serve with boiled
long grain rice.

COOK'S TIP
Dry-frying is a feature of Malay cooking
that demands the cook's close attention.
The coconut must be constantly on the
move so that it becomes crisp and
uniformly golden in colour.

BALINESE FISH CURRY

A SIMPLE FISH CURRY IS THE IDEAL DISH TO PREPARE WHEN YOU ARE IN A HURRY. THE
CURRY SAUCE CAN BE MADE IN ADVANCE, AND THE FISH TAKES ONLY MINUTES TO COOK.

SERVES FOUR TO SIX

INGREDIENTS
  675g/1½lb cod or haddock fillet
  celery leaves or chopped fresh chilli,
    to garnish
  boiled rice, to serve

For the sauce
  1cm/½in cube shrimp paste
  2 red or white onions
  2.5cm/1in fresh root ginger, peeled
    and sliced
  1cm/½in fresh galangal, peeled
    and sliced
  2 garlic cloves
  2 fresh red chillies, seeded and sliced
  90ml/6 tbsp sunflower oil
  15ml/1 tbsp dark soy sauce
  5ml/1 tsp tamarind pulp, soaked in
    30ml/2 tbsp warm water
    then strained
  250ml/8fl oz/1 cup water

1 Skin the fish, remove any bones with a pair of tweezers, and then cut the flesh into bitesize pieces. Pat dry with kitchen paper and set aside.

2 Grind the shrimp paste, onions, ginger, galangal, garlic and fresh chillies to a paste in a food processor or with a mortar and pestle.

VARIATIONS
• Use 450g/1lb cooked tiger prawns (jumbo shrimp) instead of fish. Add them 3 minutes before the end of the cooking time.
• If you don't have any fresh chillies, use 5–10ml/1–2 tsp chilli powder.

3 Heat 30ml/2 tbsp of the oil in a pan and fry the spices, stirring, for about 2 minutes. Add the soy sauce and the tamarind liquid, with the water. Cook for 2–3 minutes, stirring.

4 Heat the remaining oil in a separate pan and fry the fish for 2–3 minutes. Turn once only so that the pieces stay whole. Lift out with a slotted spoon and put into the sauce.

5 Cook the fish in the sauce for 3 minutes, until cooked through. Spoon on to a serving dish, garnish with feathery celery leaves or a little chopped fresh chilli and serve with the rice.

COOK'S TIPS
• Save time by asking the fishmonger to skin the fish for you.
• Tamarind has a refreshing acid taste.

Chillies crop up across the globe, featuring in delectable dishes from places as far apart as Thailand and Tobago. This chapter chooses some of the best, from a classic Mexican mole to a sweet and spicy Moroccan tagine. Peanuts are partnered with chillies in a Caribbean chicken dish, while China's choice is the famous Sichuan Chicken with Kung Po Sauce. The collection includes dishes that would do you proud at dinner parties, but also features such family favourites as Tandoori Chicken and Hot Pepperoni and Chilli Pizza.

Sizzling Poultry
and Meat Dishes

HOT <u>AND</u> SPICY PAN-FRIED CHICKEN

THIS TASTY MEAL CAN BE MILD OR HOT, DEPENDING ON THE TYPE OF CHILLI CHOSEN.
THE CHICKEN NEEDS TO BE FRIED OVER A FIERCE HEAT, SO CUT IT INTO SMALL PIECES.

SERVES TWO

INGREDIENTS

2 skinless chicken breast fillets
1 small fresh red or green chilli,
  seeded and thinly sliced
2 garlic cloves, thinly sliced
3 spring onions (scallions), sliced
4–5 thin slices fresh
  root ginger
2.5ml/½ tsp ground coriander
2.5ml/½ tsp ground cumin
30ml/2 tbsp olive oil
25ml/1½ tbsp lemon juice
30ml/2 tbsp pine nuts
15ml/1 tbsp raisins (optional)
oil, for frying
15ml/1 tbsp chopped fresh
  coriander (cilantro)
15ml/1 tbsp chopped fresh mint
salt and ground black pepper
fresh mint sprigs and lemon wedges,
  to garnish
bread, rice or couscous, to serve

2 In a bowl, mix the chilli, garlic, spring onions, ginger, spices, olive oil, lemon juice, pine nuts and raisins, if using. Season, then spoon the mixture over the chicken pieces, stirring so that each piece is coated. Cover with clear film (plastic wrap) and leave in a cool place for 1–2 hours.

3 Brush a wok or shallow pan with oil and heat. Lift the chicken slices out and reserve the marinade. Stir-fry them over a fairly high heat for 3–4 minutes until browned on both sides.

4 Add the reserved marinade and continue to cook over a high heat for 6–8 minutes until the chicken has browned and is cooked through. (The timing will depend on the thickness of the chicken.)

5 Reduce the heat and stir in the chopped fresh coriander and mint. Cook for 1 minute, then transfer to a heated platter and serve immediately, garnished with mint sprigs and lemon wedges. Serve with bread or with rice or couscous.

1 Cut the chicken breast portions horizontally into 3–4 thin slices: this will speed up cooking. Place the slices in a shallow bowl.

COOK'S TIPS
• It is important to cut the meat thinly. Larger portions would have less contact with the pan, tending to braise rather than fry them.
• This will be sufficient for two as a main course or four as an appetizer. Serve the chicken with bread, rather than rice or couscous, if it is to be an appetizer.

CARIBBEAN PEANUT CHICKEN

PEANUTS AND PEANUT BUTTER GO PARTICULARLY WELL WITH CHILLIES. PEANUT BUTTER MAKES THIS SAUCE GLORIOUSLY RICH AND CREAMY. USE A MEDIUM-HOT CHILLI.

SERVES FOUR

INGREDIENTS

    4 skinless chicken breast fillets, cut
      into thin strips
    225g/8oz/generous 1 cup white long
      grain rice
    15g/½oz/1 tbsp butter, plus extra
      for greasing
    30ml/2 tbsp groundnut (peanut) oil
    1 onion, finely chopped
    2 tomatoes, peeled, seeded
      and chopped
    1 fresh green chilli, seeded and sliced
    60ml/4 tbsp smooth peanut butter
    450ml/¾ pint/scant 2 cups
      chicken stock
    lemon juice, to taste
    salt and ground black pepper
    lime wedges and fresh flat leaf
      parsley sprigs, to garnish

For the marinade
    15ml/1 tbsp sunflower oil
    1–2 garlic cloves, crushed
    5ml/1 tsp chopped fresh thyme
    25ml/1½ tbsp medium curry powder
    juice of ½ lemon

1 Mix all the marinade ingredients in a large bowl and stir in the chicken. Cover loosely with clear film (plastic wrap) and set aside in a cool place for 2–3 hours.

COOK'S TIP

If the casserole is not large enough to allow you to toss the rice with the chicken mixture before serving, invert a large, deep plate over the casserole, turn both over and toss the mixture on the plate before serving.

2 Meanwhile, cook the rice in a large pan of lightly salted boiling water until tender. Drain well and turn into a generously buttered casserole.

3 Preheat the oven to 180°C/350°F/ Gas 4. Heat 15ml/1 tbsp of oil with the butter in a flameproof casserole and fry the chicken pieces for 4–5 minutes until evenly brown. Add more oil if necessary.

4 Lift out the chicken and put it on a plate. Add the finely chopped onion to the flameproof casserole and fry for 5–6 minutes until lightly browned, adding more oil if necessary. Stir in the chopped tomatoes and chilli. Cook over a gentle heat for 3–4 minutes, stirring occasionally. Switch off the heat.

5 Mix the peanut butter with the chicken stock. Stir into the tomato and onion mixture, then add the chicken. Stir in the lemon juice, season to taste, then spoon the mixture over the rice in the casserole.

6 Cover the casserole. Cook in the oven for 15–20 minutes or until piping hot. Use a large spoon to toss the rice with the chicken mixture. Serve immediately, garnished with the lime and parsley.

CHICKEN WITH CHIPOTLE CHILLI SAUCE

THIS IS AN EASY RECIPE FOR ENTERTAINING, WITH JUST A FEW KEY INGREDIENTS, INCLUDING DRIED CHILLIES. IT IS COOKED IN THE OVEN AND NEEDS NO LAST-MINUTE ATTENTION.

SERVES SIX

INGREDIENTS
  6 chipotle chillies
  chicken stock (see method
    for quantity)
  3 onions
  45ml/3 tbsp vegetable oil
  6 skinless chicken breast fillets
  salt and ground black pepper
  fresh oregano, to garnish
  boiled rice, to serve

1 Put the dried chillies in a heatproof bowl and pour over hot water to cover. Leave to stand for at least 20 minutes, until the chillies are very soft. Drain, reserving the soaking water in a liquid measure. Cut off the stalk from each chilli, then slit them lengthways and scrape out the seeds with a small sharp knife.

2 Preheat the oven to 180°C/350°F/ Gas 4. Chop the flesh of the chillies roughly and put it in a food processor or blender. Add enough chicken stock to the soaking water to make it up to 400ml/14fl oz/1⅔ cups. Pour it into the processor and process until smooth.

3 Peel the onions. Using a sharp knife, cut them in half, then slice them thinly. Separate the slices.

4 Heat the oil in a large frying pan, add the onions and cook over a low to moderate heat for about 5 minutes, or until they have softened but not coloured, stirring occasionally.

5 Using a slotted spoon, transfer the onion slices to a casserole that is large enough to hold all the chicken breast portions in a single layer. Sprinkle the onion slices with a little salt and ground black pepper.

COOK'S TIPS
• It is important to seek out chipotle chillies, as they impart a wonderfully rich and smoky flavour to the chicken.
• Dried chillies of various types can be bought by mail order, as well as from specialist food stores.
• The chilli purée can be prepared ahead of time.
• If tears come to your eyes when peeling onions, peel them under water. Then pat dry with kitchen paper before slicing.

6 Arrange the chicken on top of the onion slices. Sprinkle with a little salt and several grindings of pepper.

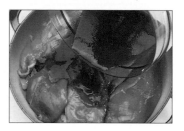

7 Pour the chipotle purée over the chicken, making sure that each piece is evenly coated.

8 Bake in the oven for 45–60 minutes or until the chicken is cooked through, but is still moist and tender. Garnish with fresh oregano and serve with boiled white rice.

VARIATION
Prepare the chipotles as in the main method. Put them in a stainless steel pan along with the soaking water; 2 peeled tomatoes, cut in wedges; ½ a sweet onion, chopped; 4 garlic cloves and 75ml/5 tbsp chopped fresh coriander (cilantro). Add water if needed to just cover. Simmer for 30 minutes. Dry-fry 15ml/1 tbsp cumin seeds, grind in a mortar or process in a blender and add to the chilli mixture. Cook for 5 minutes, season with salt, and purée. Refrigerated, it will keep for 1 week.

BARBECUE JERK CHICKEN

JERK REFERS TO THE BLEND OF HERB AND SPICE SEASONING RUBBED INTO MEAT, BEFORE IT IS ROASTED OVER CHARCOAL SPRINKLED WITH PIMIENTO BERRIES.

SERVES FOUR

INGREDIENTS
  8 chicken pieces

For the marinade
  5ml/1 tsp ground allspice
  5ml/1 tsp ground cinnamon
  5ml/1 tsp dried thyme
  1.5ml/¼ tsp freshly
    grated nutmeg
  10ml/2 tsp demerara
    (raw) sugar
  2 garlic cloves, crushed
  15ml/1 tbsp finely
    chopped onion
  15ml/1 tbsp chopped spring
    onion (scallion)
  15ml/1 tbsp vinegar
  30ml/2 tbsp oil
  15ml/1 tbsp lime juice
  1 hot chilli, chopped
  salt and ground black pepper
  salad leaves, to serve

1 Combine all the marinade ingredients in a small bowl. Using a fork, mash the ingredients together well to form a thick paste.

2 Lay the chicken pieces on a plate or board and make several lengthways slits in the flesh. Rub the seasoning all over the chicken and into the slits.

3 Place the chicken pieces in a dish, cover with clear film (plastic wrap) and marinate overnight in the refrigerator.

4 Shake off any excess seasoning from the chicken. Brush with oil and either place on a baking sheet or on a barbecue grill.

5 Cook under a preheated grill (broiler) for 45 minutes, turning frequently. Or, for the barbecue, light the coals and when ready, cook over the coals for 30 minutes, turning frequently. Serve hot with fresh salad leaves.

COOK'S TIP
The flavour is best if you marinate the chicken overnight. Sprinkle the charcoal with aromatic herbs, such as bay leaves, for even more flavour.

BON-BON CHICKEN WITH SPICY SESAME SAUCE

IN THIS RECIPE, THE CHICKEN MEAT IS TENDERIZED BY BEING BEATEN WITH A STICK (CALLED A "BON" IN CHINESE) – HENCE THE NAME FOR THIS VERY POPULAR SICHUAN DISH.

SERVES FOUR

INGREDIENTS

1 whole chicken, about 1kg/2¼lb
1.2 litres/2 pints/5 cups water
15ml/1 tbsp sesame oil
shredded cucumber, to garnish

For the sauce

30ml/2 tbsp light soy sauce
5ml/1 tsp sugar
15ml/1 tbsp finely chopped
  spring onions (scallions)
5ml/1 tsp red chilli oil
2.5ml/½ tsp Sichuan peppercorns
5ml/1 tsp white sesame seeds
30ml/2 tbsp sesame paste, or
  30ml/2 tbsp peanut butter creamed
  with a little sesame oil

1 Clean the chicken well. In a wok or pan bring the water to a rolling boil, add the chicken, reduce the heat, cover and cook for 40–45 minutes. Remove the chicken and immerse in cold water to cool.

2 After at least 1 hour, remove the chicken and drain; dry well with kitchen paper and brush with sesame oil. Carve the meat from the legs, wings and breast and pull the meat off the rest of the bones.

3 On a flat surface, pound the meat with a rolling pin, then tear the meat into shreds with your fingers.

4 Place the meat in a dish with the shredded cucumber around the edge. In a bowl, mix together all the sauce ingredients, keeping a few spring onions to garnish. Pour over the chicken and serve.

COOK'S TIP
To make chilli oil, slit and blanch chillies, pack into sterilized jars and fill with oil. Leave for 2 weeks.

TANDOORI CHICKEN

A TANDOOR IS A BELL-SHAPED CLAY OVEN FIRED BY CHARCOAL OR WOOD, WHICH REACHES A VERY HIGH TEMPERATURE — MEANING THAT THE SPICY CHICKEN IS CRISPY ON THE OUTSIDE AND MOIST INSIDE.

SERVES FOUR

INGREDIENTS

4 chicken quarters
175ml/6fl oz/¾ cup natural (plain)
  low-fat yogurt
5ml/1 tsp garam masala
5ml/1 tsp ginger pulp
5ml/1 tsp garlic pulp
7.5ml/1½ tsp chilli powder
1.5ml/¼ tsp ground turmeric
5ml/1 tsp ground coriander
15ml/1 tbsp lemon juice
5ml/1 tsp salt
few drops red food colouring
30ml/2 tbsp corn oil
mixed salad leaves, lime wedges and
  1 tomato, quartered, to garnish

1 Skin, rinse and pat dry the chicken quarters. Make two slits into the flesh of each piece, place them in a dish and set aside.

2 Mix together the yogurt, garam masala, ginger, garlic, chilli powder, turmeric, ground coriander, lemon juice, salt, red colouring and oil, and beat so that all the ingredients are well mixed together.

3 Cover the chicken quarters with the spice mixture and leave to marinate for about 3 hours.

4 Preheat the oven to 240°C/475°F/ Gas 9. Transfer the chicken pieces to an ovenproof dish.

5 Bake in the preheated oven for 20–25 minutes, or until the chicken is cooked right through and browned on top.

6 Remove from the oven, transfer to a serving dish and garnish with the salad leaves, lime and tomato.

COOK'S TIP
The red food colouring gives this dish its traditional appearance, but it can be omitted if you prefer.

SPICY MASALA CHICKEN

THESE CHICKEN PIECES ARE GRILLED AND HAVE A SWEET-AND-SOUR TASTE. THEY CAN BE SERVED COLD WITH A SALAD AND RICE, OR HOT WITH MASALA MASHED POTATOES.

SERVES FOUR

INGREDIENTS

    12 chicken thighs
    90ml/6 tbsp lemon juice
    5ml/1 tsp ginger pulp
    5ml/1 tsp garlic pulp
    5ml/1 tsp crushed dried red chillies
    5ml/1 tsp salt
    5ml/1 tsp soft light brown sugar
    30ml/2 tbsp clear honey
    30ml/2 tbsp chopped fresh
      coriander (cilantro)
    1 fresh green chilli, finely chopped
    30ml/2 tbsp vegetable oil
    fresh coriander sprigs, to garnish

1 Prick the chicken thighs with a fork. Rinse, pat dry and set aside in a bowl.

2 In a large mixing bowl, mix together the lemon juice, ginger, garlic, crushed dried red chillies, salt, sugar and honey.

3 Transfer the chicken thighs to the spice mixture and coat well. Set aside for about 45 minutes.

4 Preheat the grill (broiler) to medium. Add the fresh coriander and chopped green chilli to the chicken thighs and place them in a flameproof dish.

COOK'S TIP
Masala refers to the blend of spices used in this dish. The amounts can be varied according to taste.

5 Pour any remaining marinade over the chicken and baste with the oil, using a pastry brush.

6 Grill (broil) the chicken thighs under the preheated grill for 15–20 minutes, turning and basting occasionally, until cooked through and browned.

7 Transfer to a serving dish and garnish with the fresh coriander sprigs.

RED CHICKEN CURRY WITH BAMBOO SHOOTS

THE CHILLI PASTE THAT IS THE BASIS OF THIS DISH HAS A SUPERB FLAVOUR, USEFUL IN ALL SORTS OF SPICY DISHES, SO IT IS WORTH MAKING IT IN QUANTITY.

SERVES FOUR TO SIX

INGREDIENTS
   1 litre/1¾ pints/4 cups coconut milk
   450g/1lb skinless chicken breast
      fillets, diced
   30ml/2 tbsp Thai fish sauce
   15ml/1 tbsp granulated (white) sugar
   225g/8oz canned bamboo shoots,
      rinsed and sliced
   5 kaffir lime leaves, torn
   salt and ground black pepper
   2 fresh red chillies, chopped, 10–12
      fresh basil leaves, 10–12 fresh mint
      leaves, to garnish

For the red curry paste
   12–15 fresh red chillies, seeded
   4 shallots, thinly sliced
   2 garlic cloves, chopped
   15ml/1 tbsp chopped fresh galangal
   2 lemon grass stalks, tender
      portions chopped
   3 kaffir lime leaves, chopped
   4 coriander (cilantro) roots
   10 black peppercorns
   5ml/1 tsp coriander seeds
   2.5ml/½ tsp cumin seeds
   good pinch of ground cinnamon
   5ml/1 tsp ground turmeric
   2.5ml/½ tsp shrimp paste
   30ml/2 tbsp oil

1 Make the red curry paste. Combine all the ingredients except for the oil in a mortar. Add 5ml/1 tsp salt. Pound with a pestle, or process in a food processor, until smooth. If you are using a pestle and mortar, you might need to pound the ingredients in batches and then combine them.

2 Add the oil to the paste a little at a time and blend in well. If you are using a food processor or blender, add it slowly through the feeder tube. Scrape the paste into a jar and store in the refrigerator until ready to use.

3 Pour half the coconut milk into a large heavy pan. Gently bring to the boil, stirring all the time until the milk separates, then reduce the heat.

4 Add 30ml/2 tbsp of the red curry paste, stir to mix, and cook for a few minutes to allow the flavours to develop. The sauce should begin to thicken and may need to be stirred frequently to prevent it from sticking to the pan. Add a little more coconut milk if necessary.

5 Add the chicken, fish sauce and sugar. Fry for 3–5 minutes until the chicken changes colour, stirring constantly to prevent it from sticking.

6 Add the rest of the coconut milk, with the bamboo shoots and kaffir lime leaves. Bring back to the boil. Stir in salt and pepper to taste. Serve garnished with the chillies, basil and mint leaves.

COOK'S TIPS
• The surplus curry paste can be stored in a sealed jar in the refrigerator for 3–4 weeks. Alternatively, freeze it in small tubs, each containing about 30ml/2 tbsp.
• Young bamboo shoots are cultivated in China for the table. The preparation is laborious, so the canned shoots are used in the West. They provide a crunchy texture, and are a useful contrast to other ingredients.
• The roots of coriander (cilantro) have a deep, earthy fragrance and are used widely in Thai cooking. They can be frozen for storage until you need them. Simply cut the roots off and wrap in clear film (plastic wrap).

HOT CHICKEN CURRY

THIS CURRY HAS A NICE THICK SAUCE, AND USING RED AND GREEN PEPPERS GIVES
IT EXTRA COLOUR. SERVE WITH WHOLEMEAL CHAPATIS OR PLAIN BOILED RICE.

SERVES FOUR

INGREDIENTS
    30ml/2 tbsp corn oil
    1.5ml/¼ tsp fenugreek seeds
    1.5ml/¼ tsp onion seeds
    2 onions, chopped
    2.5ml/½ tsp garlic pulp
    2.5ml/½ tsp ginger pulp
    5ml/1 tsp ground coriander
    5ml/1 tsp chilli powder
    5ml/1 tsp salt
    400g/14oz/1¾ cups canned tomatoes
    30ml/2 tbsp lemon juice
    350g/12oz/2½ cups skinned, boned
      and cubed chicken
    30ml/2 tbsp chopped
      coriander (cilantro)
    3 fresh green chillies, chopped
    ½ red (bell) pepper, cut into chunks
    ½ green (bell) pepper, cut
      into chunks
    fresh coriander sprigs

1 In a medium pan, heat the oil and fry the fenugreek and onion seeds until they turn a shade darker.

2 Add the chopped onions, garlic and ginger and cook for about 5 minutes, until the onions turn golden brown. Turn the heat to very low.

3 Meanwhile, in a separate bowl, mix together the ground coriander, chilli powder, salt, canned tomatoes and lemon juice.

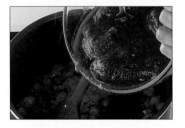

4 Pour this mixture into the pan and turn up the heat to medium. Stir-fry for about 3 minutes.

5 Add the chicken pieces and stir-fry for 5–7 minutes until golden-brown all over.

VARIATION
This recipe also works well with turkey or pork fillet (tenderloin). Increase the cooking time, if necessary, to ensure that the meat is cooked through.

6 Add the fresh coriander, green chillies and the red and green peppers. Lower the heat, cover the pan and simmer for about 10 minutes, until the chicken is cooked.

7 Serve hot, garnished with fresh coriander sprigs.

COOK'S TIP
Cucumber raita is a wonderfully refreshing dish to serve with anything spicy. To make it, dice 1 cucumber and place it in a bowl. Stir in 300ml/½ pint/ 1¼ cups natural (plain) yogurt, 1.5ml/ ¼ tsp salt and 1.5ml/¼ tsp ground cumin. A chopped fresh green chilli can be added if you like, or top the raita with a dusting of chilli powder and a fresh mint sprig.

STIR-FRIED CHICKEN WITH CHILLI AND BASIL

THIS QUICK AND EASY CHICKEN DISH IS AN EXCELLENT INTRODUCTION TO THAI CUISINE.
FIERY CHILLIES PARTNER THE HOLY BASIL, WHICH HAS A PUNGENT SPICY FLAVOUR.

2 Add the pieces of chicken to the wok and stir-fry until they change colour. Stir in the fish sauce, soy sauce and sugar. Stir-fry the mixture for 3–4 minutes or until the chicken is fully cooked.

3 Stir in the fresh basil leaves. Spoon the mixture on to a warm serving platter, or individual serving dishes, garnish with the chopped chillies and deep-fried basil, and serve.

SERVES FOUR TO SIX

INGREDIENTS
   450g/1lb skinless chicken
     breast fillets
   45ml/3 tbsp vegetable oil
   4 garlic cloves, thinly sliced
   2–4 fresh red chillies, seeded and
     finely chopped
   45ml/3 tbsp Thai fish sauce
   10ml/2 tsp dark soy sauce
   5ml/1 tsp granulated (white) sugar
   10–12 holy basil leaves
   2 fresh red chillies, seeded and
     finely chopped, to garnish
   about 20 deep-fried holy basil leaves,
     to garnish

1 Using a sharp knife, cut the chicken breasts into bitesize pieces. Heat the oil in a wok. Add the garlic and chillies and stir-fry over a medium heat for 1–2 minutes until the garlic is golden. Do not let the garlic burn or it will taste bitter.

COOK'S TIPS
• Holy basil is native to Asia and it differs from other basils in that heat develops the flavour. The leaves have the typical basil fragrance with the addition of pepper and mint. A substitute is a mix of ordinary basil and spearmint.
• To deep-fry holy basil leaves, first make sure that the leaves are completely dry or they will splutter when added to the oil. Deep-fry the leaves briefly in hot oil until they are crisp and translucent – this will only take about 30–40 seconds. Lift out the leaves using a slotted spoon or wire basket and leave them to drain on kitchen paper.

SICHUAN CHICKEN WITH KUNG PO SAUCE

THIS RECIPE COMES FROM THE SICHUAN REGION OF WESTERN CHINA, WHERE CHILLIES ARE WIDELY USED. CASHEW NUTS ARE A POPULAR INGREDIENT IN CHINESE COOKING.

SERVES THREE

INGREDIENTS

2 skinless chicken breast fillets,
   total weight about 350g/12oz
1 egg white
10ml/2 tsp cornflour (cornstarch)
2.5ml/½ tsp salt
30ml/2 tbsp yellow salted beans
15ml/1 tbsp hoisin sauce
5ml/1 tsp soft light brown sugar
15ml/1 tbsp rice wine or
   medium-dry sherry
15ml/1 tbsp wine vinegar
4 garlic cloves, crushed
150ml/¼ pint/⅔ cup chicken stock
45ml/3 tbsp sunflower oil
2–3 dried red chillies, chopped
115g/4oz/1 cup roasted cashew nuts
fresh coriander (cilantro),
   to garnish

3 Heat a wok, add the oil and stir-fry the chicken for 2 minutes until tender. Lift out the chicken and set aside.

COOK'S TIP
The yellow beans may be too salty for your taste, so if you like, rinse them in water and drain before using them.

4 Heat the oil remaining in the wok and fry the chilli pieces for 1 minute. Return the chicken to the wok and pour in the bean sauce mixture. Bring to the boil, stir in the cashew nuts and heat through. Spoon into a heated serving dish, garnish with the coriander leaves and serve immediately.

1 Cut the chicken into neat pieces. Lightly whisk the egg white in a dish, whisk in the cornflour and salt, then add the chicken and stir until coated.

2 In a bowl, mash the beans. Stir in the hoisin sauce, brown sugar, rice wine or sherry, vinegar, garlic and stock.

CRISPY AND AROMATIC DUCK

AS THIS DISH IS OFTEN SERVED WITH PANCAKES, SPRING ONIONS, CUCUMBER AND DUCK SAUCE (A SWEET BEAN PASTE), MANY PEOPLE MISTAKE IT FOR PEKING DUCK. THIS RECIPE, HOWEVER, USES A DIFFERENT COOKING METHOD. THE RESULT IS JUST AS CRISPY BUT THE DELIGHTFUL AROMA MAKES THIS DISH PARTICULARLY DISTINCTIVE.

SERVES SIX TO EIGHT

INGREDIENTS
  1 oven-ready duckling,
    about 2.25kg/5–5¼lb
  10ml/2 tsp salt
  5–6 whole star anise
  15ml/1 tbsp Sichuan peppercorns
  5ml/1 tsp cloves
  2–3 cinnamon sticks
  3–4 spring onions (scallions)
  3–4 slices fresh root ginger, unpeeled
  75–90ml/5–6 tbsp Chinese rice wine
  vegetable oil, for deep-frying
  lettuce leaves, to garnish

To serve
  Chinese pancakes
  duck sauce
  spring onions (scallions), shredded
  cucumber, diced

2 Marinate the duck with the spices, onions, ginger and wine for 4–6 hours.

3 Vigorously steam the duck with the marinade for 3–4 hours (or for longer if possible). Carefully remove the steamed duck from the cooking liquid and leave to cool for at least 5–6 hours. The duck must be cold and dry or the skin will not be crisp.

1 Remove the wings from the duck and split the body in half down the backbone. Rub salt all over the two duck halves, taking care to work it all in thoroughly.

4 Heat the vegetable oil in a wok until it is just smoking, then place the duck pieces in the oil, skin side down. Deep-fry the duck for about 5–6 minutes, or until it becomes crisp and brown. Turn the duck just once at the very last moment.

5 Remove the fried duck, drain it well and place it on a bed of lettuce leaves.

6 To serve, scrape the meat off the bone and wrap a portion in each pancake with a little duck sauce, shredded spring onions and cucumber. Eat with your fingers.

VARIATION
For those following a wheat-free diet, crispy and aromatic duck is also delicious served with fresh lettuce leaves or steamed rice pancakes.

COOK'S TIP
Small pancakes suitable for this dish can be found in most Chinese supermarkets. They can be frozen and will keep for up to 3 months in the freezer.

TURKEY STEW WITH SPICY CHOCOLATE SAUCE

A MOLE IS A RICH STEW, SERVED ON FESTIVE OCCASIONS IN MEXICO. TOASTED NUTS, FRUIT AND CHOCOLATE ARE AMONG THE CLASSIC INGREDIENTS.

SERVES FOUR

INGREDIENTS

    1 ancho chilli, seeded
    1 guajillo chilli, seeded
    115g/4oz/¾ cup sesame seeds
    50g/2oz/½ cup whole
       blanched almonds
    50g/2oz/½ cup shelled unsalted
       peanuts, skinned
    50g/2oz/¼ cup lard (shortening) or
       60ml/4 tbsp vegetable oil
    1 small onion, finely chopped
    2 garlic cloves, crushed
    50g/2oz/⅓ cup canned tomatoes in
       tomato juice
    1 ripe plaintain
    50g/2oz/⅓ cup raisins
    75g/3oz/½ cup ready-to-eat
       pitted prunes
    5ml/1 tsp dried oregano
    2.5ml/½ tsp ground cloves
    2.5ml/½ tsp crushed allspice berries
    5ml/1 tsp ground cinnamon
    25g/1oz/¼ cup unsweetned cocoa
       powder
    4 turkey breast steaks
    chopped fresh oregano, to garnish

1 Soak both types of dried chilli in a bowl of hot water for 20–30 minutes, then lift them out and chop them roughly. Reserve 250ml/8fl oz/1 cup of the soaking liquid.

COOK'S TIPS
• It is important to use good-quality cocoa powder, which is unsweetened.
• Mexican-style cocoa powder is available from specialist food stores and by mail order.

2 Spread out the sesame seeds in a heavy frying pan. Toast them over a moderate heat, shaking the pan lightly so that they turn golden all over. Do not let them burn, or the sauce will taste bitter. Set aside 45ml/3 tbsp of the toasted seeds for the garnish and tip the rest into a bowl. Toast the blanched almonds and skinned peanuts in the same way and add them to the bowl with the sesame seeds.

3 Heat half the lard or oil in a frying pan, sauté the chopped onion and garlic for 2–3 minutes, then add the chillies and tomatoes. Cook gently for 10 minutes.

4 Peel the plantain and slice it into short diagonal slices. Add it to the onion mixture with the raisins, prunes, dried oregano, spices and cocoa. Stir in the 250ml/8fl oz/1 cup of the reserved water in which the chillies were soaked. Bring to the boil, stirring, then add the toasted sesame seeds, almonds and peanuts. Cook gently for 10 minutes, stirring frequently; do not let the sauce stick to the pan and burn. Remove from the heat and leave to cool slightly.

5 Blend the sauce in batches in a food processor or blender until smooth. The sauce should be fairly thick, but a little water can be added if you think it is necessary.

6 Heat the remaining lard or oil in a flameproof casserole. Add the turkey and brown over a medium heat.

7 Pour the sauce over the steaks and cover the casserole with foil and a tight-fitting lid. Simmer over a gentle heat for 20–25 minutes or until the turkey is cooked, and the sauce has thickened. Sprinkle with the reserved sesame seeds and the chopped fresh oregano. Turkey *Mole* is traditionally served with a rice dish and warm tortillas.

MEXICAN TURKEY MOLE

MOLE POBLANO DE GUAJOLOTE IS THE GREAT FESTIVE DISH OF MEXICO. IT IS SERVED AT ANY SPECIAL OCCASION, BE IT A BIRTHDAY, WEDDING, OR FAMILY GET-TOGETHER. RICE, BEANS, TORTILLAS AND GUACAMOLE ARE THE TRADITIONAL ACCOMPANIMENTS.

SERVES SIX TO EIGHT

INGREDIENTS
2.75–3.6kg/6–8lb turkey, cut into
    serving pieces
1 onion, chopped
1 garlic clove, chopped
90ml/6 tbsp lard (shortening)
    or corn oil
salt
fresh coriander (cilantro) and 30ml/
    2 tbsp toasted sesame seeds,
    to garnish

For the sauce
6 dried ancho chillies
4 dried pasilla chillies
4 dried mulato chillies
1 drained canned chipotle chilli,
    seeded and chopped (optional)
2 onions, chopped
2 garlic cloves, chopped
450g/1lb tomatoes, peeled
    and chopped
1 stale tortilla, torn into pieces
50g/2oz/⅓ cup seedless raisins
115g/4oz/1 cup ground almonds
45ml/3 tbsp sesame seeds, ground
2.5ml/½ tsp coriander seeds, ground
5ml/1 tsp ground cinnamon
2.5ml/½ tsp ground anise
1.5ml/¼ tsp ground black peppercorns
60ml/4 tbsp lard (shortening)
    or corn oil
40g/1½oz unsweetened (bitter)
    chocolate, broken into squares
15ml/1 tbsp sugar
salt and ground pepper

1 Put the turkey pieces into a pan or flameproof casserole large enough to hold them in one layer comfortably. Add the onion and garlic, and enough cold water to cover. Season with salt, bring to a gentle simmer, cover and cook for about 1 hour, or until the turkey is tender.

2 Meanwhile, put the ancho, pasilla and mulato chillies in a dry frying pan over a low heat and roast them for a few minutes, shaking the pan frequently. Remove the stems and shake out the seeds. Tear the pods into pieces and put these into a small bowl. Add sufficient warm water to just cover and soak, turning occasionally, for 30 minutes until soft.

3 Lift out the turkey pieces and pat them dry with kitchen paper. Reserve the stock in a measuring jug (pitcher). Heat the lard or oil in a large frying pan and sauté the turkey pieces until lightly browned all over. Transfer to a plate and set aside. Reserve the oil that is left in the frying pan.

4 Tip the chillies, with the water in which they have been soaked, into a food processor. Add the chipotle chilli, if using, with the onions, garlic, tomatoes, tortilla, raisins, ground almonds and spices. Process to a purée. Do this in batches if necessary.

5 Add the lard or oil to the fat remaining in the frying pan used for sautéing the turkey. Heat the mixture, then add the chilli and spice paste. Cook, stirring, for 5 minutes.

6 Transfer the mixture to the pan or casserole in which the turkey was originally cooked. Stir in 475ml/16fl oz/ 2 cups of the turkey stock (make it up with water if necessary). Add the chocolate and season with salt and pepper. Cook over a low heat until the chocolate has melted. Stir in the sugar. Add the turkey and more stock if needed. Cover the pan and simmer very gently for 30 minutes. Serve, garnished with fresh coriander and sprinkled with the sesame seeds.

CHILLI RIBS

CHOOSE REALLY MEATY RIBS FOR THIS DISH AND TRIM OFF ANY EXCESS FAT BEFORE COOKING.

2 Heat the oil in a large pan and cook the ribs, turning until well browned. Put in a roasting pan, adding the onion.

3 Mix the braising liquid ingredients and pour over the ribs. Cover with foil then roast for 1½ hours, or until tender. Remove the foil for the last 30 minutes.

SERVES SIX

INGREDIENTS
    25g/1oz/¼ cup plain (all-purpose) flour
    5ml/1 tsp salt
    5ml/1 tsp ground black pepper
    1.6kg/3½lb pork spare ribs, cut into
      individual pieces
    30ml/2 tbsp sunflower oil
    1 onion, finely chopped
    15ml/1 tbsp cornflour (cornstarch)
    flat leaf parsley, to garnish
    sauerkraut, to serve

For the braising liquid
    1 garlic clove, crushed
    1 fresh red chilli, seeded and chopped
    45ml/3 tbsp tomato purée (paste)
    30ml/2 tbsp chilli sauce
    30ml/2 tbsp red wine vinegar
    pinch of ground cloves
    600ml/1 pint/2½ cups beef stock

1 Preheat the oven to 180°C/350°F/
Gas 4. Combine the flour, salt and black pepper in a shallow dish. Add the ribs and toss until evenly coated.

COOK'S TIP
Use mild or hot chilli sauce for this dish. If you can track some down, try using 45–60ml/3–4 tbsp ancho chilli and morello cherry glaze instead of the tomato purée and chilli sauce.

4 Tip the juices from the roasting pan into a small pan. Mix the cornflour with a little cold water in a cup, then stir the mixture into the sauce. Bring to the boil, stirring, then simmer for 2–3 minutes until thickened.

5 Serve the ribs on the sauerkraut, with a little sauce. Garnish with parsley. Serve the remaining sauce separately.

HOT PEPPERONI AND CHILLI PIZZA

THERE ARE FEW TREATS MORE TASTY THAN A HOME-MADE FRESHLY BAKED PIZZA.

SERVES FOUR

INGREDIENTS

225g/8oz/2 cups strong white
    (bread) flour
10ml/2 tsp easy-blend (rapid rise)
    dried yeast
5ml/1 tsp granulated (white) sugar
2.5ml/½ tsp salt
15ml/1 tbsp olive oil
175ml/6fl oz/¾ cup mixed hand-hot
    milk and water
fresh oregano leaves, to garnish

For the topping
400g/14oz can chopped tomatoes,
    well drained
2 garlic cloves, crushed
5ml/1 tsp dried oregano
225g/8oz mozzarella cheese,
    coarsely grated
2 dried red chillies
225g/8oz pepperoni, sliced
30ml/2 tbsp drained capers

1 Sift the flour into a bowl. Stir in the yeast, sugar and salt. Make a well in the centre. Stir the olive oil into the milk and water, then stir the mixture into the flour. Mix to a soft dough.

2 Knead the dough on a lightly floured surface for 5–10 minutes until it is smooth and elastic. Return it to the clean, lightly oiled, bowl and cover with clear film (plastic wrap). Leave in a warm place for about 30 minutes or until the dough has doubled in bulk.

3 Preheat the oven to 220°C/425°F/Gas 7. Knead the dough on a lightly floured surface for 1 minute. Divide it in half and roll each piece out to a 25cm/10in circle. Place on lightly oiled pizza trays or baking sheets.

4 Make the topping. Tip the drained tomatoes into a bowl and stir in the crushed garlic and dried oregano.

5 Spread half the mixture over each round, leaving a clear margin around the edge. Set half the mozzarella aside. Divide the rest between the pizzas. Bake for 7–10 minutes until the dough rim on each pizza is pale golden.

6 Crumble the chillies over the pizzas, then arrange the pepperoni slices and capers on top. Sprinkle with the reserved mozzarella. Return the pizzas to the oven and bake for 7–10 minutes more. Sprinkle over the fresh oregano and serve immediately.

VARIATION
Use bacon instead of sliced pepperoni. Grill (broil) about 6 slices and crumble them over the pizza with the chillies. Omit the capers.

DEEP-FRIED SPICY SPARE RIBS

IF YOU WANT THESE SPARERIBS TO BE HOTTER, JUST INCREASE THE AMOUNT OF CHILLI SAUCE.

SERVES FOUR TO SIX

INGREDIENTS

10–12 finger ribs, in total about
675g/1½ lb, with excess fat and
gristle trimmed
about 30–45ml/2–3 tbsp flour
vegetable oil, for deep-frying

For the marinade
1 garlic clove, crushed and chopped
15ml/1 tbsp light brown sugar
15ml/1 tbsp dark soy sauce
30ml/2 tbsp Chinese rice wine or
dry sherry
2.5ml/½ tsp chilli sauce
few drops sesame oil

1 Chop each rib into three to four
pieces. Combine all the marinade
ingredients in a bowl, add the spare
ribs and leave to marinate for at least
2–3 hours.

2 Coat the spare ribs with flour and
deep-fry them in medium-hot oil for
4–5 minutes, stirring to separate.
Remove and drain.

3 Heat the oil to high and deep-fry
the spare ribs once more for about
1 minute, or until the colour is an even
dark brown. Remove and drain, then
serve hot.

SPICY SALT AND PEPPER
To make Spicy Salt and Pepper, mix
15ml/1 tbsp salt with 10ml/2 tsp ground
Sichuan peppercorns and 5ml/1 tsp
fivespice powder. Heat together in a
preheated dry pan for about 2 minutes
over a low heat, stirring constantly.
This quantity is sufficient for at least
six servings.

PORK <u>WITH</u> CHILLIES <u>AND</u> PINEAPPLE

SWEET, JUICY PINEAPPLE PROVIDES THE PERFECT CONTRAST TO THE HOT CHILLI USED IN THIS DISH.

SERVES SIX

INGREDIENTS
  30ml/2 tbsp corn oil
  900g/2lb boneless pork shoulder or
    loin, cut into 5cm/2in cubes
  1 onion, finely chopped
  1 large red (bell) pepper, seeded and
    finely chopped
  1 or more jalapeño chillies, seeded
    and finely chopped
  450g/1lb fresh pineapple chunks
  8 fresh mint leaves, chopped
  250ml/8fl oz/1 cup chicken stock
  salt and ground black pepper
  fresh mint sprig, to garnish
  rice, to serve

1 Heat the oil in a large frying pan and sauté the pork, in batches, until the cubes are lightly coloured. Transfer the pork to a flameproof casserole, leaving the oil behind in the pan.

2 Add the finely chopped onion, finely chopped red pepper and the chilli(es) to the oil remaining in the pan. Sauté until the onion is tender, then add to the casserole with the pineapple. Stir to mix all together.

3 Add the mint, then cover and simmer gently for about 2 hours, or until the pork is tender. Garnish with fresh mint and serve with rice.

COOK'S TIP
If fresh pineapple is not available, use pineapple canned in its own juice.

PORK CASSEROLE <u>WITH</u> CHILLIES <u>AND</u> DRIED FRUIT

USING A TECHNIQUE TAKEN FROM SOUTH AMERICAN COOKING, THIS CASSEROLE IS BASED ON A RICH PASTE OF CHILLIES, SHALLOTS AND NUTS. SERVE WITH PLAIN BOILED RICE.

SERVES SIX

INGREDIENTS

   25ml/5 tsp plain (all-purpose) flour
   1kg/2¼lb shoulder or leg of pork,
     cut into 5cm/2in cubes
   45–60ml/3–4 tbsp olive oil
   2 large onions, chopped
   2 garlic cloves, finely chopped
   600ml/1 pint/2½ cups fruity
     white wine
   105ml/7 tbsp water
   115g/4oz/⅔ cup ready-to-eat prunes
   115g/4oz/⅔ cup ready-to-eat
     dried apricots
   grated rind and juice of 1
     small orange
   a pinch of soft light brown sugar
   30ml/2 tbsp chopped fresh parsley
   ½–1 fresh red chilli, seeded and
     finely chopped
   salt and ground black pepper

For the paste
   3 ancho chillies
   2 pasilla chillies
   30ml/2 tbsp olive oil
   2 shallots, chopped
   2 garlic cloves, chopped
   1 fresh green chilli, seeded
     and chopped
   10ml/2 tsp ground coriander
   5ml/1 tsp mild Spanish paprika
     or *pimentón dulce*
   50g/2oz/½ cup blanched
     almonds, toasted
   15ml/1 tbsp chopped fresh oregano
     or 7.5ml/1½ tsp dried oregano
   plain boiled rice, to serve

1 Make the paste first. Toast the dried chillies in a dry frying pan over a low heat for 1–2 minutes, until they are aromatic, then soak them in a bowl of warm water for 20–30 minutes.

2 Drain the chillies, reserving the soaking water, and discard their stalks and seeds. Preheat the oven to 160°C/325°F/Gas 3.

3 Heat the oil in a small frying pan. Add the shallots, garlic, fresh chilli and ground coriander, and fry over a very low heat for 5 minutes.

4 Transfer the mixture to a food processor or blender and add the drained chillies, paprika or *pimentón dulce*, almonds and oregano. Process the mixture, adding 45–60ml/3–4 tbsp of the chilli soaking liquid to make a smooth workable paste.

5 Season the flour generously with salt and black pepper, then use to coat the pork. Heat 45ml/3 tbsp of the olive oil in a large, heavy pan and fry the pork, stirring frequently, until sealed on all sides. Transfer the pork cubes to a flameproof casserole.

6 If necessary, add the remaining oil to the pan. When it is hot, fry the onions and garlic gently for 8–10 minutes.

COOK'S TIP
A Californian Chardonnay would be a suitably fruity wine to use.

7 Add the wine and water to the pan. Bring up to the boil, reduce the heat and cook for 2 minutes. Stir in half the paste, bring back to the boil and bubble for a few seconds before pouring over the pork.

8 Season lightly with salt and pepper, stir to mix, then cover and cook in the oven for 1½ hours. Increase the oven temperature to 180°C/350°F/Gas 4.

9 Add the prunes, apricots and orange juice to the casserole. Taste the sauce and add more salt and pepper if needed and a pinch of brown sugar if the orange juice has made the sauce a bit tart. Stir, cover, return to the oven and cook for a further 30–45 minutes.

10 Place the casserole over a direct heat and stir in the remaining paste. Simmer, stirring once or twice, for 5 minutes. Sprinkle with the orange rind, chopped parsley and fresh chilli. Serve with boiled rice.

STUFFED CHILLIES <u>IN A</u> WALNUT SAUCE

*THE POTATO AND MEAT FILLING IN THESE CHILLIES IS A GOOD PARTNER FOR THE RICH,
CREAMY SAUCE THAT COVERS THEM. A GREEN SALAD GOES WELL WITH THIS DISH.*

SERVES FOUR

INGREDIENTS
8 ancho chillies
1 large waxy potato, about 200g/7oz
45ml/3 tbsp vegetable oil
115g/4oz lean minced (ground) pork
50g/2oz/½ cup plain
  (all-purpose) flour
2.5ml/½ tsp ground white pepper
2 eggs, separated
oil, for deep-frying
salt
chopped fresh herbs, to garnish

For the sauce
1 onion, chopped
5ml/1 tsp ground cinnamon
115g/4oz/1 cup walnuts or pecan
  nuts, roughly chopped
50g/2oz/½ cup chopped almonds
150g/5oz/⅔ cup cream cheese
50g/2oz/½ cup soft goat's cheese
120ml/4fl oz/½ cup single (light) cream
120ml/4fl oz/½ cup dry sherry

1 Soak the dried chillies in a bowl of hot water for 20–30 minutes until softened. Drain, then slit them down one side. Scrape out the seeds, taking care to keep the chillies intact.

2 Peel the potato and cut it into 1cm/½in cubes. Heat 15ml/1 tbsp of the oil in a large frying pan, add the pork and cook, stirring, until it has browned evenly.

COOK'S TIP
The potatoes must not break or become too floury. Do not overcook.

3 Add the potato cubes and mix well. Cover and cook over a low heat for 25–30 minutes, stirring occasionally. Season with salt, then remove the filling from the heat and set it aside.

4 Make the sauce. Heat the remaining oil in a separate pan and fry the onion with the cinnamon for 3–4 minutes or until softened. Stir in the nuts and fry for 3–4 minutes more.

5 Add both types of cheese to the pan, with the single cream and dry sherry. Mix well for the flavours to blend. Reduce the heat to the lowest setting and cook until the cheese melts and the sauce starts to thicken. Taste the sauce and season it if necessary.

6 Spread out the flour on a plate or in a shallow dish. Season with the white pepper. Beat the egg yolks in a bowl until they are pale and thick.

7 In a separate, grease-free bowl, whisk the whites until they form soft peaks. Add a generous pinch of salt, then fold in the yolks, a little at a time.

8 Spoon some of the filling into each chilli. Pat the outside dry with kitchen paper. Heat the oil for deep-frying to a temperature of 180°C/350°F.

9 Coat a chilli in flour, then dip it in the egg batter, covering it completely. Drain for a few seconds, then add to the hot oil. Add several more battered chillies, but do not overcrowd the pan. Fry the chillies until golden, then lift out and drain on kitchen paper. Keep hot while cooking successive batches.

10 Reheat the walnut and cheese sauce over a low heat, if necessary. Arrange the chillies on individual plates, spoon a little sauce over each and serve immediately, sprinkled with chopped fresh herbs.

SWEET <u>AND</u> SOUR PORK

THIS CLASSIC CHINESE DISH IS A FAVOURITE, AND IT IS EASY TO SEE WHY. THE SWEET FLAVOUR COMES FROM THE SUGAR, THE SOUR FROM THE VINEGAR AND THE HOT FROM THE FRESH CHILLI.

<u>SERVES FOUR</u>

INGREDIENTS
　　350g/12oz lean pork
　　1.5ml/¼ tsp salt and 2.5ml/½ tsp
　　　ground Sichuan peppercorns
　　15ml/1 tbsp Chinese rice wine
　　115g/4oz bamboo shoots
　　30ml/2 tbsp plain (all-purpose) flour
　　1 egg, lightly beaten
　　vegetable oil, for frying
　　15ml/1 tbsp vegetable oil
　　1 garlic clove, finely chopped
　　1 spring onion (scallion), chopped
　　1 small green (bell) pepper, diced
　　1 fresh red chilli, seeded and chopped
　　15ml/1 tbsp light soy sauce
　　30ml/2 tbsp soft light brown sugar
　　45ml/3 tbsp rice vinegar
　　15ml/1 tbsp tomato purée (paste)
　　about 120ml/4fl oz/½ cup stock

1 Using a sharp knife, cut the lean pork into small bitesize cubes. Place the pork in a bowl and add the salt, ground peppercorns and Chinese wine. Cover the bowl and leave to marinate for about 15–20 minutes.

2 Cut the bamboo shoots into small cubes about the same size as the pork pieces.

3 Dust the pork with flour, dip in the beaten egg, and coat with more flour. Deep-fry in moderately hot oil for 3–4 minutes, stirring to separate the pieces. Remove.

4 Reheat the oil, add the pork and bamboo shoots and fry for 1 minute, or until golden. Drain.

5 Heat 15ml/1 tbsp oil and add the garlic, spring onion, pepper and chilli. Stir-fry for 30–40 seconds, then add the seasonings with the stock. Bring to the boil, then add the pork and bamboo shoots and heat through.

LAMB TAGINE WITH CORIANDER AND SPICES

THIS IS A VERSION OF A MOROCCAN-STYLE TAGINE IN WHICH CHOPS ARE SPRINKLED WITH
SPICES AND EITHER MARINATED FOR A FEW HOURS OR COOKED STRAIGHTAWAY.

SERVES FOUR

INGREDIENTS
    4 lamb chump (leg) chops
    2 garlic cloves, crushed
    pinch of saffron threads
    2.5ml/½ tsp ground cinnamon,
      plus extra to garnish
    2.5ml/½ tsp ground ginger
    15ml/1 tbsp chopped fresh
      coriander (cilantro)
    15ml/1 tbsp chopped fresh parsley
    1 onion, finely chopped
    45ml/3 tbsp olive oil
    300ml/½ pint/1¼ cups lamb stock
    50g/2oz/½ cup blanched almonds,
      to garnish
    5ml/1 tsp sugar
    salt and ground black pepper

1 Season the lamb with the garlic, saffron, cinnamon, ginger and a little salt and black pepper. Place on a large plate and sprinkle with the coriander, parsley and onion. Cover loosely and set aside in the refrigerator for a few hours to marinate.

2 Heat the oil in a large frying pan, over a medium heat. Add the marinated lamb and all the herbs and onion from the dish.

3 Cook for 1–2 minutes, turning once, then add the stock, bring to the boil and simmer gently for 30 minutes, turning the chops once.

4 Meanwhile, heat a small frying pan over a medium heat, add the almonds and dry-fry until golden, shaking the pan occasionally to make sure they colour evenly. Transfer to a bowl and set aside.

5 Transfer the chops to a serving plate and keep warm. Increase the heat under the pan and boil the sauce until reduced by about half. Stir in the sugar. Pour the sauce over the chops and sprinkle with the fried almonds and a little extra ground cinnamon.

COOK'S TIP
Lamb tagine is a fragrant dish, originating in North Africa. It is traditionally made in a cooking dish, known as a tagine, from where it takes its name. This dish consists of a plate with a tall lid with sloping sides. It has a narrow opening to let steam escape, while retaining the flavour.

LAMB MASALA

WHOLE SPICES ARE USED IN THIS CURRY SO REMOVE THEM BEFORE SERVING OR WARN THE DINERS OF THEIR PRESENCE IN ADVANCE! LAMB MASALA IS DELICIOUS SERVED WITH FRESHLY BAKED NAAN BREAD OR WITH A RICE ACCOMPANIMENT AND A COOL CUCUMBER RAITA. THIS DISH IS BEST MADE WITH GOOD-QUALITY SPRING LAMB.

SERVES FOUR

INGREDIENTS
   75ml/5 tbsp corn oil
   2 onions, chopped
   5ml/1 tsp grated ginger
   6 whole dried red chillies
   3 cardamom pods
   2 cinnamon sticks
   6 black peppercorns
   3 cloves
   2.5ml/½ tsp salt
   450g/1lb boned leg of
     lamb, cubed
   600ml/1 pint/2½
     cups water
   2 fresh green chillies, sliced
   30ml/2 tbsp chopped fresh
     coriander (cilantro)
   rice or naan bread,
     to serve

1 Heat the oil in a large pan. Lower the heat slightly and cook the onions until they are lightly browned.

2 Add half the ginger and half the garlic and stir well.

3 Throw in half the red chillies, the cardamoms, cinnamon, peppercorns, cloves and salt.

4 Add the lamb and cook over a medium heat. Stir constantly with a semi-circular movement, using a wooden spoon to scrape the base of the pan. Continue in this way for about 5 minutes.

5 Pour in the water, cover the stew with a lid and cook it over a medium-low heat for 35–40 minutes, or until the water has evaporated and the meat is tender.

6 Add the rest of the grated ginger, sliced garlic and the whole dried red chillies, along with the sliced fresh green chillies and the chopped fresh coriander.

7 Continue to stir over the heat until you see some free oil on the sides of the pan.

8 Transfer to a serving dish and serve immediately with fresh naan bread or boiled rice.

COOK'S TIP
The action of stirring the meat and spices together using a semi-circular motion, as described in step 4, is called bhoono-ing. It makes sure that the meat becomes well-coated and combined with the spice mixture before the cooking liquid is added.

VARIATION
Replace the lamb with cubes of braising or stewing beef for a hearty warming winter dish all the family will enjoy.

LIVELY LAMB BURGERS <u>WITH</u> CHILLI RELISH

A RED ONION RELISH CHILLI WORKS WELL WITH BURGERS. BASED ON MIDDLE-EASTERN-STYLE LAMB, SERVE WITH PITTA BREAD AND TABBOULEH OR WITH FRIES AND A SALAD.

SERVES FOUR

INGREDIENTS
 25g/1oz/3 tbsp bulgur wheat
 150ml/¼ pint/⅔ cup hot water
 500g/1¼lb lean minced
  (ground) lamb
 1 small red onion, finely chopped
 2 garlic cloves, finely chopped
 1 fresh green chilli, seeded and
  finely chopped
 5ml/1 tsp ground toasted cumin seeds
 5ml/1 tsp grated lemon rind
 60ml/4 tbsp chopped fresh flat
  leaf parsley
 30ml/2 tbsp chopped fresh mint
 olive oil, for frying
 salt and ground black pepper

For the relish
 2 red (bell) peppers, halved
  and seeded
 2 red onions, sliced into wedges
 75–90ml/5–6 tbsp extra virgin
  olive oil
 350g/12oz cherry tomatoes,
  chopped
 1 fresh red or green chilli, seeded
  and finely chopped
 30ml/2 tbsp chopped fresh mint
 30ml/2 tbsp chopped fresh parsley
 15ml/1 tbsp chopped fresh oregano
  or marjoram
 2.5–5ml/½–1 tsp ground toasted
  cumin seeds
 5ml/1 tsp grated lemon rind
 juice of ½ lemon
 granulated (white) sugar

1 Put the bulgur wheat in a bowl and pour over the hot water. Leave to stand for 15 minutes. Tip into a colander lined with a clean dishtowel. Drain well, then gather up the sides of the towel and squeeze out the excess moisture.

2 Place the bulgur in a bowl and add the lamb, onion, garlic, chilli, cumin, lemon rind, parsley and mint. Mix well, season, then form the mixture into eight small burgers. Set aside while you make the relish.

3 Grill (broil) the peppers, skin-side up, until the skin chars and blisters. Place in a strong plastic bag and tie the top to keep the steam in. Set aside for about 20 minutes, then remove the peppers from the bag, peel off the skins and dice the flesh finely. Put the diced pepper in a bowl.

4 Meanwhile, brush the onions with 15ml/1 tbsp of the oil and grill for about 5 minutes on each side, until browned. Cool, then chop. Add to the peppers.

5 Add tomatoes, chilli, mint, parsley, oregano or marjoram and the cumin. Stir in 60ml/4 tbsp of the remaining oil, with the lemon rind and juice. Season with salt, pepper and sugar and allow to stand for 20–30 minutes for the flavours to mature.

6 Heat a heavy frying pan or a ridged cast-iron griddle pan over a high heat and grease lightly with oil. Cook the burgers for about 5–6 minutes on each side, or until just cooked at the centre.

7 While the burgers are cooking, taste the relish and adjust the seasoning. Serve the burgers immediately they are cooked, with the relish.

COOK'S TIP
Oregano (*Origanum vulgare*) is also known as wild marjoram. It has a spicier flavour than marjoram (which is also known as sweet marjoram).

LAMB STEW WITH CHILLI SAUCE

THE DRIED CHILLIES IN THIS STEW ADD DEPTH AND RICHNESS TO THE SAUCE, WHILE THE
POTATO SLICES ENSURE THAT IT IS SUBSTANTIAL ENOUGH TO SERVE ON ITS OWN.

SERVES SIX

INGREDIENTS

6 guajillo chillies, seeded
2 pasilla chillies, seeded
250ml/8fl oz/1 cup hot water
3 garlic cloves, peeled
5ml/1 tsp ground cinnamon
2.5ml/½ tsp ground cloves
2.5ml/½ tsp ground black pepper
15ml/1 tbsp vegetable oil
1kg/2¼lb lean boneless lamb
  shoulder, cut into 2cm/¾in cubes
2 large potatoes, scrubbed and cut
  into 1cm/½in thick slices
salt
strips of red (bell) pepper and fresh
  oregano, to garnish

COOK'S TIP

When frying the lamb, don't be tempted
to cook too many cubes at one time, or
the meat will steam rather than fry.

1 Snap or tear the dried chillies into large pieces, put them in a bowl and pour over the hot water. Leave to soak for 20–30 minutes, then tip the contents of the bowl into a food processor or blender. Add the garlic and spices. Process until smooth.

2 Heat the oil in a large pan. Add the lamb cubes, in batches, and stir-fry over a high heat until the cubes are browned on all sides.

3 Return all the lamb cubes to the pan, spread them out, then cover them with a layer of potato slices. Add salt to taste. Put a lid on the pan and cook over a medium heat for 10 minutes.

4 Pour over the chilli mixture and mix well. Replace the lid and simmer over a low heat for about 1 hour or until the meat and the potato are tender. Serve with a rice dish, and garnish with strips of red pepper and fresh oregano.

SPICY LAMB STEW

*THIS STEW IS KNOWN AS ESTOFADO DE CARNERO IN MEXICO. THE RECIPE FOR THIS
DISH HAS AN INTERESTING MIX OF CHILLIES – THE MILD, FULL-FLAVOURED ANCHO, AND
THE PIQUANT JALAPEÑO WHICH GIVES EXTRA "BITE". THE HEAT OF THE CHILLIES IS MELLOWED
BY THE ADDITION OF GROUND CINNAMON AND CLOVES. BONELESS NECK FILLET IS VERY GOOD
FOR THIS DISH; IT IS LEAN, TENDER, FLAVOURSOME AND INEXPENSIVE.*

SERVES FOUR

INGREDIENTS

  3 dried ancho chillies
  30ml/2 tbsp olive oil
  1 jalapeño chilli, seeded
    and chopped
  1 onion, finely chopped
  2 garlic cloves, chopped
  450g/1lb tomatoes, peeled
    and chopped
  50g/2oz/⅓ cup seedless raisins
  1.5ml/¼ tsp ground cinnamon
  1.5ml/¼ tsp ground cloves
  900g/2lb boneless lamb, cut into
    5cm/2in cubes
  250ml/8fl oz/1 cup lamb stock
    or water
  salt and ground black pepper
  a few sprigs of fresh coriander
    (cilantro), to garnish
  coriander rice, to serve

COOK'S TIP
To make coriander (cilantro) rice, simply
heat 30ml/2 tbsp corn oil in a large
frying pan and gently cook 1 finely
chopped onion for about 8 minutes, or
until soft but not brown. Stir in enough
cooked, long grain rice for four and stir
gently over a medium heat until heated
through. Sprinkle over 30–45ml/
2–3 tbsp chopped fresh coriander and
stir in thoroughly.

1 Roast the ancho chillies lightly in a
dry frying pan over a low heat to bring
out the flavour.

2 Remove the stems, shake out the
seeds and tear the pods into pieces,
then put them into a bowl. Pour in
enough warm water to just cover. Leave
to soak for 30 minutes.

3 Heat the olive oil in a frying pan and
sauté the jalapeño chilli together with
the onion and garlic until the onion
is tender.

4 Add the chopped tomatoes to the pan
and cook until the mixture is thick and
well blended. Stir in the raisins, ground
cinnamon and cloves, and season to
taste with salt and pepper. Transfer the
mixture to a flameproof casserole.

5 Tip the ancho chillies and their
soaking water into a food processor and
process to a smooth purée. Add the
chilli purée to the tomato mixture in
the casserole.

6 Add the lamb cubes to the casserole,
stir to mix and pour in enough of the
lamb stock or water to just cover
the meat.

7 Bring to a simmer, then cover the
casserole and cook over a low heat for
about 2 hours, or until the lamb is
tender. Garnish with fresh coriander and
serve with coriander rice.

VARIATION
Replace some of the fresh tomatoes with
sun-dried tomatoes for a rich stew with a
delicious sauce

FIRE FRY

HERE'S ONE FOR LOVERS OF HOT, SPICY FOOD. TENDER STRIPS OF LAMB, MARINATED IN SPICES AND STIR-FRIED WITH A TOP-DRESSING OF CHILLIES, REALLY HITS THE HOT SPOT.

SERVES FOUR

INGREDIENTS
  225g/8oz lean lamb
  fillet (tenderloin)
  120ml/4fl oz/½ cup natural
  (plain) yogurt
  1.5ml/¼ tsp ground cardamom
  5ml/1 tsp grated fresh root ginger
  5ml/1 tsp crushed garlic
  5ml/1 tsp hot chilli powder
  5ml/1 tsp garam masala
  5ml/1 tsp salt
  15ml/1 tbsp corn oil
  2 onions, chopped
  1 bay leaf
  300ml/½ pint/1¼ cups water
  2 fresh red chillies, seeded and
  sliced in strips
  2 fresh green chillies, seeded and
  sliced in strips
  30ml/2 tbsp fresh coriander
  (cilantro) leaves

1 Using a sharp knife, cut the lamb into 7.5–10cm/3–4in pieces, then into strips.

2 In a bowl, whisk the yogurt with the cardamom, ginger, garlic, chilli powder, garam masala and salt. Add the lamb strips and stir to coat them in the mixture. Cover and marinate in a cool place for about 1 hour.

COOK'S TIP
This is a useful recipe for a family divided into those who love chillies and those who don't. Serve the doubters before adding the chillies, or perhaps top their portions with strips of a sweet mild chilli or even a peeled red or green (bell) pepper.

3 Heat the oil in a wok or frying pan and fry the onions for 3–5 minutes, or until they are tender and golden brown.

4 Add the bay leaf and then add the marinated lamb with the yogurt and spices, and toss over a medium heat for about 2–3 minutes.

5 Pour over the water, stir well, then cover and cook for 15–20 minutes over a low heat, stirring occasionally. Once the water has evaporated, stir-fry the mixture for 1 minute.

6 Strew the red and green chillies over the stir-fry, with the fresh coriander. Serve hot. Offer a cooling yogurt dip, if you like.

CARIBBEAN LAMB CURRY

*THIS POPULAR NATIONAL DISH OF JAMAICA IS KNOWN AS CURRY GOAT ALTHOUGH
GOAT MEAT OR LAMB CAN BE USED TO MAKE IT.*

SERVES FOUR TO SIX

INGREDIENTS
    900g/2lb boned leg of lamb
    60ml/4 tbsp curry powder
    3 garlic cloves, crushed
    1 large onion, chopped
    4 thyme sprigs or 5ml/1 tsp
        dried thyme
    3 bay leaves
    5ml/1 tsp ground allspice
    30ml/2 tbsp vegetable oil
    50g/2oz/¼ cup butter or margarine
    900ml/1½ pints/3¾ cups stock
        or water
    1 fresh hot chilli, chopped
    cooked rice, to serve
    coriander (cilantro) sprigs, to garnish

1 Cut the meat into 5cm/2in cubes,
discarding any excess fat and gristle.

2 Place the lamb, curry powder, garlic,
onion, thyme, bay leaves, allspice and
oil in a large bowl and mix. Marinate the
meat in the refrigerator for at least
3 hours or overnight.

3 Melt the butter or margarine in a large
heavy pan, add the seasoned lamb and
cook over a medium heat for about
10 minutes, turning the meat frequently.

4 Stir in the stock and chilli and bring
to the boil. Reduce the heat, cover the
pan and simmer for 1½ hours, or until
the meat is tender. Serve with rice,
garnish with coriander.

COOK'S TIP
Try goat, or mutton, if you can and enjoy
a robust curry.

INDONESIAN BEEF PATTIES

THESE SPICY LITTLE MEATBALLS COME FROM INDONESIA. SERVE THEM WITH BROAD EGG
NOODLES AND FIERY CHILLI SAMBAL AS A DIPPING SAUCE.

SERVES FOUR TO SIX

INGREDIENTS
   1cm/½in cube shrimp paste
   1 large onion, roughly chopped
   1–2 fresh red chillies, seeded
      and chopped
   2 garlic cloves, crushed
   15ml/1 tbsp coriander seeds
   5ml/1 tsp cumin seeds
   450g/1lb lean minced (ground) beef
   10ml/2 tsp dark soy sauce
   5ml/1 tsp soft dark brown sugar
   juice of 1½ lemons
   a little beaten egg
   vegetable oil, for shallow frying
   salt and ground black pepper
   1 fresh green and 1–2 fresh red
      chillies, to garnish
   Chilli Sambal (below), to serve

1 Wrap the shrimp paste in a piece of
foil and gently warm it in a dry frying
pan for 5 minutes, turning a few times.
Unwrap the paste and put in a food
processor or blender.

COOK'S TIP
When processing the shrimp paste,
onion, chillies and garlic, do not run
the machine for too long, or the onion
will become too wet and spoil the
consistency of the meatballs.

2 Add the onion, chillies and garlic to
the food processor and process until
finely chopped. Set aside. Dry-fry the
coriander and cumin seeds in a hot
frying pan for 1 minute, to release the
aroma. Tip the seeds into a mortar and
grind with a pestle.

3 Put the meat in a large bowl. Stir in
the onion mixture. Add the ground
spices, soy sauce, brown sugar, lemon
juice and beaten egg. Season to taste.

4 Shape the meat mixture into small,
even balls, and chill these for 5–10
minutes to firm them up.

5 Heat the oil in a wok or large frying pan
and fry the meatballs for 4–5 minutes,
turning often, until cooked through
and browned. You may have to do this
in batches.

6 Drain the meatballs on kitchen paper,
and then pile them on to a warm
serving platter or into a large serving
bowl. Finely slice the green chilli and
one of the red chillies, and sprinkle over
the meatballs. Garnish with a whole red
chilli, if you like. Serve with the sambal,
spooned into a small dish.

VARIATION
Beef is traditionally used for this dish,
but minced (ground) pork, lamb – or
even turkey – would also be good.

CHILLI SAMBAL

THIS FIERCE CONDIMENT IS BOTTLED AS SAMBAL OELEK, BUT IT IS EASY TO PREPARE
AND WILL KEEP FOR SEVERAL WEEKS IN A WELL-SEALED JAR IN THE REFRIGERATOR.

MAKES 450G/1LB

INGREDIENTS
   450g/1lb fresh red chillies, seeded
   10ml/2 tsp salt

COOK'S TIP
If any sambal drips on your fingers, wash
well in soapy water *immediately*.

1 Bring a pan of water to the boil, add
the seeded chillies and cook them for
5–8 minutes.

2 Drain the chillies and chop roughly.
Grind the chillies in a food processor
or blender, without making the paste
too smooth. If you like, you can do this
in batches.

3 Scrape into a screw-topped glass jar,
stir in the salt and cover with a piece of
greaseproof (waxed) paper or clear film
(plastic wrap). Screw on the lid and
store in the refrigerator. Wash all
implements in soapy water. Spoon into
dishes using a stainless-steel or plastic
spoon. Serve as an accompaniment, as
suggested in recipes.

BEEF ENCHILADAS WITH RED SAUCE

DRIED CHILLIES ARE WONDERFUL PANTRY STAPLES. IT IS WORTH HAVING A SUPPLY OF SEVERAL DIFFERENT TYPES, SO YOU'LL ALWAYS HAVE THE MEANS TO MAKE SPICY DISHES LIKE THIS.

SERVES TWO TO THREE

INGREDIENTS

   500g/1¼lb rump (round) steak,
     cut into 5cm/2in cubes
   2 ancho chillies, seeded
   2 pasilla chillies, seeded
   30ml/2 tbsp vegetable oil
   2 garlic cloves, crushed
   10ml/2 tsp dried oregano
   2.5ml/½ tsp ground cumin
   7 fresh corn tortillas
   shredded onion and fresh flat leaf
     parsley, to garnish
   mango and chilli salsa,
     to serve

1 Put the cubed rump steak in a pan and cover with water. Bring to the boil, then lower the heat and simmer for 1–1½ hours, or until very tender.

2 Meanwhile, put the dried chillies in a bowl and pour over hot water to cover. Leave to soak for 20–30 minutes, then tip the contents of the bowl into a blender and whizz to a smooth paste.

3 Drain the steak and let it cool, reserving 250ml/8fl oz/1 cup of the cooking liquid. Meanwhile, heat the oil in a large frying pan and fry the garlic, oregano and cumin for 2 minutes.

4 Stir in the chilli paste and the reserved cooking liquid from the beef. Tear 1 of the tortillas into small pieces and add it to the mixture. Bring to the boil, then lower the heat. Simmer for 10 minutes, stirring occasionally, until the sauce has thickened. Shred the steak, using 2 forks, and stir it into the sauce. Heat through for a few minutes.

5 Spoon some of the meat mixture on to each tortilla and roll it up to make an enchilada. Keep the enchiladas in a warmed dish until you have rolled them all. Garnish the enchiladas with shreds of onion and fresh flat leaf parsley, and serve immediately with mango and chilli salsa.

VARIATIONS
• For a richer version, place the rolled enchiladas side by side in a gratin dish. Pour over 300ml/½ pint/1¼ cups sour cream and 75g/3oz/¾ cup grated Cheddar cheese. Grill (broil) for 5 minutes or until the cheese melts and the sauce begins to bubble. Serve immediately, with the salsa.
• For a sharper tasting cheese topping, substitute Parmesan cheese for half the quantity of Cheddar.

MEXICAN SPICY BEEF TORTILLA

THIS DISH IS NOT UNLIKE A LASAGNE, EXCEPT THAT THE SPICY MEAT IS MIXED WITH RICE
AND IS LAYERED BETWEEN MEXICAN TORTILLAS, WITH A SALSA SAUCE FOR AN EXTRA KICK.

SERVES FOUR

INGREDIENTS
1 onion, chopped
2 garlic cloves, crushed
1 fresh red chilli, seeded and sliced
350g/12oz rump (round) steak, cut
   into small cubes
15ml/1 tbsp oil
225g/8oz/2 cups cooked long grain rice
beef stock, to moisten
salt and ground black pepper
3 large wheat tortillas

For the salsa picante
2 × 400g/14oz cans chopped tomatoes
2 garlic cloves, halved
1 onion, quartered
1–2 fresh red chillies, seeded and
   roughly chopped
5ml/1 tsp ground cumin
2.5–5ml/½–1 tsp cayenne pepper
5ml/1 tsp chopped fresh oregano
tomato juice or water, if required

For the cheese sauce
50g/2oz/¼ cup butter
50g/2oz/½ cup plain
   (all-purpose) flour
600ml/1 pint/2½ cups milk
115g/4oz/1 cup grated
   Cheddar cheese

1 Make the salsa picante. Place the first
4 ingredients in a blender or food
processor and process until smooth.

2 Pour into a pan, add the spices and
oregano, and season with salt. Bring to
the boil, stirring occasionally. Boil for
1–2 minutes, then lower the heat, cover
and simmer for 15 minutes. The sauce
should be thick, but of a pouring
consistency. If it is too thick, dilute it
with a little tomato juice or water.
Preheat the oven to 180°C/350°F/Gas 4.

COOK'S TIP
You can use any type of beef for this
dish. If stewing steak is used, it should
be very finely chopped and the cooking
time increased by 10–15 minutes.

3 Make the cheese sauce. Melt the
butter in a pan and stir in the flour.
Cook for 1 minute. Add the milk, stirring
all the time until the sauce boils and
thickens. Stir in all but 30ml/2 tbsp of
the cheese and season. Set aside.

4 Put the onion, garlic and chilli in a large
bowl. Mix in the meat. Heat the oil in a
pan and stir fry the meat for 10 minutes
or until it has browned. Stir in the rice
and stock to moisten. Season to taste.

5 Pour about one-quarter of the
cheese sauce into the base of a round
ovenproof dish. Add a tortilla and then
spread over half the salsa followed by
half the meat mixture.

6 Repeat these layers, then add half
the remaining cheese sauce and the
final tortilla. Pour over the remaining
cheese sauce and sprinkle the reserved
cheese on top. Bake in the oven for
15–20 minutes until golden on top.

CHILLI CON CARNE

THIS FAMOUS TEX-MEX STEW HAS BECOME AN INTERNATIONAL FAVOURITE. SERVE IT WITH RICE OR BAKED POTATOES AND A HEARTY GREEN SALAD.

SERVES EIGHT

INGREDIENTS
  1.2kg/2½lb lean braising steak
  30ml/2 tbsp sunflower oil
  1 large onion, chopped
  2 garlic cloves, finely chopped
  15ml/1 tbsp plain (all-purpose) flour
  300ml/½ pint/1¼ cups red wine
  300ml/½ pint/1¼ cups beef stock
  30ml/2 tbsp tomato
    purée (paste)
  salt and ground black pepper

For the beans
  30ml/2 tbsp olive oil
  1 onion, chopped
  1 fresh red chilli, seeded
    and chopped
  2 × 400g/14oz cans red kidney
    beans, drained and rinsed
  400g/14oz can chopped tomatoes

For the topping
  6 tomatoes, peeled and chopped
  1 fresh green chilli, seeded
    and chopped
  30ml/2 tbsp chopped
    fresh chives
  30ml/2 tbsp chopped fresh
    coriander (cilantro), plus sprigs
    to garnish
  150ml/¼ pint/⅔ cup sour cream

1 Cut the meat into thick strips, then cut it crossways into small cubes. Heat the oil in a large, flameproof casserole. Add the chopped onion and garlic, and cook until softened but not coloured. Season the flour and place it on a plate, then toss a batch of meat in it.

2 Use a slotted spoon to remove the onion from the pan, then add the floured beef and cook over a high heat until browned on all sides. Remove from the pan and set aside, then flour and brown another batch of meat.

3 When the last batch of meat has been browned, return the reserved meat and the onion to the pan. Stir in the wine, stock and tomato purée. Bring to the boil, reduce the heat and simmer for 45 minutes, or until the beef is tender.

4 Meanwhile, for the beans, heat the oil in a frying pan and cook the onion and chilli until softened. Stir in the kidney beans and tomatoes, and simmer gently for 20–25 minutes, or until thickened and reduced.

5 Mix the tomatoes, chilli, chives and coriander for the topping. Ladle the meat mixture on to warmed plates. Add a layer of bean mixture and tomato topping. Finish with sour cream and garnish with coriander leaves.

MEATBALLS WITH SPAGHETTI

FOR A GREAT INTRODUCTION TO THE CHARM OF CHILLIES, THIS SIMPLE PASTA DISH
IS HARD TO BEAT. CHILDREN LOVE THE GENTLE HEAT OF THE TOMATO SAUCE.

SERVES SIX TO EIGHT

INGREDIENTS
    350g/12oz minced (ground) beef
    1 egg
    60ml/4 tbsp roughly chopped fresh
      flat leaf parsley
    2.5ml/½ tsp crushed dried
      red chillies
    1 thick slice white bread,
      crusts removed
    30ml/2 tbsp milk
    about 30ml/2 tbsp olive oil
    300ml/½ pint/1¼ cups passata
      (bottled strained tomatoes)
    400ml/14fl oz/1⅔ cups
      vegetable stock
    5ml/1 tsp granulated (white) sugar
    350–450g/12oz–1lb fresh or
      dried spaghetti
    salt and ground black pepper
    shavings of Parmesan cheese,
      to serve

1 Put the beef in a large bowl. Add the egg, with half the parsley and half the crushed chillies. Season with plenty of salt and pepper.

2 Tear the bread into small pieces and place these in a small bowl. Moisten with the milk. Leave to soak for a few minutes, then squeeze out the excess milk and crumble the bread over the meat mixture. Mix everything together with a wooden spoon, then use your hands to squeeze and knead the mixture so that it becomes smooth and quite sticky.

3 Wash your hands, rinse them under the cold tap, then pick up small pieces of the mixture and roll them between your palms to make about 40–60 small balls. Place the meatballs on a tray and chill for 30 minutes.

4 Heat the oil in a large non-stick frying pan. Cook the meatballs in batches until browned on all sides. Pour the passata and stock into a large pan. Heat gently, then add the remaining chillies and the sugar, and season. Add the meatballs and bring to the boil. Reduce the heat, and simmer for 20 minutes.

5 Bring a large pan of lightly salted water to the boil and cook the pasta until it is just tender, following the instructions on the packet. Drain and tip it into a large heated bowl. Pour over the sauce and toss gently. Sprinkle with the remaining parsley and shavings of Parmesan cheese. Serve immediately.

BEEF TAGINE <u>WITH</u> SWEET POTATOES

*THIS WARMING DISH IS EATEN DURING THE WINTER IN MOROCCO WHERE, ESPECIALLY
IN THE MOUNTAINS, THE WEATHER CAN BE SURPRISINGLY COLD.*

SERVES FOUR

INGREDIENTS

900g/2lb braising or
   stewing beef
30ml/2 tbsp sunflower oil
good pinch of ground turmeric
1 large onion, chopped
1 fresh red or green chilli, seeded
   and chopped
7.5ml/1½ tsp paprika
good pinch of cayenne pepper
2.5ml/½ tsp ground cumin
450g/1lb sweet potatoes
15ml/1 tbsp chopped fresh parsley,
   plus extra to garnish
15ml/1 tbsp chopped fresh
   coriander (cilantro)
15g/½oz/1 tbsp butter
salt and ground black pepper

1 Trim the meat and cut into cubes.
Heat the oil in a flameproof casserole
and add the meat. Sprinkle with the
turmeric and fry for 3–4 minutes until
evenly brown, stirring frequently. Cover
the pan tightly and cook for 15 minutes
over a fairly gentle heat, without lifting
the lid. Preheat the oven to 180°C/
350°F/Gas 4.

2 Add the onion, chilli, paprika,
cayenne pepper and cumin to the
casserole and season. Pour in enough
water to cover the meat. Cover tightly
and cook in the oven for 1–1½ hours
until the meat is very tender, checking
occasionally and adding a little extra
water to keep the stew fairly moist.

3 Meanwhile, peel the sweet potatoes
and slice them straight into a pan of
salted water (sweet potatoes discolour
very quickly if exposed to the air).
Bring to the boil, then simmer for
2–3 minutes until just tender. Drain.

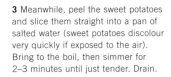

4 Stir the herbs into the meat, adding
a little extra water if the stew appears
dry. Arrange the sweet potato slices
over the meat and dot with the butter.
Cover and cook in the oven, covered,
for a further 10 minutes or until the
potatoes feel very tender when tested
with a skewer. Increase the oven
temperature to 200°C/400°F/Gas 6.

5 Remove the lid of the casserole
and cook in the oven for a further
10 minutes until the potatoes are
golden. Garnish and serve immediately.

CHILLI BEEF WITH SPICY ONION RINGS

FRUITY, SMOKY AND MILD MEXICAN CHILLIES COMBINE WELL WITH GARLIC IN THIS MARINADE FOR BEEF. THE SPICY ONION RINGS ARE HARD TO RESIST.

SERVES FOUR

INGREDIENTS
    4 rump (round) or rib-eye beef
    steaks, about 225g/8oz each

For the chilli paste
    3 large pasilla chillies
    2 garlic cloves, finely chopped
    5ml/1 tsp ground toasted cumin seeds
    5ml/1 tsp dried oregano
    60ml/4 tbsp olive oil
    salt and ground black pepper

For the spicy onion rings
    2 onions, sliced and separated
    into rings
    250ml/8fl oz/1 cup milk
    75g/3oz/½ cup coarse corn
    meal polenta
    2.5ml/½ tsp dried red chilli flakes
    5ml/1 tsp ground toasted cumin seeds
    5ml/1 tsp dried oregano
    vegetable oil, for deep-frying

1 To make the chilli paste, cut the stalks from the chillies, then slit them and shake out most of the seeds. Toast the chillies in a dry frying pan for 2–4 minutes, until they give off their aroma. Place the chillies in a bowl, cover with warm water and leave to soak for 20–30 minutes.

2 Drain the chillies, reserving the soaking water. Put them in a food processor or blender. Add the garlic, cumin, oregano and oil. Process to a smooth paste, adding a little soaking water, if necessary. It should not be too stiff. Season with pepper.

3 Pour the chilli paste all over the meat. Put the steaks in a dish, cover and leave to marinate in the refrigerator for up to 12 hours.

COOK'S TIP
It is always best to allow a few minutes resting time for the steaks after cooking. It relaxes the meat, making it more tender.

4 Make the onion rings. Soak the onions in the milk for 30 minutes. Mix the corn meal, chilli, cumin and oregano in a shallow bowl and season with salt and pepper. Heat the oil for deep-frying to 160–180°C/325–350°F or until a cube of day-old bread browns in about 45 seconds. Drain the onion rings and dip into the corn meal mixture. Fry in batches for 2–4 minutes, until browned and crisp. Do not overcrowd the pan. Drain on kitchen paper.

5 Prepare the barbecue or heat a cast-iron griddle pan. Season the steaks with salt and cook for about 5 minutes on each side for a medium result; adjust the timing for rare or well-done steak. Serve the steaks while hot with the onion rings.

BEEF WITH PEPPERS AND BLACK BEAN SAUCE

A SPICY, RICH DISH WITH A DISTINCTIVE BLACK BEAN SAUCE. THIS RECIPE WILL QUICKLY BECOME A FAVOURITE BECAUSE IT IS SO EASY TO PREPARE AND QUICK TO COOK.

SERVES FOUR

INGREDIENTS
350g/12oz rump (round) steak,
  trimmed and thinly sliced
20ml/4 tsp vegetable oil
300ml/½ pint/1¼ cups beef stock
2 garlic cloves, finely chopped
5ml/1 tsp grated fresh root ginger
1 fresh red chilli, seeded and
  finely chopped
15ml/1 tbsp black bean sauce
1 green (bell) pepper, seeded and
  cut into 2.5cm/1in squares
15ml/1 tbsp dry sherry
5ml/1 tsp cornflour (cornstarch)
5ml/1 tsp granulated (white) sugar
45ml/3 tbsp cold water
salt
cooked rice noodles,
  to serve

1 Place the rump steak in a bowl. Add 5ml/1 tsp of the oil and stir to coat.

VARIATIONS
• Use any chilli you like. Habanero, with its hint of apricot flavour, would be a good if very hot choice.
• For extra colour, use a red or orange (bell) pepper or even a yellow Hungarian wax chilli.

2 Bring the stock to the boil in a pan. Add the beef and cook for 2 minutes, stirring constantly to prevent the slices from sticking together. Drain the beef and set aside. Retain the stock for use in another recipe.

3 Heat the remaining oil in a wok. Stir-fry the garlic, ginger and chilli with the black bean sauce for a few seconds. Add the pepper squares and a little water. Cook for about 2 minutes more, then stir in the sherry. Add the beef slices to the pan, spoon the sauce over and reheat.

4 Mix the cornflour and sugar to a cream with the water. Pour the mixture into the pan. Cook, stirring, until the sauce has thickened. Season with salt. Serve immediately, with rice noodles.

COOK'S TIP
To make beef stock, brown 1kg/2¼lb beef or veal bones in an oven heated to 180°C/350°F/Gas 4 for 30 minutes. Put the bones in a pan with a bay leaf and some peppercorns. Cover with water. Add the washed skins of 2 onions, 2 chopped carrot and 1 celery stick. Bring to the boil, simmer for 40 minutes. Strain.

SHREDDED BEEF WITH CHILLIES

THE ESSENCE OF THIS RECIPE IS THAT THE BEEF IS CUT INTO VERY FINE STRIPS. THIS IS EASIER TO DO IF THE MEAT IS PLACED IN THE FREEZER FOR 30 MINUTES BEFORE IT IS SLICED.

3 Heat a wok and add half the oil. When it is hot, stir-fry the onion and ginger for 3–4 minutes, then lift out with a slotted spoon and set aside. Add the carrot, stir-fry for 3–4 minutes until slightly softened, then transfer to a plate and keep warm.

4 Heat the remaining oil in the wok, then quickly add the beef, with the marinade, followed by the chillies. Cook over high heat for 2 minutes, stirring all the time.

5 Return the fried onion and ginger to the wok and stir-fry for 1 minute more. Season with salt and pepper to taste, cover and cook for 30 seconds. Spoon the meat into two warmed bowls and add the carrot strips. Garnish with fresh chives and serve.

SERVES TWO

INGREDIENTS
225g/8oz rump (round) or fillet
   (tenderloin) of beef
15ml/1 tbsp each light and dark
   soy sauce
15ml/1 tbsp rice wine or
   medium-dry sherry
5ml/1 tsp soft dark brown sugar
90ml/6 tbsp vegetable oil
1 large onion, thinly sliced
2.5cm/1in piece fresh root ginger,
   peeled and grated
1–2 carrots, cut into matchsticks
2–3 fresh chillies, halved, seeded
   (optional) and chopped
salt and ground black pepper
fresh chives, to garnish

1 With a sharp knife, slice the beef very thinly, then cut each slice into fine strips or shreds.

2 In a bowl, mix the light and dark soy sauces with the rice wine or sherry and sugar. Add the strips of beef and stir well to ensure that they are evenly coated with the marinade. Cover and marinate in a cool place for 30 minutes.

COOK'S TIPS
• Use dried chillies if you prefer. Snap them in half, shake out the seeds, then soak them in hot water for 20–30 minutes.
• If you enjoy your food really fiery, don't bother to remove the seeds from the chillies.

BEEF <u>AND</u> AUBERGINE CURRY

*THIS SPICY THAI DISH IS PACKED WITH VEGETABLES AS WELL AS TENDER STRIPS OF STEAK,
ALL SERVED IN AN AROMATIC, FIERY COCONUT SAUCE.*

SERVES SIX

INGREDIENTS
120ml/4fl oz/½ cup sunflower oil
2 onions, thinly sliced
2.5cm/1in fresh root ginger, sliced
  and cut into batons
1 garlic clove, crushed
2 fresh red chillies, seeded and very
  finely sliced
2.5cm/1 in fresh turmeric,
  peeled and crushed, or 5ml/1 tsp
  ground turmeric
1 lemon grass stalk, lower part
  sliced finely, top bruised
675g/1½lb braising steak, cut in
  even strips
400ml/14fl oz can coconut milk
300ml/½ pint/1¼ cups water
1 aubergine (eggplant), sliced and
  patted dry
5ml/1 tsp tamarind pulp, soaked in
  60ml/4 tbsp warm water
salt and ground black pepper
finely sliced chilli and deep-fried
  onions, to garnish
boiled rice, to serve

1 Heat half the oil and cook the onions,
ginger and garlic until they give off a
rich aroma. Add the chillies, turmeric
and the lower part of the lemon grass.
Turn up the heat and add the steak,
stirring until the meat changes colour.

2 Add the coconut milk, water, lemon
grass top and seasoning to taste. Cover
and simmer gently for 1½ hours, or
until the meat is tender.

3 Towards the end of the cooking time
heat the remaining oil in a frying pan.
Cook the aubergine slices until brown
on both sides.

4 Add the browned aubergine slices to
the beef curry and cook for a further 15
minutes. Stir gently occasionally. Strain
the tamarind and stir the juice into the
curry. Taste and adjust the seasoning.

5 Put into a warm serving dish. Garnish
with the sliced chilli and deep-fried
onions and serve with boiled rice.

THAI GREEN BEEF CURRY

CHILLIES ARE THE MAIN INGREDIENT IN GREEN CURRY PASTE, WHICH IS USED FOR THIS
FRAGRANT DISH. ALSO INCLUDED ARE THAI AUBERGINES.

SERVES FOUR TO SIX

INGREDIENTS
    15ml/1 tbsp vegetable oil
    45ml/3 tbsp green curry paste
    600ml/1 pint/2½ cups coconut milk
    450g/1lb beef sirloin, cut into long,
      thin slices
    4 kaffir lime leaves, torn
    15–30ml/1–2 tbsp Thai fish sauce
    5ml/1 tsp palm sugar (jaggery)
      or soft light brown sugar
    150g/5oz small Thai aubergines
      (eggplants), halved
    a small handful of holy basil
    2 fresh green chillies,
      to garnish

1 Heat the oil in a large pan or wok.
Add the green curry paste and fry
until fragrant.

2 Stir in half the coconut milk, a little at
a time. Cook for about 5–6 minutes,
until the milk separates and an oily
sheen appears.

VARIATION
You can substitute thinly sliced chicken
breast portions for the beef.

3 Add the beef to the pan with the
kaffir lime leaves, Thai fish sauce,
palm sugar and aubergines. Cook for
2–3 minutes, then stir in the remaining
coconut milk.

4 Bring back to a simmer and cook
until the meat and aubergines are
tender. Stir in the basil just before
serving. Finely shred the green chillies
and use to garnish the curry.

COOK'S TIP
Thai aubergines look very like unripe
tomatoes. Their virtue is that they will
cook quickly in a recipe of this kind.
They have a delicate flavour and are not
so fleshy as the more common large
purple-skinned variety. These small
aubergines do not need peeling or
salting. You may also find small yellow
and purple ones.

MUSSAMAN BEEF CURRY

THIS DISH IS TRADITIONALLY BASED ON BEEF, BUT CHICKEN, LAMB OR TOFU CAN BE USED INSTEAD. IT HAS A RICH, SWEET AND SPICY FLAVOUR AND IS BEST SERVED WITH BOILED RICE.

SERVES FOUR TO SIX

INGREDIENTS
    675g/1½ lb stewing steak
    600ml/1 pint/2½ cups coconut milk
    250ml/8fl oz/1 cup coconut cream
    45ml/3 tbsp Mussaman curry paste
    30ml/2 tbsp Thai fish sauce
    15ml/1 tbsp palm sugar or light
        muscovado (brown) sugar
    60ml/4 tbsp tamarind juice (tamarind
        paste mixed with warm water)
    6 green cardamom pods
    1 cinnamon stick
    1 large potato, about 225g/8oz,
        cut into even chunks
    1 onion, cut into wedges
    50g/2oz/½ cup roasted peanuts

1 Trim off any excess fat from the stewing steak, then, using a sharp knife, cut it into 2.5cm/1in chunks.

2 Pour the coconut milk into a large, heavy pan and bring to the boil over a medium heat. Add the chunks of beef, reduce the heat to low, partially cover the pan and simmer gently for about 40 minutes, or until tender.

3 Transfer the coconut cream to a separate pan. Cook over a medium heat, stirring constantly, for about 5 minutes, or until it separates. Stir in the Mussaman curry paste and cook rapidly for 2–3 minutes, until fragrant and thoroughly blended.

4 Return the coconut cream and curry paste mixture to the pan with the beef and stir until thoroughly blended. Simmer for a further 4–5 minutes, stirring occasionally.

5 Stir the fish sauce, sugar, tamarind juice, cardamom pods, cinnamon stick, potato chunks and onion wedges into the beef curry. Continue to simmer for a further 15–20 minutes, or until the potato is cooked and tender.

6 Add the roasted peanuts to the pan and mix well to combine. Cook for about 5 minutes more, then transfer to warmed individual serving bowls and serve immediately.

COOK'S TIP
To make Mussaman curry paste, halve 12 large dried chillies and discard the seeds, then soak the chillies in hot water for about 15 minutes. Remove the chillies from the water and chop finely. Place the chopped chillies in a mortar or food processor and pound or process with 60ml/4 tbsp chopped shallots, 5 garlic cloves, the base of 1 lemon grass stalk and 30ml/2 tbsp chopped fresh galangal. Dry-fry 5ml/1 tsp cumin seeds, 15ml/1 tbsp coriander seeds, 2 cloves and 6 black peppercorns over a low heat for 1–2 minutes. Grind the toasted spices to a powder with a mortar and pestle or spice grinder, then combine with 5ml/1 tsp shrimp paste, 5ml/1 tsp salt, 5ml/1 tsp granulated (white) sugar and 30ml/2 tbsp vegetable oil. Add the shallot mixture to the spice mixture and stir well to make a paste.

CHILLI BEEF <u>WITH</u> BASIL

THIS IS A VERY EASY DISH THAT CHILLI LOVERS WILL ENJOY COOKING AND EATING. USE BIRD'S EYE CHILLIES IF YOU CAN AND FRAGRANT THAI JASMINE RICE TO SERVE.

SERVES TWO

INGREDIENTS

  16–20 large fresh basil leaves,
    plus 30ml/2 tbsp finely
    chopped basil
  about 90ml/6 tbsp groundnut
    (peanut) oil
  275g/10oz rump (round) steak
  30ml/2 tbsp Thai fish sauce
  5ml/1 tsp soft dark brown sugar
  2 fresh red chillies, sliced into rings
  3 garlic cloves, chopped
  5ml/1 tsp chopped fresh root ginger
  1 shallot, thinly sliced
  squeeze of lemon juice
  salt and ground black pepper
  Thai jasmine rice, to serve

3 Reheat the oil until hot, add the chillies, garlic, ginger and shallot, and stir-fry for 30 seconds. Add the beef and chopped basil, and stir-fry for about 3 minutes more. Flavour with lemon juice and add salt and pepper to taste.

4 Transfer to a warmed serving platter, arrange the fried basil leaves over the top and serve immediately with rice. Good accompaniments would be lightly steamed green vegetables or a crisp green salad to provide contrast.

1 Dry the basil leaves thoroughly, if necessary. Heat the oil in a wok. When it is hot, add the basil leaves and fry for about 1 minute until crisp and golden. Scoop out and drain on kitchen paper. Remove the wok from the heat and carefully pour off all but 30ml/2 tbsp of the oil.

2 Cut the steak across the grain into thin strips. In a bowl, mix together the fish sauce and sugar. Add the beef, mix well, then cover and set aside to marinate for about 30 minutes.

COOK'S TIP
Groundnut (peanut) oil is widely used in Chinese cooking. Its ability to be heated to a high temperature without burning makes it ideal for stir-frying. It has a mild, pleasant taste.

Pasta, noodles and rice lend themselves to flavouring

with mild or hot spices. Give a new twist to traditional

pasta dishes in a spicy Penne with Chilli and Broccoli

or Spaghetti with Garlic, Chilli and Oil. Try

tongue-tingling noodle dishes from China and Thailand

as Spicy Sichuan Noodles and Thai Fried Noodles are

enlivened with chillies, limes and coriander. Savour

the flavour of fish and rice with an Aromatic Mussel

Risotto or Spiced Trout Pilaff.

Flame-filled Pasta, Noodle and Rice Main Dishes

PASTA WITH SUGOCASA AND CHILLI

BOTTLED SUGOCASA IS IDEAL FOR PASTA SAUCES, BEING FINER THAN CANNED TOMATOES AND COARSER THAN PASSATA. HERE, IT IS GIVEN A FIERY KICK WITH THE ADDITION OF A LITTLE CHILLI.

SERVES FOUR

INGREDIENTS

500g/1¼lb sugocasa
2 garlic cloves, crushed
150ml/¼ pint/⅔ cup dry white wine
15ml/1 tbsp sun-dried tomato
   purée (paste)
1 fresh red chilli
300g/11oz/2¾ cups dried
   pasta shapes
60ml/4 tbsp finely chopped fresh
   flat leaf parsley
salt and ground black pepper
freshly grated Pecorino cheese,
   to serve

1 Pour the sugocasa into a pan and add the crushed garlic, white wine, sun-dried tomato purée and whole chilli. Bring to the boil. Cover and simmer for about 15 minutes.

2 Bring a large pan of lightly salted water to the boil. Stir in the pasta shapes and cook for 10–12 minutes, or for the time suggested on the packet cooking instructions, until it is al dente.

3 Remove the chilli from the sauce and stir in half the parsley. Taste for seasoning, adding salt and pepper as needed. If you prefer a hotter taste, chop some or all of the chilli and return it to the sauce and heat it through.

4 Drain the pasta and tip into a large heated bowl. Pour the sauce over the pasta and toss to mix. Serve immediately, sprinkled with grated Pecorino and the remaining parsley.

SPAGHETTI WITH GARLIC, CHILLI AND OIL

PASTA DESCRIBED AS AL DENTE *HAS A BIT OF BITE BUT IS STILL RATHER BLAND. DRIED*
RED CHILLIES GIVE MORE THAN A BIT OF AN EDGE TO THIS OTHERWISE BLAND DISH.

1 Bring a large pan of salted water to the boil and add the spaghetti, lowering it into the water gradually, as it softens. Cook for 10–12 minutes, or according to the packet instructions, until the strands are *al dente*.

2 Meanwhile, heat the oil very gently in a small pan. Add the crushed garlic and chopped dried chilli and stir over a low heat until the garlic is just beginning to brown. Remove the chilli and discard it.

3 Drain the pasta and tip it into a large heated bowl. Pour on the oil and garlic mixture, add the parsley and toss vigorously until the pasta glistens. Serve immediately, garnished with extra dried chillies.

SERVES FOUR

INGREDIENTS
400g/14oz fresh or
  dried spaghetti
90ml/6 tbsp extra virgin olive oil
2–4 garlic cloves, crushed
1 dried red chilli, chopped, plus
  extra dried chillies to garnish
1 small handful fresh flat leaf
  parsley, roughly chopped
salt

COOK'S TIPS
• Use a fresh chilli, if you prefer.
• For extra heat, substitute chilli oil for some or all of the olive oil. Be careful when using chilli oil because the flavour becomes very concentrated, so use it sparingly.
• If you like, hand round separately a bowl of freshly grated Parmesan cheese. The delicious flavour of this cheese is better appreciated when fresh. A block will keep well in the refrigerator, wrapped in clear film (plastic wrap).

PENNE WITH CHILLI AND BROCCOLI

THIS QUICK-COOK PASTA DISH IS PACKED FULL OF FLAVOUR AS WELL AS BEING COLOURFUL, DELICIOUS AND NUTRITIOUS. ADJUST THE AMOUNT OF CHILLI ACCORDING TO TASTE.

SERVES FOUR

INGREDIENTS
  450g/1lb/3 cups penne
  450g/1lb small broccoli florets
  30ml/2 tbsp stock
  1 garlic clove, crushed
  1 small red chilli, sliced, or
   2.5ml/½ tsp chilli sauce
  60ml/4 tbsp natural (plain) yogurt
  30ml/2 tbsp toasted pine nuts
   or cashews
  salt and ground black pepper

VARIATION
Green chillies can be used instead of red chillies and toasted almonds make a good substitute for pine nuts.

1 Add the pasta to a large pan of lightly salted, boiling water and return to the boil. Place the broccoli in a steamer basket over the top. Cover and cook for 8–10 minutes, until both the pasta and the broccoli are just tender. Drain.

2 Heat the stock to simmering point and add the crushed garlic and the sliced chilli or chilli sauce. Stir over a low heat for 2–3 minutes.

3 Stir in the broccoli, pasta and yogurt. Adjust the seasoning, sprinkle with toasted pine nuts or cashew nuts and serve hot.

BLACK PASTA <u>WITH</u> SQUID SAUCE

ANOTHER SHELLFISH DISH WITH A SUBTLE, RATHER THAN A STRIDENT, CHILLI FLAVOUR.
DON'T BE TEMPTED TO OMIT THE CHILLI FLAKES.

SERVES FOUR

INGREDIENTS
    105ml/7 tbsp olive oil
    2 shallots, finely chopped
    3 garlic cloves, crushed
    45ml/3 tbsp chopped fresh parsley
    675g/1½lb cleaned squid, cut into
       rings and rinsed
    150ml/¼ pint/⅔ cup dry white wine
    400g/14oz can chopped tomatoes
    2.5ml/½ tsp dried chilli flakes
       or powder
    450g/1lb squid ink tagliatelle
    salt and ground black pepper

1 Heat the oil in a pan and cook the shallots until pale golden, then add the garlic. When the garlic colours a little, add 30ml/2 tbsp of the parsley, stir, then add the squid and stir again. Cook for 3–4 minutes, then pour in the dry white wine.

2 Simmer for a few seconds, then add the tomatoes and chilli flakes. Season with salt and pepper. Cover and simmer gently for about 1 hour, until the squid is tender. Add more water during the cooking time if necessary.

3 Bring a large pan of lightly salted water to the boil and cook the squid ink tagliatelle, following the instructions on the packet, or until it is *al dente*. Drain and return the pasta to the pan. Add the squid sauce and mix well to coat the tagliatelle evenly. Serve in warmed dishes, sprinkling each portion with the remaining chopped parsley.

COOK'S TIPS
• Tagliatelle flavoured with squid ink looks amazing and tastes deliciously of the sea. Look for it in good Italian delicatessens and better supermarkets.
• If you make your own pasta, you can buy sachets of squid ink from delicatessens.
• If you prepare the squid yourself, you will find the ink sac in the innards.

VERMICELLI WITH SPICY CLAM SAUCE

THERE'S A SUBTLE CHILLI FLAVOUR IN THIS ITALIAN DISH. THE TRICK IS TO USE ENOUGH TO MAKE IT LIVELY, AS HERE, BUT NOT SO MUCH THAT YOU CAN'T TASTE THE CLAMS.

SERVES FOUR

INGREDIENTS

  1kg/2¼lb fresh clams, well scrubbed
  250ml/8fl oz/1 cup dry white wine
  2 garlic cloves, bruised
  1 large handful fresh flat leaf parsley
  30ml/2 tbsp olive oil
  1 small onion, finely chopped
  8 ripe Italian plum tomatoes, peeled,
    seeded and finely chopped
  ½–1 fresh red chilli, seeded and
    finely chopped
  350g/12oz dried vermicelli
  salt and ground black pepper

1 Discard any clams that are open or that do not close when sharply tapped against the work surface.

2 Put the wine, garlic and half the parsley into a pan, then the clams. Cover and bring to the boil. Cook for 5 minutes, shaking the pan.

3 Tip the clams into a large colander set over a bowl and let the liquid drain through. Leave the clams until cool enough to handle, then remove about two-thirds of them from their shells, tipping the clam liquor into the bowl of cooking liquid. Discard any clams that have failed to open. Set both shelled and unshelled clams aside, keeping the unshelled clams warm in a bowl covered with a lid.

4 Heat the olive oil in a pan, add the onion and stir over the heat for about 5 minutes until softened and lightly coloured. Add the tomatoes, then strain in the clam cooking liquid. Stir in the chilli and salt and pepper to taste.

5 Bring to the boil, half-cover the pan and simmer gently for 15–20 minutes. Meanwhile, cook the pasta according to the instructions on the packet. Chop the remaining parsley finely.

6 Add the shelled clams to the tomato sauce, stir well and heat through very gently for 2–3 minutes.

7 Drain the cooked pasta well and tip it into a warmed bowl. Taste the sauce for seasoning, then pour the sauce over the pasta and toss everything together well. Garnish with the reserved unshelled clams, arranging them attractively on top of the pasta. Sprinkle the chopped parsley over the pasta and serve immediately.

CHILLI RAVIOLI <u>WITH</u> CRAB

CHILLI PASTA LOOKS AND TASTES SENSATIONAL. ADD A CREAMY CRAB FILLING AND YOU'VE GOT A GREAT TALKING POINT FOR A DINNER PARTY.

SERVES FOUR

INGREDIENTS
 300g/11oz/2¾ cups strong white
  (bread) flour
 5ml/1 tsp salt
 5–10ml/1–2 tsp crushed dried
  red chillies
 3 eggs
 75g/3oz/6 tbsp butter
 juice of 1 lemon

For the filling
 175g/6oz/¾ cup mascarpone
 175g/6oz crab meat
 30ml/2 tbsp finely chopped
  fresh flat leaf parsley
 finely grated rind of 1 lemon
 pinch of crushed dried chillies
 salt and ground black pepper

1 Put the flour, salt and dried chillies in a food processor. Add 1 egg and pulse until mixed. Switch the processor to maximum speed and add the remaining eggs through the feeder tube. As soon as the mixture forms a dough, transfer it to a clean work surface and knead for 5 minutes, until smooth and elastic. Wrap in clear film (plastic wrap) and leave to rest for 15 minutes.

2 Make the filling. Put the mascarpone in a bowl and mash it with a fork. Add the crab meat, parsley, lemon rind and crushed dried chillies, with salt and pepper to taste. Stir well.

3 Using a pasta machine, roll out one-quarter of the pasta dough into a 90cm–1 metre/36–39in strip. Cut into two 45–50cm/18–20in lengths. With a 6cm/2½in fluted cutter, firmly cut out 8 squares from each strip.

4 Using a teaspoon, put a mound of filling in the centre of half the squares. Brush a little water around the edge of the filled squares, then top with the plain squares and press the edges to seal. For a decorative finish, press the edges with the tines of a fork.

5 Put the ravioli on floured dishtowels, sprinkle lightly with flour and leave to dry while repeating the process with the remaining dough to make 32 ravioli altogether.

6 Bring a large pan of lightly salted water to the boil and cook the ravioli for 4–5 minutes. Meanwhile, melt the butter and lemon juice in a small pan until sizzling.

7 Drain the ravioli and divide them among 4 warmed bowls. Drizzle the lemon butter over the ravioli and serve.

CRISPY FRIED RICE VERMICELLI

*MEE KROB IS USUALLY SERVED AT THAI CELEBRATION MEALS. IT IS A CRISP TANGLE OF
FRIED RICE VERMICELLI, TOSSED IN A PIQUANT GARLIC, SWEET AND SOUR SAUCE.*

SERVES FOUR TO SIX

INGREDIENTS
 oil, for frying
 175g/6oz rice vermicelli
 15ml/1 tbsp chopped garlic
 4–6 dried chillies, seeded
  and chopped
 30ml/2 tbsp chopped shallot
 15ml/1 tbsp dried shrimp, rinsed
 115g/4oz/1 cup minced
  (ground) pork
 115g/4oz/1 cup raw prawns
  (shrimp), peeled and chopped
 30ml/2 tbsp brown bean sauce
 30ml/2 tbsp rice wine vinegar
 45ml/3 tbsp Thai fish sauce
 75g/3 tbsp palm sugar (jaggery)
 30ml/2 tbsp tamarind or
  lime juice
 115g/4oz/2 cups beansprouts

For the garnish
 2 spring onions (scallions), shredded
 30ml/2 tbsp fresh coriander
  (cilantro) leaves
 2 heads pickled garlic (optional)
 2-egg omelette, rolled and sliced
 2 red chillies, chopped

3 Add the minced pork and stir-fry until
it is no longer pink, about 3–4 minutes.
Add the prawns and stir-fry for a further
2 minutes. Remove the mixture and
set aside.

4 To the same wok, add the brown
bean sauce, vinegar, fish sauce and
palm sugar. Bring to a gentle boil, stir
to dissolve the sugar and cook until
thick and syrupy.

5 Add the tamarind or lime juice and
adjust the seasoning. It should be
sweet, sour and salty.

6 Reduce the heat. Add the pork and
prawn mixture and the beansprouts to
the sauce, stir to mix.

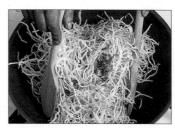

7 Add the rice noodles and toss gently
to coat them with the sauce without
breaking the noodles too much.

8 Transfer the noodles to a platter.
Garnish with spring onions, coriander
leaves, pickled garlic, omelette strips
and red chillies.

1 Heat the oil in a wok. Break the rice
vermicelli apart into small handfuls
about 7.5cm/3in long. Deep-fry in the
hot oil until they puff up. Remove and
drain on kitchen paper.

2 Leave 30ml/2 tbsp of the hot oil in
the wok, add the garlic, chillies,
shallots and shrimp. Fry until fragrant.

THAI FRIED NOODLES

THE CHILLI FLAVOUR SIMPLY TEASES THE TASTE BUDS IN THIS CLASSIC THAI RECIPE. IT IS MADE WITH RICE NOODLES AND IS ONE OF THE NATIONAL DISHES OF THAILAND.

SERVES FOUR TO SIX

INGREDIENTS
350g/12oz rice noodles
45ml/3 tbsp vegetable oil
15ml/1 tbsp chopped garlic
16 raw king prawns (jumbo shrimp),
  shelled, tails left intact
  and deveined
2 eggs, lightly beaten
15ml/1 tbsp dried shrimps, rinsed
30ml/2 tbsp pickled white radish
50g/2oz fried tofu, cut into
  small slivers
2.5ml/½ tsp dried chilli flakes
115g/4oz chives, preferably garlic
  chives, cut into 5cm/2in lengths
225g/8oz/3–4 cups beansprouts
50g/2oz/½ cup roasted peanuts,
  coarsely ground
5ml/1 tsp granulated (white) sugar
15ml/1 tbsp dark soy sauce
30ml/2 tbsp Thai fish sauce
30ml/2 tbsp tamarind or
  lime juice
30ml/2 tbsp coriander (cilantro)
  leaves, to garnish
kaffir lime wedges, to garnish

1 Soak the noodles in warm water for 20–30 minutes, then drain.

2 Heat 15ml/1 tbsp of the oil in a wok. Add the garlic and fry until golden. Stir in the prawns and cook for about 1–2 minutes until pink, tossing from time to time. Remove and set aside.

VARIATION
If you are unable to find kaffir limes use the juiciest variety available.

3 Heat another 15ml/1 tbsp of oil in the wok. Add the eggs and tilt the wok to spread them into a thin sheet. Stir to scramble and break the egg into small pieces. Remove from the wok and set aside with the prawns.

4 Heat the remaining oil in the same wok. Add the dried shrimps, pickled radish, tofu and chilli flakes. Stir briefly. Add the soaked noodles and stir-fry for 5 minutes.

5 Add the chives, half the beansprouts and half the peanuts. Season with the sugar, soy sauce, fish sauce and tamarind or lime juice. Mix well and cook until the noodles are heated through.

6 Return the prawn and egg mixture to the wok and mix with the noodles. Serve immediately, garnished with the rest of the beansprouts, peanuts, the coriander leaves and lime wedges.

SPICY SICHUAN NOODLES

ROASTED NUTS PROVIDE CRUNCH AND A SPICY DRESSING ADDS FLAVOUR IN THIS DISH.

SERVES FOUR

INGREDIENTS
  350g/12oz thick noodles
  175g/6oz cooked chicken, shredded
  50g/2oz/½ cup roasted
    cashew nuts

For the dressing
  4 spring onions (scallions), chopped
  30ml/2 tbsp chopped
    coriander (cilantro)
  2 garlic cloves, chopped
  30ml/2 tbsp smooth peanut butter
  30ml/2 tbsp sweet chilli sauce
  15ml/1 tbsp soy sauce
  15ml/1 tbsp sherry vinegar
  15ml/1 tbsp sesame oil
  30ml/2 tbsp olive oil
  30ml/2 tbsp chicken stock
    or water
  10 toasted Sichuan
    peppercorns, ground

1 Cook the noodles in a pan of boiling water until just tender, following the directions on the packet. Drain, rinse under cold running water and drain well.

2 While the noodles are cooking combine all the ingredients for the dressing in a large bowl and whisk together well.

3 Add the noodles, chicken and nuts to the dressing, toss gently to coat and season to taste. Serve immediately.

SESAME NOODLES WITH SPRING ONIONS

THIS SIMPLE BUT TASTY WARM SALAD CAN BE PREPARED AND COOKED IN JUST A FEW MINUTES.

SERVES FOUR

INGREDIENTS
  2 garlic cloves, peeled and
    coarsely chopped
  30ml/2 tbsp Chinese
    sesame paste
  15ml/1 tbsp dark
    sesame oil
  30ml/2 tbsp soy sauce
  30ml/2 tbsp rice wine
  15ml/1 tbsp honey
  pinch of five-spice powder
  350g/12oz soba or
    buckwheat noodles
  4 spring onions (scallions),
    finely sliced diagonally
  50g/2oz/1 cup beansprouts
  7.5cm/3in piece of cucumber,
    cut into batons
  toasted sesame seeds
  salt and ground black pepper

1 Process the garlic, sesame paste, oil, soy sauce, rice wine, honey and five-spice powder with a pinch each of salt and pepper in a blender or food processor until smooth.

2 Cook the noodles in a pan of boiling water until just tender, following the directions on the packet. Drain the noodles immediately and tip them into a bowl.

3 Toss the hot noodles with the dressing and the spring onions. Top with the beansprouts, cucumber and sesame seeds and serve.

COOK'S TIP
If you can't find Chinese sesame paste, then use either tahini paste or smooth peanut butter instead.

THAI MIXED VEGETABLE CURRY <u>WITH</u> LEMON GRASS RICE

FRAGRANT JASMINE RICE, SUBTLY FLAVOURED WITH LEMON GRASS AND CARDAMOM, IS THE PERFECT ACCOMPANIMENT TO THIS VEGETABLE CURRY.

SERVES FOUR

INGREDIENTS
   10ml/2 tsp vegetable oil
   400ml/14fl oz/1⅔ cups coconut milk
   300ml/½ pint/1¼ cups
      vegetable stock
   225g/8oz new potatoes, halved or
      quartered if large
   130g/4½oz baby corn cobs
   5ml/1 tsp granulated (white) sugar
   185g/6½oz/generous 1 cup
      broccoli florets
   1 red (bell) pepper, seeded and
      sliced lengthways
   115g/4oz spinach, tough stalks
      removed, leaves shredded
   30ml/2 tbsp chopped fresh
      coriander (cilantro)
   salt and ground black pepper

For the spice paste
   1 fresh red chilli, seeded and chopped
   3 fresh green chillies, seeded and
      roughly chopped
   1 lemon grass stalk, outer layers
      removed and lower 5cm/2in chopped
   2 shallots, chopped
   finely grated rind of 1 lime
   2 garlic cloves, chopped
   5ml/1 tsp ground coriander
   2.5ml/½ tsp ground cumin
   1cm/½in fresh galangal,
      chopped (optional)
   30ml/2 tbsp chopped fresh
      coriander (cilantro)

For the rice
   225g/8oz/generous 1 cup jasmine
      rice, rinsed and drained
   1 lemon grass stalk, outer leaves
      removed, cut into 3 pieces
   6 cardamom pods, bruised
   475ml/16fl oz/2 cups water

1 Make the spice paste by grinding all the ingredients to a coarse paste in a food processor or blender. Scrape the paste out of the food processor or blender into a bowl, using a plastic spatula.

2 Heat the oil in a large heavy pan and fry the spice paste for 1–2 minutes, stirring constantly.

3 Pour in the coconut milk and stock, stir well and bring to the boil. Reduce the heat, add the potatoes and simmer for 15 minutes.

4 Meanwhile, prepare the rice. Tip the rice into a large pan and add the lemon grass and cardamom pods. Pour over the measured water.

COOK'S TIP
Save preparation time by making the spice paste the day before it is required. Cover and refrigerate.

5 Bring to the boil, then reduce the heat, cover, and cook for 10–15 minutes until the water has been absorbed and the rice is tender and slightly sticky. Season with salt, and leave to stand, covered, for 10 minutes.

6 Add the baby corn to the potatoes in the pan, with salt and pepper to taste, and cook for 2 minutes. Stir in the sugar, broccoli and red pepper, and cook for 2 minutes or until the vegetables are tender. Stir in the shredded spinach and half the fresh coriander. Cook for 2 minutes.

7 Remove the whole spices from the rice, fluff up the grains with a fork, then spoon into heated bowls. Top with the curry, sprinkled with the remaining fresh coriander.

VARIATIONS
• Substitute Thai aubergines (eggplant) for the potatoes.
• Use baby carrots instead of corn cobs.
• For non-vegetarians, add cooked prawns (shrimp) and just heat through.
• For protein, add toasted cashew nuts.

PERSIAN RICE <u>WITH A</u> TAHDEEG

PERSIAN OR IRANIAN CUISINE IS EXOTIC AND DELICIOUS. A TAHDEEG IS THE GLORIOUS,
GOLDEN RICE CRUST OR "DIG" THAT FORMS ON THE BASE OF THE PAN.

SERVES EIGHT

INGREDIENTS

   450g/1lb/generous 2¼ cups basmati
     rice, rinsed thoroughly and soaked
   2 garlic cloves, crushed
   2 onions, 1 chopped, 1 thinly sliced
   150ml/¼ pint/⅔ cup sunflower oil
   150g/5oz/⅔ cup green lentils, soaked
   600ml/1 pint/2½ cups stock
   50g/2oz/⅓ cup raisins
   10ml/2 tsp ground coriander
   45ml/3 tbsp tomato purée (paste)
   a few saffron threads
   1 egg yolk, beaten
   10ml/2 tsp natural (plain) yogurt
   75g/3oz/6 tbsp butter, melted
     and strained
   extra oil, for frying
   salt and ground black pepper

1 Drain the soaked rice, then cook it in plenty of boiling salted water for 10–12 minutes or until tender. Drain again.

2 Soak the saffron threads in a little hot water.

3 In a large pan, cook the garlic and chopped onion in 30ml/2 tbsp oil for 5 minutes, Then add the lentils, stock, raisins, coriander, tomato purée and seasoning. Bring the lentils to the boil, then cover and simmer for 20 minutes.

4 Remove about 120ml/8 tbsp of the cooked rice and mix with the egg yolk and yogurt. Season well.

5 In a large pan, heat about two-thirds of the remaining oil and sprinkle the egg and yogurt rice evenly over the base.

6 Sprinkle the remaining rice into the pan, alternating it with the lentil mixture. Build up in a pyramid shape away from the sides of the pan, finishing with plain rice on top.

7 With a long wooden spoon handle, make three holes down to the base of the pan and drizzle over the butter. Bring to a high heat, then wrap the pan lid in a clean, wet dishtowel and place firmly on top. When a good head of steam appears, turn the heat down to low. Cook for about 30 minutes.

8 Meanwhile, cook the sliced onion in the remaining oil until browned and crisp. Drain well and set aside.

9 Remove the rice and lentil pan from the heat, still covered, and stand it briefly in a sink of cold water for a minute or two to loosen the base. Remove the lid and mix a few spoons of the white rice with the saffron water.

10 Toss the rice and lentils together in the pan and spoon on to a serving dish in a mound. Sprinkle the saffron rice on top. Break up the rice crust on the pan base and place pieces of it around the mound. Sprinkle over the crispy fried onions and serve.

FESTIVE RICE

THIS THAI DISH IS TRADITIONALLY SERVED SHAPED INTO A CONE AND SURROUNDED BY A VARIETY OF ACCOMPANIMENTS.

SERVES EIGHT

INGREDIENTS

450g/1lb/generous 2¼ cups
   Thai fragrant rice
60ml/4 tbsp oil
2 garlic cloves, crushed
2 onions, finely sliced
5cm/2in fresh turmeric, peeled
   and crushed
750ml/1¼ pints/3 cups water
400ml/14fl oz can coconut milk
1–2 lemon grass
   stalks, bruised

For the accompaniments
   omelette strips
   2 fresh red chillies, finely chopped
   cucumber chunks
   tomato wedges
   deep-fried onions
   prawn (shrimp) crackers

1 Wash the rice in several changes of water. Drain well.

2 Heat the oil in a wok and gently cook the garlic, onions and turmeric for a few minutes, until they are softened but not browned.

3 Add the rice and stir well so that each grain is thoroughly coated. Pour in the water and coconut milk and add the lemon grass.

4 Bring to the boil, stirring well. Cover the pan and cook gently for 15–20 minutes, or until all of the liquid has been completely absorbed.

5 Remove the pan from the heat. Cover with a clean dishtowel, put on the lid and leave to stand in a warm place for 15 minutes.

6 Remove the lemon grass, turn out on to a serving platter and garnish the dish with the accompaniments.

INDIAN PILAU RICE

THIS LIGHTLY SPICED DISH CAN BE SERVED ON ITS OWN OR AS AN ACCOMPANIMENT TO A CURRY.

SERVES FOUR

INGREDIENTS

225g/8oz/generous 1 cup basmati
  rice, rinsed well
30ml/2 tbsp vegetable oil
1 small onion, finely chopped
1 garlic clove, crushed
5ml/1 tsp fennel seeds
15ml/1 tbsp sesame seeds
2.5ml/½ tsp ground turmeric
5ml/1 tsp ground cumin
1.5ml/½ tsp salt
2 whole cloves
4 green cardamom pods,
  lightly crushed
5 black peppercorns
450ml/¾ pint/scant 2 cups
  vegetable stock
15ml/1 tbsp ground almonds
coriander (cilantro) sprigs,
  to garnish

1 Soak the basmati rice in a pan of cold water for 30 minutes. Heat the vegetable oil in a pan, and then add the chopped onion and crushed garlic, and cook all together gently for 5–6 minutes, stirring occasionally, until softened.

2 Stir in the fennel and sesame seeds, the turmeric, cumin, salt, cloves, cardamom pods and peppercorns and cook for about 1 minute.

3 Drain the rice well, add it to the pan and stir-fry for a further 3 minutes.

4 Pour in the vegetable stock. Bring to the boil, then cover the pan, reduce the heat to very low and simmer very gently for 20 minutes, without removing the lid, until all the liquid has been absorbed.

5 Remove from the heat and leave to stand for 2–3 minutes. Fork up the rice and stir in the ground almonds. Garnish the rice with coriander sprigs.

OKRA FRIED RICE

SLICED OKRA PROVIDES A WONDERFUL CREAMY TEXTURE TO THIS DELICIOUS, SIMPLE DISH.

SERVES THREE TO FOUR

INGREDIENTS

30ml/2 tbsp vegetable oil
15ml/1 tbsp butter or margarine
1 garlic clove, crushed
½ red onion, finely chopped
115g/4oz okra, trimmed
30ml/2 tbsp diced green and red
  (bell) peppers
2.5ml/½ tsp dried thyme
2 green chillies, finely chopped
2.5ml/½ tsp five-spice powder
1 vegetable stock (bouillon) cube
30ml/2 tbsp soy sauce
15ml/1 tbsp chopped
  coriander (cilantro)
225g/8oz/3 cups cooked rice
salt and ground black pepper
coriander sprigs, to garnish

1 Heat the oil and the butter or margarine in a frying pan, add the garlic and onion and cook over a medium heat for 5 minutes, until soft.

2 Thinly slice the okra, add to the frying pan and stir-fry gently for a further 6–7 minutes.

3 Add the green and red peppers, thyme, chillies and five-spice powder and cook for 3 minutes, then crumble in the stock cube.

4 Add the soy sauce, coriander and rice and heat through, stirring. Season with salt and pepper. Serve hot, garnished with coriander sprigs.

CHILLI CHIVE RICE WITH MUSHROOMS

WHILE COOKING, THIS RICE DISH DEVELOPS A WONDERFUL AROMA, WHICH IS MATCHED BY THE COMPLEMENTARY FLAVOURS OF CHILLI, GARLIC CHIVES AND FRESH CORIANDER.

3 Add the rice to the onions and fry over a low heat, stirring frequently, for 4–5 minutes. Pour in the stock mixture, then stir in the salt and a good grinding of black pepper.

4 Bring to the boil, stir and reduce the heat to very low. Cover tightly and cook for 15–20 minutes, until the rice has absorbed all the liquid.

5 Remove from the heat. Lay a clean, folded dishtowel over the open pan and press on the lid, jamming it firmly in place. Leave to stand for 10 minutes. The towel will absorb the steam while the rice becomes completely tender.

6 Meanwhile, heat the remaining oil in a frying pan and cook the mushrooms for 5–6 minutes, until tender and browned. Add the remaining chives and cook for a further 1–2 minutes.

7 Stir the mixed, sliced mushrooms and chopped fresh coriander leaves into the cooked rice. Adjust the seasoning, transfer to a warmed serving dish and serve immediately, sprinkled with the cashew nuts.

SERVES FOUR

INGREDIENTS
- 350g/12oz/1¾ cups long grain rice
- 60ml/4 tbsp groundnut (peanut) oil
- 1 small onion, finely chopped
- 2 fresh green chillies, seeded and finely chopped
- a handful of garlic chives, chopped
- 15g/½oz/¼ cup fresh coriander (cilantro)
- 600ml/1 pint/2½ cups vegetable or mushroom stock
- 5ml/1 tsp salt
- 250g/9oz/3–3½ cups mixed mushrooms, thickly sliced
- 50g/2oz/½ cup cashew nuts, fried in 15ml/1 tbsp oil until golden brown
- ground black pepper

1 Wash and drain the rice. Heat half the oil in a pan and cook the onion and chillies over a low heat, stirring occasionally, for 10–12 minutes, until soft, but not browned.

2 Set half the garlic chives aside. Cut the stalks off the coriander and set the leaves aside. Purée the remaining chives and the coriander stalks with the stock in a blender or food processor.

COOK'S TIP
Wild mushrooms are often expensive, but they do have distinctive flavours. Mixing them with cultivated mushrooms is an economical way of using them. Look for ceps, chanterelles, oyster, morels and horse mushrooms.

BROWN RICE <u>WITH</u> LIME <u>AND</u> LEMON GRASS

IT IS UNUSUAL TO FIND BROWN RICE GIVEN THE THAI TREATMENT, BUT THE NUTTY FLAVOUR OF THE GRAINS IS HERE ENHANCED BY THE FRAGRANCE OF LIMES AND LEMON GRASS.

SERVES FOUR

INGREDIENTS

2 limes
1 lemon grass stalk
225g/8oz/generous 1 cup brown
  long grain rice
15ml/1 tbsp olive oil
1 onion, chopped
2.5cm/1in piece fresh root ginger,
  peeled and finely chopped
7.5ml/1½ tsp coriander seeds
7.5ml/1½ tsp cumin seeds
750ml/1¼ pints/3 cups
  vegetable stock
60ml/4 tbsp chopped fresh
  coriander (cilantro)
spring onion (scallion) green and
  toasted coconut strips, to garnish
lime wedges, to serve

1 Pare the limes, using a cannelle knife (zester) or fine grater, taking care to avoid cutting the bitter pith. Set the rind aside. Finely chop the lower portion of the lemon grass stalk and set it aside.

2 Rinse the rice in plenty of cold water until the water runs clear. Tip it into a sieve (strainer) and drain thoroughly.

3 Heat the oil in a large pan. Add the onion, ginger, coriander and cumin seeds, lemon grass and lime rind and cook over a low heat for 2–3 minutes.

4 Add the rice to the pan and cook, stirring constantly, for 1 minute, then pour in the stock and bring to the boil. Reduce the heat to very low and cover the pan. Cook gently for 30 minutes, then check the rice. If it is still crunchy, cover the pan and cook for 3–5 minutes more. Remove from the heat.

5 Stir in the fresh coriander, fluff up the rice grains with a fork, cover the pan and leave to stand for 10 minutes. Transfer to a warmed dish, garnish with spring onion green and toasted coconut strips, and serve with lime wedges.

RICE WITH DILL AND SPICY BEANS

THIS SPICED RICE DISH IS A FAVOURITE IN IRAN, WHERE IT IS KNOWN AS BAGHALI POLO.
SAFFRON ADDS A WONDERFUL COLOUR AS WELL AS FLAVOUR TO THE RICE.

4 Pour the remaining melted butter over the rice. Sprinkle with the cinnamon and cumin. Cover the pan with a clean dishtowel and secure with a tight-fitting lid, lifting the corners of the cloth back over the lid. Steam over a low heat for 30–45 minutes.

5 Mix 45ml/3 tbsp of the rice with the saffron water. Spoon the remaining rice on to a large serving plate and sprinkle on the saffron-flavoured rice to decorate. Serve with lamb or chicken.

COOK'S TIP
Saffron may seem expensive, however you only need a little to add flavour and colour to a variety of savoury and sweet dishes. And, as long as it is kept dry and dark, it never goes off.

SERVES FOUR

INGREDIENTS
   275g/10oz/scant 1½ cups basmati
     rice, soaked in salted water for
     3 hours
   45ml/3 tbsp melted butter
   175g/6oz/1½ cups broad (fava)
     beans, fresh or frozen
   90ml/6 tbsp finely chopped fresh dill
   5ml/1 tsp ground cinnamon
   5ml/1 tsp ground cumin
   2–3 saffron threads, soaked in
     15ml/ 1 tbsp boiling water
   salt

1 Drain the rice and then boil it in fresh salted water for 5 minutes. Reduce the heat and simmer very gently for 10 minutes, until half cooked. Drain and rinse in warm water.

2 Put 15ml/1 tbsp of the butter in a non-stick pan and add enough rice to cover the base. Add a quarter of the beans and a little dill.

3 Add another layer of rice, then a layer of beans and dill and continue layering until all the beans and dill are used up, finishing with a layer of rice. Cook over a low heat for 10 minutes.

MEXICAN RICE

CHILLIES PLAY A SUPPORTING ROLE IN THIS SOUTH AMERICAN RECIPE. LEAVING THEM
WHOLE LIMITS THEIR IMPACT, BUT STILL MAKES A CONTRIBUTION TO THE FINISHED DISH.

SERVES SIX

INGREDIENTS
200g/7oz/1 cup long grain rice
200g/7oz can chopped tomatoes in
  tomato juice
½ onion, roughly chopped
2 garlic cloves, roughly chopped
30ml/2 tbsp vegetable oil
450ml/¾ pint/scant 2 cups
  vegetable stock
2.5ml/½ tsp salt
3 fresh green fresno chillies or other
  fresh green chillies
150g/5oz/1 cup frozen peas
ground black pepper

1 Put the rice in a large heatproof bowl
and pour over boiling water to cover.
Stir once, then leave to stand for
10 minutes. Drain, rinse under cold
water, then drain again. Leave in the
strainer and set aside to dry slightly.

2 Meanwhile, pour the tomatoes and
juice into a food processor or blender,
add the onion and garlic, and process
until smooth.

3 Heat the oil in a large, heavy pan, add
the rice and cook over a medium heat
until it becomes a delicate golden
brown. Stir occasionally to ensure that
the rice does not stick to the base of the
pan. Reduce the heat if the rice begins
to darken too much.

4 Add the tomato mixture and stir over
a medium heat until all the liquid has
been absorbed. Stir in the stock, salt,
whole chillies and peas.

5 Continue to cook the mixture, stirring
occasionally, until all the liquid has
been absorbed and the rice is just
tender. Season with pepper.

6 Remove the pan from the heat, cover
it with a tight-fitting lid and leave it to
stand in a warm place for 5–10 minutes.
Remove the chillies, fluff up the rice
lightly and serve, sprinkled with black
pepper. The chillies can be used as a
garnish, if you like.

COOK'S TIP
Do not stir the rice too often after you
add the stock or the grains will break
down and the mixture will quickly
become starchy.

SPICY RICE CAKES

THESE FLAVOURSOME SPICED CAKES ARE AN IDEAL WAY TO USE UP LEFTOVER RICE.

MAKES SIXTEEN

INGREDIENTS
1 garlic clove, crushed
1cm/½ in piece fresh root ginger,
   peeled and finely chopped
1.5ml/¼ tsp ground turmeric
5ml/1 tsp sugar
2.5ml/½ tsp salt
5ml/1 tsp chilli sauce
10ml/2 tsp fish or soy sauce
30ml/2 tbsp chopped fresh
   coriander (cilantro)
juice of ½ lime
115g/4oz/generous ½ cup dry weight
   long grain rice, cooked
peanuts, chopped
vegetable oil, for deep-frying
coriander sprigs, to garnish

1 In a food processor, process the garlic, ginger and turmeric. Add the sugar, salt, chilli and fish or soy sauce, coriander and lime juice.

2 Add three-quarters of the cooked rice and process until smooth and sticky. Transfer to a mixing bowl and stir in the remainder of the rice. Wet your hands and shape into thumb-size balls.

3 Roll the balls in chopped peanuts to coat evenly. Then set aside until ready to cook and serve.

VARIATION
Replace the chilli sauce with a small red chilli, such as a red serranos or a mild red wax chilli.

4 Heat the vegetable oil in a deep frying pan or wok. Prepare a tray lined with kitchen paper to drain the rice cakes. Deep-fry three cakes at a time until crisp and golden, remove with a slotted spoon, then drain on the kitchen paper and continue cooking the remaining mixture in the same way. Serve hot.

RED RICE RISSOLES

A MELTING CHEESE CENTRE MAKES THESE SPICED RICE RISSOLES A REAL TREAT.

SERVES SIX

INGREDIENTS
1 large red onion, chopped
1 red (bell) pepper, chopped
2 garlic cloves, crushed
1 red chilli, finely chopped
30ml/2 tbsp olive oil
25g/1oz/2 tbsp butter
225g/8oz/generous 1 cup risotto rice
1 litre/1¾ pints/4 cups stock
4 sun-dried tomatoes, chopped
30ml/2 tbsp tomato purée (paste)
10ml/2 tsp dried oregano
45ml/3 tbsp chopped fresh parsley
150g/6oz cheese, e.g. red Leicester
   or smoked Cheddar
1 egg, beaten
115g/4oz/1 cup dried breadcrumbs
oil, for deep-frying
salt and ground black pepper

1 Cook the onion, pepper, garlic and chilli in a pan with the olive oil and butter for 5 minutes. Stir in the rice and cook for a further 2 minutes.

2 Pour in the stock and add the sun-dried tomatoes, purée, oregano and seasoning. Bring to the boil, stirring occasionally, then cover and simmer for 20 minutes.

3 Stir in the parsley, then turn into a shallow dish and chill until firm. When cold, divide into 12 and shape into equal balls.

4 Cut the cheese into 12 pieces and press a piece into the centre of each rice rissole. Shape the rissole mixture around the cheese to form a seal.

5 Put the beaten egg in one bowl and the breadcrumbs into another. Dip the rissoles first into the egg, then into the breadcrumbs, coating each of them evenly and completely.

6 Place the rissoles on a plate and chill again for 30 minutes. Fill a deep frying pan one-third full of oil and heat until a cube of day-old bread browns in under a minute.

7 Fry the rissoles, in batches, for about 3–4 minutes, reheating the oil in between. Drain on kitchen paper and keep warm, uncovered. Serve with a side salad.

PISTACHIO PILAFF

SAFFRON AND GINGER ARE TRADITIONAL RICE SPICES AND ESPECIALLY DELICIOUS WHEN MIXED WITH FRESH PISTACHIOS.

SERVES FOUR

INGREDIENTS
3 onions
60ml/4 tbsp olive oil
2 garlic cloves, crushed
2.5cm/1in piece fresh root
   ginger, grated
1 green chilli, chopped
2 carrots, coarsely grated
225g/8oz/generous 1 cup basmati
   rice, rinsed
1.5ml/¼ tsp saffron threads, crushed
450ml/¾ pint/scant 2 cups stock
5cm/2in cinnamon stick
5ml/1 tsp ground coriander
75g/3oz/¾ cup fresh pistachios
450g/1lb fresh leaf spinach
5ml/1 tsp garam masala
salt and ground black pepper
tomato salad, to serve

1 Coarsely chop two of the onions. Heat half the oil in a large pan and cook the chopped onions with half the garlic, the ginger and the chilli for 5 minutes, until softened.

COOK'S TIP
Saffron adds an exquisite scent that is not equalled by any other spice, but turmeric will supply a delicate yellow colour if used in moderate quantities.

2 Mix in the carrots and rice, cook for 1 more minute and then add the saffron, stock, cinnamon and coriander. Season well. Bring to the boil, then cover and simmer gently for 10 minutes without lifting the lid.

3 Remove from the heat and leave to stand, uncovered, for 5 minutes. Add the pistachios, mixing them in with a fork. Remove the cinnamon stick and keep the rice warm.

4 Thinly slice the third onion and cook in the remaining oil for about 3 minutes. Stir in the spinach. Cover and cook for another 2 minutes.

5 Add the garam masala powder. Cook until just tender, then drain and coarsely chop the spinach.

6 Spoon the spinach around the edge of a round serving dish and pile the pilaff in the centre. Serve immediately with a tomato salad.

BASMATI <u>AND</u> NUT PILAFF

USE WHATEVER NUTS ARE YOUR FAVOURITE IN THIS DISH — EVEN UNSALTED PEANUTS ARE GOOD, ALTHOUGH ALMONDS, CASHEW NUTS OR PISTACHIOS ARE MORE EXOTIC.

SERVES FOUR TO SIX

INGREDIENTS
  225g/8oz/generous 1 cup
    basmati rice
  1 onion, chopped
  1 garlic clove, crushed
  1 large carrot,
    coarsely grated
  15–30ml/1–2 tbsp
    sunflower oil
  5ml/1 tsp cumin seeds
  10ml/2 tsp ground coriander
  10ml/2 tsp black mustard
    seeds (optional)
  4 green cardamom pods
  450ml/¾ pint/scant 2 cups
    stock or water
  1 bay leaf
  75g/3oz/¾ cup
    unsalted nuts
  salt and ground black pepper
  fresh chopped parsley or coriander
    (cilantro), to garnish

1 Wash the rice in a sieve (strainer) under cold running water. If there is time, soak the rice for 30 minutes, then drain it well in a sieve.

2 In a large shallow frying pan, gently cook the onion, garlic and carrot in the oil for 3–4 minutes.

3 Stir in the rice and spices and cook for a further 1–2 minutes so that the grains are coated in oil.

4 Pour in the stock or water, add the bay leaf and season well. Bring to the boil, cover and simmer very gently.

5 Remove from the heat without lifting the lid. Leave to stand on one side for about 5 minutes.

6 If the rice is cooked, there will be steam holes in the centre of the pan. Discard the bay and cardamom pods.

7 Stir in the nuts and check the seasoning. Sprinkle over the chopped parsley or coriander.

SPICED TROUT PILAFF

SMOKED TROUT MIGHT SEEM AN UNUSUAL PARTNER FOR RICE, BUT THIS IS A WINNING COMBINATION,
AND THE ADDITION OF HERBS AND SPICES HELPS CUT THROUGH THE RICHNESS OF THE FISH.

SERVES FOUR

INGREDIENTS

225g/8oz/generous 1 cup
  basmati rice
40g/1½oz/3 tbsp butter
2 onions, sliced into rings
1 garlic clove, crushed
2 bay leaves
2 whole cloves
2 green cardamom pods
2.5cm/2in cinnamon sticks
5ml/1 tsp cumin seeds
4 hot-smoked trout fillets, skinned
50g/2oz/½ cup slivered (sliced)
  almonds, toasted
50g/2oz/scant ½ cup seedless raisins
30ml/2 tbsp chopped fresh parsley
mango chutney and poppadums,
  to serve

1 Wash the rice thoroughly in several changes of water and drain well. Set aside. Melt the butter in a large frying pan and cook the onions until well browned, stirring frequently.

2 Add the garlic, bay leaves, cloves, cardamom pods, cinnamon and cumin seeds and stir-fry for 1 minute.

3 Stir in the rice, then add 600ml/ 1 pint/2½ cups boiling water. Bring to the boil. Cover the pan tightly, reduce the heat and cook very gently for 20–25 minutes, until the water has been absorbed and the rice is tender.

4 Flake the smoked trout and add to the pan with the almonds and raisins. Fork through gently. Cover the pan and allow the smoked trout to warm in the rice for a few minutes.

5 Sprinkle over the parsley and serve with mango chutney and poppadums.

AROMATIC MUSSEL RISOTTO

*FRESH ROOT GINGER ADDS A DISTINCTIVE FLAVOUR TO THIS DISH, WHILE THE GREEN
CHILLIES GIVE IT A LITTLE HEAT. USE JALAPEÑOS OR SERRANOS.*

SERVES THREE TO FOUR

INGREDIENTS
   900g/2lb live mussels
   about 250ml/8fl oz/1 cup dry
     white wine
   30ml/2 tbsp olive oil
   1 onion, chopped
   2 garlic cloves, crushed
   1–2 fresh green chillies, seeded and
     finely sliced
   2.5cm/1in piece of fresh root
     ginger, grated
   275g/10oz/1½ cups risotto rice
   900ml/1½ pints/3¾ cups simmering
     fish stock
   30ml/2 tbsp chopped fresh
     coriander (cilantro)
   30ml/2 tbsp double (heavy) cream
   salt and ground black pepper

1 Scrub the mussels, discarding any
that do not close when sharply tapped.
Place in a large pan. Add half the wine
and bring to the boil. Cover the pan and
cook the mussels for 4–5 minutes until
they have opened, shaking the pan
occasionally. Drain, reserving the liquid
and discarding any mussels that have
failed to open. Remove most of the
mussels from their shells, reserving a
few in their shells for decoration. Strain
the mussel liquid.

2 Heat the oil and fry the onion and
garlic for 3–4 minutes until beginning to
soften. Stir in the chillies. Continue to
cook over a low heat for 1–2 minutes,
stirring frequently, then stir in the
grated ginger and fry very gently for
1 minute more.

3 Add the rice and cook over a medium
heat for 2 minutes, stirring, until the
rice is coated in oil and the grains
become translucent.

4 Stir in the reserved cooking liquid
from the mussels. When this has been
absorbed, add the remaining wine and
cook, stirring, until this has been
absorbed. Now add the hot fish stock, a
little at a time, making sure that each
addition has been absorbed before
adding the next.

5 When the rice is about three-quarters
cooked, stir in the shelled mussels. Add
the coriander and season. Continue
adding stock to the risotto until it is
creamy and the rice is tender but
slightly firm in the centre.

6 Remove the risotto from the heat, stir
in the cream, cover and leave to rest for
a few minutes. Warm a serving dish and
spoon in the risotto, garnish with the
reserved mussels in their shells, and
serve immediately.

SQUID AND CHILLI RISOTTO

SQUID NEEDS TO BE COOKED VERY QUICKLY OR VERY SLOWLY. HERE THE SQUID IS MARINATED IN LIME AND KIWI FRUIT — A POPULAR METHOD IN NEW ZEALAND FOR TENDERIZING SQUID.

SERVES THREE TO FOUR

INGREDIENTS
about 450g/1lb squid
about 45ml/3 tbsp olive oil
15g/½oz/1 tbsp butter
1 onion, finely chopped
2 garlic cloves, crushed
1 fresh red chilli, seeded and
    finely sliced
275g/10oz/1½ cups risotto rice
175ml/6fl oz/¾ cup dry white wine
1 litre/1¾ pints/4 cups simmering
    fish stock
30ml/2 tbsp chopped fresh
    coriander (cilantro)
salt and ground black pepper

For the marinade
2 ripe kiwi fruit, chopped
    and mashed
1 fresh red chilli, seeded and sliced
30ml/2 tbsp lime juice

1 If not already cleaned, prepare the squid by cutting off the tentacles at the base and pulling to remove the quill. Discard the quill and intestines, if necessary, and pull away the thin outer skin. Rinse the body and cut into thin strips: cut the tentacles into short pieces, discarding both the beak and the eyes.

2 Put the kiwi fruit for the marinade in a bowl, then stir in the chilli and lime juice. Add the squid, stirring to coat all the strips in the mixture. Season with salt and pepper, cover with clear film (plastic wrap) and set aside in the refrigerator for 4 hours or overnight.

3 Drain the squid. Heat 15ml/1 tbsp of the olive oil in a frying pan and cook the strips, in batches if necessary, for about 30–60 seconds over a high heat. It is important that the squid cooks very quickly to keep it tender.

4 Transfer the cooked squid to a plate and set aside. Don't worry if some of the marinade clings to the squid, but if too much juice accumulates in the pan, pour this into a jug and add more olive oil when cooking the next batch, so that the squid fries rather than simmers. Reserve the accumulated juices in a jug.

5 Heat the remaining oil with the butter in a large pan and gently fry the onion and garlic for 5–6 minutes until soft. Add the sliced chilli to the pan and fry for 1 minute more.

COOK'S TIPS
• You can only make a true risotto with Italian risotto rice. Names to look for are Arborio, Carnaroli, Roma and Baldo. These are the rices that give the right kind of creamy texture.
• As in this recipe, always use a well-flavoured stock.

6 Add the rice. Cook for a few minutes, stirring, until the rice is coated with oil and is slightly translucent, then stir in the wine until it has been absorbed.

7 Gradually add the hot stock and the reserved cooking liquid from the squid, a ladleful at a time, stirring the rice constantly and waiting until each quantity of stock has been absorbed before adding the next.

8 When the rice is about three-quarters cooked, stir in the squid and continue cooking the risotto until all the stock has been absorbed and the rice is tender, but retains a bit of "bite". Stir in the chopped coriander, cover with the lid or a dishtowel, and leave to rest for a few minutes before serving.

VARIATIONS
• Use a long hot chilli, such as cayenne, for this dish, or try a milder variety, such as a red fresno.
• You can use a habanero if you like, but one-quarter or half will probably be sufficient, and remember to wear gloves when you handle it.

LOUISIANA SHELLFISH GUMBO

GUMBO IS A SOUP, BUT IS SERVED OVER RICE AS A MAIN COURSE. IN THIS VERSION,
CHILLI IS ADDED TO THE "HOLY TRINITY" OF ONION, CELERY AND SWEET PEPPER.

SERVES SIX

INGREDIENTS

450g/1lb fresh mussels
450g/1lb raw prawns (shrimp),
    in the shell
1 cooked crab, about 1kg/2¼lb
a small bunch of parsley, leaves
    chopped and stalks reserved
150ml/¼ pint/⅔ cup vegetable oil
115g/4oz/1 cup plain
    (all-purpose) flour
1 green (bell) pepper, seeded
    and chopped
1 large onion, chopped
2 celery sticks, sliced
1 fresh green chilli, seeded
    and chopped
3 garlic cloves, finely chopped
75g/3oz smoked spiced sausage,
    skinned and sliced
275g/10oz/1½ cups white long
    grain rice
6 spring onions (scallions), sliced
Tabasco sauce, to taste
salt

1 Wash the mussels in several changes of cold water, pulling away the black "beards". Discard broken mussels or any that do not close when tapped firmly.

2 Bring 250ml/8fl oz/1 cup water to the boil in a deep pan. Add the prepared mussels, cover the pan tightly and cook over a high heat, shaking frequently, for 3 minutes. As the mussels open, lift them out with tongs into a strainer set over a bowl. Discard any that fail to open. Shell the mussels, discarding most of the shells but reserving a few.

3 Peel the prawns and set them aside, reserving a few for the garnish. Put the shells and heads into the pan.

4 Remove all the meat from the crab, separating the brown and white meat. Add all the pieces of shell to the pan and stir in 5ml/1 tsp salt.

5 Return the mussel liquid from the bowl to the pan and make it up to 2 litres/3½ pints/8 cups with water. Bring the shellfish stock to the boil, skimming it regularly. When there is no more froth on the surface, add the parsley stalks and simmer for 15 minutes. Cool the reduced stock, then strain into a liquid measure and make it up to 2 litres/3½ pints/8 cups with water.

6 Heat the oil in a heavy pan and stir in the flour. Stir constantly over a medium heat with a wooden spoon or whisk until the roux reaches a golden-brown colour. Immediately add the pepper, onion, celery, chilli and garlic. Continue cooking for about 3 minutes until the onion is soft. Stir in the sausage. Reheat the stock.

7 Stir the brown crab meat into the roux, then ladle in the hot stock a little at a time, stirring constantly until it has all been smoothly incorporated. Bring to a low boil, partially cover the pan, then simmer for 30 minutes.

8 Meanwhile, cook the rice in plenty of lightly salted boiling water until the grains are tender.

9 Add the prawns, mussels, white crab meat and spring onions to the gumbo. Return to the boil and season with salt if necessary. Taste and add a dash or two of Tabasco sauce to heighten the heat generated by the chilli. Simmer for a further minute, then add the chopped parsley leaves. Serve immediately, ladling the soup over the hot rice in soup plates.

COOK'S TIP
It is vital to stir constantly to darken the roux without burning. Should black specks occur at any stage of cooking, discard the roux and start again. Have the pepper, onion, celery, chilli and garlic ready to add to the roux the minute it reaches the correct golden-brown stage, as this stops it from becoming too dark.

SHELLFISH AND RICE

CAYENNE PEPPER GIVES THIS COLOURFUL RICE AND FISH DISH A FLAVOUR BOOST.

SERVES SIX

INGREDIENTS
30ml/2 tbsp oil
115g/4oz rindless smoked bacon, diced
1 onion, chopped
2 celery sticks, chopped
2 large garlic cloves, chopped
10ml/2 tsp cayenne pepper
2 bay leaves
5ml/1 tsp dried oregano
2.5ml/½ tsp dried thyme
4 tomatoes, peeled and chopped
150ml/¼ pint/⅔ cup tomato sauce
350g/12oz/1¾ cups long grain rice
475ml/16fl oz/2 cups fish stock
175g/6oz cod, or haddock, skinned, boned and cubed
115g/4oz/1 cup cooked, peeled prawns (shrimp)
salt and ground black pepper
2 spring onions (scallions), chopped, to garnish

1 Preheat the oven to 180°C/350°F/ Gas 4. Heat the oil in a large pan and fry the bacon until crisp. Add the onion and celery and stir until beginning to stick to the pan.

2 Add the garlic, cayenne pepper, herbs, tomatoes and seasoning and mix well. Stir in the tomato sauce, rice and stock and bring to the boil.

3 Stir in the fish and transfer to an ovenproof dish. Cover and bake for 20–30 minutes, until the rice is tender. Stir in the prawns and heat through. Serve sprinkled with the spring onions.

CHICKEN JAMBALAYA

THIS SPICY CREOLE DISH CONTAINS A TASTY MIXTURE OF CHICKEN, HAM AND PRAWNS.

SERVES TEN

INGREDIENTS
2 × 1.5kg/3–3½ lb chickens
450g/1lb raw smoked gammon (cured ham)
50g/2oz/4 tbsp bacon fat
50g/2oz/½ cup plain (all-purpose) flour
3 onions, finely sliced
2 green (bell) peppers, seeded and sliced
675g/1½ lb tomatoes, chopped
2–3 garlic cloves, crushed
10ml/2 tsp chopped fresh thyme or 5ml/1 tsp dried thyme
24 prawns (shrimp), peeled
500g/1¼ lb/scant 3 cups long grain rice
2–3 dashes Tabasco sauce
6 spring onions (scallions), finely chopped
45ml/3 tbsp chopped fresh parsley
salt and ground black pepper

1 Cut each chicken into 10 pieces and season. Dice the gammon, discarding the rind and fat.

2 In a large casserole, melt the lard or bacon fat and brown the chicken pieces all over, lifting them out and setting them aside as they are done.

3 Turn the heat down, sprinkle the flour on to the fat in the pan and stir until the roux turns golden brown.

4 Return the chicken pieces to the pan, add the diced gammon, onions, green peppers, tomatoes, garlic and thyme and cook, stirring regularly, for 10 minutes, then stir in the prawns.

5 Stir the rice into the pan with one-and-a-half times the rice's volume in cold water. Season with salt, pepper and Tabasco sauce. Bring to the boil and cook over a low heat until the rice is tender and the liquid absorbed. Add a little extra boiling water if the rice dries out before it is cooked.

6 Mix the spring onions and parsley into the finished dish, reserving a little of the mixture to sprinkle over the jambalaya. Serve hot.

VARIATION
Jambalaya can be made with almost any kind of meat, poultry or shellfish.

YOGURT CHICKEN <u>AND</u> RICE

THIS SUSTAINING CHICKEN DISH IS FLAVOURED WITH ZERESHK, WHICH ARE SMALL, SOUR DRIED BERRIES THAT ARE AVAILABLE FROM MIDDLE EASTERN STORES.

<u>SERVES SIX</u>

INGREDIENTS

40g/1½oz/3 tbsp butter
1.5kg/3–3½lb chicken pieces
1 large onion, chopped
250ml/8fl oz/1 cup chicken stock
2 eggs
475ml/16fl oz/2 cups natural
  (plain) yogurt
2–3 saffron threads, dissolved in
  15ml/1 tbsp boiling water
5ml/1 tsp ground cinnamon
450g/1lb/generous 2¼ cups
  basmati rice, soaked in salted
  water for 2 hours
75g/3oz/⅓ cup zereshk
salt and ground black pepper
herb salad, to serve

1 Melt two-thirds of the butter in a large, flameproof casserole and cook the chicken and onion for 4–5 minutes, until the onion is softened and the chicken browned.

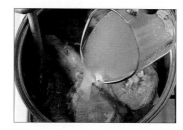

2 Add the stock and salt and pepper, bring to the boil and then simmer for 45 minutes, or until the chicken is cooked and the stock reduced by half.

3 Skin and bone the chicken. Cut the flesh into large pieces and place in a large bowl. Reserve the stock.

4 Beat the eggs and blend with the yogurt. Add the saffron water and cinnamon and season. Pour over the chicken and leave to marinate on one side for up to 2 hours.

5 Drain the rice and then boil in salted water for 5 minutes, reduce the heat and simmer for 10 minutes, until half cooked. Drain and rinse in warm water.

6 Transfer the chicken from the yogurt mixture to a dish and mix half the rice into the yogurt.

7 Preheat the oven to 160°C/325°F/ Gas 3 and grease a large 10cm/4in deep ovenproof dish.

8 Place the rice and yogurt mixture in the base of the dish, arrange the chicken pieces in a layer on top and then add the plain rice. Warm the zereshk thoroughly, then sprinkle over.

9 Mix the remaining butter with the chicken stock and pour over the rice. Cover tightly with foil and cook in the oven for 35–45 minutes.

10 Leave the dish to cool for a few minutes. Place on a cold, damp dishtowel which will help lift the rice from the base of the dish, then run a knife around the inside edge of the dish. Place a large flat plate over the dish and turn out. You should have a rice "cake" which can be cut into wedges. Serve hot with a herb salad.

VARIATION
If you cannot obtain zereshk, this dish is just as delicious with raisins or sultanas (golden raisins).

THAI FRIED RICE <u>WITH</u> CHILLIES

THIS SUBSTANTIAL DISH IS BASED ON THAI FRAGRANT RICE, WHICH IS SOMETIMES KNOWN AS JASMINE RICE. CHICKEN, RED PEPPER AND CHILLIES ADD COLOUR AND EXTRA FLAVOUR.

SERVES FOUR

INGREDIENTS

    475ml/16fl oz/2 cups water
    50g/2oz/½ cup coconut
      milk powder
    350g/12oz/1¾ cups Thai fragrant
      rice, rinsed and well drained
    30ml/2 tbsp groundnut (peanut) oil
    2 garlic cloves, chopped
    1 small onion, finely chopped
    2.5cm/1in piece fresh root
      ginger, grated
    225g/8oz skinless chicken breast
      fillets, cut into 1cm/½in dice
    1 red (bell) pepper, seeded
      and sliced
    1 fresh red chilli, seeded
      and chopped
    115g/4oz/⅔ cup drained canned
      corn kernels
    5ml/1 tsp chilli oil
    5ml/1 tsp curry powder
    2 eggs, beaten
    salt
    spring onion (scallion) shreds,
      to garnish

1 Pour the water into a pan and whisk in the coconut milk powder. Add the rice and bring to the boil. Reduce the heat, cover and cook for 12 minutes or until the rice is tender and the liquid has been absorbed. Remove from the heat immediately and spread the rice on a baking sheet and leave until cold.

COOK'S TIP
It is important that the rice is completely cold before being fried. The oil should be very hot when the rice is added.

2 Heat the oil in a wok, add the garlic, onion and ginger, and stir-fry over a medium heat for 2 minutes.

3 Push the vegetables to the sides of the wok, add the chicken to the centre and stir-fry for 2 minutes. Add the rice. Stir-fry over a high heat for 3 minutes.

4 Stir in the sliced red pepper, chilli, corn, chilli oil and curry powder, with salt to taste. Toss over the heat for 1 minute. Stir in the beaten eggs and cook for 1 minute more. Everything should be piping hot before serving. Transfer to a heated serving dish, garnish with spring onion shreds and serve.

MADRAS CURRY WITH SPICY RICE

CHILLIES ARE AN INDISPENSABLE INGREDIENT OF A HOT MADRAS CURRY. AFTER LONG, GENTLE SIMMERING, THEY MERGE WITH THE OTHER FLAVOURINGS TO GIVE A DELECTABLE RESULT.

SERVES FOUR

INGREDIENTS
    30ml/2 tbsp vegetable oil
    25g/1oz/2 tbsp ghee or butter
    675g/1½lb stewing beef, cut into
        bitesize cubes
    1 onion, chopped
    3 green cardamom pods
    2 fresh green chillies, seeded and
        finely chopped
    2.5cm/1in piece of fresh root
        ginger, grated
    2 garlic cloves, crushed
    15ml/1 tbsp Madras curry paste
    5ml/1 tsp ground cumin
    5ml/1 tsp ground coriander
    150ml/¼ pint/⅔ cup beef stock
    salt

For the rice
    225g/8oz/generous 1 cup basmati rice
    15ml/1 tbsp sunflower oil
    25g/1oz/2 tbsp ghee or butter
    1 onion, finely chopped
    1 garlic clove, crushed
    5ml/1 tsp ground cumin
    2.5ml/½ tsp ground coriander
    4 green cardamom pods
    1 cinnamon stick
    1 small red (bell) pepper, seeded
        and diced
    1 small green (bell) pepper, seeded
        and diced
    300ml/½ pint/1¼ cups chicken stock

1 Heat half the oil with half the ghee or butter in a large, shallow pan. Fry the meat, in batches if necessary, until browned on all sides. Transfer to a plate and set aside.

2 Heat the remaining oil and ghee or butter and fry the onion for about 3–4 minutes until softened. Add the cardamom pods and fry for 1 minute, then stir in the chillies, ginger and garlic, and fry for 2 minutes more.

3 Stir in the curry paste, ground cumin and coriander, then return the meat to the pan. Stir in the stock. Season with salt, bring to the boil, then reduce the heat and simmer very gently for 1–1½ hours, until the meat is tender.

4 When the curry is almost ready, prepare the rice. Put it in a bowl and pour over boiling water to cover. Set aside for 10 minutes, then drain, rinse under cold water and drain again. The rice will still be uncooked but should have lost its brittleness.

VARIATION
If you like, you can serve plain boiled rice with this curry. Put the rice in a sieve (strainer) and rinse it under cold water. Place in a pan with 5ml/1 tsp salt, and add water to come 5cm/2in above the level of the rice. Bring to the boil and simmer for 9–12 minutes. Drain and serve.

5 Heat the oil and ghee or butter in a flameproof casserole and fry the onion and garlic gently for 3–4 minutes until softened and lightly browned.

6 Stir in the ground cumin and coriander, green cardamom pods and cinnamon stick. Fry for 1 minute, then add the diced peppers.

7 Add the rice, stirring to coat the grains in the spice mixture, and pour in the chicken stock. Bring to the boil, then reduce the heat, cover the pan tightly and simmer for about 8–10 minutes, or until the rice is tender and the stock has been absorbed. Spoon into a bowl and serve with the curry.

COOK'S TIPS
• The curry should be fairly dry, but take care that it does not catch on the base of the pan. If you want to leave it unattended, cook it in a heavy pan. Alternatively, cook it in a flameproof casserole, in an oven preheated to 180°C/350°F/Gas 4.
• Offer a little mango chutney, if you like, and if you want to cool the heat, a bowl of yogurt raita.

Get into the habit of buying fresh chillies whenever
you see them on sale, and you'll be surprised how
often you'll use them in cooking, not necessarily as
the principal ingredient, but for pungent punctuation.
Chillies are great for highlighting other flavours, and
nowhere is this more apparent than when they are added
to vegetable and vegetarian dishes. Try Mushrooms with
Chipotle Chillies, Peppers Filled with Spiced Vegetables
or Jalapeño and Onion Quiche.

Vibrant Vegetarian and Side Dishes

MUSHROOMS <u>WITH</u> CHIPOTLE CHILLIES

CHIPOTLE CHILLIES ARE JALAPEÑOS THAT HAVE BEEN SMOKE-DRIED. THEIR SMOKY FLAVOUR IS THE PERFECT FOIL FOR THE MUSHROOMS IN THIS SIMPLE SALAD.

SERVES SIX

INGREDIENTS
  2 chipotle chillies
  450g/1lb/6 cups button
    (white) mushrooms
  60ml/4 tbsp vegetable oil
  1 onion, finely chopped
  2 garlic cloves, crushed or chopped
  salt
  small bunch of fresh coriander
    (cilantro), to garnish

VARIATION
Use cascabel instead of chipotle chillies. The name "cascabel" means "little rattle" and accurately describes the sound they make when shaken. Cascabel's nutty flavour is best appreciated when the skin is removed. Soak as for chipotle chillies, scoop out the flesh and add it to the onion and garlic.

1 Put the dried chillies in a heatproof bowl and pour over hot (not boiling) water to cover. Leave to stand for 20–30 minutes until they have softened. Drain, cut off the stalks, then slit the chillies and scrape out the seeds. Chop the flesh finely.

2 Trim the mushrooms, then clean them with a damp cloth or kitchen paper. If they are large, cut them in half.

3 Heat the oil in a large frying pan. Add the onion, garlic, chillies and mushrooms, and stir until evenly coated in the oil. Fry for 6–8 minutes, stirring occasionally, until the onion and mushrooms are tender.

4 Season with salt and spoon into a serving dish. Chop some of the coriander, leaving some whole leaves, and use to garnish. Serve hot.

RED HOT CAULIFLOWER

VEGETABLES ARE SELDOM SERVED PLAIN IN MEXICO. THE CAULIFLOWER HERE IS FLAVOURED WITH A SIMPLE SERRANO AND TOMATO SALSA AND FRESH CHEESE.

SERVES SIX

INGREDIENTS
1 small onion
1 lime
1 medium cauliflower
400g/14oz can chopped tomatoes
4 fresh serrano chillies, seeded and
  finely chopped
1.5ml/¼ tsp granulated (white) sugar
75g/3oz feta cheese, crumbled
salt
chopped fresh flat leaf parsley,
  to garnish

1 Chop the onion very finely and place in a bowl. With a zester or sharp knife, peel away the zest of the lime in thin strips. Add the lime zest to the finely chopped onion.

2 Cut the lime in half and use a reamer or citrus squeezer to extract the juice from each half in turn, adding it to the onion and lime zest mixture. Set aside for the lime juice to soften the onion.

COOK'S TIP
A zester enables you to pare off tiny strips of lime rind with no pith.

3 Cut the cauliflower into florets. Tip the tomatoes into a pan and add the chillies and sugar. Heat gently. Meanwhile, bring a pan of water to the boil, add the cauliflower florets and cook gently for 5–8 minutes until tender.

4 Add the chopped onion mixture to the tomato salsa, with salt to taste. Stir and heat through, then spoon about one-third of the salsa into a serving dish.

5 Arrange the drained cauliflower florets on top of the salsa and spoon the remaining salsa on top.

6 Sprinkle with the feta, which should soften a little on contact. Serve immediately, sprinkled with chopped fresh flat leaf parsley.

BEANS <u>IN</u> HOT SAUCE

*THIS TASTY DISH CONSISTS OF NUTRITIOUS BEANS SERVED WITH A TOMATO AND CHILLI SAUCE.
IT CAN BE SERVED ON ITS OWN, OR WITH COOKED RICE OR SOME BREAD*

SERVES FOUR

INGREDIENTS

    450g/1lb green lima or broad (fava)
      beans, thawed if frozen
    30ml/2 tbsp olive oil
    1 onion, finely chopped
    2 garlic cloves, chopped
    350g/12oz tomatoes, peeled, seeded
      and chopped
    1 or 2 drained canned jalapeño
      chillies, seeded and chopped
    salt
    fresh coriander (cilantro) sprigs,
      to garnish

1 Cook the beans in a pan of boiling water for 15–20 minutes, until tender. Drain and keep hot, to one side, in the covered pan.

2 Heat the olive oil in a frying pan and sauté the onion and garlic until the onion is soft but not brown. Add the tomatoes and cook until the mixture is thick and flavoursome.

3 Add the jalapeños and cook for 1–2 minutes. Season with salt.

4 Pour the mixture over the reserved beans and check that they are hot. If not, return everything to the frying pan and cook over a low heat for just long enough to heat through. Put into a warm serving dish, garnish with the coriander and serve.

BROAD BEAN AND CAULIFLOWER CURRY

THIS IS A HOT AND SPICY VEGETABLE CURRY, IDEAL WHEN SERVED WITH BROWN BASMATI
RICE, SMALL POPPADUMS AND MAYBE A COOLING CUCUMBER RAITA AS WELL.

SERVES FOUR

INGREDIENTS

2 garlic cloves, chopped
2.5cm/1 in cube fresh root ginger
1 fresh green chilli, seeded
  and chopped
15ml/1 tbsp oil
1 onion, sliced
1 large potato, chopped
30ml/2 tbsp ghee or softened butter
15ml/1 tbsp curry powder, mild
  or hot
1 cauliflower, cut into small florets
600ml/1 pint/2½ cups stock
30ml/2 tbsp creamed coconut or
  coconut cream
275g/10oz can broad (fava) beans
juice of ½ lemon (optional)
salt and ground black pepper
fresh coriander (cilantro), chopped,
  to garnish

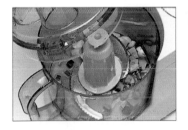

1 Blend the garlic, ginger, chilli and oil in a food processor or blender until they form a smooth paste.

2 In a large pan, cook the onion and potato in the ghee or butter for 5 minutes, then stir in the spice paste and curry powder. Cook for 1 minute.

VARIATION
Try using broccoli florets instead of cauliflower in this recipe. Top with toasted pine nuts to add flavour and contrast to the dish.

3 Add the cauliflower florets and stir well into the spicy mixture, then pour in the stock. Bring to the boil and mix in the coconut, stirring until it melts and is combined.

4 Season well, then cover and simmer for 10 minutes. Add the beans and their can juices and cook, uncovered, for a further 10 minutes.

5 Check the seasoning and add a good squeeze of lemon juice, if you like. Serve hot, garnished with chopped coriander.

THAI ASPARAGUS

THIS IS AN EXCITINGLY DIFFERENT WAY OF COOKING ASPARAGUS. THE FLAVOUR IS COMPLEMENTED BY THE ADDITION OF GALANGAL AND CHILLI.

SERVES FOUR

INGREDIENTS

   350g/12oz asparagus stalks
   30ml/2 tbsp vegetable oil
   1 garlic clove, crushed
   15ml/1 tbsp sesame seeds, toasted
   2.5cm/1in piece fresh galangal,
     finely grated
   1 fresh red chilli, seeded and
     finely chopped
   15ml/1 tbsp Thai fish sauce
   15ml/1 tbsp light soy sauce
   45ml/3 tbsp water
   5ml/1 tsp palm sugar (jaggery) or
     light muscovado (brown) sugar

VARIATIONS
Try this with broccoli or pak choi (bok choy). The sauce also works very well with green beans.

1 Snap the asparagus stalks. They will break naturally at the junction between the woody base and the more tender portion of the stalk. Discard the woody parts of the stems.

2 Heat the oil in a wok and stir-fry the garlic, sesame seeds and galangal for 3–4 seconds, until the garlic is just beginning to turn golden.

3 Add the asparagus stalks and chilli, toss to mix, then add the fish sauce, soy sauce, water and sugar. Using two spoons, toss over the heat for a further 2 minutes, or until the asparagus just begins to soften and the liquid is reduced by half.

4 Carefully transfer to a warmed platter and serve immediately.

SPRING ONIONS <u>WITH</u> ROMESCO SAUCE

SPRING ONIONS ARE DELICIOUS WHEN CHARGRILLED ON A GRIDDLE, UNDER A GRILL OR ON A BARBECUE. THE SPICY, FLAVOURSOME ROMESCO SAUCE COMPLEMENTS THEM PERFECTLY.

SERVES SIX

INGREDIENTS

3 bunches of plump spring onions (scallions), or Chinese green onions, about 2.5cm/1in across the bulb
olive oil, for brushing

For the romesco sauce
2–3 *ñoras* or other mild dried red chillies, such as Mexican *anchos* or *guajillos*
1 large red (bell) pepper, halved and seeded
2 large tomatoes, halved and seeded
4–6 large garlic cloves, unpeeled
75–90ml/5–6 tbsp olive oil
25g/1oz/¼ cup hazelnuts, blanched
4 slices French bread, each about 2cm/¾in thick
15ml/1 tbsp sherry vinegar
squeeze of lemon juice (optional)
chopped fresh parsley, to garnish

1 Prepare the sauce. Soak the dried chillies in hot water for about 30 minutes. Preheat the oven to 220°C/425°F/Gas 7.

2 Place the pepper, tomatoes and garlic on a baking sheet and drizzle with 15ml/1 tbsp olive oil. Roast, uncovered, for 30–40 minutes, until the pepper is blistered and blackened and the garlic is soft. Cool slightly, then peel the pepper, tomatoes and garlic.

COOK'S TIP
This piquant romesco sauce is a variation on the classic, roasting the vegetables rather than frying them.

3 Heat the remaining oil in a small frying pan and fry the hazelnuts until lightly browned, then transfer them to a plate. Fry the bread in the same oil until light brown on both sides, then transfer to the plate with the nuts and leave to cool. Reserve the oil from cooking.

4 Drain the chillies, discard as many of their seeds as you can, then place the chillies in a food processor. Add the red pepper halves, tomatoes, garlic, hazelnuts and bread chunks together with the reserved olive oil. Add the vinegar and process to a paste. Check the seasoning and thin the sauce with a little more oil or lemon juice, if necessary. Set aside.

5 Trim the roots from the spring onions or trim the Chinese onion leaves so that they are about 15–18cm/6–7in long. Brush with oil.

6 Heat an oiled ridged grill pan and cook the onions for about 2 minutes on each side, turning once and brushing with oil. (Alternatively, place under a preheated grill (broiler) 10cm/4in away from the heat and cook for 3 minutes on each side, brushing with more oil when turned; roast in a preheated oven at 200°C/400°F/Gas 6 for 5–6 minutes; or barbecue over grey charcoal for 3–4 minutes on each side, brushing with oil as needed.) Serve immediately with the sauce.

MASALA MASHED POTATOES

THESE POTATOES ARE HERBY, HOT AND SPICY AND WILL PERK UP ANY MEAL.

SERVES FOUR

INGREDIENTS
3 potatoes
15ml/1 tbsp chopped fresh mint
  and coriander (cilantro), mixed
5ml/1 tsp mango powder
5ml/1 tsp salt
5ml/1 tsp crushed black peppercorns
1 fresh red chilli, chopped
1 fresh green chilli, chopped
50g/2oz/4 tbsp margarine

1 Boil the potatoes until soft enough to be mashed. Mash the potatoes down using a masher.

2 Blend together the chopped herbs, mango powder, salt, pepper, chillies and margarine to form a paste.

3 Stir the mixture into the mashed potatoes and mix together thoroughly with a fork. Serve warm as an accompaniment.

VARIATION
Instead of potatoes, try sweet potatoes. Cook them until tender, mash and continue from step 2.

SPICY CABBAGE

AN EXCELLENT VEGETABLE ACCOMPANIMENT, THIS IS A VERY VERSATILE SPICY DISH THAT CAN ALSO BE SERVED AS A WARM SIDE SALAD. IT'S SO QUICK TO MAKE THAT IT CAN BE A HANDY LAST MINUTE ADDITION TO ANY MEAL.

SERVES FOUR

INGREDIENTS
50g/2oz/4 tbsp margarine
2.5ml/½ tsp white cumin seeds
3–8 dried red chillies, to taste
1 small onion, sliced
225g/8oz/2½ cups cabbage
2 carrots, grated
2.5ml/½ tsp salt
30ml/2 tbsp lemon juice

1 Melt the margarine in a pan and stir-fry the white cumin seeds and dried red chillies for about 30 seconds.

2 Add the sliced onion and cook for about 2 minutes. Add the cabbage and carrots and stir-fry for a further 5 minutes, until the cabbage is soft.

3 Finally, stir in the salt and lemon juice and serve.

SICHUAN SIZZLER

THIS DISH IS ALSO KNOWN AS FISH-FRAGRANT AUBERGINE, AS THE FLAVOURINGS OFTEN ACCOMPANY FISH. IF YOU USE TINY AUBERGINES, OMIT THE SALTING PROCESS.

SERVES FOUR

INGREDIENTS

   2 medium aubergines (eggplants)
   5ml/1 tsp salt
   3 dried red chillies
   groundnut (peanut) oil, for
     deep-frying
   3–4 garlic cloves, finely chopped
   1cm/½in piece fresh root ginger,
     finely chopped
   4 spring onions (scallions), cut into
     2.5cm/1in lengths (white and green
     parts kept separate)
   15ml/1 tbsp Chinese rice wine or
     medium-dry sherry
   15ml/1 tbsp light soy sauce
   5ml/1 tsp granulated (white) sugar
   1.5ml/¼ tsp ground roasted
     Sichuan peppercorns
   15ml/1 tbsp Chinese rice vinegar
   5ml/1 tsp sesame oil

1 Trim the aubergines and cut them into strips, about 4cm/1½in wide and 7.5cm/3in long. Place the aubergines in a colander and sprinkle over the salt. Leave for 30 minutes, then rinse them thoroughly under cold running water. Pat dry with kitchen paper.

2 Meanwhile, soak the chillies in a bowl of warm water for 20–30 minutes. Then drain and pat dry with kitchen paper.

3 Cut each chilli into 3–4 pieces, discarding the seeds.

4 Half-fill a wok with oil and heat to 180°C/350°F. Deep-fry the aubergine pieces until golden brown. Drain on kitchen paper. Pour off most of the oil from the wok.

5 Reheat the oil left in the wok and add the garlic, ginger, chillies and the white spring onion. Stir-fry for 30 seconds.

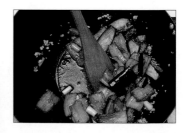

6 Add the aubergine and toss over the heat for 1–2 minutes. Stir in the rice wine or sherry, soy sauce, sugar, ground peppercorns and rice vinegar. Stir-fry for 1–2 minutes. Sprinkle over the sesame oil and green spring onion, and serve.

STEAMED VEGETABLES WITH THAI SPICY DIP

IN THAILAND, STEAMED VEGETABLES ARE OFTEN PARTNERED WITH RAW ONES TO CREATE THE CONTRASTING TEXTURES THAT ARE SUCH A FEATURE OF THE NATIONAL CUISINE.

SERVES FOUR

INGREDIENTS
    1 head broccoli, divided into florets
    130g/4½oz 1 cup green
      beans, trimmed
    130g/4½oz asparagus, trimmed
    ½ head cauliflower, divided
      into florets
    8 baby corn cobs
    130g/4½oz mangetouts (snow peas)
      or sugar snap peas
    salt

For the dip
    1 fresh green chilli, seeded
    4 garlic cloves, peeled
    4 shallots, peeled
    2 tomatoes, halved
    5 pea aubergines (eggplant)
    30ml/2 tbsp lemon juice
    30ml/2 tbsp soy sauce
    2.5ml/½ tsp salt
    5ml/1 tsp granulated (white) sugar

COOK'S TIP
Cauliflower varieties with pale green curds have a more delicate flavour than those with white curds.

1 Place the broccoli, green beans, asparagus and cauliflower in a steamer and steam over boiling water for about 4 minutes, until just tender but still with a "bite". Transfer them to a bowl and add the corn cobs and mangetouts or sugar snap peas. Season to taste with a little salt. Toss to mix, then set aside.

2 Make the dip. Preheat the grill (broiler). Wrap the chilli, garlic cloves, shallots, tomatoes and aubergines in a foil package. Grill (broil) for 10 minutes, until the vegetables have softened, turning the package over once or twice.

3 Unwrap the foil and tip its contents into a mortar or food processor. Add the lemon juice, soy sauce, salt and sugar. Pound with a pestle or process to a fairly liquid paste.

4 Scrape the dip into a serving bowl or four individual bowls. Serve, surrounded by the steamed and raw vegetables.

VARIATIONS
You can use a combination of other vegetables if you like. Use pak choi (bok choy) instead of the cauliflower or substitute raw baby carrots for the corn cobs and mushrooms in place of the mangetouts (snow peas).

PANCAKES STUFFED WITH LIGHTLY SPICED SQUASH

IN ORDER TO APPRECIATE THE INDIVIDUAL FLAVOURS OF THE BUTTERNUT SQUASH, LEEKS AND CHICORY IN THESE PANCAKES, IT IS IMPORTANT NOT TO OVERDO THE CHILLI.

SERVES FOUR

INGREDIENTS
    115g/4oz/1 cup plain (all-purpose) flour
    50g/2oz ⅓ cup yellow corn meal
    2.5ml/½ tsp salt
    2.5ml/½ tsp chilli powder
    2 large (US extra large) eggs
    450ml/¾ pint/scant 2 cups milk
    65g/2½oz/5 tbsp butter
    vegetable oil, for greasing
    25g/1oz/⅓ cup freshly grated
        Parmesan cheese

For the filling
    30ml/2 tbsp olive oil
    450g/1lb butternut squash (peeled
        weight), seeded
    a large pinch of dried red chilli flakes
    2 large leeks, thickly sliced
    2.5ml/½ tsp chopped fresh or
        dried thyme
    3 chicory (Belgian endive) heads,
        thickly sliced
    115g/4oz full-flavoured goat's
        cheese, cut into cubes
    90g/3½oz/scant 1 cup walnuts or
        pecan nuts, roughly chopped
    30ml/2 tbsp chopped fresh flat
        leaf parsley
    salt and ground black pepper

2 When ready to cook the pancakes, melt 25g/1oz/2 tbsp of the butter and stir it into the batter. Heat a lightly greased 18cm/7in heavy frying pan or crêpe pan. Pour about 60ml/4 tbsp of the batter into the pan, tilt it so that the batter forms a pancake and cook for 2–3 minutes, until set and lightly browned underneath. Turn and cook the pancake on the other side for 2–3 minutes. Lightly grease the pan after every second pancake.

3 Make the filling. Heat the oil in a large pan. Add the squash and cook, stirring frequently, for 10 minutes, until almost tender. Add the chilli flakes and cook, stirring, for a further 1–2 minutes. Stir in the leeks and thyme, and cook for 4–5 minutes more.

5 Preheat the oven to 200°C/400°F/ Gas 6. Lightly grease an ovenproof dish. Either layer the pancakes with the filling to make a stack in the dish or stuff each pancake with 30–45ml/2–3 tbsp filling. Roll or fold the pancakes to enclose the filling and place in the dish.

6 Sprinkle the grated Parmesan over the pancakes. Melt the remaining butter and drizzle it over the layered or filled pancakes. Bake for 10–15 minutes, until the cheese is bubbling and the pancakes are piping hot. Serve immediately.

COOK'S TIP
This can all be prepared in advance, but make sure the filling is cold before adding to the pancakes.

VARIATIONS
• Fennel could be used instead of chicory, and pumpkin, other varieties of winter squash or courgette (zucchini) instead of butternut squash.
• If you like, you can add a fresh chilli, but make it a mild one, such as Anaheim. Roast and peel it first.

1 Sift the flour, corn meal, salt and chilli powder into a bowl. Make a well in the centre. Add the eggs and a little of the milk. Whisk the eggs and milk, gradually incorporating the dry ingredients and adding more milk to make a batter with a consistency like that of thick cream.

4 Add the chicory and cook, stirring frequently, for 4–5 minutes, until the leeks are cooked and the chicory is hot, but still with some bite to its texture. Cool slightly, then stir in the cheese, nuts and parsley. Season the mixture well with salt and pepper.

CHILLI <u>AND</u> PAK CHOI OMELETTE PARCELS

*COLOURFUL STIR-FRIED VEGETABLES AND CORIANDER IN BLACK BEAN SAUCE MAKE
A REMARKABLY GOOD OMELETTE FILLING, WHICH IS QUICK AND EASY TO PREPARE.*

SERVES FOUR

INGREDIENTS

130g/4½oz broccoli, cut into
    small florets
30ml/2 tbsp groundnut (peanut) oil
1cm/½in piece fresh root ginger,
    finely grated
1 large garlic clove, crushed
2 fresh red chillies, seeded and
    finely sliced
4 spring onions (scallions),
    diagonally sliced
175g/6oz/3 cups pak choi
    (bok choy), shredded
50g/2oz/2 cups fresh coriander
    (cilantro) leaves, plus extra
    to garnish
115g/4oz/2 cups beansprouts
45ml/3 tbsp black bean sauce
4 eggs
salt and ground black pepper

1 Bring a pan of lightly salted water to the boil and blanch the broccoli for 2 minutes. Drain, then refresh under cold running water, and drain again.

2 Heat 15ml/1 tbsp of the oil in a frying pan and stir-fry the ginger, garlic and half the chilli for 1 minute. Add the spring onions, broccoli and pak choi, and toss the mixture over the heat for 2 minutes more.

3 Chop three-quarters of the coriander and add to the frying pan. Add the beansprouts and stir-fry for 1 minute, then add the black bean sauce and heat through for 1 minute more. Remove the pan from the heat and keep warm.

4 Mix the eggs lightly with a fork and season well. Heat a little of the remaining oil in a small frying pan and add one-quarter of the beaten egg. Tilt the pan so that the egg covers the base, then sprinkle over one-quarter of the reserved coriander leaves. Cook until set, then turn out the omelette on to a plate and keep warm while you make 3 more omelettes.

5 Spoon one-quarter of the stir-fry on to each omelette and roll up. Cut in half crossways and serve, garnished with coriander leaves and chilli slices.

COOK'S TIP
If you overdo the chilli, don't reach for a glass of water. Drinking it will simply spread the discomfort. Instead, eat something starchy, such as a piece of bread, or try a spoonful of yogurt.

SPICY ROOT VEGETABLE GRATIN

SUBTLY SPICED WITH CURRY POWDER, TURMERIC, CORIANDER AND MILD CHILLI POWDER,
THIS RICH GRATIN IS SUBSTANTIAL ENOUGH TO SERVE ON ITS OWN.

2 Preheat the oven to 180°C/350°F/Gas 4. Heat half the butter in a heavy pan, and add the curry powder, turmeric and coriander. Stir in half the chilli powder. Cook for 2 minutes, then put aside to cool slightly.

3 Drain the vegetable slices, then pat them dry with kitchen paper. Place in a bowl, add the spice mixture and the shallots, and mix well.

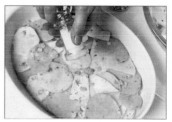

4 Arrange the vegetables in a gratin dish, adding salt and pepper to each layer. Mix together the cream and milk, pour the mixture over the vegetables, then sprinkle the remaining chilli powder on top.

SERVES FOUR

INGREDIENTS
2 large potatoes, total weight about 450g/1lb
2 sweet potatoes, total weight about 275g/10oz
175g/6oz celeriac
15ml/1 tbsp unsalted butter
5ml/1 tsp curry powder
5ml/1 tsp ground turmeric
2.5ml/½ tsp ground coriander
5ml/1 tsp mild chilli powder
3 shallots, chopped
150ml/¼ pint/⅔ cup single (light) cream
150ml/¼ pint/⅔ cup milk
salt and ground black pepper
chopped fresh flat leaf parsley, to garnish

1 Thinly slice the potatoes, sweet potatoes and celeriac, using a sharp knife or the slicing attachment in a food processor. Immediately place the slices in a bowl of cold water to prevent discolouring. Set aside.

VARIATION
Substitute parsnips or carrots for the sweet potatoes, and turnips for the celeriac.

5 Cover with baking parchment and bake for about 45 minutes. Remove the parchment, dot with the remaining butter and bake for 50 minutes more until the top is golden. Serve garnished with the chopped fresh parsley.

COOK'S TIP
A salad of mixed leaves could be served separately with the gratin then some fresh fruit, such as mango, to follow.

COURGETTE TORTE

THIS DISH LOOKS RATHER LIKE A SPANISH OMELETTE, WHICH IS TRADITIONALLY SERVED AT ROOM TEMPERATURE. SERVE WARM OR LEAVE TO COOL.

2 Slice the onion and add it to the oil remaining in the pan, with most of the jalapeño strips, reserving some for the garnish. Fry until the onions have softened and are golden. Using a slotted spoon, add the onions and jalapeños to the courgettes.

3 Beat the eggs in a large bowl. Add the self-raising flour, cheese and cayenne. Mix well, then stir in the courgette mixture, with salt to taste.

4 Grease a 23cm/9in round shallow ovenproof dish with the butter. Pour in the courgette mixture and bake for 30 minutes until risen, firm to the touch and golden. Allow to cool.

5 Serve the courgette torte in thick wedges, garnished with the remaining jalapeño strips. A tomato salad, sprinkled with chives, makes a colourful accompaniment.

SERVES FOUR TO SIX

INGREDIENTS
  500g/1¼lb courgettes (zucchini)
  60ml/4 tbsp vegetable oil
  1 small onion
  3 fresh jalapeño chillies, seeded
    and cut in strips
  3 large (US extra large) eggs
  50g/2oz/½ cup self-raising
    (self-rising) flour
  115g/4oz/1 cup grated Monterey
    Jack or mild Cheddar cheese
  2.5ml/½ tsp cayenne pepper
  15g/½oz/1 tbsp butter
  salt

1 Preheat the oven to 180°C/350°F/ Gas 4. Top and tail the courgettes, then slice them thinly. Heat the oil in a large frying pan. Add the courgettes and cook for a few minutes, turning them over at least once, until they are soft and beginning to brown. Using a slotted spoon, transfer them to a bowl.

OKRA, CHILLI AND TOMATO TAGINE

THE WORD "TAGINE" USUALLY CONJURES UP AN IMAGE OF A SPICY LAMB AND APRICOT STEW, BUT THIS VEGETARIAN VERSION IS EQUALLY AUTHENTIC.

SERVES FOUR

INGREDIENTS
350g/12oz okra
5–6 tomatoes
2 small onions
2 garlic cloves, crushed
1 fresh green chilli, seeded
5ml/1 tsp paprika
small handful of fresh
  coriander (cilantro)
175ml/6fl oz/¾ cup water
30ml/2 tbsp sunflower oil
juice of 1 lemon

1 Trim the okra and then cut into 1cm/½in lengths. Peel and seed the tomatoes and chop roughly.

2 Roughly chop 1 of the onions and place in a food processor or blender with the garlic, chilli, paprika, coriander and 60ml/4 tbsp of the water. Blend to a paste.

COOK'S TIP
A tagine is an earthenware dish with a tall conical lid, which has given its name to slowly simmered stews. It is used in North African cooking.

3 Heat the sunflower oil in a large pan. Thinly slice the second onion in rings and fry in the oil for 5–6 minutes until golden brown. Using a slotted spoon, transfer the fried onion rings to a plate lined with crumpled kitchen paper. Set aside.

4 Reduce the heat and scrape the onion and coriander mixture into the pan. Cook for 1–2 minutes, stirring frequently, and then add the okra, tomatoes, lemon juice and remaining water. Stir well to mix, cover tightly and simmer over a low heat for about 15 minutes until the okra is tender.

5 Transfer the tagine to a warmed serving dish, sprinkle with the fried onion rings and serve immediately while hot.

VARIATION
To make this more substantial, add extra vegetables, such as aubergine (eggplant), carrots and leeks.

PEPPERS <u>FILLED WITH</u> SPICED VEGETABLES

JALAPEÑO CHILLIES AND INDIAN SPICES SEASON THE VEGETABLE STUFFING IN THESE BAKED PEPPERS. SERVE WITH PLAIN RICE, CUCUMBER SLICES AND A LENTIL DHAL.

SERVES SIX

INGREDIENTS
6 large evenly shaped red or yellow (bell) peppers
500g/1¼lb potatoes, peeled, halved if large
1–2 jalapeños or other fresh green chillies, seeded and chopped
1 small onion, chopped
4–5 garlic cloves, chopped
5cm/2in piece of fresh root ginger, chopped
105ml/7 tbsp water
90–105ml/6–7 tbsp groundnut (peanut) oil
1 aubergine (eggplant), cut into 1cm/½in dice
10ml/2 tsp cumin seeds
5ml/1 tsp kalonji seeds
2.5ml/½ tsp ground turmeric
5ml/1 tsp ground coriander
5ml/1 tsp ground toasted cumin seeds
1–2 pinches of cayenne pepper
about 30ml/2 tbsp lemon juice
salt and ground black pepper
30ml/2 tbsp chopped fresh coriander (cilantro), to garnish

1 Cut the tops off the peppers and pull out the central core from each, keeping the shells intact. Shake out any remaining seeds. Cut a thin slice off the base of the peppers, if necessary, to make them stand upright.

2 Bring a large pan of lightly salted water to the boil. Add the peppers and cook for 5–6 minutes. Lift out and drain them upside down in a colander.

3 Bring the water in the pan back to the boil, add the potatoes and cook for 10–12 minutes, until just tender. Drain thoroughly, put on one side to cool, then cut into 1cm/½in dice.

4 Put the green chillies, onion, garlic and ginger in a food processor or blender with 60ml/4 tbsp of the water and process to a purée. Preheat the oven to 190°C/375°F/Gas 5.

5 Heat 45ml/3 tbsp of the oil in a large, deep frying pan and cook the aubergine, stirring occasionally, until browned on all sides. Remove from the pan and set aside. Add another 30ml/2 tbsp of the oil to the pan and sauté the potatoes until lightly browned. Remove from the pan and set aside.

6 If necessary, add another 15ml/1 tbsp oil to the pan, then add the cumin and kalonji seeds. Fry briefly until the seeds darken, then add the turmeric, coriander and ground cumin. Cook for 15 seconds. Stir in the chilli purée and fry, scraping the pan with a spatula, until the mixture begins to brown. Do not let it burn.

7 Return the potatoes and aubergines to the pan, and season with salt, pepper and 1–2 pinches of cayenne. Pour in the remaining measured water and 15ml/1 tbsp lemon juice. Cook, stirring, until the liquid evaporates.

8 Place the peppers on a baking tray and fill with the potato mixture. Brush the pepper skins with a little oil and bake for 30–35 minutes, until cooked. Allow to cool a little, then sprinkle with a little more lemon juice, garnish with the coriander and serve.

COOK'S TIPS
• Try using poblano chillies instead of the sweet peppers.
• The spice kalonji, also known as nigella, is a very tiny black seed that closely resembles the onion seed. It is available from most supermarkets and Indian foodstores.

VARIATIONS
• Instead of serving with rice and a lentil dhal, try Indian breads and a cucumber or mint yogurt raita.
• Substitute carrots and parsnips for the potatoes.

CHILLI, TOMATO <u>AND</u> SPINACH PIZZA

THIS RICHLY FLAVOURED TOPPING WITH A HINT OF SPICE MAKES A COLOURFUL PIZZA.
ADDED TO A READY-MADE PIZZA BASE, IT MAKES THE COOK'S LIFE REALLY EASY.

SERVES THREE

INGREDIENTS
  1–2 fresh red chillies
  50g/2oz/½ cup sun-dried tomatoes in
    oil, drained, plus 45ml/3 tbsp oil
    from the jar
  1 onion, chopped
  2 garlic cloves, chopped
  400g/14oz can chopped tomatoes
  15ml/1 tbsp tomato purée (paste)
  175g/6oz fresh spinach
  1 ready-made pizza base,
    25–30cm/10–12in in diameter
  75g/3oz/¾ cup grated smoked
    Bavarian cheese
  75g/3oz/¾ cup grated mature (sharp)
    Cheddar cheese
  salt and ground black pepper

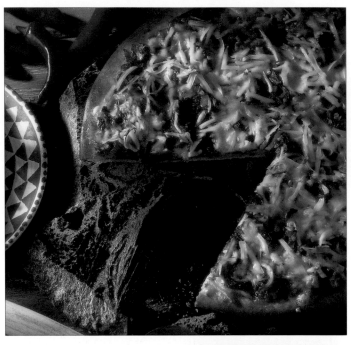

1 Slit the chillies, open them out and use a sharp knife to scrape out the seeds. Chop the flesh finely.

3 Roughly chop the sun-dried tomatoes. Add them to the pan with the canned chopped tomatoes, tomato purée and seasoning. Simmer uncovered, stirring occasionally, for 15 minutes.

5 Add the spinach to the sauce and stir gently. Cook, stirring, for a further 5–10 minutes until the spinach has wilted and no excess moisture remains.

2 Heat 30ml/2 tbsp of the oil from the sun-dried tomatoes in a pan, add the chopped onion, garlic and chillies, and fry gently for about 5 minutes until the onions are soft. Do not let them brown.

4 Preheat the oven to 220°C/425°F/ Gas 7. Remove the stalks from the spinach and wash the leaves in plenty of cold water. Drain well and pat dry with kitchen paper. Roughly chop the spinach.

6 Brush the pizza base with the remaining tomato oil, then spoon over the sauce. Sprinkle over the cheeses and bake for 15–20 minutes or for the time recommended on the packaging of the pizza base, until crisp and golden. Serve immediately.

JALAPEÑO <u>AND</u> ONION QUICHE

CANNED OR BOTTLED JALAPEÑO CHILLIES ARE USEFUL IN A RANGE OF DISHES,
FROM DIPS AND SALADS TO SNACKS AND MAIN COURSES.

SERVES SIX

INGREDIENTS
  15g/½oz/1 tbsp butter
  2 onions, sliced
  4 spring onions (scallions)
  2.5ml/½ tsp ground cumin
  15–30ml/1–2 tbsp chopped canned
    or bottled jalapeño chillies
  75g/3oz/¾ cup grated Cheddar or
    Monterey Jack cheese
  4 eggs
  300ml/½ pint/1¼ cups milk
  2.5ml/½ tsp salt
  flat leaf parsley, to garnish

For the pastry
  175g/6oz/1½ cups plain
    (all-purpose) flour
  1.5ml/¼ tsp salt
  1.5ml/¼ tsp cayenne pepper
  75g/3oz/6 tbsp cold butter
  75g/3oz/6 tbsp cold margarine
  30–60ml/2–4 tbsp iced water

1 Make the pastry. Sift the flour, salt
and cayenne pepper into a bowl. Rub in
the butter and margarine until the
mixture resembles coarse breadcrumbs.

2 Sprinkle in 30ml/2 tbsp iced water
and mix until the dough holds together.
If the dough is too crumbly, add a little
more water, 15ml/1 tbsp at a time.
Gather the dough into a ball and flatten
slightly. Wrap in clear film (plastic wrap)
and chill for at least 30 minutes.

3 Preheat the oven to 190°C/375°F/
Gas 5. Roll out the pastry to a thickness
of about 3mm/⅛in. Use to line a
23cm/9in fluted quiche tin (tart pan)
that has a removable base. Prick the
base of the pastry case all over with a
fork. Line the case with foil and fill with
baking beans.

4 Bake for 12–15 minutes, until the
pastry has just set. Remove from the
oven and carefully lift out the foil and
beans. Return it to the oven and bake
for 5–8 minutes more, until golden.

5 While the pastry case is baking, melt
the butter in a frying pan and cook the
onions over a medium heat for
5 minutes, until softened. Cut the
spring onions into 1cm/½in pieces and
cook for 1 minute more. Stir in the
cumin and jalapeños, and set aside.

6 Spoon the onion mixture into the
pastry shell. Sprinkle with the cheese.
In a bowl, whisk the eggs, milk and salt
together. Pour the egg mixture into the
pastry case. Bake for 30–40 minutes,
until the filling has set. Serve warm or
cold, garnished with parsley.

JAMAICAN BLACK BEAN POT

MOLASSES IMPARTS A RICH SYRUPY FLAVOUR TO THE SPICY SAUCE, WHICH MATCHES
HOT CHILLI WITH BLACK BEANS, VIBRANT PEPPERS AND ORANGE BUTTERNUT SQUASH.

SERVES FOUR

INGREDIENTS
    225g/8oz/1¼ cups dried black beans,
        soaked overnight in water to cover
    1 bay leaf
    30ml/2 tbsp vegetable oil
    1 large onion, chopped
    1 garlic clove, chopped
    ½–1 Scotch bonnet chilli, seeded
        and finely chopped
    5ml/1 tsp English mustard powder
    15ml/1 tbsp blackstrap molasses
    30ml/2 tbsp soft dark brown sugar
    5ml/1 tsp dried thyme
    5ml/1 tsp vegetable bouillon powder
        or 1 vegetable stock (bouillon) cube
    1 red (bell) pepper, seeded and diced
    1 yellow (bell) pepper, seeded
        and diced
    675g/1½lb/5¼ cups butternut
        squash or pumpkin, seeded and cut
        into 1cm/½in dice
    salt and ground black pepper
    fresh thyme sprigs, to garnish

2 Heat the oil in the pan and sauté the onion, garlic and chilli for about 5 minutes, or until softened, stirring occasionally. Add the mustard powder, molasses, sugar and thyme. Cook for 1 minute, stirring. Stir in the black beans, mix well and spoon the mixture into a flameproof casserole.

3 Add enough water to the reserved cooking liquid to make 400ml/14fl oz/ 1⅔ cups, then mix in the bouillon powder or crumbled stock cube. Pour into the casserole and mix well. Bake in the oven for 25 minutes.

4 Add the peppers and squash or pumpkin to the casserole and mix well. Season to taste. Cover, then bake for 45 minutes more, or until the vegetables are tender. Serve garnished with thyme.

COOK'S TIP
The Scotch bonnet chilli, like its close relative, the habanero, is blisteringly hot. Handle it with great care (wearing gloves is wise) and use only as much as you dare. The uninitiated may find even half too much, and may prefer to substitute a milder variety, but it would be a shame to miss the chilli flavour.

1 Drain the beans, rinse and drain again. Place in a large pan, cover with fresh water and add the bay leaf. Bring to the boil, then boil rapidly for 10 minutes. Reduce the heat, cover, and simmer for 30 minutes until tender. Drain, reserving the cooking water. Preheat the oven to 180°C/350°F/Gas 4.

VARIATIONS
• This dish is delicious served with cornbread or plain rice.
• If you like, you could substitute red kidney beans for the black beans, and still retain the authentic Caribbean flavour.

CHILLI CHEESE TORTILLA WITH SALSA

GOOD WARM OR COLD, THIS IS LIKE A SLICED POTATO QUICHE WITHOUT THE PASTRY BASE,
AND IS WELL SPIKED WITH CHILLI. IT MAKES A SATISFYING LUNCH.

SERVES FOUR

INGREDIENTS
    45ml/3 tbsp sunflower or olive oil
    1 small onion, thinly sliced
    2–3 fresh green jalapeño chillies,
       seeded and sliced
    200g/7oz cold cooked
       potato, sliced
    150g/5oz/1¼ cups grated cheese
    6 eggs, beaten
    salt and ground black pepper
    fresh herbs and chilli, to garnish

For the salsa
    500g/1¼lb fresh, flavoursome
       tomatoes, peeled, seeded and
       finely chopped
    1 fresh mild green chilli, seeded
       and finely chopped
    2 garlic cloves, crushed
    45ml/3 tbsp chopped fresh
       coriander (cilantro)
    Juice of 1 lime
    2.5ml/½ tsp salt

1 Make the salsa by mixing all the ingredients in a bowl. Mix well, cover and set aside.

2 Heat 15ml/1 tbsp of the oil in a large frying pan and gently fry the onion and jalapeños for 5 minutes, stirring until softened. Add the potato and cook for 5 minutes until lightly browned, keeping the slices whole. Using a slotted spoon, transfer the vegetables to a warm plate.

COOK'S TIP
Use a firm but not hard cheese, such as Double Gloucester or Monterey Jack.

3 Wipe the pan with kitchen paper, then add the remaining oil and heat until really hot. Return the vegetables to the pan. Sprinkle the cheese over the top and season.

4 Pour in the beaten egg, making sure that it seeps under the vegetables. Cook over a low heat, stirring, until set. Serve hot or cold, in wedges, with the salsa. Garnish with fresh herbs and chilli.

BLACK BEAN AND CHILLI BURRITOS

TORTILLAS ARE A WONDERFULLY ADAPTABLE FOOD. HERE THEY ARE FILLED WITH BEANS, CHEESE AND SALSA, AND SPIKED WITH CHILLI.

SERVES FOUR

INGREDIENTS
225g/8oz/1¼ cups dried black
  beans, soaked in water overnight
1 bay leaf
45ml/3 tbsp coarse salt
1 small red onion, finely chopped
225g/8oz/2 cups grated Cheddar
  cheese or Monterey Jack
45ml/3 tbsp chopped pickled
  jalapeño chillies
15ml/1 tbsp chopped fresh
  coriander (cilantro)
900ml/1½ pints/3¾ cups
  tomato salsa
8 wheat flour tortillas
salt and ground black pepper
diced avocado, to serve

1 Drain the beans and put them in a large pan. Add fresh cold water to cover and the bay leaf. Bring to the boil, then reduce the heat, cover and simmer for 30 minutes. Add the salt and continue simmering for about 30 minutes more, or until the beans are tender. Drain and tip into a bowl. Discard the bay leaf.

2 Grease a rectangular baking dish. Add the onion, half the cheese, the jalapeños, coriander and 250ml/8fl oz/ 1 cup of the salsa to the beans. Stir well and add salt and pepper if needed. Preheat the oven to 180°C/350°F/Gas 4.

3 Place 1 tortilla on a board. Spread a large spoonful of the filling down the middle, then roll up to enclose the filling. Place the burrito in the dish, seam side down. Repeat to make 7 more.

4 Sprinkle the remaining cheese over the burritos. Bake for 15 minutes, until all the cheese melts.

5 Serve the burritos immediately, with avocado and the remaining salsa.

KENYAN MUNG BEAN STEW

THE KENYAN NAME FOR THIS SIMPLE AND TASTY STEW IS DENGU. IT CONTAINS A HEALTHY MIXTURE OF MUNG BEANS, ONION, PEPPERS AND CHILLI.

SERVES FOUR

INGREDIENTS

225g/8oz/1¼ cups mung beans,
   soaked overnight
25g/1oz/2 tbsp ghee or butter
2 garlic cloves, crushed
1 red onion, chopped
30ml/2 tbsp tomato purée (paste)
½ green (bell) pepper, seeded and
   cut into small cubes
½ red (bell) pepper, seeded and cut
   into small cubes
1 green chilli, seeded and
   finely chopped
300ml/½ pint/1¼ cups water

1 Put the mung beans in a large pan, cover with water and boil until the beans are soft and the water has evaporated. Remove from the heat and mash coarsely with a fork or potato masher.

2 Heat the ghee or butter in a separate pan, add the garlic and onion and cook for 4–5 minutes, until golden brown, then add the tomato purée and cook for a further 2–3 minutes, stirring constantly.

3 Stir in the mashed beans, then the green and red peppers and chilli.

4 Add the water, stirring well to mix all the ingredients together.

5 Pour back into a clean pan and simmer for about 10 minutes, then spoon the stew into a serving dish and serve immediately.

COOK'S TIP
If you prefer a more traditional, smoother texture, cook the mung beans until they are very soft, then mash them thoroughly until smooth.

BLACK-EYED BEAN STEW <u>WITH</u> SPICY PUMPKIN

THIS DELICIOUS, SUSTAINING DISH CONTAINS A DOUBLE HIT OF CHILLI, AS BOTH THE BLACK-EYED BEANS AND THE PUMPKIN ARE SEASONED WITH FIERY HOT PEPPER SAUCE.

SERVES THREE TO FOUR

INGREDIENTS

225g/8oz/1¼ cups black-eyed beans
  (peas), soaked for 4 hours
1 onion, chopped
1 green or red (bell) pepper, seeded
  and chopped
2 garlic cloves, chopped
1 vegetable stock (bouillon) cube
1 thyme sprig or 5ml/1 tsp dried thyme
5ml/1 tsp paprika
2.5ml/½ tsp mixed (apple pie) spice
2 carrots, sliced
15–30ml/1–2 tbsp palm oil
salt and hot pepper sauce

For the spicy pumpkin
  675g/1½lb pumpkin
  1 onion
  25g/1oz/2 tbsp butter or margarine
  2 garlic cloves, crushed
  3 tomatoes, peeled and chopped
  2.5ml/½ tsp ground cinnamon
  10ml/2 tsp curry powder
  pinch of grated nutmeg
  300ml/½ pint/⅔ cup water
  salt, hot pepper sauce and
    ground black pepper

1 Drain the beans, place in a pan and cover generously with water. Bring the beans to the boil.

2 Add the onion, green or red pepper, garlic, stock cube, herbs and spices. Simmer for 45 minutes, or until the beans are just tender. Season to taste with the salt and a little hot pepper sauce.

VARIATION
Replace the black-eyed beans (peas) with a mixture of borlotti beans, pinto beans and red kidney beans for a colourful variation on this dish.

3 Add the carrots and palm oil and continue cooking for about 10–12 minutes, until the carrots are cooked, adding a little more water if necessary. Remove from the heat and set aside.

4 To make the spicy pumpkin, cut the pumpkin into cubes and finely chop the onion.

5 Melt the butter or margarine in a large pan, and add the pumpkin, onion garlic, tomatoes, spices and water. Stir well to combine and simmer until the pumpkin is soft.

6 Season the pumpkin with salt, hot pepper sauce and black pepper, to taste. Serve with the black-eyed beans.

RED BEAN CHILLI

THIS VEGETARIAN CHILLI CAN BE ADAPTED TO ACCOMMODATE MEAT EATERS BY ADDING EITHER MINCED BEEF OR LAMB IN PLACE OF THE LENTILS.

SERVES FOUR

INGREDIENTS

30ml/2 tbsp vegetable oil
1 onion, chopped
400g/14oz can chopped tomatoes
2 garlic cloves, crushed
300ml/½ pint/1¼ cups white wine
about 300ml/½ pint/1¼ cups
  vegetable stock
115g/4oz/½ cup red lentils
2 thyme sprigs or 5ml/1 tsp
  dried thyme
10ml/2 tsp ground cumin
45ml/3 tbsp dark soy sauce
½ hot chilli pepper,
  finely chopped
5ml/1 tsp mixed (apple pie) spice
15ml/1 tbsp oyster sauce (optional)
225g/8oz can red kidney
  beans, drained
10ml/2 tsp sugar
salt
boiled rice and corn,
  to serve

1 Heat the oil in a large pan and cook the onion over a medium heat for a few minutes until slightly softened.

2 Add the tomatoes and garlic, cook for 10 minutes, then stir in the wine and stock.

COOK'S TIP
Fiery chillies can irritate the skin, so always wash your hands well after handling them and take care not to touch your eyes. If you like really hot, spicy food, then add the seeds from the chilli, too.

3 Add the lentils, thyme, cumin, soy sauce, hot pepper, mixed spice and oyster sauce, if using.

4 Cover and simmer for 40 minutes, or until the lentils are cooked, stirring occasionally and adding more water if the lentils begin to dry out.

5 Stir in the kidney beans and sugar and continue cooking for 10 minutes, adding a little extra stock or water if necessary. Season to taste with salt and serve hot with boiled rice and corn.

EGG AND GREEN LENTIL CURRY WITH GREEN CHILLIES AND GINGER

THIS SIMPLE AND NOURISHING CURRY CAN BE COOKED IN HALF AN HOUR. SERVE THE DISH WITH YOUR FAVOURITE CHUTNEY.

2 Boil the eggs for 10 minutes, then plunge them straight into cold water. When cool enough to handle, shell them and cut them in half lengthways.

3 Heat the oil in a large frying pan and fry the cloves and peppercorns for 2 minutes. Stir in the onion, chillies, garlic and ginger, and fry for a further 5–6 minutes, stirring frequently.

4 Stir in the curry paste and fry for a further 2 minutes, stirring constantly. Add the chopped tomatoes, sugar and water. Simmer for about 5 minutes until the sauce thickens, stirring occasionally. Add the boiled eggs, drained lentils and garam masala. Cover and simmer for 10 minutes, then serve.

SERVES FOUR

INGREDIENTS

75g/3oz/scant ½ cup green lentils
750ml/1¼ pints/3 cups stock
6 eggs
30ml/2 tbsp oil
3 cloves
1.5ml/¼ tsp black peppercorns
1 onion, finely chopped
2 fresh green chillies, finely chopped
2 garlic cloves, crushed
2.5cm/1in piece fresh root ginger, peeled and chopped
30ml/2 tbsp curry paste
400g/14oz can chopped tomatoes
2.5ml/½ tsp granulated (white) sugar
175ml/6fl oz/¾ cup water
2.5ml/½ tsp garam masala

1 Wash the lentils thoroughly under cold running water. Drain and check for small stones. Put the lentils in a large, heavy pan. Pour in the stock. Bring to the boil, then reduce the heat, cover and simmer gently for about 15 minutes or until the lentils are soft. Drain and set aside.

COOK'S TIPS
• If you haven't got any fresh chillies, substitute dried ones. Reconstitute them by soaking in hot water for at least 20 minutes.
• A little sugar is often added to chilli beans, to soften the flavour. If you have any, try stirring in a spoonful of chilli jam instead, or a dash of Tabasco sauce.

LENTIL DHAL WITH CHILLIES AND ROASTED GARLIC

FRESH AND DRIED CHILLIES FEATURE IN THIS SPICY LENTIL DHAL, WHICH MAKES A COMFORTING, STARCHY MEAL WHEN SERVED WITH BOILED RICE OR INDIAN BREADS.

SERVES FOUR TO SIX

INGREDIENTS
40g/1½oz/3 tbsp butter or ghee
1 onion, chopped
2 fresh green chillies, seeded
  and chopped
15ml/1 tbsp chopped fresh root ginger
225g/8oz/1 cup yellow or red lentils
900ml/1½ pints/3¾ cups water
1 head of garlic
5ml/1 tsp ground cumin
5ml/1 tsp ground coriander
2 tomatoes, peeled and diced
a little lemon juice
salt and ground black pepper
30–45ml/2–3 tbsp fresh coriander
  (cilantro) sprigs, to garnish

For the whole spice mix
30ml/2 tbsp groundnut (peanut) oil
4–5 shallots, sliced
2 garlic cloves, thinly sliced
15g/½oz/1 tbsp butter or ghee
5ml/1 tsp cumin seeds
5ml/1 tsp mustard seeds
3–4 small dried red chillies
8–10 fresh curry leaves

1 Melt the butter or ghee in a large pan and gently cook the onion, chillies and ginger for 10 minutes, stirring the mixture occasionally until golden.

2 Stir in the lentils and water. Bring to the boil, then reduce the heat and partially cover the pan. Simmer, stirring occasionally, for 50–60 minutes, until the texture resembles that of a very thick soup.

3 Meanwhile, preheat the oven to 180°C/350°F/Gas 4. Put the whole head of garlic in a small baking dish and roast for 30–45 minutes until soft.

4 Slice the top off the head of garlic. Scoop the roasted flesh into the lentil mixture, then stir in the cumin and ground coriander. Cook for a further 10–15 minutes, stirring frequently. Stir in the tomatoes, then season the mixture, adding lemon juice to taste.

5 For the spice mix, heat the oil in a small, heavy pan and fry the shallots until crisp and browned. Add the garlic and cook, stirring, until it colours slightly. Remove with a slotted spoon and set aside.

6 Melt the butter or ghee in the same pan and fry the cumin and mustard seeds until the mustard seeds pop. Stir in the chillies, curry leaves and the shallot mixture, then swirl most of the hot mixture into the dhal. Season. Top with the remaining spice mixture, garnish with coriander sprigs and serve.

SICHUAN SPICY TOFU

*SICHUAN PEPPER ADDS A SPICY, WOODY AROMA TO TOFU IN THIS DISH, WHICH ALSO CONTAINS
BEEF, SO IS NOT SUITABLE FOR VEGETARIANS.*

SERVES FOUR

INGREDIENTS
  1 packet tofu
  1 leek
  115g/4oz/1 cup minced (ground) beef
  45ml/3 tbsp vegetable oil
  15ml/1 tbsp black bean sauce
  15ml/1 tbsp light soy sauce
  5ml/1 tsp chilli bean sauce
  15ml/1 tbsp Chinese rice wine
    or dry sherry
  about 45–60ml/3–4 tbsp water or
    vegetable stock
  10ml/2 tsp cornflour
    (cornstarch) paste
  ground Sichuan peppercorns,
    to taste
  a few drops sesame oil

1 Cut the tofu into 1cm/½in cubes and
blanch them in a pan of boiling water
for about 2–3 minutes, until they
harden. Remove and drain. Cut the
leek into short sections.

2 Stir-fry the beef in oil until the colour
changes, then add the chopped leek
and black bean sauce. Add the tofu
with the soy sauce, chilli bean sauce
and wine or sherry. Stir for 1 minute.

3 Add the vegetable stock or water,
bring to the boil and braise for about
2–3 minutes.

4 Thicken the spicy sauce with the
cornflour paste, season with the ground
Sichuan peppercorns and sprinkle with
some drops of sesame oil. Serve the
dish immediately.

TOFU AND GREEN BEAN RED CURRY

THE CHILLIES ARE STIRRED INTO THIS CURRY JUST BEFORE SERVING, SO CHOOSE A VARIETY
WHOSE HEAT WILL BE TOLERABLE TO ALL YOUR GUESTS, OR OFFER THE CHILLIES SEPARATELY.

SERVES FOUR TO SIX

INGREDIENTS

600ml/1 pint/2½ cups coconut milk
15ml/1 tbsp red curry paste
45ml/3 tbsp Thai fish sauce
10ml/2 tsp palm sugar (jaggery) or
  soft dark brown sugar
225g/8oz/3 cups button
  (white) mushrooms
115g/4oz green beans, trimmed
175g/6oz firm tofu, rinsed and cut
  into 2cm/¾in cubes
4 kaffir lime leaves, torn
2 fresh red chillies, seeded
  and sliced
coriander (cilantro) leaves,
  to garnish

1 Pour about one-third of the coconut milk into a pan. Cook until it starts to separate and an oily sheen appears.

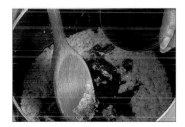

2 Add the red curry paste, fish sauce and sugar to the coconut milk. Mix together thoroughly, then stir in the mushrooms and cook for 1 minute. Stir in the rest of the coconut milk and bring back to the boil.

COOK'S TIP

Firm tofu is suitable for stir-frying, braising and poaching. You can keep it in the refrigerator for up to 5 days by changing the water daily.

VARIATION

This works equally well with aubergines (eggplant), cauliflower, broccoli, bamboo shoots or a mixture of vegetables.

3 Add the green beans and cubes of tofu, and simmer gently for a further 4–5 minutes.

4 Stir in the kaffir lime leaves and chillies. Serve garnished with the coriander leaves.

BENGALI-STYLE VEGETABLES

THIS HOT DRY CURRY USES SPICES THAT DO NOT REQUIRE LONG SLOW COOKING. PARTIALLY COOK THE VEGETABLES IN ADVANCE AND COMPLETE THE DISH QUICKLY LATER IN THE DAY.

3 Drain the vegetables and tip them into a bowl. Add the chilli and ginger mixture, with the yogurt, ground coriander and turmeric. Season with plenty of salt and pepper, and mix well.

4 Heat the ghee in a large frying pan. Add the vegetable mixture and cook over a high heat for 2 minutes, stirring from time to time.

SERVES FOUR

INGREDIENTS

½ cauliflower, broken into florets
1 large potato, peeled and cut into
  2.5cm/1in dice
115g/4oz green beans, trimmed
2 courgettes (zucchini), halved
  lengthways and sliced
2 fresh green chillies
2.5cm/1in piece of fresh root
  ginger, peeled
120ml/4fl oz/½ cup natural
  (plain) yogurt
10ml/2 tsp ground coriander
2.5ml/½ tsp ground turmeric
25g/1oz/2 tbsp ghee
2.5ml/½ tsp garam masala
5ml/1 tsp cumin seeds
10ml/2 tsp granulated (white) sugar
pinch each of ground cloves, ground
  cinnamon and ground cardamom
salt and ground black pepper

1 Bring a large pan of water to the boil. Add the cauliflower florets and diced potato, and cook for 5 minutes. Add the beans and courgettes, and cook for 2–3 minutes.

2 Meanwhile, cut the chillies in half, then scrape out and discard the seeds using a very sharp knife. Roughly chop the flesh. Finely chop the ginger. Mix the chillies and ginger together in a small bowl.

5 Stir in the garam masala and cumin seeds, and cook for 2 minutes. Stir in the sugar, ground cloves, cinnamon and cardamom, and cook for 1 minute or until all the liquid has evaporated. Serve immediately.

COOK'S TIPS
• Ghee has a burning point higher than the best oils, so it is very good for frying and searing.
• An alternative to ghee is to add a little groundnut (peanut) oil to ordinary butter. It allows the frying temperature to be reached without burning.

BALTI-STYLE VEGETABLES WITH CASHEW NUTS

IT IS THE PREPARATION THAT TAKES THE TIME HERE. DO IT IN ADVANCE AND EVERYONE WILL BE IMPRESSED WITH THE SPEED AT WHICH YOU CAN PRODUCE A DELICIOUS MEAL.

SERVES FOUR

INGREDIENTS
  2 carrots
  1 red (bell) pepper, seeded
  1 green (bell) pepper, seeded
  2 courgettes (zucchini)
  115g/4oz green beans, trimmed
  1 medium bunch spring
    onions (scallions)
  15ml/1 tbsp extra virgin olive oil
  4–6 curry leaves
  2.5ml/½ tsp white cumin seeds
  4 dried red chillies
  10–12 cashew nuts
  5ml/1 tsp salt
  30ml/2 tbsp lemon juice
  fresh mint leaves, to garnish
  cooked rice, to serve (optional)

1 Prepare the vegetables: cut the carrots, peppers and courgettes into matchsticks, halve the beans and chop the spring onions. Set aside.

VARIATION
Use peanuts instead of cashew nuts, and baby leeks for spring onions.

2 Heat the oil in a wok or frying pan and fry the curry leaves, cumin seeds and dried chillies for about 1 minute, until aromatic. Be careful with the timing, as curry leaves quickly burn.

3 Add the vegetables and nuts, and stir-fry for 3–4 minutes. Add the salt and lemon juice. Toss the vegetables over the heat for 3–5 minutes more, until they are crisp-tender.

4 Lift out and discard the curry leaves. Spoon the fragrant stir-fry on to a heated serving dish and garnish with mint leaves. Serve immediately, with boiled rice, if you like.

BALTI SPLIT PEAS WITH GREEN AND RED CHILLIES

URAD DHAL, OFF-WHITE HULLED, SPLIT PEAS, IS JUST ONE OF MANY DIFFERENT TYPES OF BEANS, PEAS AND LENTILS SOLD IN INDIAN FOOD STORES. HERE, THEY ARE COMBINED WITH AROMATIC HERBS AS WELL AS BOTH RED AND GREEN CHILLIES.

2 Heat the oil in a wok or frying pan over a medium heat. Fry the bay leaf with the onions and cinnamon bark.

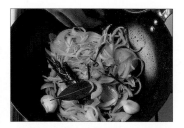

3 Add the ginger, whole garlic cloves and half the green and red chillies.

4 Drain almost all the water from the split peas. Add to the wok or frying pan, followed by the remaining green and red chillies and finally the fresh mint. Heat through briefly and serve.

COOK'S TIP
For a milder curry, replace some of the chillies with green or red (bell) peppers which will also add colour to the dish.

SERVES FOUR

INGREDIENTS
115g/4oz/½ cup urad dhal or
  yellow split peas
30ml/2 tbsp corn oil
1 bay leaf
2 onions, sliced
1 piece cinnamon bark
15ml/1 tbsp grated fresh root ginger
2 garlic cloves
2 fresh green chillies, seeded and
  sliced lengthways
2 fresh red chillies, seeded and
  sliced lengthways
15ml/1 tbsp chopped
  fresh mint

1 Put the dhal or split peas in a bowl and pour in enough cold water to cover by at least 2.5cm/1in. Cover and leave to soak overnight. Next day, drain the dhal and boil it in water until the individual grains are soft enough to break into two. Set aside.

HOT <u>AND</u> SPICY POTATOES

THERE ARE SEVERAL VARIATIONS ON THIS CHILLI AND POTATO DISH, BUT THE
MOST IMPORTANT THING IS THE SPICING, WHICH IS MADE HOTTER STILL BY
ADDING VINEGAR. THE CLASSIC VERSION IS MADE WITH FRESH TOMATO SAUCE
FLAVOURED WITH GARLIC AND CHILLI.

<u>SERVES FOUR</u>

INGREDIENTS
  675g/1½lb small new potatoes
  75ml/5 tbsp olive oil
  2 garlic cloves, sliced
  3 dried chillies, seeded
    and chopped
  2.5ml/½ tsp ground cumin
  10ml/2 tsp paprika
  30ml/2 tbsp red or white
    wine vinegar
  1 red or green (bell) pepper,
    seeded and sliced
  coarse sea salt, for sprinkling
    (optional)

1 Scrub the potatoes and put them into a pan of salted water. Bring to the boil and cook for 10 minutes, or until almost tender. Drain and leave to cool slightly. Peel, if you like, then cut into chunks.

2 Heat the oil in a large frying or sauté pan and fry the potatoes, turning them frequently, until golden.

3 Meanwhile, crush together the garlic, chillies and cumin using a mortar and pestle. Mix the paste with the paprika and wine vinegar, then add to the potatoes with the sliced pepper and cook, stirring, for 2 minutes. Scatter with salt, if using, and serve hot as a tapas dish or cold as a side dish.

POTATOES WITH RED CHILLIES

IF YOU LIKE CHILLIES, YOU'LL LOVE THESE POTATOES! THE RED CHILLIES ADD COLOUR, FLAVOUR AND FIRE TO THE DISH, WHICH IS FRAGRANCED WITH WARMING SPICES.

SERVES FOUR

INGREDIENTS

  12–14 small new or salad
    potatoes, halved
  30ml/2 tbsp vegetable oil
  2.5ml/½ tsp crushed dried
    red chillies
  2.5ml/½ tsp white cumin seeds
  2.5ml/½ tsp fennel seeds
  2.5ml/½ tsp crushed coriander seeds
  5ml/1 tsp salt
  1 onion, sliced
  1–4 fresh red chillies, chopped
  45ml/3 tbsp chopped fresh
    coriander (cilantro)

COOK'S TIP

After draining the cooked potatoes, cover with kitchen paper and put on the lid. The paper will absorb the steam and leave the potatoes dry.

1 Bring a pan of lightly salted water to the boil and cook the potatoes for about 15 minutes until tender but still firm. Remove from the heat and drain off the water. Set aside until needed.

2 Heat the oil in a deep frying pan and add the crushed chillies, cumin, fennel and coriander seeds. Sprinkle the salt over and fry, stirring continuously, for 30–40 seconds.

3 Add the sliced onion and fry until golden brown. Tip in the dry potatoes, add the chopped red chillies and 15ml/ 1 tbsp of the chopped coriander and stir well.

4 Reduce the heat to very low, then cover and cook for 5–7 minutes. Serve the potatoes hot, on a heated dish, garnished with the remaining chopped fresh coriander.

BOMBAY POTATOES

THIS CLASSIC GUJARATI (INDIAN VEGETARIAN) DISH OF POTATOES IS SLOWLY COOKED
IN A RICHLY FLAVOURED CURRY SAUCE WITH FRESH CHILLIES FOR AN ADDED KICK.

SERVES FOUR TO SIX

INGREDIENTS
450g/1lb new or small salad potatoes
5ml/1 tsp ground turmeric
60ml/4 tbsp vegetable oil
2 dried red chillies
6–8 curry leaves
2 onions, finely chopped
2 fresh green chillies, finely chopped
50g/2oz/1 cup coriander (cilantro)
    leaves, coarsely chopped
1.5ml/¼ tsp asafoetida
2.5ml/½ tsp each cumin, mustard,
    onion, fennel and kalonji seeds
lemon juice, to taste
salt
fried fresh curry leaves, to garnish

VARIATION
This works very well with cauliflower
florets. Just reduce the cooking time.

1 Chop the potatoes into small chunks.
Bring a pan of lightly salted water to the
boil and add the potatoes with half the
turmeric. Cook for 15–20 minutes, or
until tender. Drain and set aside a few,
then coarsely mash the rest. Set aside.

2 Heat the oil in a large heavy pan and
fry the red chillies and curry leaves until
the chillies begin to char. Do not let
them burn or they will taste bitter.

3 Add the onions, fresh green chillies,
coriander, remaining turmeric,
asafoetida and spice seeds, and cook,
stirring, until the onions are tender.

4 Fold in the potatoes and add a few
drops of water. Cook over a low heat for
about 10 minutes, stirring gently so that
the potatoes absorb the spices without
starting to break up. Remove the dried
chillies and curry leaves.

5 Serve the potatoes hot, with lemon
juice squeezed or poured over, and
seasoned with salt. Garnish with the
fried fresh curry leaves, if you like.

COOK'S TIP
Asafoetida is a spice with a pungent,
rather unpleasant odour, which vanishes
when it is cooked. It is widely used in
Indian vegetarian cooking.

Chillies taste great in all sorts of salads, from a simple mixture of spinach and serranos to the colourful combination of fruit and vegetables that is known as Gado-gado, served here with a peanut and chilli sauce. Not surprisingly, they have a great affinity for sweet peppers, but also work well with shellfish, especially squid. Some fresh chillies are tender enough to use as they are, seeded and sliced, but others benefit from being roasted so that the flesh takes on a smoky flavour. Do this over a flame or under the grill, or use a culinary blow torch so that only the outer skin is charred.

Piquant Salads

ROASTED PEPPER AND TOMATO SALAD

CHILLIES DO NOT NEED TO DOMINATE TO MAKE THEIR PRESENCE FELT IN A DISH. HERE
THEY ARE USED TO ACCENTUATE THE FLAVOUR OF THEIR MILDER RELATIONS, THE SWEET PEPPERS.

SERVES FOUR

INGREDIENTS
   3 red (bell) peppers
   6 large plum tomatoes
   2.5ml/½ tsp dried red chilli flakes
   1 red onion, finely sliced
   3 garlic cloves, finely chopped
   grated rind and juice of 1 lemon
   45ml/3 tbsp chopped fresh flat
     leaf parsley
   30ml/2 tbsp extra virgin olive oil
     or chilli oil
   salt
   black and green olives and extra
     chopped flat leaf parsley, to garnish

COOK'S TIPS
• (Bell) peppers roasted this way will
keep for several weeks. After peeling off
the skins, place the pepper pieces in a
jar with a tight-fitting lid. Pour over olive
oil to cover. Store in the refrigerator.
• For an intense flavour, roast fresh red
chillies with the peppers and tomatoes.

1 Preheat the oven to 220°C/425°F/
Gas 7. Place the peppers on a baking
tray and roast, turning occasionally, for
10 minutes or until the skins are almost
blackened. Add the tomatoes to the
baking tray, return to the oven and roast
for 5 minutes more.

2 Place the roasted peppers in a plastic
bag, close the top loosely, trapping in
the steam to loosen the skins, and then
set them aside, with the tomatoes, until
they are cool enough to handle, which
should take about 15 minutes.

3 Carefully pull off the skin from the
peppers. Remove the seeds, then chop
the peppers and tomatoes roughly and
place in a mixing bowl.

4 Add the chilli flakes, onion slices,
chopped garlic, lemon rind and juice.
Sprinkle over the parsley. Mix well, then
transfer to a serving dish.

5 Sprinkle with a little salt, drizzle over
the olive oil or chilli oil and sprinkle
olives and extra parsley over the top.
Serve at room temperature.

SPINACH AND SERRANO CHILLI SALAD

YOUNG SPINACH LEAVES MAKE A WELCOME CHANGE FROM LETTUCE AND ARE EXCELLENT IN SALADS. THE ROASTED GARLIC IS AN INSPIRED ADDITION TO THE DRESSING.

SERVES SIX

INGREDIENTS

500g/1¼lb baby spinach leaves
50g/2oz/⅓ cup sesame seeds
50g/2oz/¼ cup butter
30ml/2 tbsp olive oil
6 shallots, sliced
8 fresh serrano chillies, seeded and
  cut into strips
4 tomatoes, sliced

For the dressing
8 smoked or roasted garlic cloves
120ml/4fl oz/½ cup white wine vinegar
2.5ml/½ tsp ground white pepper
1 bay leaf
2.5ml/½ tsp ground allspice
30ml/2 tbsp chopped fresh thyme,
  plus extra sprigs, to garnish

1 Pull any coarse stalks from the spinach leaves, rinse the leaves and dry them in a salad spinner or clean dishtowel. Put them in a plastic bag in the refrigerator.

2 Make the dressing. Remove the skins from the garlic, then chop the flesh and put it in a jar that has a screw-top lid. Add the vinegar, pepper, bay leaf, allspice and chopped thyme. Close tightly, shake well, then set aside.

COOK'S TIP
You can buy smoked garlic from most supermarkets. If you prefer to use roasted garlic, place the cloves in a roasting pan in an oven preheated to 180°C/350°F/Gas 4 and cook for about 15 minutes until soft.

3 Toast the sesame seeds in a dry frying pan, shaking frequently over a medium heat until golden. Set aside.

4 Heat the butter and oil in a frying pan. Fry the shallots for 4–5 minutes, until softened, then stir in the chilli strips and fry for 2–3 minutes more.

5 In a large bowl, layer the spinach with the shallot and chilli mixture, and the tomato slices. Pour over the dressing. Sprinkle with sesame seeds and serve, garnished with thyme sprigs.

VARIATION
For a crunchy salad, use finely sliced red or white cabbage instead of spinach

VINEGARED CHILLI CABBAGE

A HOT CABBAGE DISH THAT WILL CERTAINLY ADD A BIT OF SPICE TO EVERY MEAL.
THE ADDITION OF VINEGAR AT THE END GIVES THIS DISH ITS DISTINCT FLAVOUR.

SERVES FOUR TO SIX

INGREDIENTS
    1 fresh red chilli, halved, seeded
        and cut into strips
    25g/1oz/2 tbsp lard (shortening)
        or butter
    2 garlic cloves, crushed (optional)
    1 white cabbage, cored
        and shredded
    10ml/2 tsp cider vinegar
    5ml/1 tsp cayenne pepper
    salt

1 Put the chilli with the lard or butter into a large pan and cook over a medium heat until the chilli sizzles and curls at the edges.

2 Add the garlic and cabbage and stir, over the heat, until the cabbage is coated and warm. Add salt to taste and 75ml/5 tbsp water. Bring to the boil, cover and lower the heat.

3 Cook, shaking the pan regularly, for 3–4 minutes, until the cabbage wilts. Remove the lid, raise the heat and cook off the liquid. Check the seasoning and sprinkle with vinegar and cayenne pepper.

VARIATION
For a very savoury dish, replace the white cabbage with 450g/1lb sauerkraut. Rinse the sauerkraut well before use and take care not to add too much salt.

COOK'S TIP
A wok with a domed lid is good for this part-frying, part-steaming method of cooking cabbage.

COLESLAW ᴵᴺ TRIPLE-HOT DRESSING

THE TRIPLE HOTNESS IN THIS COLESLAW IS SUPPLIED BY MUSTARD, HORSERADISH AND TABASCO.

SERVES SIX

INGREDIENTS
    ½ white cabbage, cored and shredded
    2 celery sticks, finely sliced
    1 green (bell) pepper, seeded and
        finely sliced
    4 spring onions (scallions), shredded
    30ml/2 tbsp chopped fresh dill
    cayenne pepper

For the dressing
    15ml/1 tbsp Dijon mustard
    10ml/2 tsp creamed horseradish
    5ml/1 tsp Tabasco sauce
    30ml/2 tbsp red wine vinegar
    75ml/5 tbsp olive oil
    salt and ground black pepper

1 Mix the cabbage, celery, pepper and spring onions in a salad bowl.

2 Mix the mustard, horseradish and Tabasco sauce, then gradually stir in the vinegar with a fork and finally beat in the oil and seasoning. Toss the salad in the dressing and leave to stand, if possible, for at least 1 hour, turning it once or twice.

3 Immediately before serving, season the salad if necessary, toss again and sprinkle with dill and cayenne.

COOK'S TIP
This is a good salad for a buffet table or picnic as it improves after standing in its dressing (it could be left overnight in the refrigerator) and travels well in a covered plastic bowl or box.

KACHUMBALI SALAD

THIS IS A PEPPERY RELISH FROM TANZANIA, WHERE IT IS SERVED WITH GRILLED POULTRY, MEAT OR FISH DISHES, TOGETHER WITH RICE — THIS SALAD USES THE SAME COMBINATION OF VEGETABLES AND FLAVOURS.

SERVES FOUR TO SIX

INGREDIENTS
  2 red onions
  4 tomatoes
  1 green chilli
  ½ cucumber
  1 carrot
  juice of 1 lemon
  salt and ground black pepper

1 Slice the onions and tomatoes very thinly and place in a bowl.

2 Slice the chilli lengthways, discard the seeds, then chop very finely. Peel and slice the cucumber and carrot and add to the onions and tomatoes.

COOK'S TIP
Traditional *Kachumbali* is made by very finely chopping the onions, tomatoes, cucumber and carrot. This produces a very moist, sauce-like mixture, which is good when served inside chapatis and eaten as a snack.

3 Squeeze the lemon juice over the salad. Season with salt and freshly ground black pepper and toss together to mix. Serve as an accompaniment, salad or relish.

COCONUT CHILLI RELISH

THIS SIMPLE BUT DELICIOUS RELISH IS WIDELY MADE IN TANZANIA. ONLY THE WHITE PART OF THE COCONUT FLESH IS USED — EITHER SHRED IT FAIRLY COARSELY, OR GRATE IT FINELY FOR A MOISTER RESULT.

MAKES ABOUT 50G/2OZ

INGREDIENTS
  50g/2oz fresh or desiccated
    (dry unsweetened
    shredded) coconut
  10ml/2 tsp lemon juice
  1.5ml/¼ tsp salt
  10ml/2 tsp water
  1.5ml/¼ tsp finely chopped
    red chilli

1 Grate the coconut and place in a mixing bowl. If using desiccated coconut, add just enough water to moisten it.

2 Add the lemon juice, salt, water and chilli. Stir thoroughly and serve as a relish with meats or as an accompaniment to a main dish.

STIR-FRIED CHILLI GREENS

*THIS ATTRACTIVE DISH IS SPICED WITH GINGER AND RED CHILLIES, AND GIVEN ADDED
ZEST BY THE ADDITION OF OYSTER SAUCE.*

SERVES FOUR

INGREDIENTS

2 bunches spinach or chard or
   1 head Chinese leaves (Chinese
   cabbage) or 450g/1lb curly kale
3 garlic cloves, crushed
5cm/2in fresh root ginger, peeled
   and cut in thin batons
45–60ml/3–4 tbsp groundnut
   (peanut) oil
115g/4oz skinless chicken breast
   fillet, or pork fillet (tenderloin), or
   a mixture of both, very finely sliced
12 quail's eggs, hard-boiled
   and shelled
1 fresh red chilli, seeded
   and cut into strips
30–45ml/2–3 tbsp oyster sauce
15ml/1 tbsp soft light brown sugar
10ml/2 tsp cornflour (cornstarch),
   mixed with 50ml/2fl oz/¼ cup
   cold water
salt

2 Stir-fry the garlic and ginger in the hot oil, without browning, for a minute. Add the chicken and/or pork and keep stirring it in the wok until the meat changes colour. When the meat looks cooked, add the sliced stems first and cook them quickly; then add the torn leaves, quail's eggs and chilli. Spoon in the oyster sauce and a little boiling water, if necessary. Cover and cook for 1–2 minutes only.

3 Remove the cover, stir and add sugar and salt to taste. Stir in the cornflour and water mixture and toss thoroughly. Cook until the mixture is well coated in a glossy sauce.

4 Serve immediately, while still very hot and the colours are bright and positively jewel-like.

COOK'S TIP
As with all stir-fries, don't start cooking until you have prepared all the ingredients and arranged them to hand. Cut everything into small, even pieces so the food can be cooked very quickly and all the colours and flavours preserved.

1 Wash the chosen leaves well and shake them dry. Strip the tender leaves from the stems and tear them into pieces. Discard the lower, tougher part of the stems and slice the remainder evenly.

GREEN BEAN <u>AND</u> CHILLI PEPPER SALAD

*THIS PIQUANT MIXTURE OF GREEN BEANS, PEPPERS, ONIONS AND CHILLIES IS SERVED ON
A BED OF COOLING SHREDDED LETTUCE WITH A TANGY DRESSING.*

SERVES FOUR

INGREDIENTS
350g/12oz/2¼ cups cooked green
   beans, quartered
2 red (bell) peppers, seeded
   and chopped
2 spring onions (scallions) (white
   and green parts), chopped
1 or more drained pickled serrano
   chillies, well rinsed and then
   seeded and chopped
1 iceberg lettuce, coarsely shredded,
   or mixed salad leaves
olives, to garnish

For the dressing
45ml/3 tbsp red wine vinegar
135ml/9 tbsp olive oil
salt and ground black pepper

1 Combine the cooked green beans,
chopped peppers, chopped spring
onions and chillies in a salad bowl.

2 Make the salad dressing. Pour the red
wine vinegar into a bowl or jug (pitcher).
Add salt and ground black pepper to
taste, then gradually whisk in the olive
oil until well combined.

3 Pour the salad dressing over the
prepared vegetables and toss lightly
together to mix and coat thoroughly.

4 Line a large platter with the shredded
lettuce leaves and arrange the salad
attractively on top. Garnish with the
olives and serve.

SPICY VEGETABLE RIBBONS

*FEW SALADS LOOK PRETTIER THAN THIS COMBINATION OF CUCUMBER, CARROT
AND MOOLI RIBBONS, TOSSED WITH BEANSPROUTS AND SPIKED WITH CHILLI.*

2 Wash the beansprouts and drain them thoroughly in a colander. Pat them dry with kitchen paper.

3 Peel the cucumber, cut it in half lengthwise and scoop out and discard the seeds. Peel the cucumber flesh into long ribbon strips, using a swivel vegetable peeler or mandoline.

SERVES FOUR

INGREDIENTS
   225g/8oz/4 cups beansprouts
   1 cucumber
   2 carrots
   1 small mooli (daikon)
   1 small red onion, thinly sliced
   2.5cm/1in fresh root ginger, peeled
     and cut into thin matchsticks
   1 small fresh red chilli, seeded and
     thinly sliced
   handful of fresh coriander (cilantro)
     leaves or fresh mint leaves

For the dressing
   15ml/1 tbsp rice vinegar
   15ml/1 tbsp light soy sauce
   15ml/1 tbsp Thai fish sauce
   1 garlic clove, finely chopped
   15ml/1 tbsp sesame oil
   45ml/3 tbsp groundnut (peanut) oil
   30ml/2 tbsp sesame seeds,
     lightly toasted

1 First make the dressing by mixing all the ingredients in a bottle or screw-top jar and shaking vigorously.

COOK'S TIPS
• Keep beansprouts refrigerated and use within a day of purchase.
• Mooli, which looks like a white parsnip, has a fresh, peppery taste. Eat it raw or cooked, but as it has a high water content it needs to be salted before cooking.
• Refrigerated, the dressing will keep for a couple of days.

4 Peel the carrots and mooli into ribbons as for the cucumber.

5 Place the carrots, mooli and cucumber ribbons in a large shallow serving dish, add the beansprouts, onion, ginger, chilli and coriander or mint and toss to mix. Pour the dressing over the salad just before serving.

GREEN PAPAYA AND CHILLI SALAD

THIS SALAD APPEARS IN MANY GUISES IN SOUTH-EAST ASIA. AS GREEN PAPAYA IS NOT EASY TO FIND, FINELY SHREDDED CARROTS, CUCUMBER OR GREEN APPLE CAN BE USED INSTEAD.

SERVES FOUR

INGREDIENTS

1 green papaya
4 garlic cloves, roughly chopped
15ml/1 tbsp chopped shallots
3–4 fresh red chillies, seeded and sliced, plus extra sliced fresh red chillies to garnish (optional)
2.5ml/½ tsp salt
2–3 snake beans or 6 green beans, cut into 2cm/¾in lengths
2 tomatoes, cut into thin wedges
45ml/3 tbsp Thai fish sauce
15ml/1 tbsp granulated (white) sugar
juice of 1 lime
30ml/2 tbsp crushed roasted peanuts

3 Add the sliced beans and wedges of tomato to the mortar and crush them lightly with the pestle.

VARIATION
Use cashew nuts instead of peanuts.

4 Flavour the mixture with the fish sauce, sugar and lime juice – you will not need extra salt. Transfer the salad to a serving dish and sprinkle with crushed peanuts. Garnish with the extra sliced red chillies, if using, and serve.

1 Cut the papaya in half lengthways. Scrape out the seeds with a spoon, then peel, using a swivel vegetable peeler or a small sharp knife. Shred the flesh finely using a food processor or grater.

2 Put the garlic, shallots, sliced chillies and salt in a large mortar and grind to a paste with a pestle. Add the shredded papaya, a little at a time, pounding until it becomes slightly limp and soft.

BUTTERNUT SQUASH AND FETA SALAD

THIS IS ESPECIALLY GOOD SERVED WITH A SALAD BASED ON RICE OR COUSCOUS.
SERVE THE DISH WITH PLENTY OF GOOD, WARM, CRUSTY BREAD.

SERVES FOUR TO SIX

INGREDIENTS

   75ml/5 tbsp olive oil
   15ml/1 tbsp balsamic vinegar, plus
     a little extra if needed
   15ml/1 tbsp sweet soy sauce
   350g/12oz shallots, peeled but
     left whole
   3 fresh red chillies
   1 butternut squash, peeled, seeded
     and cut into chunks
   5ml/1 tsp finely chopped fresh thyme
   60ml/4 tbsp chopped fresh flat
     leaf parsley
   1 small garlic clove, finely chopped
   75g/3oz/¾ cup walnuts or pecan
     nuts, chopped
   150g/5oz feta cheese
   salt and ground black pepper

1 Preheat the oven to 200°C/400°F/
Gas 6. Beat the oil, vinegar and soy
sauce together in a large bowl.

2 Toss the shallots and 2 of the chillies
in the oil mixture and turn into a large,
shallow roasting pan or ovenproof dish.
Season with salt and pepper. Roast,
uncovered, for 25 minutes, stirring once
or twice.

3 Add the butternut squash and roast
for a further 35–40 minutes, stirring
once, until the squash is tender and
browned. Remove from the oven, stir
in the chopped thyme and set the
vegetable mixture aside to cool.

4 Mix the parsley and garlic together
and stir in the nuts. Seed and finely
chop the remaining chilli.

5 Stir the parsley, garlic and nut mixture
into the cooled vegetables. Add chopped
chilli to taste and adjust the seasoning,
adding a little extra balsamic vinegar if
you like. Crumble the feta cheese and
add it to the salad, tossing together
lightly. Transfer to a serving dish and
serve immediately, at room temperature
rather than chilled.

COUSCOUS AND CHILLI SALAD

THIS IS A SPICY VARIATION ON A CLASSIC TABBOULEH, TRADITIONALLY MADE WITH
BULGUR WHEAT AND NOT COUSCOUS, WHICH IS ACTUALLY A FORM OF SEMOLINA GRAIN.

SERVES FOUR

INGREDIENTS
  45ml/3 tbsp olive oil
  5 spring onions (scallions), chopped
  1 garlic clove, crushed
  5ml/1 tsp ground cumin
  350ml/12fl oz/1½ cups
    vegetable stock
  175g/6oz/1 cup couscous
  2 tomatoes, peeled and chopped
  60ml/4 tbsp chopped fresh parsley
  60ml/4 tbsp chopped fresh mint
  1 fresh green chilli, seeded and
    finely chopped
  30ml/2 tbsp lemon juice
  salt and ground black pepper
  crisp lettuce leaves, to serve
  toasted pine nuts and grated lemon
    rind, to garnish

1 Heat the oil in a pan. Add the spring onions and garlic. Stir in the cumin and cook over a medium heat for 1 minute. Pour in the stock and bring to the boil.

2 Remove the pan from the heat, stir in the couscous, cover the pan tightly and leave to stand for 10 minutes, until all the liquid has been absorbed.

3 Tip the couscous into a bowl. Stir in the tomatoes, parsley, mint, chilli and lemon juice, and season. Leave to stand for 1 hour for the flavours to develop.

4 To serve, line a bowl with lettuce leaves and spoon the couscous salad into the centre. Sprinkle toasted pine nuts and lemon rind over, to garnish.

VARIATIONS
• You can use fine bulgur wheat instead of couscous. Follow the packet instructions for its preparation.
• It is very important for the flavour of the salad to use fresh mint. If it is not available, substitute fresh coriander. The flavour will not be quite the same but dried or freeze-dried mint are not suitable alternatives.

SWEET POTATO, PEPPER AND CHILLI SALAD

*THIS SALAD IS COMPOSED OF A DELICIOUS BLEND OF INGREDIENTS AND HAS A TRULY
TROPICAL TASTE. IT IS IDEAL SERVED WITH ASIAN OR CARIBBEAN DISHES.*

2 Meanwhile, mix the dressing
ingredients together in a bowl and
season to taste.

3 Put the red pepper in a large bowl
and add the celery and onion. Tip in the
finely chopped chilli and mix with a
wooden spoon.

SERVES FOUR TO SIX

INGREDIENTS
   1kg/2¼lb sweet potatoes
   1 red (bell) pepper, seeded and diced
   3 celery sticks, finely diced
   ¼ red skinned onion, finely chopped
   1 fresh red chilli, finely chopped
   salt and ground black pepper

For the dressing
   45ml/3 tbsp chopped fresh coriander
     (cilantro), plus extra to garnish
   juice of 1 lime
   150ml/¼ pint/⅔ cup natural
     (plain) yogurt

1 Preheat the oven to 200°C/400°F/
Gas 6. Wash the potatoes and pat dry
with kitchen paper, pierce them all over
and bake in the oven for 40 minutes or
until tender.

4 Remove the sweet potatoes from the
oven. When they are cool enough to
handle, peel them. Cut them into cubes
and add them to the large bowl. Drizzle
the dressing over and toss carefully.
Season again to taste and serve,
garnished with fresh coriander.

VARIATION
This would work well with potatoes.

GADO-GADO WITH PEANUT AND CHILLI SAUCE

A BANANA LEAF, WHICH CAN BE BOUGHT FROM ASIAN FOOD STORES, CAN BE USED AS WELL AS THE MIXED SALAD LEAVES TO LINE THE PLATTER FOR A SPECIAL OCCASION.

SERVES SIX

INGREDIENTS

½ cucumber
2 pears (not too ripe) or 175g/6oz
  wedge of yam bean (jicama)
1–2 eating apples
juice of ½ lemon
mixed salad leaves
6 small tomatoes, cut in wedges
3 slices fresh pineapple, cored and
  cut in wedges
3 eggs, hard-boiled (hard-cooked)
  and shelled
175g/6oz egg noodles, cooked,
  cooled and chopped
deep-fried onions, to garnish

For the peanut sauce
2–4 fresh red chillies, seeded and
  ground, or 15ml/1 tbsp chilli sambal
300ml/½ pint/1¼ cups coconut milk
350g/12oz/1¼ cups crunchy
  peanut butter
15ml/1 tbsp dark soy sauce or soft
  dark brown sugar
5ml/1 tsp tamarind pulp, soaked in
  45ml/3 tbsp warm water
coarsely crushed peanuts
salt

2 Simmer gently until the sauce thickens, then stir in the soy sauce or sugar. Strain in the tamarind juice, add salt to taste and stir well. Spoon into a bowl and sprinkle with a few coarsely crushed peanuts.

VARIATION
Quail's eggs can be used instead of hen's eggs and look very attractive in this dish. Hard-boil for 3 minutes, shell, then halve or leave whole.

3 To make the salad, core the cucumber and peel the pears or yam bean. Cut them into matchsticks. Finely shred the apples and sprinkle them with the lemon juice. Spread a bed of salad leaves on a flat platter, then pile the fruit and vegetables on top.

4 Add the sliced or quartered hard-boiled eggs, the chopped noodles and the deep-fried onions. Serve immediately, with the sauce.

1 Make the peanut sauce. Put the chillies or chilli sambal in a pan. Pour in the coconut milk. Stir in the peanut butter. Heat gently, stirring, until mixed.

COOK'S TIP
To make your own peanut butter, process roasted peanuts in a food processor, slowly adding vegetable oil to achieve the right texture. Add salt to taste.

HOT HOT CAJUN POTATO SALAD

IN CAJUN COUNTRY, WHERE TABASCO ORIGINATES, HOT MEANS REALLY HOT, SO YOU CAN GO TO TOWN WITH THIS SALAD IF YOU THINK YOU CAN TAKE IT!

2 Place the potatoes in a large bowl and add the green pepper, gherkin, spring onions and eggs. Mix gently.

3 In a separate bowl, mix the mayonnaise with the mustard and season with salt, black pepper and Tabasco sauce to taste.

4 Add the dressing to the potato mixture, toss gently to coat, then sprinkle a pinch or 2 of cayenne on top. Garnish with fanned, sliced gherkin.

COOK'S TIP
To hard-boil eggs, pierce the round end so air can escape to prevent cracking. Place in boiling water for 8 minutes. Remove into cold water, then peel.

<u>SERVES SIX TO EIGHT</u>

INGREDIENTS
  8 waxy potatoes
  1 green (bell) pepper, seeded
    and diced
  1 large gherkin, chopped
  4 spring onions (scallions), shredded
  3 eggs, hard-boiled (hard-cooked),
    shelled and chopped
  250ml/8fl oz/1 cup mayonnaise
  15ml/1 tbsp Dijon mustard
  Tabasco sauce, to taste
  pinch or 2 of cayenne
  salt and ground black pepper
  fanned, sliced gherkin, to garnish
  salad leaves, to serve

1 Put the unpeeled potatoes in a pan of cold salted water, bring to the boil and cook for 20–30 minutes, until tender. Drain. When the potatoes are cool enough to handle, peel them and cut into large chunks.

CHAYOTE SALAD

COOL AND REFRESHING, THIS SALAD IS IDEAL ON ITS OWN OR WITH FISH OR CHICKEN DISHES. THE SOFT FLESH OF THE CHAYOTES ABSORBS THE FLAVOUR OF THE DRESSING.

SERVES FOUR

INGREDIENTS

    2 *chayotes*, peeled, halved and seeded
    2 firm tomatoes
    1 small onion, finely chopped
    finely sliced strips of fresh red and
      green chilli, to garnish

For the dressing
    2.5ml/½ tsp Dijon mustard
    2.5ml/½ tsp ground anise
    90ml/6 tbsp white wine vinegar
    60ml/4 tbsp olive oil
    salt and ground black pepper

1 Bring a pan of water to the boil. Add the *chayotes* to the boiling water. Lower the heat and simmer for 20 minutes or until the *chayotes* are tender. Drain and set them aside to cool.

2 Meanwhile, peel the tomatoes. Cut a cross in the base of each tomato. Place them in a heatproof bowl and pour over boiling water to cover. After 3 minutes, lift the tomatoes out on a slotted spoon and plunge them into a bowl of cold water. Drain. The skins will have begun to peel back from the crosses. Remove the skins completely and cut the tomatoes into wedges.

3 Make the dressing by combining all the ingredients in a screw top jar. Close the lid tightly and shake the jar vigorously.

4 Cut the *chayotes* into wedges and place in a bowl with the tomato and onion. Pour over the dressing and serve garnished with strips of fresh red and green chilli.

SPICY POTATO SALAD

THIS TASTY SALAD IS QUICK TO PREPARE, AND MAKES A SATISFYING ACCOMPANIMENT TO MEAT OR FISH COOKED ON THE BARBECUE.

SERVES SIX

INGREDIENTS

900g/2lb potatoes, peeled
2 red (bell) peppers
2 celery sticks
1 shallot
2–3 spring onions (scallions)
1 green chilli, finely chopped
1 garlic clove, crushed
10ml/2 tsp finely chopped
   fresh chives
10ml/2 tsp finely chopped
   fresh basil
15ml/1 tbsp finely chopped
   fresh parsley
15ml/1 tbsp single (light) cream
30ml/2 tbsp salad cream
15ml/1 tbsp mayonnaise
5ml/1 tsp mild mustard
7.5ml/½ tbsp sugar
chopped fresh chives, to garnish

1 Boil the potatoes until tender but still firm. Drain and cool, then cut into 2.5cm/1in cubes and place in a large salad bowl.

2 Halve the peppers, cut away and discard the core and seeds and cut into small pieces. Finely chop the celery, shallot, and spring onions and slice the chilli very thinly, discarding the seeds. Add the vegetables to the potatoes together with the garlic and chopped herbs.

3 Blend the cream, salad cream, mayonnaise, mustard and sugar in a small bowl, stirring until the mixture is well combined.

4 Pour the dressing over the potato and vegetable salad and stir gently to coat evenly. Serve, garnished with the chopped chives.

PEPPERY BEAN SALAD

THIS PRETTY SALAD USES CANNED BEANS FOR SPEED AND CONVENIENCE. YOU COULD ADD EXTRA HOT PEPPER SAUCE IF YOU PREFER A MORE FIERY FLAVOUR.

SERVES FOUR TO SIX

INGREDIENTS

425g/15oz can kidney beans, drained
425g/15oz can black-eyed beans (peas), drained
425g/15oz can chickpeas, drained
¼ red (bell) pepper
¼ green (bell) pepper
6 radishes
15ml/1 tbsp chopped spring onion (scallion)
5ml/1 tsp ground cumin
15ml/1 tbsp tomato ketchup
30ml/2 tbsp olive oil
15ml/1 tbsp white wine vinegar
1 garlic clove, crushed
½ tsp hot pepper sauce
salt
sliced spring onion (scallion), to garnish

1 Drain the beans and chickpeas and rinse. Shake off the excess water and tip them into a large salad bowl.

2 Core, seed and chop the peppers. Trim the radishes and slice thinly. Add to the beans with the pepper and spring onion.

3 Mix together the cumin, ketchup, oil, vinegar and garlic in a small bowl. Add a little salt and hot pepper sauce to taste and stir again thoroughly.

4 Pour the dressing over the salad and mix. Chill for at least 1 hour before serving, garnished with spring onion.

COOK'S TIP
For an even tastier salad, allow the ingredients to marinate for a few hours.

PIQUANT SHELLFISH SALAD

THE FISH SAUCE DRESSING ADDS A SUPERB FLAVOUR TO THE NOODLES AND PRAWNS.

SERVES FOUR

INGREDIENTS

    200g/7oz rice vermicelli
    8 baby corn cobs, halved
    150g/5oz mangetouts (snow peas)
    15ml/1 tbsp vegetable oil
    2 garlic cloves, finely chopped
    2.5cm/1in piece fresh root ginger,
      peeled and finely chopped
    1 fresh red or green chilli, seeded
      and finely chopped
    450g/1lb raw peeled tiger prawns
      (jumbo shrimp)
    4 spring onions (scallions), sliced
    15ml/1 tbsp sesame seeds, toasted
    1 lemon grass stalk, thinly shredded

For the dressing
    15ml/1 tbsp chopped fresh chives
    15ml/1 tbsp Thai fish sauce
    5ml/1 tsp soy sauce
    45ml/3 tbsp groundnut (peanut) oil
    5ml/1 tsp sesame oil
    30ml/2 tbsp rice vinegar

1 Put the rice vermicelli in a wide heatproof bowl, pour over boiling water and leave to soak for 10 minutes. Drain, refresh under cold water and drain well again. Tip into a large serving bowl and set aside until required.

2 Boil or steam the corn cobs and mangetouts for about 3 minutes, until tender but still crunchy. Refresh under cold running water and drain. Make the dressing by mixing all the ingredients in a screw-top jar. Close tightly and shake vigorously to combine.

3 Heat the oil in a large frying pan or wok. Add the garlic, ginger and red or green chilli and cook for 1 minute. Add the tiger prawns and toss over the heat for about 3 minutes, until they have just turned pink. Stir in the spring onions, corn cobs, mangetouts and sesame seeds, and toss lightly to mix.

4 Tip the contents of the pan or wok over the rice vermicelli. Pour the dressing on top and toss well. Sprinkle with lemon grass and serve, or chill for 1 hour before serving.

PINK AND GREEN SALAD

THERE'S JUST ENOUGH CHILLI IN THIS STUNNING SALAD TO BRING A ROSY BLUSH TO YOUR CHEEKS.

SERVES FOUR

INGREDIENTS

225g/8oz/2 cups dried farfalle or
other pasta shapes
juice of ½ lemon
1 small fresh red chilli, seeded and
very finely chopped
60ml/4 tbsp chopped fresh basil
30ml/2 tbsp chopped fresh
coriander (cilantro)
60ml/4 tbsp extra virgin olive oil
15ml/1 tbsp mayonnaise
250g/9oz peeled cooked
prawns (shrimp)
1 avocado
salt and ground black pepper

1 Bring a large pan of lightly salted water to the boil and cook the pasta for 10–12 minutes, following the packet instructions, or until it is *al dente*.

2 Meanwhile, put the lemon juice and chilli in a bowl with half the basil and coriander. Add salt and pepper to taste. Whisk well to mix, then whisk in the oil and mayonnaise until thick. Add the prawns and stir to coat in the dressing.

3 Drain the pasta in a colander, and rinse under cold running water until cold. Leave to drain and dry, shaking the colander occasionally.

4 Halve, stone (pit) and peel the avocado, then cut the flesh into dice. Add to the prawns and dressing with the pasta, toss well to mix and taste for seasoning. Serve immediately, sprinkled with the remaining basil and coriander.

COOK'S TIP
Keep a few chillies in the freezer and you'll never need to worry about getting fresh supplies just when you want them.

THAI SHELLFISH SALAD WITH CHILLI DRESSING AND FRIZZLED SHALLOTS

IN THIS INTENSELY FLAVOURED SALAD, SWEET PRAWNS AND MANGO ARE PARTNERED WITH A SWEET-SOUR GARLIC DRESSING HEIGHTENED WITH THE HOT TASTE OF CHILLI.

SERVES FOUR TO SIX

INGREDIENTS

675g/1½lb raw prawns (shrimp),
   shelled and deveined, with
   tails on
finely grated rind of 1 lime
½ fresh red chilli, seeded and
   finely chopped
30ml/2 tbsp olive oil, plus extra
   for brushing
1 ripe but firm mango
2 carrots, cut into long
   thin shreds
10cm/4in piece cucumber, sliced
1 small red onion, halved and
   thinly sliced
45ml/3 tbsp roasted peanuts,
   roughly chopped
salt and ground black pepper

For the dressing
1 large garlic clove, chopped
10–15ml/2–3 tsp granulated
   (white) sugar
juice of 1½–2 limes
15–30ml/1–2 tbsp Thai fish sauce
1 fresh red chilli, seeded
5–10ml/1–2 tsp light rice vinegar

For the frizzled shallots
30ml/2 tbsp groundnut (peanut) oil
4 large shallots, thinly sliced

COOK'S TIPS
• For an authentic flavour, use Pacific shrimp, which are a wonderful brownish blue when raw. If they are frozen, make sure they are thawed before using.
• When searing the prawnsm (shrimp), make sure that they have all turned pink, as undercooked prawns are unpleasant to eat and may be harmful. However, do not overcook, which spoils the texture.
• Mangoes vary considerably. Some are ripe when the skin is green flushed with red; others when they are red-gold or yellow. Ripe mangoes give gently when squeezed lightly in the palm of the hand.

1 Place the prawns in a glass or china dish and add the lime rind and chilli. Season with salt and pepper, and spoon the oil over. Toss to mix, cover and leave to marinate for 30–40 minutes.

2 Make the dressing. Place the garlic in a mortar with 10ml/2 tsp sugar. Pound until smooth, then work in the juice of 1½ limes and 15ml/1 tbsp of the fish sauce.

3 Transfer the dressing to a jug (pitcher). Finely chop half the fresh red chilli, and add it to the dressing. Taste the mixture and add more sugar, lime juice, fish sauce and the rice vinegar to taste.

4 Cut through the mango lengthwise 1cm/½in from each side of the centre to free the stone (pit). Remove all the peel and cut the flesh away from the stone. Cut all the flesh into fine strips. Set the mango aside. Make the frizzled shallots by heating the oil in a wok or frying pan and frying them until crisp. Drain on kitchen paper and set aside.

5 In a bowl, toss the mango, carrots, cucumber and onion with half the dressing. Arrange the salad on individual plates or in bowls.

6 Heat a ridged, cast-iron griddle pan or heavy frying pan until very hot. Brush the prawns with a little oil, then sear them for 2–3 minutes on each side, until they turn pink and are patched with brown on the outside. Arrange the prawns on the salads.

7 Sprinkle the remaining dressing over the salads. Finely shred the remaining chilli and sprinkle it over the salads with the crisp-fried shallots. Serve, with the peanuts handed around separately.

VARIATIONS
• Use scallops or chicken breast fillets instead of prawns (shrimp).
• Chop cashew nuts in place of peanuts.
• Substitute finely sliced baby leeks for the shallots.
• Make into a more substantial meal by mixing with cooked pasta shapes.

SCALLOP CONCHIGLIE

*SCALLOPS, PASTA AND ROCKET ARE FLAVOURED WITH PEPPER, CHILLI AND BALSAMIC VINEGAR
IN THIS ELEGANT, LIGHT AND SUMMERY PASTA DISH.*

2 Make the vinaigrette. Put the vinegar in a bowl and stir in the honey until dissolved. Add the chopped pepper, chillies and garlic, then whisk in the oil.

3 Bring a large pan of lightly salted water to the boil and cook the pasta for 10–12 minutes, or until *al dente*.

4 Meanwhile, heat the oil and butter in a frying pan until sizzling. Add half the scallops and toss over a high heat for 2 minutes. Remove with a slotted spoon and keep warm. Cook the remaining scallops in the same way.

5 Add the wine to the liquid in the pan and stir over a high heat until the mixture has reduced to a few tablespoons. Remove from the heat and keep warm.

6 Drain the pasta and tip it into a warmed bowl. Add the rocket, scallops, the reduced cooking juices and the vinaigrette, and toss well to combine.

COOK'S TIP

This is best prepared using fresh scallops, which look creamy-grey. If pure white they will have been frozen.

SERVES FOUR

INGREDIENTS

8 large fresh scallops
300g/11oz/2¾ cups dried conchiglie
  or other pasta shapes
15ml/1 tbsp olive oil
15g/½oz/1 tbsp butter
120ml/4fl oz/½ cup dry white wine
90g/3½oz/1½–2 cups rocket
  (arugula) leaves, stalks trimmed
salt and ground black pepper

For the vinaigrette
15ml/1 tbsp balsamic vinegar
5–10ml/1–2 tsp clear honey, to taste
1 piece bottled roasted (bell) pepper,
  drained and finely chopped
1–2 fresh red chillies, seeded
  and chopped
1 garlic clove, crushed
60ml/4 tbsp extra virgin olive oil

1 Unless the fishmonger has already done so, remove the dark beard-like fringe and tough muscle from the scallops. Cut each of the scallops into 2–3 pieces. If the corals are attached, pull them off and cut each piece in half. Season with salt and pepper.

VARIATION

Use prawns (shrimp) instead of scallops.

SPICY SQUID SALAD

THIS COLOURFUL SALAD IS A REFRESHING WAY OF SERVING SQUID. THE GINGER AND CHILLI
DRESSING IS ADDED WHILE THE SQUID IS STILL HOT, AND FLAVOURS THE SHELLFISH AND BEANS.

SERVES FOUR

INGREDIENTS
   450g/1lb squid
   300ml/½ pint/1¼ cups fish stock
   175g/6oz green beans, trimmed
      and halved
   45ml/3 tbsp fresh coriander
      (cilantro) leaves
   10ml/2 tsp granulated (white) sugar
   30ml/2 tbsp rice vinegar
   5ml/1 tsp sesame oil
   15ml/1 tbsp light soy sauce
   15ml/1 tbsp vegetable oil
   2 garlic cloves, finely chopped
   10ml/2 tbsp finely chopped fresh
      root ginger
   1 fresh chilli, seeded and chopped
   salt

1 Prepare the squid. Holding the body
in one hand, gently pull away the head
and tentacles. Discard the head then
trim and reserve the tentacles. Remove
the transparent "quill" from inside the
body of the squid and peel off the
purplish skin on the outside.

2 Cut the body of the squid open
lengthways and wash thoroughly. Score
criss-cross patterns on the inside,
taking care not to cut through the flesh
completely, then cut into 7.5 × 5cm/
3 × 2in pieces.

COOK'S TIPS
• If you hold your knife at an angle when
scoring the squid, there is less of a risk
of cutting right through it.
• Always make sure your knives are kept
sharp to make cutting easier.

3 Bring the fish stock to the boil in a
wok or pan. Add all the squid pieces,
then lower the heat and cook for about
2 minutes until they are tender and
have curled. Drain.

4 Bring a pan of lightly salted water to
the boil, add the beans and cook them
for 3–5 minutes, until they are crisp-
tender. Drain, refresh under cold water
or turn into a bowl of iced water, then
drain again. Mix the squid and beans in
a serving bowl.

5 In a bowl, mix the coriander leaves,
sugar, rice vinegar, sesame oil and soy
sauce. Pour the mixture over the squid
and beans, and toss lightly, using a
spoon, to coat.

6 Heat the vegetable oil in a wok or
small pan. When it is very hot, stir-fry
the garlic, ginger and chilli for a few
seconds, then pour the dressing over
the squid mixture. Toss gently and leave
for at least 5 minutes. Add salt to taste
and serve warm or cold.

CHILLI CHICKEN SALAD

ANYONE WHO HAS TRAVELLED THROUGH NORTH-EAST THAILAND WILL HAVE ENCOUNTERED THIS TRADITIONAL DISH, IN WHICH CHICKEN IS COATED IN A HOT AND SHARP CHILLI SAUCE.

SERVES FOUR TO SIX

INGREDIENTS
    450g/1lb minced (ground) chicken
    1 lemon grass stalk, trimmed
    3 kaffir lime leaves,
      finely chopped
    4 fresh red chillies, seeded
      and chopped
    60ml/4 tbsp lime juice
    30ml/2 tbsp Thai fish sauce
    15ml/1 tbsp roasted ground rice
      (see Cook's Tip)
    2 spring onions (scallions), chopped
    30ml/2 tbsp fresh coriander
      (cilantro) leaves
    thinly sliced kaffir lime leaves,
      mixed salad leaves and fresh
      mint sprigs, to garnish

1 Heat a large non-stick frying pan. Add the chicken and moisten with a little water. Stir constantly over a medium heat for 7–10 minutes until it is cooked.

2 While the chicken is cooking, cut off the lower 5cm/2in of the lemon grass stalk and chop finely.

3 Transfer the cooked chicken to a bowl and add the chopped lemon grass, lime leaves, chillies, lime juice, fish sauce, ground rice, spring onions and coriander leaves. Mix thoroughly.

4 Spoon the chicken mixture into a salad bowl. Sprinkle sliced kaffir lime leaves over the top and garnish with salad leaves and sprigs of mint.

COOK'S TIP
Use glutinous rice (a short to medium grain rice) for the roasted ground rice. Put in a frying pan and dry-roast it until golden brown. Remove and grind to a powder, using a mortar and pestle or a food processor. When the rice is cold, store it in a glass jar in a cool, dry place.

THAI BEEF SALAD

A HEARTY MAIN MEAL SALAD, THIS COMBINES TENDER STRIPS OF STEAK WITH A WONDERFUL CHILLI AND LIME DRESSING. SERVE IT WITH WARM CRUSTY BREAD OR A BOWL OF RICE.

SERVES FOUR

INGREDIENTS
    oil, for frying
    2 sirloin steaks, each
      about 225g/8oz
    1 lemon grass stalk, trimmed
    1 red onion, finely sliced
    ½–1 fresh red chilli,
      finely chopped
    ½ cucumber, cut into strips
    30ml/2 tbsp chopped spring
      onion (scallion)
    juice of 2 limes
    15–30ml/1–2 tbsp Thai
      fish sauce
    Chinese mustard cress, or fresh
      herbs, to garnish

COOK'S TIP
Look out for gui chai leaves in Thai groceries. These look like very thin spring onions (scallions) and are often used as a substitute for the more familiar vegetable.

1 Heat a large frying pan until hot, add a little oil and pan-fry the steaks for 6–8 minutes for medium-rare. If you prefer, cook the steaks under a preheated medium grill (broiler). Allow to rest for 10–15 minutes.

2 Cut off the lower 5cm/2in of the lemon grass stalk and chop it finely.

3 When the meat is cool, slice it thinly on a cutting board and put the slices in a large bowl.

4 Add the sliced onion, chilli, cucumber, lemon grass and chopped spring onion to the meat slices.

5 Toss the salad and flavour with the lime juice and fish sauce. Transfer to a serving bowl or plate and serve at room temperature or chilled, garnished with Chinese mustard cress or fresh herbs.

VARIATION
Instead of beef, use pork, chicken or meaty tuna steaks.

CHICKEN, VEGETABLE AND CHILLI SALAD

*THIS VIETNAMESE SALAD IS FULL OF SURPRISING TEXTURES AND FLAVOURS. SERVE AS A
LIGHT LUNCH DISH OR FOR SUPPER WITH CRUSTY FRENCH BREAD.*

SERVES FOUR

INGREDIENTS
  225g/8oz Chinese leaves
    (Chinese cabbage)
  2 carrots, cut in matchsticks
  ½ cucumber, cut in matchsticks
  2 fresh red chillies, seeded and cut
    into thin strips
  1 small onion, sliced into fine rings
  4 pickled gherkins, sliced into fine
    rings, plus 45ml/3 tbsp of the
    liquid from the jar
  50g/2oz/½ cup peanuts, lightly ground
  225g/8oz cooked chicken, sliced
  1 garlic clove, crushed
  5ml/1 tsp granulated (white) sugar
  30ml/2 tbsp cider or white
    wine vinegar
  salt

COOK'S TIP
Add extra cider or white wine vinegar to
the dressing for a sharper taste.

1 Discard any tough, outer leaves from
the Chinese leaves, then stack the
remainder on a board. Using a sharp
knife, cut them into shreds that are
about the same width as the carrot
matchsticks. Put the Chinese leaves
and carrot matchsticks in a salad bowl.

2 Spread out the cucumber matchsticks
in a colander and sprinkle with salt.
Stand the colander on a plate and set
aside for 15 minutes, to extract the
excess liquid.

3 Mix the chillies and onion rings in a
small bowl. Add the sliced gherkins and
peanuts. Rinse the salted cucumber
thoroughly, drain well and pat dry with
kitchen paper.

4 Add the cucumber matchsticks to
the salad bowl and toss together lightly.
Stir in the chilli mixture. Arrange the
chicken on top. In a bowl, whisk the
gherkin liquid with the garlic, sugar and
vinegar. Pour over the salad, toss lightly
and serve.

THAI BEEF AND MUSHROOM SALAD

ALL THE INGREDIENTS FOR THIS TRADITIONAL THAI DISH — KNOWN AS YAM NUA YANG
— ARE WIDELY AVAILABLE IN LARGER SUPERMARKETS.

SERVES FOUR

INGREDIENTS
    675g/1½lb fillet (tenderloin) or
      rump (round) steak
    30ml/2 tbsp olive oil
    2 small mild red chillies, seeded
      and sliced
    225g/8oz/3¼ cups fresh shiitake
      mushrooms, stems removed and
      caps sliced

For the dressing
    3 spring onions (scallions),
      finely chopped
    2 garlic cloves, finely chopped
    juice of 1 lime
    15–30ml/1–2 tbsp Thai fish sauce
    5ml/1 tsp soft light brown sugar
    30ml/2 tbsp chopped fresh
      coriander (cilantro)

To serve
    1 cos or romaine lettuce, torn
      into strips
    175g/6oz cherry tomatoes, halved
    5cm/2in piece cucumber, peeled,
      halved and thinly sliced
    45ml/3 tbsp toasted sesame seeds

1 Preheat the grill (broiler) to medium, then cook the steak for 2–4 minutes on each side, depending on how well done you like it. (In Thailand, the beef is traditionally served quite rare.) Leave to cool for at least 15 minutes.

2 Slice the meat as thinly as possible and place the slices in a bowl.

3 Heat the olive oil in a small frying pan. Add the seeded and sliced red chillies and the sliced shiitake mushroom caps. Cook for 5 minutes, stirring occasionally. Turn off the heat and add the steak slices to the pan. Stir well to coat the beef slices in the chilli and mushroom mixture.

4 Make the dressing by mixing all the ingredients in a bowl, then pour it over the meat mixture and toss gently.

5 Arrange the lettuce, tomatoes and cucumber on a plate. Spoon the steak mixture in the centre and sprinkle the sesame seeds over. Serve immediately.

Warm spices, such as nutmeg, ginger, cinnamon and cardamom, enliven fresh fruit salads, ice creams, pastries, hot desserts and cakes. Indulge yourself with Fresh Pineapple with Ginger and wickedly sweet spicy Baklava from Persia. Give your friends a dessert to remember with an Egyptian version of Spiced Bread Pudding, scented with rose-water and flavoured with chopped pistachio nuts, almonds and hazelnuts.

Sweet and
Spicy Dishes

FRESH PINEAPPLE <u>WITH</u> GINGER

THIS REFRESHING DESSERT CAN ALSO BE MADE WITH VACUUM-PACKED PINEAPPLE.
ALTHOUGH THIS MAKES A GOOD SUBSTITUTE, FRESH PINEAPPLE IS BEST.

SERVES FOUR

INGREDIENTS
   1 fresh pineapple, peeled
   slivers of fresh coconut
   300ml/½ pint/1¼ cups pineapple juice
   60ml/4 tbsp coconut liqueur
   2.5cm/1in piece preserved stem
      ginger, plus 45ml/3 tbsp of
      the syrup

1 Peel and slice the pineapple, arrange in a serving dish and sprinkle the coconut slivers on top.

2 Place the pineapple juice and coconut liqueur in a pan and heat gently.

3 Thinly slice the preserved stem ginger and add to the pan with the syrup. Bring just to the boil and then simmer gently until the liquid is slightly reduced and the sauce is fairly thick.

4 Pour the sauce over the pineapple and coconut, leave to cool, then chill before serving.

COOK'S TIP
If fresh coconut is not available, use desiccated (dry unsweetened shredded) coconut instead.

COCONUT AND NUTMEG ICE CREAM

AN EASY-TO-MAKE, QUITE HEAVENLY, ICE CREAM THAT WILL BE LOVED BY ALL THE FAMILY FOR ITS TRULY TROPICAL TASTE.

<u>SERVES EIGHT</u>

INGREDIENTS
   400g/14oz can evaporated
      (unsweetened condensed) milk
   400g/14oz can sweetened
      condensed milk
   400g/14oz can coconut milk
   freshly grated nutmeg
   5ml/1 tsp almond extract
   lemon balm sprigs, lime slices and
      shredded coconut, to decorate

1 In a large freezerproof bowl mix together the evaporated, condensed and coconut milks and stir in the nutmeg and the almond extract.

2 Chill in a freezer for about an hour or two until the mixture is semi-frozen.

3 Remove from the freezer and whisk the mixture with a hand or electric whisk until it is fluffy and almost doubled in volume.

4 Pour into a freezer container, then cover and freeze. Soften slightly before serving, decorated with lemon balm, lime slices and shredded coconut.

SPICY NOODLE PUDDING

A TRADITIONAL JEWISH RECIPE, SPICY NOODLE PUDDING HAS A WARM AROMATIC FLAVOUR AND MAKES A DELICIOUS DESSERT.

SERVES FOUR TO SIX

INGREDIENTS
    175g/6oz wide egg noodles
    225g/8oz/1 cup cottage cheese
    115g/4oz/½ cup cream cheese
    75g/3oz/scant ½ cup caster
      (superfine) sugar
    2 eggs
    120ml/4fl oz/½ cup sour cream
    5ml/1 tsp vanilla extract
    pinch of ground cinnamon
    pinch of grated nutmeg
    2.5ml/½ tsp grated lemon rind
    50g/2oz/¼ cup butter
    25g/1oz/¼ cup nibbed almonds
    25g/1oz/scant ½ cup fine dried
      white breadcrumbs
    icing (confectioners') sugar
      for dusting

1 Preheat the oven to 180°C/350°F/ Gas 4. Grease a shallow ovenproof dish. Cook the noodles in a large pan of boiling water until just tender. Drain well.

2 Beat the cottage cheese, cream cheese and sugar together in a bowl. Add the eggs, one at a time, and stir in the sour cream. Stir in the vanilla extract, cinnamon, nutmeg and lemon rind.

3 Fold the noodles into the cheese mixture. Spoon into the prepared dish and level the surface.

4 Melt the butter in a frying pan. Add the almonds and cook for about 1 minute. Remove from the heat.

5 Stir in the breadcrumbs, mixing well. Sprinkle the mixture over the pudding. Bake for 30–40 minutes, or until the mixture is set. Serve hot, dusted with a little icing sugar.

SPICED NUTTY BANANAS

CINNAMON AND NUTMEG ARE SPICES WHICH PERFECTLY COMPLEMENT THE BANANAS AND COCONUT IN THIS DELECTABLE DESSERT.

SERVES THREE

INGREDIENTS

   6 ripe, but firm, bananas
   30ml/2 tbsp chopped unsalted
     cashew nuts
   30ml/2 tbsp chopped
     unsalted peanuts
   30ml/2 tbsp desiccated (dry
     unsweetened shredded) coconut
   7.5–15ml/½–1 tbsp demerara
     (raw) sugar
   5ml/1 tsp ground cinnamon
   2.5ml/½ tsp freshly grated nutmeg
   150ml/¼ pint/⅔ cup orange juice
   60ml/4 tbsp rum
   15g/½ oz/1 tbsp butter or margarine
   double (heavy) cream, to serve

1 Preheat the oven to 200°C/400°F/ Gas 6. Slice the bananas and place in a greased, shallow ovenproof dish.

2 Mix together the cashew nuts, peanuts, coconut, sugar, cinnamon and nutmeg in a small bowl.

3 Pour the orange juice and rum over the bananas, then sprinkle with the nut and sugar mixture.

4 Dot the top with butter or margarine, then bake in the oven for 15–20 minutes, or until the bananas are golden and the sauce is bubbly. Serve with double cream.

VARIATIONS
Freshly grated nutmeg makes all the difference to this dish. More rum can be added if you like. Chopped mixed nuts can be used instead of peanuts.

CARAMEL RICE PUDDING

THIS RICE PUDDING IS DELICIOUS SERVED WITH CRUNCHY FRESH FRUIT.

SERVES FOUR

INGREDIENTS
  50g/2oz/4 tbsp short grain rice
  75ml/5 tbsp demerara (raw) sugar
  5ml/1 tsp ground cinnamon
  400g/14oz can evaporated (unsweetened
    condensed) milk made up to
    600ml/1 pint/2½ cups with water
  a knob (pat) of butter
  1 small fresh pineapple
  2 crisp eating apples
  10ml/2 tsp lemon juice

1 Preheat the oven to 150°C/300°F/
Gas 2. Put the rice in a sieve (strainer)
and wash under cold water. Drain well
and put into a lightly greased soufflé dish.

2 Add 30ml/2 tbsp sugar and the
cinnamon to the dish. Add the diluted
milk and stir gently.

3 Dot the surface of the rice with butter
and bake for 2 hours, then leave to cool
for 30 minutes.

4 Meanwhile, peel, core and slice the
pineapple and apples and then cut
the pineapple into chunks. Toss the fruit
in lemon juice and set aside.

5 Preheat the grill (broiler) and sprinkle
the remaining sugar over the rice. Grill
(broil) for 5 minutes, or until the sugar
has caramelized. Leave the rice to stand
for 5 minutes to allow the caramel to
harden, then serve with the fresh fruit.

SPICED RICE PUDDING

BOTH MUSLIM AND HINDU COMMUNITIES PREPARE THIS TRADITIONAL PUDDING.

SERVES FOUR TO SIX

INGREDIENTS
  15ml/1 tbsp ghee or melted
    unsalted butter
  5cm/2in piece cinnamon stick
  225g/8oz/1 cup soft light
    brown sugar
  115g/4oz/½ cup ground rice
  1.2 litres/2 pints/5 cups milk
  5ml/1 tsp ground cardamom seeds
  50g/2oz/scant ½ cup sultanas
    (golden raisins)
  25g/1oz/¼ cup slivered almonds
  2.5ml/½ tsp grated nutmeg, to serve

1 In a heavy pan, heat the ghee or
butter and cook the cinnamon and
sugar. Keep cooking until the sugar
begins to caramelize. Reduce the heat
immediately when this happens.

2 Add the rice and half of the milk.
Bring to the boil, stirring constantly
to avoid the milk boiling over. Reduce
the heat and simmer until the rice is
cooked, stirring frequently.

3 Add the remaining milk, cardamom,
sultanas and almonds and leave to
simmer, but keep stirring to prevent
the rice from sticking to the base of the
pan. When the mixture has thickened,
serve hot or cold, sprinkled with the
grated nutmeg.

BAKLAVA

THIS IS THE QUEEN OF ALL PASTRIES WITH ITS EXOTIC FLAVOURS AND IS USUALLY SERVED
FOR THE PERSIAN NEW YEAR ON 21 MARCH, CELEBRATING THE FIRST DAY OF SPRING.

SERVES SIX TO EIGHT

INGREDIENTS
350g/12oz/3 cups ground
  pistachio nuts
150g/5oz/1¼ cups icing
  (confectioners') sugar
15ml/1 tbsp ground cardamom
150g/5oz/⅔ cup unsalted
  butter, melted
450g/1lb filo pastry

For the syrup
450g/1lb/2 cups granulated
  (white) sugar
300ml/½ pint/1¼ cups water
30ml/2 tbsp rose-water

1 First make the syrup: place the sugar and water in a pan, bring to the boil and then simmer for 10 minutes, until syrupy. Stir in the rose-water and leave to cool.

2 Mix together the nuts, icing sugar and cardamom. Preheat the oven to 160°C/325°F/Gas 3 and brush a large rectangular baking tin (pan) with a little melted butter.

3 Taking one sheet of filo pastry at a time, and keeping the remainder covered with a damp cloth, brush with melted butter and lay on the base of the tin. Continue until yoy have six buttered layers in the tin. Spread half of the nut mixture over, pressing down with a spoon.

4 Take another six sheets of filo pastry, brush with butter and lay over the nut mixture. Sprinkle over the remaining nuts and top with a final layer of six filo sheets brushed again with butter. Cut the pastry diagonally into small lozenge shapes using a sharp knife. Pour the remaining melted butter evenly over the top.

5 Bake for 20 minutes, then increase the heat to 200°C/400°F/Gas 6 and bake for 15 minutes, until light golden in colour and puffed.

6 Remove from the oven and drizzle about three-quarters of the syrup over the pastry, reserving the remainder for serving. Arrange the baklava lozenges on a large glass dish and serve with extra syrup.

SPICED BREAD PUDDING

HERE'S A SPICY EGYPTIAN VERSION OF THE CLASSIC BREAD AND BUTTER PUDDING,
MADE WITH FILO PASTRY IN PLACE OF THE BREAD AND FLAVOURED WITH ROSE-WATER.

SERVES FOUR

INGREDIENTS
    10–12 sheets filo pastry
    600ml/1 pint/2½ cups milk
    250ml/8fl oz/1 cup double
      (heavy) cream
    1 egg, beaten
    30ml/2 tbsp rose-water
    50g/2oz/½ cup each chopped pistachio
      nuts, almonds and hazelnuts
    115g/4oz/⅔ cup raisins
    15ml/1 tbsp ground cinnamon
    single (light) cream, to serve

1 Preheat the oven to 160°C/325°F/ Gas 3. Bake the filo pastry, on a baking sheet, for 15–20 minutes, until crisp. Remove the sheet from the oven and raise the temperature to 200°C/400°F/Gas 6.

2 Scald the milk and cream by pouring into a pan and heating the mixture very gently until it is hot but not boiling. Gradually add the beaten egg and the rose-water.

3 Cook over a low heat until the mixture begins to thicken, stirring constantly.

4 Crumble the pastry using your hands and then spread in layers with the nuts and raisins into the base of a shallow ovenproof dish.

5 Pour the custard mixture over the nut and pastry base and bake in the oven for 20 minutes, until golden. Sprinkle with cinnamon and serve with single cream.

DATE AND NUT PASTRIES

THESE ARABIC SWEETMEATS CONTAIN A DELICIOUS, AND NUTRITIOUS, MIXTURE OF DATES
AND THREE TYPES OF NUTS, AND ARE FLAVOURED WITH CINNAMON AND ROSE-WATER.

MAKES THIRTY FIVE TO FORTY

INGREDIENTS
    450g/1lb/4 cups plain
      (all-purpose) flour
    225g/8oz/1 cup unsalted butter, cubed
    45ml/3 tbsp rose-water
    60–75ml/4–5 tbsp milk
    icing (confectioners') sugar,
      for sprinkling

For the filling
    225g/8oz/1¼ cups dates, stoned
      (pitted) and chopped
    175g/6oz/1½ cups walnuts, chopped
    115g/4oz/1 cup blanched
      almonds, chopped
    50g/2oz/½ cup pistachio nuts, chopped
    120ml/4fl oz/½ cup water
    115g/4oz/½ cup sugar
    10ml/2 tsp ground cinnamon

1 Preheat the oven to 160°C/325°F/ Gas 3. Make the filling: place the dates, walnuts, almonds, pistachios, water, sugar and cinnamon in a small pan and cook over a low heat until the dates are soft and the water has been absorbed.

2 Place the flour in a large bowl and add the butter, working it into the flour with your fingertips.

3 Add the rose-water and milk and knead the dough until it's soft.

4 Take walnut-size lumps of dough. Roll each into a ball and hollow with your thumb. Pinch the sides.

5 Place a spoonful of date mixture in the hollow and then press the dough back over the filling to seal.

6 Arrange the pastries on a large baking sheet. Press to flatten slightly. Make little dents with a fork.

7 Bake in the oven for 20 minutes. Do not let them change colour or the pastry will become hard. Cool slightly and then sprinkle with icing sugar and serve.

CINNAMON BALLS

GROUND ALMONDS OR HAZELNUTS FORM THE BASIS OF MOST PASSOVER CAKES AND COOKIES.
THESE BALLS SHOULD BE SOFT INSIDE, WITH A VERY STRONG CINNAMON FLAVOUR.

MAKES ABOUT FIFTEEN

INGREDIENTS
175g/6oz/1½ cups ground almonds
75g/3oz/scant ½ cup caster
  (superfine) sugar
15ml/1 tbsp ground cinnamon
2 egg whites
oil, for greasing
icing (confectioners') sugar,
  for dredging

1 Preheat the oven to 180°C/350°F/
Gas 4. Grease a large baking sheet
with oil.

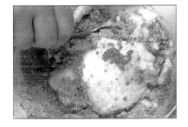

2 Mix together the ground almonds,
sugar and cinnamon.

3 Whisk the egg whites until they
begin to stiffen and fold enough egg
white into the almonds to make a
fairly firm mixture.

COOK'S TIP
The balls harden with keeping, so it is a
good idea to cook only what you need
and freeze the rest of the raw balls.
Defrost as required and then bake as
per the recipe.

4 Wet your hands with cold water and
roll small spoonfuls of the mixture into
balls. Place these at intervals on the
baking sheet. Bake for about 15 minutes
in the centre of the oven. They should
be slightly soft inside – too much
cooking will make them hard and tough.

5 Slide a spatula under the balls to
release them from the baking sheet and
leave to cool. Sift a little icing sugar on
to a plate and when the balls are cold
slide them on to the plate. Shake gently
to cover the balls in sugar and store in
an airtight container or in the freezer.

APPLE <u>AND</u> CINNAMON CRUMBLE CAKE

THIS SCRUMPTIOUS CAKE HAS LAYERS OF SPICY FRUIT AND CRUMBLE AND IS QUITE
DELICIOUS SERVED WARM WITH FRESH CREAM.

MAKES ONE CAKE

INGREDIENTS
    3 large cooking apples
    2.5ml/½ tsp ground cinnamon
    250g/9oz/1 cup butter
    250g/9oz/1¼ cups caster
      (superfine) sugar
    4 eggs
    450g/1lb/4 cups self-raising
      (self-rising) flour

For the crumble topping
    175g/6oz/¾ cup demerara (raw) sugar
    125g/4¼ oz/generous 1 cup plain
      (all-purpose) flour
    5ml/1 tsp ground cinnamon
    65g/2½ oz/about 4½ tbsp desiccated
      (dry unsweetened shredded) coconut
    115g/4oz/½ cup butter

1 Preheat the oven to 180°C/350°F/
Gas 4. Grease a 25cm/10in round
cake tin (pan) and line the base with
greaseproof (waxed) paper. To make
the crumble topping, mix together the
sugar, flour, cinnamon and coconut in a
bowl, then rub in the butter with your
fingertips and set aside.

2 Peel and core the apples, then
grate them coarsely. Place them in a
bowl, sprinkle with the cinnamon and
set aside.

3 Cream the butter and sugar in a bowl
with an electric mixer, until light and
fluffy. Beat in the eggs, one at a time,
beating well after each addition.

4 Sift in half the flour, mix well, then
add the remaining flour and stir
until smooth.

5 Spread half the cake mixture evenly
over the base of the prepared tin.
Spoon the apples on top and sprinkle
over half the crumble topping.

6 Spread the remaining cake mixture
over the crumble and finally top with
the remaining crumble topping.

7 Bake for 1 hour 10 minutes – 1 hour
20 minutes, covering the cake with foil
if it browns too quickly. Leave in the tin
for about 5 minutes, before turning out
on to a wire rack. Once cool, cut into
slices to serve.

COOK'S TIP
To make the topping in a food processor,
add all the ingredients and process for a
few seconds until the mixture resembles
bread-crumbs. You can also grate the
apples using the grating disc. If you
don't have a 25cm/10in round tin (pan),
you can use a 20cm/8in square cake tin.

BANANA GINGER CAKE

A CLEVER TWIST ON TWO CLASSIC FAVOURITES, GINGER CAKE AND BANANA CAKE, THIS MOIST,
TANGY RECIPE USES BOTH GROUND AND PRESERVED STEM GINGER TO PACK SOME PUNCH.

MAKES ONE CAKE

INGREDIENTS
    200g/7oz/1¾ cups plain
      (all-purpose) flour
    10ml/2 tsp bicarbonate of soda
      (baking soda)
    10ml/2 tsp ground ginger
    150g/5oz/1¼ cups medium oatmeal
    60ml/4 tbsp dark muscovado
      (molasses) sugar
    75g/3oz/6 tbsp sunflower margarine
    150g/5oz/¾ cup golden (light
      corn) syrup
    1 egg, beaten
    3 ripe bananas, mashed
    75g/3oz/¾ cup icing
      (confectioners') sugar
    preserved stem ginger, to decorate

1 Preheat the oven to 160°C/325°F/
Gas 3. Grease and line an 18 x 28cm/
7 x 11in cake tin (pan).

2 Stir together the flour, bicarbonate
of soda and ginger, then stir in the
oatmeal and combine.

3 Heat the sugar, margarine and
golden syrup in a pan, until melted,
then stir into the flour mixture.

4 Beat in the egg and mashed bananas
until thoroughly combined.

5 Spoon into the tin and bake for about
1 hour, or until firm to the touch. Leave
to cool in the tin, then turn out and cut
into squares.

6 Sift the icing sugar into a bowl and
stir in just enough water to make a
smooth, runny icing. Drizzle the icing
over each square and top with a piece
of preserved stem ginger.

COOK'S TIP
This is a nutritious, energy-giving
cake that is a really good choice for
packed lunches as it doesn't break
up too easily.

SPICED DATE AND WALNUT CAKE

MIXED SPICE ADDS A WARM FLAVOUR TO THIS LOW-FAT, HIGH-FIBRE CAKE. SIMPLY SERVE
IT ON ITS OWN, OR SPREAD IT WITH BUTTER AND HONEY FOR AN EXTRA SPECIAL SNACK.

MAKES ONE CAKE

INGREDIENTS

300g/11oz/2⅔ cups wholemeal
   (whole-wheat) self-raising
   (self-rising) flour
10ml/2 tsp mixed (apple pie) spice
150g/5oz/scant 1 cup chopped dates
50g/2oz/½ cup chopped walnuts
60ml/4 tbsp sunflower oil
115g/4oz/½ cup dark muscovado
   (molasses) sugar
300ml/½ pint/1¼ cups skimmed milk
walnut halves, to decorate

VARIATION
Pecan nuts can be used in place of the
walnuts in this cake, if you like.

1 Preheat the oven to 180°C/350°F/
Gas 4. Grease and line a 900g/2lb loaf tin
(pan) with greaseproof (waxed) paper.

2 Sift together the self-raising flour and
mixed spice, adding back any bran from
the sieve. Stir in the dates and walnuts.

3 Mix the oil, sugar and milk, then add
to the dry ingredients. Mix well, then
spoon the mixture into the prepared tin.

4 Arrange the walnut halves over the
top of the cake mixture. Bake the cake
for 45–50 minutes, or until golden
brown and firm. Turn out the cake,
remove the lining paper and leave to
cool on a wire rack.

MEXICAN BREAD PUDDING

MEXICAN COOKS BELIEVE IN MAKING GOOD USE OF EVERYTHING AVAILABLE TO THEM.
THIS PUDDING WAS INVENTED AS A WAY OF USING UP FOOD BEFORE THE LENTEN FAST,
BUT IS NOW EATEN AT OTHER TIMES TOO.

SERVES SIX

INGREDIENTS
    1 small French stick, a few days old
    75–115g/3–4oz/⅓–½ cup butter,
      softened, plus extra for greasing
    200g/7oz/scant 1 cup soft dark
      brown sugar
    1 cinnamon stick, about 15cm/
      6in long
    400ml/14fl oz/1⅔ cups water
    45ml/3 tbsp dry sherry
    75g/3oz/¾ cup flaked almonds,
      plus extra, to decorate
    75g/3oz/½ cup raisins
    115g/4oz/1 cup grated Monterey Jack
      or mild Cheddar cheese
    single (light) cream, for pouring

1 Slice the bread into about 30 rounds,
each 1cm/½in thick. Lightly butter on
both sides. Cook in batches in a warm
frying pan until browned, turning over
once. Set the slices aside.

2 Place the sugar, cinnamon stick and
water in a pan. Heat gently, stirring all
the time, until the sugar has dissolved.
Bring to the boil, then lower the heat
and simmer for 15 minutes without
stirring. Remove the cinnamon stick,
then stir in the sherry.

COOK'S TIP
This recipe works well with older bread
that is quite dry. If you only have fresh
bread, slice it and dry it out for a few
minutes in a low oven.

3 Preheat the oven to 180°C/350°F/
Gas 4. Grease a 20cm/8in square
baking dish with butter. Layer the bread
rounds, almonds, raisins and cheese in
the dish, pour the syrup over, letting it
soak into the bread. Bake the pudding
for about 30 minutes until golden brown.

4 Remove from the oven, leave to stand
for 5 minutes, then cut into squares.
Serve cold, with single cream poured
over and decorated with the extra
flaked almonds.

DRUNKEN PLANTAIN

MEXICANS ENJOY THEIR NATIVE FRUITS AND UNTIL THEIR CUISINE WAS INFLUENCED BY
THE SPANISH AND THE FRENCH, THEY HAD NO PASTRIES OR CAKES, PREFERING TO END
THEIR MEALS WITH FRUIT. THIS DELICIOUS DESSERT IS QUICK AND EASY TO PREPARE.

SERVES SIX

INGREDIENTS
    3 ripe plantains
    50g/2oz/¼ cup butter, diced
    45ml/3 tbsp rum
    grated rind and juice of
      1 small orange
    5ml/1 tsp ground cinnamon
    50g/2oz/¼ cup soft dark brown sugar
    50g/2oz/½ cup whole almonds,
      in their skins
    fresh mint sprigs, to decorate
    crème fraîche or thick double (heavy)
      cream, to serve

1 Preheat the oven to 180°C/350°F/
Gas 4. Peel the plantains and cut them
in half lengthways. Put the pieces in a
shallow baking dish, dot them all over
with butter, then spoon over the rum
and orange juice.

2 Mix the orange rind, cinnamon and
brown sugar in a bowl. Sprinkle the
mixture over the plantains.

3 Bake for 25–30 minutes, until the
plantains are soft and the sugar has
melted into the rum and orange juice
to form a sauce.

4 Meanwhile, slice the almonds and dry
fry them in a heavy-based frying pan
until the cut sides are golden. Serve the
plantains in individual bowls, with some
of the sauce spooned over. Sprinkle the
almonds on top, decorate with the fresh
mint sprigs and offer crème fraîche or
double cream separately.

CINNAMON ROLLS

SIMILAR TO A CHELSEA BUN, BUT WITHOUT THE ICING, THESE FLAVOURSOME FRUITY ROLLS FILL THE HOUSE WITH THE APPETIZING AROMA OF CINNAMON AND SUGAR AS THEY COOK.

MAKES TWENTY FOUR SMALL ROLLS

INGREDIENTS

For the dough
    400g/14oz/3½ cups strong
        white bread flour
    2.5ml/½ tsp salt
    30ml/2 tbsp sugar
    5ml/1 tsp easy-blend (rapid-rise)
        dried yeast
    45ml/3 tbsp oil
    1 egg
    120ml/4fl oz/½ cup warm milk
    120ml/4fl oz/½ cup warm water

For the filling
    25g/1oz/2 tbsp butter, softened
    25g/1oz/2 tbsp soft dark brown sugar
    2.5–5ml/½–1 tsp ground cinnamon
    15ml/1 tbsp raisins

1 Sift the flour, salt and sugar and sprinkle over the yeast. Mix the oil, egg, milk and water and add to the flour. Mix to a dough, then knead until smooth. Leave to rise until doubled in size and then knock back (punch down).

2 Roll out the dough into a large rectangle and cut in half vertically. Spread over the soft butter, reserving 15ml/1 tbsp for brushing. Mix the sugar and cinnamon and sprinkle over the top. Dot with the raisins.

3 Roll each piece into a long Swiss (jelly) roll shape, to enclose the filling. Cut into 2.5cm/1in slices, arrange flat on a greased baking sheet and brush with the remaining butter. Leave to rise again for about 30 minutes.

4 Preheat the oven to 200°C/400°F/ Gas 6 and bake the cinnamon rolls for about 20 minutes. Leave to cool on a wire rack. Serve fresh for breakfast or tea, with extra butter if you like.

PEACH KUCHEN

THE JOY OF THIS CAKE IS ITS ALL-IN-ONE SIMPLICITY. IT CAN BE SERVED STRAIGHT FROM THE OVEN, OR CUT INTO SQUARES WHEN COLD.

SERVES EIGHT

INGREDIENTS

350g/12oz/3 cups self-raising
  (self-rising) flour
225g/8oz/1 cup caster
  (superfine) sugar
175g/6oz/¾ cup unsalted
  butter, softened
2 eggs
120ml/4fl oz/½ cup milk
6 large peeled peaches, sliced or
  450g/1lb plums or cherries, pitted
115g/4oz/½ cup soft light brown sugar
2.5ml/½ tsp ground cinnamon
sour cream or crème fraîche, to serve

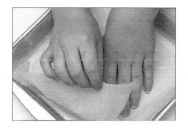

1 Preheat the oven to 190°C/375°F/
Gas 5. Grease and line a 20 x 25 x
2.5cm/8 x 10 x 1in cake tin (pan).

2 Put the flour, sugar, butter, eggs and
milk into a large bowl and beat for a few
minutes until you have a smooth batter.
Spoon it into the prepared cake tin.

COOK'S TIP
To peel ripe peaches, cover with boiling
water for 20 seconds. The skin will then
slip off easily.

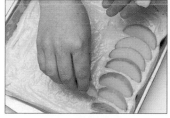

3 Arrange the peaches, plums or
cherries over the cake mixture. Mix the
brown sugar and cinnamon and
sprinkle over the fruit.

4 Bake for about 40 minutes, testing for
doneness by inserting a cocktail stick
(toothpick) in the centre.

5 Serve the cake warm or cool with the
sour cream or crème fraîche.

CARIBBEAN FRUIT AND RUM CAKE

THIS IS A DELICIOUS RECIPE FOR A CAKE THAT IS EATEN AT CHRISTMAS, WEDDINGS AND OTHER SPECIAL OCCASIONS. IT IS KNOWN AS BLACK CAKE, BECAUSE, TRADITIONALLY, THE RECIPE USES BURNT SUGAR.

MAKES ONE CAKE

INGREDIENTS
    450g/1lb/2 cups currants
    450g/1lb/3 cups raisins
    225g/8oz/1 cup prunes, pitted
    115g/4oz/⅔ cup mixed
      (candied) peel
    400g/14oz/2¼ cups soft dark
      brown sugar
    5ml/1 tsp mixed (apple pie) spice
    90ml/6 tbsp rum, plus more
      if needed
    300ml/½ pint/1¼ cups sherry,
      plus more if needed
    450g/1lb/2 cups softened butter
    10 eggs, beaten
    450g/1lb/4 cups self-raising
      (self-rising) flour
    5ml/1 tsp vanilla extract

1 Wash the currants, raisins, prunes and mixed peel, then pat dry. Place in a food processor and process until finely chopped. Transfer to a large, clean jar or bowl, add 115g/4oz of the sugar, the mixed spice, rum and sherry. Mix very well and then cover with a lid and set aside for anything from 2 weeks to 3 months – the longer it is left, the better the flavour will be.

2 Stir the fruit mixture occasionally and keep covered, adding more alcohol, if you like.

3 Preheat the oven to 160°C/325°F/ Gas 3. Grease and line a 25cm/10in round cake tin (pan) with a double layer of greaseproof (waxed) paper.

4 Sift the flour and set aside. Cream together the butter and remaining sugar and beat in the eggs until the mixture is smooth and creamy.

5 Add the fruit mixture, then gradually stir in the flour and vanilla extract. Mix well, adding 15–30ml/1–2 tbsp sherry if the mixture is too stiff; it should just fall off the back of the spoon, but should not be too runny.

6 Spoon the mixture into the prepared tin, cover loosely with foil and bake for about 2½ hours, until the cake is firm and springy. Leave to cool in the tin overnight, then sprinkle with more rum if the cake is not to be used immediately. Wrap the cake in foil to keep it moist.

COOK'S TIP
Although the dried fruits are chopped in a food processor, they can be marinated whole, if you prefer. If you don't have enough time to marinate the fruit, simmer the fruit in the alcohol mixture for about 30 minutes, and leave overnight.

Add colour and fire to Mexican Sangrita, a refreshing drink based on tomatoes — and chillies! Bring a touch of fire to a Bloody Maria cocktail by pepping it up with Worcestershire and Tabasco sauces. Try a Caribbean pick-me-up with Caribbean Cream Stout Punch or Demerara Rum Punch, sprinkled with freshly grated nutmeg. Finally, as your friends gather round the fireside on a chilly winter day, warm their hearts with tumblers of Spiced Mocha Drink or Mulled Wine.

Spiced Drinks

SPICED MOCHA DRINK

THIS SPICY CHOCOLATE MILK DRINK CAN BE SERVED EITHER HOT OR COLD — DEPENDING ON THE WEATHER AND YOUR PREFERENCE.

SERVES FOUR

INGREDIENTS

175g/6oz milk chocolate
120ml/4fl oz/½ cup single
(light) cream
750ml/1¼ pints/3 cups hot
black coffee
2.5ml/½ tsp ground cinnamon
whipped cream or ice, to serve

1 Using a sharp knife, cut the chocolate into small pieces to enable it to melt quickly and evenly.

2 Put the chocolate into a double saucepan or a bowl set over a pan of almost simmering water. The base of the bowl should not touch the water.

3 Add the single cream to the chocolate melting in the bowl, then stir together well to mix.

4 Continue to heat gently until the chocolate is melted and smooth, stirring occasionally. Remove the bowl from the heat.

5 Add the coffee and cinnamon to the chocolate and whisk until foamy. Divide among four serving glasses, then either serve hot with a spoonful of cream, or cool and chill, and serve over ice.

COOK'S TIP
If any steam gets into the chocolate while you are melting it, it may turn into a solid mass. If this should happen, stir in about 5ml/1 tsp butter or margarine for each 25g/1oz of chocolate.

MULLED WINE

CLOVES, CINNAMON AND NUTMEG ADD SPICY FLAVOUR TO THIS DELICIOUS MULLED WINE. IT MAKES A WARMING DRINK FOR A WINTER PARTY.

MAKES SIXTEEN ×
150ml/¼ PINT/⅔ CUP GLASSES

INGREDIENTS
1 orange
60ml/4 tbsp demerara (raw) sugar
grated nutmeg
2 cinnamon sticks
a few cloves, plus extra for studding
30ml/2 tbsp seedless raisins
75ml/5 tbsp clear honey
2 clementines
1.5 litres/2½ pints/6¼ cups red wine
750ml/1¼ pints/3 cups medium
(hard) cider
300ml/½ pint/1¼ cups orange juice

1 With a sharp knife or a vegetable peeler, pare off a long strip of orange rind.

VARIATION
Vary the spices used in this mulled wine – whole allspice can be added instead of cinnamon sticks. If you like, you can also add a selection of sliced citrus fruits.

2 Place the sugar, nutmeg, cinnamon, cloves, raisins, honey and rind in a large pan. Stud the clementines with cloves and add them to the pan. Add the wine and heat gently until the sugar is dissolved. Pour in the cider and continue to heat gently. Do not boil.

3 Add the orange juice to the pan and warm through. Remove the clementines and cinnamon sticks and strain the mulled wine into a warmed punch bowl or other serving bowl. Add the clove-studded clementines and serve hot in warmed glasses, or in glasses containing a small spoon (to prevent the glass from breaking).

SANGRITA

THE BLOOD-RED COLOUR OF THIS VERY FIERY YET COOLING BEVERAGE IS REFLECTED IN ITS NAME, WHIH IS DERIVED FROM THE SPANISH WORD FOR "BLOOD".

SERVES EIGHT

INGREDIENTS

    450g/1lb tomatoes, peeled, seeded and chopped
    120ml/4fl oz/½ cup orange juice
    60ml/4 tbsp freshly squeezed lime juice
    1 small onion, chopped
    2.5ml/½ tsp granulated (white) sugar
    6 small fresh green chillies, seeded and chopped
    50ml/2oz aged tequila *(Tequila Anejo)* per person
    salt

1 Put the chopped tomatoes, orange juice, lime juice, chopped onion, granulated sugar and chopped green chillies into a food processor.

2 Process the tomato mixture until very smooth, scraping down the sides if necessary.

3 Pour the tomato mixture into a jug (pitcher) and chill well.

4 To serve, pour into small glasses, allowing about 90ml/6 tbsp per portion. Pour the tequila into separate small glasses. Sip the tomato juice and tequila alternately.

COOK'S TIP
Plain white tequila is not suitable for this. Choose one of the amber aged tequilas *(Añejos)*, which are smoother and more gentle on the palate.

SANGRIA

THIS VERY POPULAR SUMMER DRINK WAS BORROWED FROM SPAIN. THE MEXICAN VERSION IS VERY SLIGHTLY LESS ALCOHOLIC THAN THE SPANISH ORIGINAL.

SERVES SIX

INGREDIENTS

    ice cubes
    1 litre/1¾ pints/4 cups dry red table wine
    150ml/¼ pint/⅔ cup orange juice
    50ml/2fl oz/¼ cup freshly squeezed lime juice
    115g/4oz/generous ½ cup caster (superfine) sugar
    2 limes or 1 apple, sliced, to serve

1 Half fill a large jug (pitcher) with ice cubes. Pour in the wine and the orange and lime juices.

2 Add the sugar and stir well until it has dissolved completely.

3 Pour into tall glasses and float the lime or apple slices on top. Serve the sangria immediately.

COOK'S TIP
Sugar does not dissolve readily in alcohol. It is easier to use simple sugar syrup, which is very easy to make and gives a smoother drink. Combine 475ml/16fl oz/2 cups granulated (white) sugar and 450g/1lb water in a jug (pitcher) and set aside until the sugar has dissolved. Stir from time to time. 15ml/1 tbsp simple syrup is the equivalent of 7.5ml/1½ tsp sugar.

VARIATION
Substitute sparkling lemonade for the orange juice for a lighter drink.

BLOODY MARIA

A CLOSE COUSIN OF THE ORIGINAL VODKA-BASED BLOODY MARY, THIS SIMPLE COCKTAIL CONSISTS OF WHITE TEQUILA AND TOMATO JUICE MIXED TOGETHER WITH SPICY SEASONINGS. BE CAREFUL WHEN ADDING THE TABASCO SAUCE — IT'S WICKEDLY HOT.

SERVES TWO

INGREDIENTS
175ml/6fl oz/¾ cup tomato juice
90ml/3fl oz/6 tbsp white tequila
a dash each of Worcestershire and
    Tabasco sauces
30ml/2 tbsp lemon juice
salt and ground black pepper
8 ice cubes

COOK'S TIP
When drinks are to be served with ice, make sure all the ingredients are thoroughly chilled ahead of time.

1 Combine the tomato juice, tequila, Worcestershire and Tabasco sauces, and lemon juice in a cocktail shaker. Add salt and pepper to taste, and four ice cubes. Shake very vigorously.

2 Place the remaining ice cubes in two heavy-based glasses and strain the tequila over them.

MARGARITA

TEQUILA IS MADE FROM THE SAP OF A FLESHY-LEAFED PLANT CALLED THE BLUE AGAVE AND GETS ITS NAME FROM THE TOWN OF TEQUILA, WHERE IT HAS BEEN MADE FOR OVER 200 YEARS. THE MARGARITA IS THE BEST-KNOWN DRINK MADE WITH TEQUILA.

SERVES TWO

INGREDIENTS
½ lime or lemon
120ml/4fl oz/½ cup white tequila
30ml/2 tbsp Triple Sec or Cointreau
30ml/2 tbsp freshly squeezed lime or
    lemon juice
4 or more ice cubes
salt

1 Rub the rims of two cocktail glasses with the lime or lemon. Pour some salt into a saucer and dip in the glasses so that the rims are frosted.

COOK'S TIP
It really is worth going to the trouble of buying limes for this recipe. Lemons will do, but something of the special flavour of the drink will be lost in the substitution.

2 Combine the tequila, Triple Sec or Cointreau, and lime and lemon juice in a jug (pitcher) and stir to mix well.

3 Pour the tequila mixture into the prepared glasses. Add the ice cubes and serve immediately.

DEMERARA RUM PUNCH

THE INSPIRATION FOR THIS PUNCH CAME FROM THE RUM DISTILLERY AT PLANTATION DIAMOND ESTATE IN GUYANA WHERE SOME OF THE FINEST RUM IN THE WORLD IS MADE.

SERVES FOUR

INGREDIENTS

150ml/¼ pint/⅔ cup orange juice
150ml/¼ pint/⅔ cup pineapple juice
150ml/¼ pint/⅔ cup mango juice
120ml/4fl oz/½ cup water
250ml/8fl oz/1 cup dark rum
a dash of angostura bitters
freshly grated nutmeg
25g/1oz/2 tbsp demerara
   (raw) sugar
1 small banana
1 large orange

1 Pour the orange, pineapple and mango juices into a large punch bowl. Stir in the water.

2 Add the rum, bitters, nutmeg and sugar. Stir gently until the sugar dissolves.

3 Slice the banana and stir gently into the punch.

4 Slice the orange and add to the punch. Chill and serve with ice.

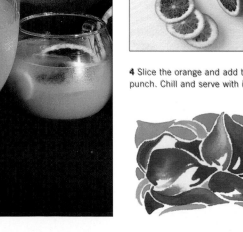

CARIBBEAN CREAM STOUT PUNCH

A WELL-KNOWN "PICK-ME-UP" THAT IS POPULAR ALL OVER THE CARIBBEAN, THIS SATISFYING DRINK COMBINES STOUT, SHERRY AND MILK WITH AROMATIC NUTMEG AND VANILLA.

SERVES TWO

INGREDIENTS
  475ml/16fl oz/2 cups stout
  300ml/½ pint/1¼ cups evaporated
    (unsweetened condensed) milk
  75ml/5 tbsp sweetened
    condensed milk
  75ml/5 tbsp sherry
  2 or 3 drops vanilla extract
  freshly grated nutmeg

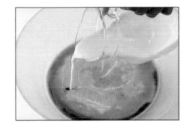

1 Mix together the stout, evaporated and condensed milks, sherry and vanilla extract in a blender or food processor, or whisk together in a large mixing bowl, until creamy.

2 Add a little grated nutmeg to the stout mixture and blend or whisk again for a few minutes.

COOK'S TIP
Stout is a strong, dark beer that originated in the British Isles. It has a strong taste of hops and is made with roasted barley, which gives it its dark colour and bittersweet flavour.

3 Chill for at least 45 minutes. Serve.

NUTRITIONAL INFORMATION

The nutritional analysis below is
per portion, unless otherwise stated.

p30 Salsa Verde Energy 216Kcal/888kJ;
Protein 1g; Carbohydrate 2g, of which
sugars 2g; Fat 3g, of which saturates
0g; Cholesterol 0mg; Calcium 16mg;
Fibre 0.5g; Sodium 0.1g.
p30 Avocado and Sweet Red Pepper Salsa
Energy 235Kcal/968kJ; Protein 3g;
Carbohydrate 7g, of which sugars 5g;
Fat 22g, of which saturates 4g;
Cholesterol 0mg; Calcium 35mg;
Fibre 3.6g; Sodium 0.1g.
p31 Chilli and Pesto Salsa Energy 310Kcal/
1277kJ; Protein 5g; Carbohydrate 2g, of
which sugars 1g; Fat 31g, of which
saturates 5g; Cholesterol 6mg; Calcium
99mg; Fibre 1.0g; Sodium 0.2g.
p32 Fiery Citrus Salsa Energy 36Kcal/
153kJ; Protein 1g; Carbohydrate 8g, of
which sugars 8g; Fat 0g, of which
saturates 0g; Cholesterol 0mg; Calcium
23mg; Fibre 1.4g; Sodium 0.1g.
p33 Classic Mexican Tomato Salsa
Energy 42Kcal/176kJ; Protein 2g;
Carbohydrate 8g, of which sugars 7g;
Fat 1g, of which saturates 0g; Cholesterol
0mg; Calcium 31mg; Fibre 1.7g;
Sodium 0.1g.
p34 Roasted Tomato Salsa Energy
67Kcal/278kJ; Protein 1g; Carbohydrate
7g, of which sugars 5g; Fat 4g, of which
saturates 1g; Cholesterol 0mg; Calcium
18mg; Fibre 1.5g; Sodium 0.1g.
p36 Mango and Chilli Salsa Energy
68Kcal/288kJ; Protein 2g; Carbohydrate
16g, of which sugars 14g; Fat 0g, of
which saturates 0g; Cholesterol 0mg;
Calcium 33mg; Fibre 2.8g; Sodium 0g.
p36 Roasted Serrano and Tomato Salsa
Energy 27Kcal/116kJ; Protein 1g;
Carbohydrate 5g, of which sugars 4g;
Fat 0g, of which saturates 0g; Cholesterol
0mg; Calcium 23mg; Fibre 1.2g;
Sodium 0.1g.
p38 Hot Hot Habanero Salsa Serves 4:
Energy 22Kcal/92kJ; Protein 1g;
Carbohydrate 4g, of which sugars 4g;
Fat 0g, of which saturates 0g; Cholesterol
0mg; Calcium 20mg; Fibre 0.1g;
Sodium 0.1g.
p39 Sweet Potato and Jalapeño Salsa
Energy 161Kcal/688kJ; Protein 3g;
Carbohydrate 39g, of which sugars 13g;
Fat 2g, of which saturates 0g; Cholesterol
0mg; Calcium 61mg; Fibre 4.7g;
Sodium 0.2g.
p40 Cactus Pear Salsa Energy 58Kcal/
243kJ; Protein 2g; Carbohydrate 11g,
of which sugars 10g; Fat 0g, of which
saturates 0g; Cholesterol 0mg; Calcium
58mg; Fibre 0.9g; Sodium 0.3g.
p42 Pinto Bean Salsa Energy 146Kcal/
621kJ; Protein 10g; Carbohydrate 26g,
of which sugars 4g; Fat 1g, of which
saturates 0g; Cholesterol 0mg; Calcium
75mg; Fibre 8.0g; Sodium 0.1g.
p43 Black Bean Salsa Energy 78Kcal/
27kJ; Protein 3g; Carbohydrate 10g, of
which sugars 3g; Fat 3g, of which
saturates 0g; Cholesterol 0mg; Calcium
25mg; Fibre 2.2g; Sodium 0.1g.
p44 Guacamole Energy 209Kcal/862kJ;
Protein 3g; Carbohydrate 6g, of which
sugars 3g; Fat 20g, of which saturates
4g; Cholesterol 0mg; Calcium 25mg;
Fibre 4.2g; Sodium 0.1g.

p45 Spicy Tomato and Chilli Dip Energy
99Kcal/412kJ; Protein 2g; Carbohydrate
6g, of which sugars 5g; Fat 8g, of which
saturates 1g; Cholesterol 0mg; Calcium
28mg; Fibre 1.5g; Sodium 0.1g.
p46 Spiced Carrot Dip Energy 74Kcal/
311kJ; Protein 3g; Carbohydrate 13g, of
which sugars 12g; Fat 1g, of which
saturates 0g; Cholesterol 0mg; Calcium
95mg; Fibre 2.0g; Sodium 0.2g.
p47 Chilli Bean Dip Energy 196Kcal/
880kJ; Protein 9g; Carbohydrate 12g, of
which sugars 4g; Fat 13g, of which
saturates 5g; Cholesterol 18mg; Calcium
200mg; Fibre 3.5g; Sodium 0.7g.
p48 Chilli and Red Onion Raita
Energy 54Kcal/225kJ; Protein 3g;
Carbohydrate 8g, of which sugars 7g;
Fat 1g, of which saturates 1g; Cholesterol
4mg; Calcium 98mg; Fibre 0.9g; Sodium
0.1g.
p49 Pumpkin Seed Sauce Energy
215Kcal/894kJ; Protein 8g; Carbohydrate
10g, of which sugars 6g; Fat 16g, of
which saturates 2g; Cholesterol 0mg;
Calcium 23mg; Fibre 2.9g; Sodium 0.5g.
p50 Smoky Chipotle Sauce Energy
67Kcal/286kJ; Protein 1g; Carbohydrate
11g, of which sugars 11g; Fat 0g, of
which saturates 0g; Cholesterol 0mg;
Calcium 14mg; Fibre 0.9g; Sodium 0.1g.
p50 Guajillo Chilli Sauce Energy
52Kcal/219kJ; Protein 2g; Carbohydrate
9g, of which sugars 9g; Fat 1g, of
which saturates 0g; Cholesterol 0mg;
Calcium 19mg; Fibre 2g; Sodium 0.2g.
p52 Thai Red Curry Sauce Energy 386Kcal/
1595kJ; Protein 5g; Carbohydrate 5g,
of which sugars 4g; Fat 38g, of which
saturates 30g; Cholesterol 0mg; Calcium
33mg; Fibre 0.6g; Sodium 0.3g.
p53 Mexican Vinegar Seasoning Energy
17Kcal/70kJ; Protein 1g; Carbohydrate
2g, of which sugars 1g; Fat 0g, of which
saturates 0g; Cholesterol 0mg; Calcium
22mg; Fibre .03g; Sodium 0.7g.
p54 Chilli Relish Energy 86Kcal/363kJ;
Protein 1g; Carbohydrate 15g, of which
sugars 14g; Fat 3g, of which saturates
0g; Cholesterol 0mg; Calcium 23mg;
Fibre 1.3g; Sodium 0.3g.
p55 Spicy Corn Relish Energy
115Kcal/482kJ; Protein 3g; Carbohydrate
19g, of which sugars 9g; Fat 4g, of
which saturates 0g; Cholesterol 0mg;
Calcium 40mg; Fibre 1.8g; Sodium 0.2g.
p56 Red Onion, Garlic and Chilli Relish
Energy 122Kcal/505kJ; Protein 3g;
Carbohydrate 15g, of which sugars 10g;
Fat 6g, of which saturates 1g; Cholesterol
0mg; Calcium 42mg; Fibre 2.4g;
Sodium 0.1g.

p57 Piquant Pineapple Relish
Energy 80Kcal/341kJ; Protein 1g;
Carbohydrate 20g, of which sugars 20g;
Fat 0g, of which saturates 0g; Cholesterol
0mg; Calcium 18mg; Fibre 0.7g; Sodium
0.1g.
p58 Chilli Strips with Lime Per recipe:
Energy 55Kcal/229kJ; Protein 4g;
Carbohydrate 8g, of which sugars 6g;
Fat 1g, of which saturates 0g; Cholesterol
0mg; Calcium 72mg; Fibre 1g;
Sodium 0.4g.
**p59 Hot Thai Pickled Shallots with
Chillies** Energy 171Kcal/715kJ; Protein
4g; Carbohydrate 31g, of which sugars
27g; Fat 1g, of which saturates 0g;
Cholesterol 0mg; Calcium 71mg;
Fibre 2.3g; Sodium 1.3g.
**p60 Coconut Chutney with Onion and
Chilli** Energy 239Kcal/984kJ; Protein 2g;
Carbohydrate 4g, of which sugars 4g;
Fat 24g, of which saturates 17g;
Cholesterol 0mg; Calcium 31mg;
Fibre 3.9g; Sodium 0.3g.
p60 Onion, Mango and Chilli Relish
Energy 197Kcal/819kJ; Protein 7g;
Carbohydrate 13g, of which sugars 10g;
Fat 14g, of which saturates 3g;
Cholesterol 0mg; Calcium 53mg; Fibre
3.1g; Sodium 0.1g.
p62 Mixed Vegetable Pickle 1 of 3 jars:
Energy 592Kcal/2458kJ; Protein 19g;
Carbohydrate 41g, of which sugars
35g; Fat 40g, of which saturates 6g;
Cholesterol 0mg; Calcium 165mg;
Fibre 10.3g; Sodium 4.4g.
p63 Spicy Fried Dumplings Energy
193Kcal/819kJ; Protein 5g; Carbohydrate
36g, of which sugars 3g; Fat 4g, of which
saturates 1g; Cholesterol 2mg; Calcium
195mg; Fibre 1.4g; Sodium 0.3g.
p64 Chickpea Breads Energy 270Kcal/
1136kJ; Protein 10g; Carbohydrate 34g,
of which sugars 2g; Fat 12g, of which
saturates 6g; Cholesterol 24mg; Calcium
71mg; Fibre 5.9g; Sodium 0.3g.
p65 Chilli Poori Puffs Energy 106Kcal/
445kJ; Protein 2g; Carbohydrate 14g,
of which sugars 0g; Fat 5g, of which
saturates 1g; Cholesterol 0mg; Calcium
18mg; Fibre 1.2g; Sodium 0.1g.
p66 Mixed Spiced Nuts Energy 966Kcal/
4001kJ; Protein 23g; Carbohydrate 31g,
of which sugars 22g; Fat 84g, of which
saturates 21g; Cholesterol 0mg; Calcium
161mg; Fibre 8.6g; Sodium 0.3g.
p66 Red-hot Roots Energy 191Kcal/
805kJ; Protein 4g; Carbohydrate 30g,
of which sugars 15g; Fat 7g, of which
saturates 1g; Cholesterol 0mg; Calcium
73mg; Fibre 7.7g; Sodium 0.6g.
p67 Chilli-spiced Plantain Chips
Energy 201Kcal/844kJ; Protein 1g;
Carbohydrate 26g, of which sugars 5g;
Fat 11g, of which saturates 1g;
Cholesterol 0mg; Calcium 17mg;
Fibre 1.1g; Sodium 0g.
p67 Popcorn with Lime and Chilli
Energy 484Kcal/2021kJ; Protein 8g;
Carbohydrate 39g, of which sugars
5g; Fat 34g, of which saturates 4g;
Cholesterol 0mg; Calcium 12mg;
Fibre 3.4g; Sodium 0g.
p68 Tortilla Chips Energy 194Kcal/
816kJ; Protein 4g; Carbohydrate 33g,
of which sugars 1g; Fat 6g, of which
saturates 1g; Cholesterol 0mg; Calcium
61mg; Fibre 1.3g; Sodium 0.4g.

p68 Hot Pumpkin Seeds Energy
193Kcal/803kJ; Protein 8g;
Carbohydrate 7g, of which sugars 2g;
Fat 15g, of which saturates 2g;
Cholesterol 0mg; Calcium 14mg;
Fibre 1.8g; Sodium 0g.
p72 Hot and Sour Soup Energy 172Kcal/
717kJ; Protein 12g; Carbohydrate 13g,
of which sugars 1g; Fat 9g, of which
saturates 2g; Cholesterol 51mg; Calcium
149mg; Fibre 0.2g; Sodium 1.1g.
p73 Warming Spinach and Rice Soup
Energy 289Kcal/1201kJ; Protein 14g;
Carbohydrate 26g, of which sugars
4g; Fat 15g, of which saturates 4g;
Cholesterol 14mg; Calcium 451mg;
Fibre 3.1g; Sodium 1.1g.
**p74 Hot and Sweet Vegetable and Tofu
Soup** Energy 109Kcal/459kJ; Protein 7g;
Carbohydrate 14g, of which sugars 12g;
Fat 4g, of which saturates 0g; Cholesterol
0mg; Calcium 339mg; Fibre 0.9g;
Sodium 1.1g.
p75 Hot and Spicy Miso Broth with Tofu
Energy 90Kcal/376kJ; Protein 8g;
Carbohydrate 7g, of which sugars 3g;
Fat 4g, of which saturates 0g;
Cholesterol 0mg; Calcium 314mg;
Fibre 1.1g; Sodium 1.8g.
p76 Coconut and Pumpkin Soup
Energy 567Kcal/2342kJ; Protein 9g;
Carbohydrate 16g, of which sugars
12g; Fat 52g, of which saturates g45;
Cholesterol 19mg; Calcium 120mg;
Fibre 2.2g; Sodium 1.0g.
p77 Spiced Red Lentil and Coconut Soup
Energy 265Kcal/1119kJ; Protein 14g;
Carbohydrate 40g, of which sugars 11g;
Fat 7g, of which saturates 0g; Cholesterol
0mg; Calcium 84mg; Fibre 3.7g;
Sodium 0.4g.
p78 Spicy Bean Soup Energy 209Kcal/
885kJ; Protein 13g; Carbohydrate 33g,
of which sugars 8g; Fat 4g, of which
saturates 1g; Cholesterol 0mg; Calcium
79mg; Fibre 5.2g; Sodium 0.3g.
p79 Gazpacho with Avocado Salsa
Energy 299Kcal/1251kJ; Protein 7g;
Carbohydrate 31g, of which sugars
13g; Fat 17g, of which saturates 3g;
Cholesterol 0mg; Calcium 86mg;
Fibre 5.6g; Sodium 0.3g.
p80 Spicy Yogurt Soup Energy 241Kcal/
1005kJ; Protein 10g; Carbohydrate 17g,
of which sugars 9g; Fat 15g, of which
saturates 3g; Cholesterol 12mg; Calcium
257mg; Fibre 1.7g; Sodium 0.2g.
**p81 Tamarind Soup with Peanuts and
Vegetables** Energy 179Kcal/747kJ;
Protein 7g; Carbohydrate 13g, of which
sugars 1g; Fat 12g, of which saturates
2g; Cholesterol 0mg; Calcium 24mg;
Fibre 1.9g; Sodium 0.7g.

p82 Plantain Soup with Corn and Chilli
Energy 206Kcal/867kJ; Protein 4g;
Carbohydrate 34g, of which sugars
8g; Fat 7g, of which saturates 3g;
Cholesterol 13mg; Calcium 24mg;
Fibre 2.8g; Sodium 0.9g.

p82 Spicy Groundnut Soup Energy
152Kcal/639kJ; Protein 5g; Carbohydrate
19g, of which sugars 4g; Fat 7g, of
which saturates 2g; Cholesterol 0mg;
Calcium 37mg; Fibre 2g; Sodium 0.7g.

p84 Spicy Pepper Soup Energy 65Kcal/
271kJ; Protein 1g; Carbohydrate 3g,
of which sugars 3g; Fat 6g, of which
saturates 1g; Cholesterol 0mg, Calcium
18mg; Fibre 0.5g; Sodium 0.3g.

p85 Provençal Fish Soup with Rouille
Energy 313Kcal/1315kJ; Protein 46g;
Carbohydrate 15g, of which sugars 9g;
Fat 8g, of which saturates 1g; Cholesterol
296mg; Calcium 155mg; Fibre 3.4g;
Sodium 0.9g.

p86 Spiced Mussel Soup Energy 145Kcal/
609kJ; Protein 11g; Carbohydrate 9g, of
which sugars 3g; Fat 5g, of which
saturates 1g; Cholesterol 35mg; Calcium
54mg; Fibre 1.2g; Sodium 0.2g.

p87 Hot and Spicy Shellfish Soup
Energy 626Kcal/2622kJ; Protein 30g;
Carbohydrate 87g, of which sugars 12g;
Fat 17g, of which saturates 2g;
Cholesterol 252mg; Calcium 150mg;
Fibre 1.2g; Sodium 0.8g.

p88 Coconut and Shellfish Soup
Energy 288Kcal/1216kJ; Protein 40g;
Carbohydrate 13g, of which sugars
8g; Fat 9g, of which saturates 1g;
Cholesterol 473mg; Calcium 174mg;
Fibre 0.8g; Sodium 1.4g.

p89 Chilli Squash and Shellfish Soup
Energy 102Kcal/433kJ; Protein 13g;
Carbohydrate 11g, of which sugars 6g;
Fat 1g, of which saturates 0g; Cholesterol
111mg; Calcium 105mg; Fibre 2.2g;
Sodium 0.9g.

p90 Malaysian Prawn Soup Energy
831Kcal/3508kJ; Protein 57g;
Carbohydrate 104g, of which sugars
16g; Fat 24g, of which saturates 2g;
Cholesterol 296mg; Calcium 418mg;
Fibre 8g; Sodium 1.8g.

p92 Thai Chicken and Chilli Soup
Energy 148Kcal/632kJ; Protein 20g;
Carbohydrate 13g, of which sugars
11g; Fat 2g, of which saturates 1g;
Cholesterol 53mg; Calcium 73mg;
Fibre 0.6g; Sodium 1.0g.

p92 Hot-and-sour Shellfish Soup Energy
115Kcal/486kJ; Protein 22g; Carbohydrate
3g, of which sugars 1g; Fat 2g, of which
saturates 0g; Cholesterol 219mg; Calcium
104mg; Fibre 0.7g; Sodium 1.4g.

p94 Mulligatawny Soup Energy 440Kcal/
1836kJ; Protein 33g; Carbohydrate 22g,
of which sugars 13g; Fat 25g, of which
saturates 9g; Cholesterol 136mg;
Calcium 83mg; Fibre 3.6g; Sodium 0.9g.

p95 Chicken Pepper Soup Energy
372Kcal/1554kJ; Protein 36g;
Carbohydrate 6g, of which sugars 5g;
Fat 23g, of which saturates 18g;
Cholesterol 135mg; Calcium 44mg;
Fibre 0.6g; Sodium 225g.

p96 Rice Porridge Energy 468Kcal/
1959kJ; Protein 27g; Carbohydrate 37g,
of which sugars 1g; Fat 24g, of which
saturates 7g; Cholesterol 74mg; Calcium
48mg; Fibre 1.2g; Sodium 1.7g.

p97 Thai Chicken and Noodle Soup
Energy 591Kcal/2503kJ; Protein 31g;
Carbohydrate 92g, of which sugars
10g; Fat 14g, of which saturates 4g;
Cholesterol 113mg; Calcium 101mg;
Fibre 3.3g; Sodium 1.8g.

p98 Spiced Lamb Soup Energy 517Kcal/
2306kJ; Protein 30g; Carbohydrate 37g,
of which sugars 6g; Fat 26g, of which
saturates 17g; Cholesterol 95mg;
Calcium 84mg; Fibre 5.0g; Sodium 0.7g.

p99 Beef and Turmeric Soup Energy
330Kcal/1391kJ; Protein 16g;
Carbohydrate 45g, of which sugars
5g; Fat 11g, of which saturates 4g;
Cholesterol 26mg; Calcium 57mg;
Fibre 2.4g; Sodium 0.1g.

p102 Spicy Peanut Balls Energy 124Kcal/
520kJ; Protein 3g; Carbohydrate 14g,
of which sugars 1g; Fat 7g, of which
saturates 1g; Cholesterol 0mg; Calcium
13mg; Fibre 0.5g; Sodium 0g.

p103 Little Onions Cooked with Chillies
Energy 244Kcal/1012kJ; Protein 3g;
Carbohydrate 16g, of which sugars
13g; Fat 18g, of which saturates 2g;
Cholesterol 0mg, Calcium 48mg;
Fibre 1.9g; Sodium 0g.

p104 Chilli Spiced Onion Koftas Energy
190Kcal/793kJ; Protein 7g; Carbohydrate
25g, of which sugars 10g; Fat 8g, of
which saturates 1g; Cholesterol 0mg;
Calcium 102mg; Fibre 4.8g; Sodium 0.6g

p105 Chilli Yogurt Cheese in Olive Oil
Per jar: Energy 1886Kcal/7773kJ;
Protein 23g; Carbohydrate 20g, of which
sugars 18g; Fat 191g, of which saturates
48g; Cholesterol 67mg; Calcium 541mg;
Fibre 0g; Sodium 0.8g.

**p105 Spiced Feta with Chilli Seeds and
Olives** Per jar: Energy 2012Kcal/8282kJ;
Protein 20g; Carbohydrate 20g, of which
sugars 2g; Fat 214g, of which saturates
44g; Cholesterol 88mg; Calcium 465mg;
Fibre 0.4g; Sodium 2.0g.

p106 Courgette Fritters with Chilli Jam
Energy 183Kcal/762kJ; Protein 5g;
Carbohydrate 15g, of which sugars
8g; Fat 12g, of which saturates 2g;
Cholesterol 43mg; Calcium 88mg;
Fibre 1.7g; Sodium 0.1g.

p107 Samosas Energy 86Kcal/359kJ;
Protein 1g; Carbohydrate 7g, of which
sugars 1g; Fat 6g, of which saturates
1g; Cholesterol 0mg; Calcium 4mg;
Fibre 0.5g; Sodium 0.1g.

**p108 Thai Tempeh Cakes with Chilli
Sauce** Energy 147Kcal/616kJ; Protein 9g;
Carbohydrate 11g, of which sugars 4g;
Fat 7g, of which saturates 1g; Cholesterol
29mg; Calcium 59mg; Fibre 1.7g;
Sodium 0.1g.

p109 Potato Skins with Cajun Dip
Energy 226Kcal/943kJ; Protein 6g;
Carbohydrate 23g, of which sugars 6g;
Fat 13g, of which saturates 2g;
Cholesterol 7mg; Calcium 128mg; Fibre
1.4g; Sodium 0.5g.

**p110 Spicy Potato Wedges with Chilli
Dip** Energy 388Kcal/1626kJ; Protein 8g;
Carbohydrate 52g, of which sugars
6g; Fat 18g, of which saturates 2g;
Cholesterol 0mg; Calcium 4.6mg;
Fibre 4.6g; Sodium 0.1g.

p111 Spicy Potatoes Energy 133Kcal/
557kJ; Protein 2g; Carbohydrate 19g,
of which sugars 1g; Fat 6g, of which
saturates 1g; Cholesterol 0mg; Calcium
23mg; Fibre 1.1g; Sodium 0.5g.

p112 Fried Dough Balls with Fiery Salsa
Energy 221Kcal/933kJ; Protein 5g;
Carbohydrate 38g, of which sugars 3g;
Fat 6g, of which saturates 1g; Cholesterol
0mg; Calcium 73mg; Fibre 2.1g;
Sodium 0.2g.

p114 Stuffed Chillies with Cheese
Energy 489Kcal/2031kJ; Protein 16g;
Carbohydrate 28g, of which sugars
3g; Fat 35g, of which saturates 18g;
Cholesterol 141mg; Calcium 329mg;
Fibre 1.5g; Sodium 0.4g.

**p116 Peppers with Cheese and Chilli
Filling** Energy 491Kcal/2048kJ; Protein
20g; Carbohydrate 41g, of which sugars
21g; Fat 28g, of which saturates 10g;
Cholesterol 263mg; Calcium 265mg;
Fibre 6g; Sodium 0.7g.

**p117 Courgettes with Cheese and Green
Chillies** Energy 148Kcal/610kJ; Protein
3g; Carbohydrate 5g, of which sugars
4g; Fat 13g, of which saturates 6g;
Cholesterol 18mg; Calcium 51mg;
Fibre 1.4g; Sodium 0.1g.

p118 Toasted Cheese Tortillas Energy
418Kcal/1764kJ; Protein 17g;
Carbohydrate 66g, of which sugars
1g; Fat 11g, of which saturates 7g;
Cholesterol 29mg; Calcium 303mg;
Fibre 2.6g; Sodium 0.5g.

p119 Pimiento Tartlets Energy 476Kcal/
1984kJ; Protein 7g; Carbohydrate 39g,
of which sugars 6g; Fat 33g, of which
saturates 21g; Cholesterol 85mg;
Calcium 124mg; Fibre 2.7g; Sodium 0.3g.

p120 Desert Nachos Energy 1223Kcal/
5129kJ; Protein 45g; Carbohydrate 135g,
of which sugars 3g; Fat 60g, of which
saturates 27g; Cholesterol 109mg; Calcium
1098mg; Fibre 5.4g; Sodium 1.4g.

p120 Tortillas with Enchilada Sauce
Energy 750Kcal/3145kJ; Protein 38g;
Carbohydrate 65g, of which sugars 11g;
Fat 40g, of which saturates 14g;
Cholesterol 269mg; Calcium 492mg;
Fibre 10.7g; Sodium 2.9g.

p122 Peri-peri Prawns with Aioli
Energy 373Kcal/1543kJ; Protein 14g;
Carbohydrate 2g, of which sugars 1g;
Fat 35g, of which saturates 5g;
Cholesterol 174mg; Calcium 68mg;
Fibre 0.1g; Sodium 0.5g.

p123 Fiendish Fritters Energy 719Kcal/
3038kJ; Protein 33g; Carbohydrate 115g,
of which sugars 11g; Fat 17g, of which
saturates 3g; Cholesterol 272mg;
Calcium 312mg; Fibre 7.2g; Sodium 1.2g.

p124 Pan-steamed Chilli Mussels
Energy 77Kcal/328kJ; Protein 11g;
Carbohydrate 5g, of which sugars 2g;
Fat 2g, of which saturates 0g; Cholesterol
36mg; Calcium 41mg; Fibre 0.4g;
Sodium 0.4g.

p125 Spicy Shellfish Wontons Energy
283Kcal/1176kJ; Protein 18g;
Carbohydrate 10g, of which sugars
4g; Fat 19g, of which saturates 3g;
Cholesterol 130mg; Calcium 55mg;
Fibre 0.9g; Sodium 0.5g.

p126 Ceviche of Fish with Citrus Fruits
Energy 699Kcal/1235kJ; Protein 40g,
Carbohydrate 16g, of which sugars 14g;
Fat 8g, of which saturates 1g; Cholesterol
220mg; Calcium 137mg; Fibre 1.9g;
Sodium 1.1g.

p127 Thai-style Marinated Salmon Energy
509Kcal/2108kJ; Protein 26g; Carbo
hydrate 7g, of which sugars 6g; Fat 42g,
of which saturates 7g; Cholesterol 91mg;
Calcium 44mg; Fibre 0g; Sodium 1.7g.

p128 Singapore Crabs Energy 389Kcal/
1619kJ; Protein 24g; Carbohydrate 22g,
of which sugars 20g; Fat 23g, of which
saturates 3g; Cholesterol 84mg; Calcium
1/mg; Fibre 0.3g; Sodium 2.4g.

p128 Pork Satay Sticks Energy 156Kcal/
653kJ; Protein 14g; Carbohydrate 9g,
of which sugars 8g; Fat 8g, of which
saturates 2g; Cholesterol 39mg; Calcium
43mg; Fibre 0.6g; Sodium 0.5g.

p130 San Francisco Chicken Wings
Energy 865Kcal/3620kJ; Protein 83g;
Carbohydrate 4g, of which sugars
18g; Fat 50g, of which saturates 14g;
Cholesterol 360mg; Calcium 135mg;
Fibre 0g; Sodium 1.5g.

p131 Chicken Satay Energy 636Kcal/
2655kJ; Protein 46g; Carbohydrate 34g,
of which sugars 29g; Fat 37g, of which
saturates 6g; Cholesterol 94mg; Calcium
154mg; Fibre 5.1g; Sodium 0.4g.

p132 Chicken Tortillas with Fresno Salsa
Energy 363Kcal/1519kJ; Protein 11g;
Carbohydrate 35g, of which sugars 3g;
Fat 21g, of which saturates 4g;
Cholesterol 20mg; Calcium 120mg;
Fibre 3.8g; Sodium 0.6g.

p134 Chicken Naan Pockets Energy
327Kcal/1381kJ; Protein 33g; Carbohydrate 29g, of which sugars 4g; Fat
10g, of which saturates 2g; Cholesterol
116mg, Calcium 156mg; Fibre 1.8g;
Sodium 0.9g.

p134 Chicken Tikka Energy 126Kcal/
531kJ; Protein 18g; Carbohydrate 3g,
of which sugars 3g; Fat 5g, of which
saturates 1g; Cholesterol 70mg; Calcium
61mg; Fibre 0.2g; Sodium 0.4g.

p136 Stuffed Rolls with Spicy Salsa
Energy 461Kcal/1922kJ; Protein 18g;
Carbohydrate 28g, of which sugars 2g;
Fat 31g, of which saturates 16g;
Cholesterol 64mg; Calcium 360mg;
Fibre 4.7g; Sodium 0.8g.

p136 Eggs with Tortillas and Beans
Energy 519Kcal/2191kJ; Protein 38g; Carbohydrate 64g, of which sugars 6g; Fat 13g, of which saturates 5g; Cholesterol 267mg; Calcium 270mg; Fibre 3.4g; Sodium 1.5g.

p138 Rolls with Refried Beans and Chilli
Energy 497Kcal/2090kJ; Protein 39g; Carbohydrate 38g, of which sugars 6g; Fat 22g, of which saturates 9g; Cholesterol 104mg; Calcium 124mg; Fibre 5.6g; Sodium 0.5g.

p139 Spring Rolls with Fiery Chilli Sauce
Energy 131Kcal/548kJ; Protein 6g; Carbohydrate 13g, of which sugars 2g; Fat 6g, of which saturates 1g; Cholesterol 9mg; Calcium 5mg; Fibre 0.6g; Sodium 0.2g.

p140 Firecrackers Energy 43Kcal/180kJ; Protein 2g; Carbohydrate 2g, of which sugars 0g; Fat 3g, of which saturates 0g; Cholesterol 18mg; Calcium 8mg; Fibre 0.1g; Sodium 0.1g.

p141 Chilli Crab Claws Energy 212Kcal/890kJ; Protein 14g; Carbohydrate 28g, of which sugars 13g; Fat 5g, of which saturates 1g; Cholesterol 95mg; Calcium 19mg; Fibre 0.3g; Sodium 0.5g.

p144 Salt and Pepper Prawns Energy 123Kcal/511kJ; Protein 10g; Carbohydrate 4g, of which sugars 3g; Fat 8g, of which saturates 1g; Cholesterol 98mg; Calcium 52mg; Fibre 0.6g; Sodium 1.4g.

p145 Spicy Prawns with Okra Energy 246Kcal/1023kJ; Protein 22g; Carbohydrate 6g, of which sugars 5g; Fat 15g, of which saturates 2g; Cholesterol 219mg; Calcium 193mg; Fibre 2.4g; Sodium 0.3g.

p146 Stir-fried Prawns with Tamarind Energy 219Kcal/922kJ; Protein 21g; Carbohydrate 19g, of which sugars 17g; Fat 7g, of which saturates 1g; Cholesterol 219mg; Calcium 116mg; Fibre 0.4g; Sodium 0.4g.

p147 Spicy Prawns with Cornmeal Energy 529Kcal/2211kJ; Protein 50g; Carbohydrate 25g, of which sugars 0g; Fat 25g, of which saturates 8g; Cholesterol 467mg; Calcium 404mg; Fibre 0.8g; Sodium 1.1g.

p148 Chilli Crabs Energy 286Kcal/1194kJ; Protein 14g; Carbohydrate 26g, of which sugars 25g; Fat 14g, of which saturates 2g; Cholesterol 49mg; Calcium 31mg; Fibre 0.9g; Sodium 1.5g.

p149 Caribbean Chilli Crab Cakes Energy 69Kcal/286kJ; Protein 4g; Carbohydrate 2g, of which sugars 1g; Fat 5g, of which saturates 1g; Cholesterol 28mg; Calcium 6mg; Fibre 0.2g; Sodium 0.1g.

p150 Flash-fried Squid with Paprika and Garlic Energy 292Kcal/1218kJ; Protein 21g; Carbohydrate 10g, of which sugars 0g; Fat 19g, of which saturates 3g; Cholesterol 281mg; Calcium 38mg; Fibre 0.5g; Sodium 0.2g.

p151 Five-spice Squid with Chilli and Black Bean Sauce Energy 133Kcal/556kJ; Protein 13g; Carbohydrate 4g, of which sugars 3g; Fat 7g, of which saturates 0g; Cholesterol 169mg; Calcium 23mg; Fibre 0.9g; Sodium 0.3g.

p152 Spiced Scallops in their Shells Energy 143Kcal/604kJ; Protein 24g; Carbohydrate 5g, of which sugars 1g; Fat 3g, of which saturates 1g; Cholesterol 47mg; Calcium 37mg; Fibre 0.2g; Sodium 0.7g.

p153 Mussels in Chilli and Black Bean Sauce Energy 136Kcal/569kJ; Protein 12g; Carbohydrate 5g, of which sugars 2g; Fat 7g, of which saturates 1g; Cholesterol 40mg; Calcium 43mg; Fibre 0.2g; Sodium 0.5g.

p154 Three-Colour Fish Kebabs Energy 715Kcal/2976kJ; Protein 50g; Carbohydrate 12g, of which sugars 11g; Fat 52g, of which saturates 8g; Cholesterol 92mg; Calcium 56mg; Fibre 3.4g; Sodium 0.3g.

p155 Seared Tuna with Red Onion Salsa Energy 463Kcal/1935kJ; Protein 46g; Carbohydrate 9g, of which sugars 7g; Fat 27g, of which saturates 5g; Cholesterol 53mg; Calcium 64mg; Fibre 2.6g; Sodium 0.3g.

p156 Baked or Grilled Spiced Whole Fish Energy 211Kcal/887kJ; Protein 30g; Carbohydrate 1g, of which sugars 0g; Fat 10g, of which saturates 1g; Cholesterol 63mg; Calcium 71mg; Fibre 0.2g; Sodium 0.2g.

p156 Vinegar Chilli Fish Energy 481Kcal/1993kJ; Protein 25g; Carbohydrate 7g, of which sugars 5g; Fat 39g, of which saturates 6g; Cholesterol 68mg; Calcium 41mg; Fibre 1.3g; Sodium 0.1g.

p158 Mexican Spicy Fish Energy 238Kcal/983kJ; Protein 6g; Carbohydrate 6g, of which sugars 4g; Fat 21g, of which saturates 3g; Cholesterol 20mg; Calcium 49mg; Fibre 1.3g; Sodium 0.1g.

p159 Citrus Fish with Chillies Energy 284Kcal/1185kJ; Protein 34g; Carbohydrate 8g, of which sugars 3g; Fat 13g, of which saturates 2g; Cholesterol 81mg; Calcium 45mg; Fibre 0.7g; Sodium 0.5g.

p160 Saffron Fish Energy 346Kcal/1439kJ; Protein 32g; Carbohydrate 0g, of which sugars 0g; Fat 24g, of which saturates 4g; Cholesterol 176mg; Calcium 43mg; Fibre 0g; Sodium 0.1g.

p160 Pan-fried Spicy Sardines Energy 310Kcal/1296kJ; Protein 22g; Carbohydrate 10g, of which sugars 0g; Fat 20g, of which saturates 4g; Cholesterol 0mg; Calcium 108mg; Fibre 0.6g; Sodium 0.2g.

p162 Spiced Fish with Chillies, Lemon and Red Onions Energy 279Kcal/1165kJ; Protein 34g; Carbohydrate 8g, of which sugars 3g; Fat 13g, of which saturates 2g; Cholesterol 81mg; Calcium 43mg; Fibre 0.8g; Sodium 0.5g.

p163 Red Snapper with Chilli, Gin and Ginger Sauce Energy 289Kcal/1217kJ; Protein 45g; Carbohydrate 7g, of which sugars 3g; Fat 9g, of which saturates 1g; Cholesterol 83mg; Calcium 109mg; Fibre 0.9g; Sodium 0.6g.

p164 Whole Fish with Sweet and Sour Sauce Energy 1003Kcal/4200kJ; Protein 21g; Carbohydrate 210g, of which sugars 9g; Fat 7g, of which saturates 0g; Cholesterol 0mg; Calcium 83mg; Fibre 1.9g; Sodium 0.1g.

p165 Turkish Cold Fish Energy 431Kcal/1804kJ; Protein 45g; Carbohydrate 14g, of which sugars 12g; Fat 22g, of which saturates 2g; Cholesterol 0mg; Calcium 196mg; Fibre 4.2g; Sodium 0.7g.

p166 Cajun Blackened Fish with Papaya Salsa Energy 297Kcal/1240kJ; Protein 42g; Carbohydrate 5g, of which sugars 4g; Fat 12g, of which saturates 7g; Cholesterol 130mg; Calcium 50mg; Fibre 1.0g; Sodium 0.3g.

p166 Caribbean Fish Steaks Energy 256Kcal/1070kJ; Protein 31g; Carbohydrate 11g, of which sugars 9g; Fat 10g, of which saturates 1g; Cholesterol 69mg; Calcium 123mg; Fibre 3.6g; Sodium 0.2g.

p168 Coconut Salmon Energy 418Kcal/1740kJ; Protein 37g; Carbohydrate 6g, of which sugars 4g; Fat 28g, of which saturates 4g; Cholesterol 88mg; Calcium 73mg; Fibre 0.6g; Sodium 0.3g.

p169 Salmon with Tequila Cream Sauce Energy 528Kcal/2192kJ; Protein 38g; Carbohydrate 3g, of which sugars 2g; Fat 41g, of which saturates 10g; Cholesterol 104mg; Calcium 75mg; Fibre 1.5g; Sodium 0.2g.

p170 Salmon Parcels with Spiced Leeks Energy 394Kcal/1644kJ; Protein 37g; Carbohydrate 5g, of which sugars 4g; Fat 25g, of which saturates 4g; Cholesterol 88mg; Calcium 64mg; Fibre 2.8g; Sodium 0.2g.

p171 Trout with Tamarind and Chilli Sauce Energy 312Kcal/1311kJ; Protein 37g; Carbohydrate 14g, of which sugars 11g; Fat 12g, of which saturates 2g; Cholesterol 117mg; Calcium 64mg; Fibre 0.4g; Sodium 1.4g.

p172 Swordfish Tacos Energy 357Kcal/1507kJ; Protein 32g; Carbohydrate 36g, of which sugars 3g; Fat 11g, of which saturates 2g; Cholesterol 62mg; Calcium 80mg; Fibre 2.1g; Sodium 0.4g.

p172 Swordfish with Chilli and Lime Sauce Energy 420Kcal/1746kJ; Protein 29g; Carbohydrate 4g, of which sugars 4g; Fat 32g, of which sat. 14g; Cholesterol 111mg; Calcium 39mg; Fibre 0.9g; Sodium 0.5g.

p174 Fiery Fish Stew Energy 310Kcal/1306kJ; Protein 33g; Carbohydrate 31g, of which sugars 8g; Fat 8g, of which saturates 1g; Cholesterol 69mg; Calcium 61mg; Fibre 3.6g; Sodium 0.5g.

p175 Creole Fish Stew Energy 340Kcal/1424kJ; Protein 37g; Carbohydrate 11g, of which sugars 5g; Fat 17g, of which saturates 4g; Cholesterol 73mg; Calcium 124mg; Fibre 2.9g; Sodium 0.5g.

p176 Curried Shellfish with Coconut Milk Energy 243Kcal/1024kJ; Protein 41g; Carbohydrate 8g, of which sugars 6g; Fat 5g, of which saturates 1g; Cholesterol 288mg; Calcium 119mg; Fibre 0.2g; Sodium 0.7g.

p178 Coconut Fish Curry Energy 333Kcal/1390kJ; Protein 26g; Carbohydrate 15g, of which sugars 13g; Fat 20g, of which saturates 8g; Cholesterol 58mg; Calcium 95mg; Fibre 2.6g; Sodium 0.6g.

p179 Balinese Fish Curry Energy 322Kcal/1342kJ; Protein 33g; Carbohydrate 8g, of which sugars 5g; Fat 18g, of which saturates 2g; Cholesterol 84mg; Calcium 53mg; Fibre 1.1g; Sodium 0.2g.

p182 Hot and Spicy Pan-fried Chicken Energy 483Kcal/2017kJ; Protein 34g; Carbohydrate 23g, of which sugars 22g; Fat 29g, of which saturates 3g; Cholesterol 88mg; Calcium 61mg; Fibre 1.2g; Sodium 0.3g.

p183 Caribbean Peanut Chicken Energy 574Kcal/2412kJ; Protein 39g; Carbohydrate 56g, of which sugars 5g; Fat 23g, of which saturates 6g; Cholesterol 95mg; Calcium 73mg; Fibre 2.6g; Sodium 0.6g.

p184 Chicken with Chipotle Chilli Sauce Energy 214Kcal/898kJ; Protein 36g; Carbohydrate 1g, of which sugars 1g; Fat 7g, of which saturates 1g; Cholesterol 105mg; Calcium 13mg; Fibre 0.1g; Sodium 0.2g.

p186 Barbecue Jerk Chicken Energy 210Kcal/882kJ; Protein 31g; Carbohydrate 6g, of which sugars 5g; Fat 7g, of which saturates 1g; Cholesterol 88mg; Calcium 38mg; Fibre 0.6g; Sodium 0.2g.

p187 Bon-Bon Chicken with Spicy Sesame Sauce Energy 232Kcal/974kJ; Protein 30g; Carbohydrate 2g, of which sugars 1g; Fat 11g, of which saturates 2g; Cholesterol 113mg; Calcium 42mg; Fibre 0.7g; Sodium 0.2g.

p188 Tandoori Chicken Energy 227Kcal/956kJ; Protein 31g; Carbohydrate 4g, of which sugars 4g; Fat 10g, of which saturates 2g; Cholesterol 117mg; Calcium 109mg; Fibre 0g; Sodium 0.7g.

p189 Spicy Masala Chicken Energy 241Kcal/1010kJ; Protein 26g; Carbohydrate 7g, of which sugars 6g; Fat 13g, of which saturates 3g; Cholesterol 130mg; Calcium 19mg; Fibre 0g; Sodium 0.4g.

p190 Red Chicken Curry with Bamboo Shoots Energy 230Kcal/968kJ; Protein 28g; Carbohydrate 12g, of which sugars 9g; Fat 8g, of which saturates 1g; Cholesterol 108mg; Calcium 69mg; Fibre 1.5g; Sodium 0.5g.

p192 Hot Chicken Curry Energy 176Kcal/740kJ; Protein 21g; Carbohydrate 5g, of which sugars 5g; Fat 8g, of which saturates 1g; Cholesterol 79mg; Calcium 28mg; Fibre 1.4g; Sodium 0.6g.

p194 Stir-fried Chicken with Chilli and Basil Energy 214Kcal/899kJ; Protein 28g; Carbohydrate 4g, of which sugars 10g; Fat 10g, of which saturates 1g; Cholesterol 79mg; Calcium 14mg; Fibre 0g; Sodium 0.7g.

p195 Sichuan Chicken with Kung Po Sauce Energy 504Kcal/2101kJ; Protein 38g; Carbohydrate 15g, of which sugars 6g; Fat 32g, of which saturates 6g; Cholesterol 82mg; Calcium 37mg; Fibre 1.7g; Sodium 1.0g.

p196 Crispy and Aromatic Duck Energy 390Kcal/1627kJ; Protein 40g; Carbohydrate 1g, of which sugars 0g; Fat 24g, of which saturates 5g; Cholesterol 220mg; Calcium 38mg; Fibre 0.1g; Sodium 0.9g.

p198 Turkey Stew with Spicy Chocolate Sauce Energy 824Kcal/3435kJ; Protein 45g; Carbohydrate 39g, of which sugars 21g; Fat 56g, of which saturates 12g; Cholesterol 83mg; Calcium 286mg; Fibre 7.2g; Sodium 0.2g.

p200 Mexican Turkey Mole Energy 728Kcal/3040kJ; Protein 66g; Carbohydrate 28g, of which sugars 20g; Fat 40g, of which saturates 7g; Cholesterol 175mg; Calcium 168mg; Fibre 4.4g; Sodium 0.4g.

p202 Chilli Ribs Energy 460Kcal/1912kJ; Protein 40g; Carbohydrate 7g, of which sugars 3g; Fat 30g, of which saturates 10g; Cholesterol 141mg; Calcium 33mg; Fibre 0.8g; Sodium 0.8g.

p203 Hot Pepperoni and Chilli Pizza Energy 690Kcal/2885kJ; Protein 32g; Carbohydrate 49g, of which sugars 7g; Fat 42g, of which saturates 19g; Cholesterol 36mg; Calcium 333mg; Fibre 2.5g; Sodium 1.5g.

p204 Deep-fried Spicy Spare Ribs Energy 549Kcal/2284kJ; Protein 34g; Carbohydrate 8g, of which sugars 2g; Fat 43g, of which saturates 13g; Cholesterol 101mg; Calcium 29mg; Fibre 0.3g; Sodium 0.3g.

p205 Pork with Chillies and Pineapple Energy 267Kcal/1122kJ; Protein 32g; Carbohydrate 12g, of which sugars 11g; Fat 10g, of which saturates 3g; Cholesterol 96mg; Calcium 33mg; Fibre 1.7g; Sodium 0.3g.

p206 Pork Casserole with Chillies and Dried Fruit Energy 740Kcal/3101kJ; Protein 75g; Carbohydrate 28g, of which sugars 22g; Fat 30g, of which saturates 7g; Cholesterol 213mg; Calcium 123mg; Fibre 4.9g; Sodium 0.3g.

p208 Stuffed Chillies in a Walnut Sauce Energy 912Kcal/3781kJ; Protein 26g; Carbohydrate 30g, of which sugars 11g; Fat 74g, of which saturates 23g; Cholesterol 199mg; Calcium 220mg; Fibre 3.7g; Sodium 0.3g.

p210 Sweet and Sour Pork Energy 254Kcal/1065kJ; Protein 23g; Carbohydrate 16g, of which sugars 10g; Fat 11g, of which saturates 2g; Cholesterol 113mg; Calcium 43mg; Fibre 1.6g; Sodium 0.4g.

p211 Lamb Tagine with Coriander and Spices Energy 331Kcal/1374kJ; Protein 21g; Carbohydrate 6g, of which sugars 4g; Fat 25g, of which saturates 6g; Cholesterol 67mg; Calcium 64mg; Fibre 1.6g; Sodium 0.3g.

p212 Lamb Masala Energy 327Kcal/1357kJ; Protein 24g; Carbohydrate 6g, of which sugars 5g; Fat 23g, of which saturates 6g; Cholesterol 83mg; Calcium 42mg; Fibre 1.1g; Sodium 0.3g.

p214 Lively Lamb Burgers with Chilli Relish Energy 476Kcal/1979kJ; Protein 28g; Carbohydrate 22g, of which sugars 14g; Fat 32g, of which saturates 10g; Cholesterol 96mg; Calcium 89mg; Fibre 3.6g; Sodium 0.2g.

p215 Lamb Stew with Chilli Sauce Energy 385Kcal/1613kJ; Protein 36g; Carbohydrate 15g, of which sugars 1g; Fat 21g, of which saturates 9g; Cholesterol 127mg; Calcium 38mg; Fibre 1.1g; Sodium 0.3g.

p216 Spicy Lamb Stew Energy 474Kcal/1987kJ; Protein 47g; Carbohydrate 16g, of which sugars 15g; Fat 25g, of which saturates 12g; Calcium 62mg; Fibre 2g; Sodium 0.7g.

p218 Fire Fry Energy 193Kcal/803kJ; Protein 14g; Carbohydrate 9g, of which sugars 7g; Fat 12g, of which saturates 5g; Cholesterol 45mg; Calcium 89mg; Fibre 1.1g; Sodium 0.6g.

p219 Caribbean Lamb Curry Energy 609Kcal/2535kJ; Protein 46g; Carbohydrate 7g, of which sugars 14g; Fat 44g, of which saturates 20g; Cholesterol 203mg; Calcium 89mg; Fibre 2.5g; Sodium 0.6g.

p220 Indonesian Beef Patties Energy 298Kcal/1241kJ; Protein 28g; Carbohydrate 7g, of which sugars 6g; Fat 18g, of which saturates 6g, Cholesterol 114mg; Calcium 66mg; Fibre 0.9g; Sodium 0.3g.

p220 Chilli Sambal Energy 117Kcal/491kJ; Protein 8g; Carbohydrate 19g, of which sugars 19g; Fat 1g, of which saturates 0g; Cholesterol 0mg; Calcium 73mg; Fibre 0g; Sodium 4.0g.

p222 Beef Enchiladas with Red Sauce Energy 856Kcal/3612kJ; Protein 69g; Carbohydrate 100g, of which sugars 2g; Fat 23g, of which saturates 6g; Cholesterol 148mg; Calcium 222mg; Fibre 4.1g; Sodium 0.6g.

p223 Mexican Spicy Beef Tortilla Energy 860Kcal/3614kJ; Protein 42g; Carbohydrate 99g, of which sugars 15g; Fat 35g, of which saturates 19g; Cholesterol 127mg; Calcium 523mg; Fibre 3.5g; Sodium 0.7g.

p224 Chilli Con Carne Energy 404Kcal/1688kJ; Protein 38g; Carbohydrate 16g, of which sugars 9g; Fat 18g, of which saturates 7g; Cholesterol 106mg; Calcium 82mg; Fibre 4.0g; Sodium 0.3g.

p225 Meatballs with Spaghetti Energy 425Kcal/1797kJ; Protein 24g; Carbohydrate 58g, of which sugars 8g; Fat 12g, of which saturates 4g; Cholesterol 72mg; Calcium 57mg; Fibre 3.0g; Sodium 0.5g.

p226 Beef Tagine with Sweet Potatoes Energy 516Kcal/2163kJ; Protein 52g; Carbohydrate 29g, of which sugars 10g; Fat 22g, of which saturates 8g; Cholesterol 150mg; Calcium 71mg; Fibre 3.7g; Sodium 0.2g.

p227 Chilli Beef with Spicy Onion Rings Energy 521Kcal/2176kJ; Protein 55g; Carbohydrate 23g, of which sugars 8g; Fat 24g, of which saturates 7g; Cholesterol 142mg; Calcium 126mg; Fibre 1.1g; Sodium 0.3g.

p228 Beef with Peppers and Black Bean Sauce Energy 159Kcal/667kJ; Protein 20g; Carbohydrate 5g, of which sugars 3g; Fat 7g, of which saturates 2g; Cholesterol 52mg; Calcium 12mg; Fibre 0.8g; Sodium 0.4g.

p229 Shredded Beef with Chillies Energy 508Kcal/2108kJ; Protein 28g; Carbohydrate 15g, of which sugars 10g; Fat 38g, of which saturates 6g; Cholesterol 66mg; Calcium 49mg; Fibre 1.7g; Sodium 0.3g.

p230 Beef and Aubergine Curry Energy 394Kcal/1638kJ; Protein 26g; Carbohydrate 12g, of which sugars 10g; Fat 27g, of which saturates 5g; Cholesterol 71mg; Calcium 54mg; Fibre 2.3g; Sodium 0.2g.

p231 Thai Green Beef Curry Energy 252Kcal/1059kJ; Protein 28g; Carbohydrate 11g, of which sugars 10g; Fat 11g, of which saturates 3g; Cholesterol 57mg; Calcium 72mg; Fibre 0.8g; Sodium 0.7g.

p232 Mussaman Beef Curry Energy 449Kcal/1886kJ; Protein 43g; Carbohydrate 30g, of which sugars 17g; Fat 18g, of which saturates 5g; Cholesterol 106mg; Calcium 93mg; Fibre 2.0g; Sodium 0.8g.

p233 Chilli Beef with Basil Energy 619Kcal/2566kJ; Protein 32g; Carbohydrate 9g, of which sugars 5g; Fat 51g, of which saturates 11g; Cholesterol 81mg; Calcium 34mg; Fibre 0.6g; Sodium 0.9g.

p236 Pasta with Sugocasa and Chilli Energy 281Kcal/1198kJ; Protein 10g; Carbohydrate 60g, of which sugars 5g; Fat 2g, of which saturates 0g; Cholesterol 6mg; Calcium 38mg; Fibre 3.3g; Sodium 0.2g.

p237 Spaghetti with Garlic, Chilli and Oil Energy 549Kcal/2308kJ; Protein 12g; Carbohydrate 75g, of which sugars 4g; Fat 24g, of which saturates 3g; Cholesterol 0mg; Calcium 33mg; Fibre 3.2g; Sodium 0.1g.

p238 Penne with Chilli and Broccoli Energy 493Kcal/2092kJ; Protein 20g; Carbohydrate 89g, of which sugars 6g; Fat 9g, of which saturates 1g; Cholesterol 2mg; Calcium 123mg; Fibre 6.6g; Sodium 0.2g.

p239 Black Pasta with Squid Sauce Energy 726Kcal/3064kJ; Protein 41g; Carbohydrate 92g, of which sugars 6g; Fat 24g, of which saturates 4g; Cholesterol 380mg; Calcium 73mg; Fibre 4.6g; Sodium 0.3g.

p240 Vermicelli with Spicy Clam Sauce Energy 466Kcal/1953kJ; Protein 23g; Carbohydrate 78g, of which sugars 7g; Fat 7g, of which saturates 1g; Cholesterol 55mg; Calcium 106mg; Fibre 2.5g; Sodium 1.1g.

p241 Chilli Ravioli with Crab Energy 712Kcal/2973kJ; Protein 25g; Carbohydrate 57g, of which sugars 1g; Fat 45g, of which saturates 275g; Cholesterol 287mg; Calcium 184mg; Fibre 2.4g; Sodium 1.5g.

p242 Crispy Fried Rice Vermicelli Energy 385Kcal/1614kJ; Protein 18g; Carbohydrate 59g, of which sugars 22g; Fat 9g, of which saturates 2g; Cholesterol 81mg; Calcium 73mg; Fibre 0.8g; Sodium 0.8g.

p243 Thai Fried Noodles Energy 597Kcal/2491kJ; Protein 24g; Carbohydrate 79g, of which sugars 4g; Fat 20g, of which saturates 3g; Cholesterol 213mg; Calcium 177mg; Fibre 202g; Sodium 0.7g.

p244 Spicy Sichuan Noodles Energy 626Kcal/2631kJ; Protein 27g; Carbohydrate 72g, of which sugars 5g; Fat 27g, of which saturates 4g; Cholesterol 46mg; Calcium 41mg; Fibre 3.6g; Sodium 0.5g.

p244 Sesame Noodles with Spring Onions Energy 463Kcal/1950kJ; Protein 11g; Carbohydrate 72g, of which sugars 7g; Fat 15g, of which saturates 1g; Cholesterol 0mg; Calcium 82mg; Fibre 3.6g; Sodium 0.4g.

p246 Thai Mixed Vegetable Curry with Lemon Grass Rice Energy 330Kcal/1388kJ; Protein 10g, Carbohydrate 66g, of which sugars 12g; Fat 3g, of which saturates 1g; Cholesterol 0mg; Calcium 96mg; Fibre 3.3g; Sodium 0.4g.

p248 Persian Rice with a Tahdeeg Energy 555Kcal/2307kJ; Protein 10g; Carbohydrate 63g, of which sugars 8g; Fat 30g, of which saturates 8g; Cholesterol 45mg; Calcium 49mg; Fibre 2.5g; Sodium 0.3g.

p249 Festive Rice Energy 277Kcal/1155kJ; Protein 5g; Carbohydrate 50g, of which sugars 5g; Fat 6g, of which saturates 1g; Cholesterol 0mg; Calcium 37mg; Fibre 0.6g; Sodium 0.1g.

p250 Indian Pilau Rice Energy 309Kcal/1286kJ; Protein 6g; Carbohydrate 47g, of which sugars 1g; Fat 11g, of which saturates 4g; Cholesterol 11mg; Calcium 44mg; Fibre 0.6g; Sodium 0.5g.

p250 Okra Fried Rice Energy 247Kcal/1034kJ; Protein 5g; Carbohydrate 29g, of which sugars 3g; Fat 13g, of which saturates 4g; Cholesterol 0mg; Calcium 99mg; Fibre 2.2g; Sodium 1.1g.

p252 Chilli Chive Rice with Mushrooms Energy 735Kcal/3040kJ; Protein 14g; Carbohydrate 106g, of which sugars 2g; Fat 32g, of which saturates 6g; Cholesterol 0mg; Calcium 87mg; Fibre 2.3g; Sodium 1.1g.

p253 Brown Rice with Lime and Lemon Grass Energy 253Kcal/1070kJ; Protein 5g; Carbohydrate 50g, of which sugars 3g; Fat 5g, of which saturates 1g; Cholesterol 0mg; Calcium 38mg; Fibre 1.6g; Sodium 0.6g.

p254 Rice with Dill and Spicy Beans Energy 357Kcal/1490kJ; Protein 8g; Carbohydrate 58g, of which sugars 1g; Fat 10g, of which saturates 6g; Cholesterol 24mg; Calcium 55mg; Fibre 2.8g; Sodium 0.2g.

p255 Mexican Rice Energy 192Kcal/811kJ; Protein 5g; Carbohydrate 33g, of which sugars 2g; Fat 5g, of which saturates 1g; Cholesterol 0mg; Calcium 35mg; Fibre 1.9g; Sodium 0.4g.

p256 Spicy Rice Cakes Energy 132Kcal/549kJ; Protein 1g; Carbohydrate 7g, of which sugars 1g; Fat 11g, of which saturates 1g; Cholesterol 0mg; Calcium 7mg; Fibre 0.2g; Sodium 0.1g.
p256 Red Rice Rissoles Energy 471Kcal/1972kJ; Protein 14g; Carbohydrate 51g, of which sugars 3g; Fat 25g, of which saturates 9g; Cholesterol 73mg; Calcium 231mg; Fibre 1.3g; Sodium 0.8g.
p258 Pistachio Pilaff Energy 506Kcal/2100kJ; Protein 13g; Carbohydrate 61g, of which sugars 12g; Fat 23g, of which saturates 3g; Cholesterol 0mg; Calcium 267mg; Fibre 6.1g; Sodium 0.6g.
p259 Basmati and Nut Pilaff Energy 388Kcal/1615kJ; Protein 11g; Carbohydrate 53g, of which sugars 6g; Fat 16g, of which saturates 2g; Cholesterol 0mg; Calcium 62mg; Fibre 2.6g; Sodium 0.4g.
p260 Spiced Trout Pilaff Energy 603Kcal/2519kJ; Protein 38g; Carbohydrate 61g, of which sugars 13g; Fat 24g, of which saturates 7g; Cholesterol 122mg; Calcium 111mg; Fibre 2.3g; Sodium 0.3g.
p261 Aromatic Mussel Risotto Energy 610Kcal/2573kJ; Protein 20g; Carbohydrate 83g, of which sugars 1g; Fat 24g, of which saturates 9g; Cholesterol 70mg; Calcium 102mg; Fibre 0.4g; Sodium 1.2g.
p262 Squid and Chilli Risotto Energy 645Kcal/2722kJ; Protein 31g; Carbohydrate 86g, of which sugars 5g; Fat 22g, of which saturates 6g; Cholesterol 348mg; Calcium 84mg; Fibre 1.2g; Sodium 1.0g.
p264 Louisiana Shellfish Gumbo Energy 639Kcal/2674kJ; Protein 28g; Carbohydrate 59g, of which sugars 4g; Fat 33g, of which saturates 5g; Cholesterol 131mg; Calcium 113mg; Fibre 2.1g; Sodium 1.0g.
p266 Shellfish and Rice Energy 360Kcal/1513kJ; Protein 24g; Carbohydrate 38g, of which sugars 8g; Fat 13g, of which saturates 3g; Cholesterol 116mg; Calcium 95mg; Fibre 2.0g; Sodium 1.5g.
p266 Chicken Jambalaya Energy 486Kcal/2053kJ; Protein 45g; Carbohydrate 50g, of which sugars 3g; Fat 13g, of which saturates 4g; Cholesterol 184mg; Calcium 82mg; Fibre 1.7g; Sodium 0.9g.
p268 Yogurt Chicken and Rice Energy 606Kcal/2542kJ; Protein 43g; Carbohydrate 78g, of which sugars 17g; Fat 14g, of which saturates 6g; Cholesterol 220mg; Calcium 223mg; Fibre 0.8g; Sodium 0.5g.

p269 Thai Fried Rice with Chillies Energy 562Kcal/2347kJ; Protein 23g; Carbohydrate 81g, of which sugars 5g; Fat 16g, of which saturates 8g; Cholesterol 39mg; Calcium 35mg; Fibre 3.4g; Sodium 0.1g.
p270 Madras Curry with Spicy Rice Energy 647Kcal/2699kJ; Protein 46g; Carbohydrate 53g, of which sugars 6g; Fat 29g, of which saturates 10g; Cholesterol 128mg; Calcium 82mg; Fibre 1.9g; Sodium 0.6g.
p274 Mushrooms with Chipotle Chillies Energy 87Kcal/359kJ; Protein 2g; Carbohydrate 3g, of which sugars 2g; Fat 8g, of which saturates 1g; Cholesterol 0mg; Calcium 12mg; Fibre 1.2g; Sodium 0.1g.
p275 Red Hot Cauliflower Energy 65Kcal/271kJ; Protein 5g; Carbohydrate 5g, of which sugars 4g; Fat 3g, of which saturates 2g; Cholesterol 9mg; Calcium 67mg; Fibre 1.5g; Sodium 0.3g.
p276 Beans in Hot Sauce Energy 149Kcal/621kJ; Protein 8g; Carbohydrate 15g, of which sugars 7g; Fat 7g, of which saturates 1g; Cholesterol 0mg; Calcium 49mg; Fibre 8.1g; Sodium 0.1g.
p277 Bean and Cauliflower Curry Energy 262Kcal/1094kJ; Protein 11g; Carbohydrate 25g, of which sugars 6g; Fat 14g, of which saturates 8g; Cholesterol 11mg; Calcium 82mg; Fibre 6.6g; Sodium 0.6g.
p278 Thai Asparagus Energy 414Kcal/1738kJ; Protein 14g; Carbohydrate 65g, of which sugars 23g; Fat 12g, of which saturates 2g; Cholesterol 0mg; Calcium 157mg; Fibre 1.8g; Sodium 0.2g.
p279 Spring Onions with Romesco Sauce Energy 202Kcal/840kJ; Protein 3g; Carbohydrate 16g, of which sugars 4g; Fat 14g, of which saturates 2g; Cholesterol 0mg; Calcium 39mg; Fibre 1.9g; Sodium 0.1g.
p280 Masala Mashed Potatoes Energy 208Kcal/869kJ; Protein 3g; Carbohydrate 26g, of which sugars 1g; Fat 11g, of which saturates 2g; Cholesterol 0mg; Calcium 14mg; Fibre 2.0g; Sodium 0.6g.
p280 Spicy Cabbage Energy 132Kcal/544kJ; Protein 2g; Carbohydrate 8g, of which sugars 7g; Fat 11g, of which saturates 2g; Cholesterol 0mg; Calcium 49mg; Fibre 2.4g; Sodium 0.3g.
p282 Sichuan Sizzler Energy 95Kcal/395kJ; Protein 2g; Carbohydrate 6g, of which sugars 5g; Fat 7g, of which saturates 1g; Cholesterol 0mg; Calcium 24mg; Fibre 3.3g; Sodium 0.5g.
p283 Steamed Vegetables with Thai Spicy Dip Energy 114Kcal/479kJ; Protein 10g; Carbohydrate 14g, of which sugars 11g; Fat 2g, of which saturates 0g; Cholesterol 0mg; Calcium 116mg; Fibre 7.4g; Sodium 1.0g.
p284 Pancakes Stuffed with Lightly Spiced Squash Energy 784Kcal/3261kJ; Protein 26g; Carbohydrate 53g, of which sugars 14g; Fat 54g, of which saturates 21g; Cholesterol 199mg; Calcium 424mg; Fibre 6.5g; Sodium 0.8g.
p286 Chilli and Pak Choi Omelette Parcels Energy 183Kcal/759kJ; Protein 12g; Carbohydrate 5g, of which sugars 4g; Fat 13g, of which saturates 3g; Cholesterol 232mg; Calcium 111mg; Fibre 2.2g; Sodium 0.5g.

p287 Spicy Root Vegetable Gratin Energy 284Kcal/1192kJ; Protein 7g; Carbohydrate 39g, of which sugars 9g; Fat 13g, of which saturates 8g; Cholesterol 35mg; Calcium 130mg; Fibre 5.1g; Sodium 0.2g.
p288 Courgette Torte Energy 387Kcal/1604kJ; Protein 17g; Carbohydrate 13g, of which sugars 4g; Fat 30g, of which saturates 11g; Cholesterol 210mg; Calcium 321mg; Fibre 1.7g; Sodium 0.4g.
p289 Okra, Chilli and Tomato Tagine Energy 116Kcal/485kJ; Protein 4g; Carbohydrate 10g, of which sugars 8g; Fat 7g, of which saturates 1g; Cholesterol 0mg; Calcium 164mg; Fibre 5.4g; Sodium 0.1g.
p290 Peppers Filled with Spiced Vegetables Energy 141Kcal/582kJ; Protein 1g; Carbohydrate 5g, of which sugars 3g; Fat 14g, of which saturates 3g; Cholesterol 0mg; Calcium 25mg; Fibre 1.6g; Sodium 0.1g.
p292 Chilli, Tomato and Spinach Pizza Energy 559Kcal/2345kJ; Protein 26g; Carbohydrate 59g, of which sugars 12g; Fat 26g, of which saturates 9g; Cholesterol 35mg; Calcium 603mg; Fibre 4.9g; Sodium 1.0g.
p293 Jalapeño and Onion Quiche Energy 465Kcal/1934kJ; Protein 14g; Carbohydrate 29g, of which sugars 6g; Fat 34g, of which saturates 15g; Cholesterol 210mg; Calcium 238mg; Fibre 1.7g; Sodium 0.6g.
p294 Jamaican Black Bean Pot Energy 259Kcal/1093kJ; Protein 8g; Carbohydrate 44g, of which sugars 28g; Fat 7g, of which saturates 1g; Cholesterol 0mg; Calcium 157mg; Fibre 4.9g; Sodium 0.4g.
p295 Chilli Cheese Tortilla with Fresh Tomato and Coriander Salsa Energy 432Kcal/1798kJ; Protein 24g; Carbohydrate 14g, of which sugars 5g; Fat 32g, of which saturates 12g; Cholesterol 384mg; Calcium 352mg; Fibre 2.1g; Sodium 0.8g.
p296 Black Bean and Chilli Burritos Energy 742Kcal/3119kJ; Protein 38g; Carbohydrate 77g, of which sugars 12g; Fat 33g, of which saturates 16g; Cholesterol 77mg; Calcium 611mg; Fibre 4.7g; Sodium 1.9g.
p297 Kenyan Mung Bean Stew Energy 235Kcal/990kJ; Protein 16g; Carbohydrate 31g, of which sugars 5g; Fat 6g, of which saturates 3g; Cholesterol 13mg; Calcium 32mg; Fibre 1.2g; Sodium 0.1g.
p298 Black-eyed Bean Stew with Spicy Pumpkin Energy 453Kcal/1906kJ; Protein 22g; Carbohydrate 58g, of which sugars 16g; Fat 17g, of which saturates 9g; Cholesterol 18mg; Calcium 182mg; Fibre 12.0g; Sodium 0.2g.
p299 Red Bean Chilli Energy 240Kcal/1011kJ; Protein 13g; Carbohydrate 35g, of which sugars 10g; Fat 7g, of which saturates 1g; Cholesterol 0mg; Calcium 79mg; Fibre 5.4g; Sodium 1.2g.
p300 Egg and Green Lentil Curry with Green Chillies and Ginger Energy 298Kcal/1248kJ; Protein 18g; Carbohydrate 17g, of which sugars 6g; Fat 18g, of which saturates 3g; Cholesterol 357mg; Calcium 104mg; Fibre 3.0g; Sodium 0.9g.

p301 Lentil Dhal with Chillies and Roasted Garlic Energy 383Kcal/1606kJ; Protein 17g; Carbohydrate 42g, of which sugars 8g; Fat 18g, of which saturates 8g; Cholesterol 29mg; Calcium 79mg; Fibre 4.8g; Sodium 0.2g.
p302 Sichuan Spicy Tofu Energy 189Kcal/787kJ; Protein 12g; Carbohydrate 5g, of which sugars 2g; Fat 14g, of which saturates 3g; Cholesterol 16mg; Calcium 301mg; Fibre 0.5g; Sodium 0.2g.
p303 Tofu and Green Bean Red Curry Energy 97Kcal/412kJ; Protein 5g; Carbohydrate 14g, of which sugars 11g; Fat 3g, of which saturates 1g; Cholesterol 0mg; Calcium 214mg; Fibre 1.3g; Sodium 0.7g.
p304 Bengali-style Vegetables Energy 161Kcal/673kJ; Protein 6g; Carbohydrate 17g, of which sugars 8g; Fat 8g, of which saturates 5g; Cholesterol 21mg; Calcium 106mg; Fibre 2.4g; Sodium 0.1g.
p305 Balti-style Vegetables Energy 89Kcal/371kJ; Protein 3g; Carbohydrate 9g, of which sugars 8g; Fat 5g, of which saturates 1g; Cholesterol 0mg; Calcium 46mg; Fibre 3.1g; Sodium 0.5g.
p306 Balti Split Peas with Green and Red Chillies Energy 176Kcal/740kJ; Protein 8g; Carbohydrate 23g, of which sugars 5g; Fat 6g, of which saturates 1g; Cholesterol 0mg; Calcium 36mg; Fibre 2.9g; Sodium 0.1g.
p307 Hot and Spicy Potatoes Energy 255Kcal/1070kJ; Protein 4g; Carbohydrate 29g, of which sugars 3g; Fat 15g, of which saturates 2g; Cholesterol 0mg; Calcium 20mg; Fibre 2.4g; Sodium 0.1g.
p308 Potatoes with Red Chillies Energy 131Kcal/551kJ; Protein 2g; Carbohydrate 19g, of which sugars 2g; Fat 6g, of which saturates 1g; Cholesterol 0mg; Calcium 17mg; Fibre 1.1g; Sodium 0.5g.
p309 Bombay Potatoes Energy 208Kcal/869kJ; Protein 4g; Carbohydrate 24g, of which sugars 6g; Fat 12g, of which saturates 1g; Cholesterol 0mg; Calcium 59mg; Fibre 2.2g; Sodium 0.1g.
p312 Roasted Pepper and Tomato Salad Energy 143Kcal/594kJ; Protein 2g; Carbohydrate 14g, of which sugars 12g; Fat 9g, of which saturates 1g; Cholesterol 0mg; Calcium 31mg; Fibre 3.4g; Sodium 0.1g.
p313 Spinach and Serrano Chilli Salad Energy 194Kcal/801kJ; Protein 5g; Carbohydrate 7g, of which sugars 5g; Fat 16g, of which saturates 6g; Cholesterol 18mg; Calcium 221mg; Fibre 3.4g; Sodium 0.2g.

p314 Vinegared Chilli Cabbage Energy 80Kcal/333kJ; Protein 2g; Carbohydrate 6g, of which sugars 6g; Fat 5g, of which saturates 3g; Cholesterol 13mg; Calcium 58mg; Fibre 2.4g; Sodium 0.1g.

p314 Coleslaw in Triple-hot Dressing Energy 113Kcal/466kJ; Protein 1g; Carbohydrate 4g, of which sugars 4g; Fat 10g, of which saturates 1g; Cholesterol 0mg; Calcium 36mg; Fibre 1.6g; Sodium 0.2g.

p316 Kachumbali Salad Energy 54Kcal/228kJ; Protein 2g; Carbohydrate 11g, of which sugars 9g; Fat 1g, of which saturates 0g; Cholesterol 0mg; Calcium 39mg; Fibre 2.7g; Sodium 0.1g.

p316 Coconut Chilli Relish Energy 179Kcal/737kJ; Protein 2g; Carbohydrate 2g, of which sugars 2g; Fat 18g, of which saturates 16g; Cholesterol 0mg; Calcium 9mg; Fibre 3.7g; Sodium 0.4g.

p318 Stir-fried Chilli Greens Energy 265Kcal/1101kJ; Protein 17g; Carbohydrate 11g, of which sugars 6g; Fat 17g, of which saturates 4g; Cholesterol 191mg; Calcium 226mg; Fibre 2.4g; Sodium 0.8g.

p319 Green Bean and Chilli Pepper Salad Energy 284Kcal/1175kJ; Protein 3g; Carbohydrate 11g, of which sugars 9g; Fat 25g, of which saturates 4g; Cholesterol 0mg; Calcium 73mg; Fibre 5.4g; Sodium 0.1g.

p320 Spicy Vegetable Ribbons Energy 143Kcal/593kJ; Protein 5g; Carbohydrate 10g, of which sugars 7g; Fat 10g, of which saturates 2g; Cholesterol 0mg; Calcium 94mg; Fibre 3.1g; Sodium 0.2g.

p321 Green Papaya and Chilli Salad Energy 95Kcal/397kJ; Protein 3g; Carbohydrate 13g, of which sugars 8g; Fat 4g, of which saturates 1g; Cholesterol 0mg; Calcium 30mg; Fibre 1.9g; Sodium 0.6g.

p322 Butternut Squash and Feta Salad Energy 421Kcal/1746kJ; Protein 11g; Carbohydrate 17g, of which sugars 11g; Fat 35g, of which saturates 8g; Cholesterol 26mg; Calcium 234mg; Fibre 3.7g; Sodium 0.9g.

p323 Couscous and Chilli Salad Energy 192Kcal/799kJ; Protein 4g; Carbohydrate 25g, of which sugars 2g; Fat 9g, of which saturates 1g; Cholesterol 0mg; Calcium 36mg; Fibre 0.8g; Sodium 0.4g.

p324 Sweet Potato, Pepper and Chilli Salad Energy 270Kcal/1151kJ; Protein 6g; Carbohydrate 61g, of which sugars 21g; Fat 2g, of which saturates 1g; Cholesterol 4mg; Calcium 156mg; Fibre 7.2g; Sodium 0.2g.

p325 Gado-gado with Peanut and Chilli Sauce Energy 613Kcal/2560kJ; Protein 24g; Carbohydrate 45g, of which sugars 22g; Fat 39g, of which saturates 8g; Cholesterol 125mg; Calcium 98mg; Fibre 7.7g; Sodium 0.6g.

p326 Hot Hot Cajun Potato Salad Energy 402Kcal/1666kJ; Protein 6g; Carbohydrate 15g, of which sugars 3g; Fat 35g, of which saturates 6g; Cholesterol 147mg; Calcium 34mg; Fibre 1.4g; Sodium 0.4g.

p327 Chayote Salad Energy 132Kcal/546kJ; Protein 1g; Carbohydrate 6g, of which sugars 5g; Fat 11g, of which saturates 2g; Cholesterol 0mg; Calcium 23mg; Fibre 1.5g; Sodium 0.1g.

p328 Spicy Potato Salad Energy 179Kcal/754kJ; Protein 4g; Carbohydrate 32g, of which sugars 7g; Fat 5g, of which saturates 1g; Cholesterol 5mg; Calcium 34mg; Fibre 3.1g; Sodium 0.1g.

p329 Peppery Bean Salad Energy 312Kcal/1317kJ; Protein 18g; Carbohydrate 43g, of which sugars 6g; Fat 9g, of which saturates 1g; Cholesterol 0mg; Calcium 112mg; Fibre 10.9g; Sodium 0.7g.

p330 Piquant Shellfish Salad Energy 397Kcal/1699kJ; Protein 28g; Carbohydrate 44g, of which sugars 2g; Fat 12g, of which saturates 2g; Cholesterol 219mg; Calcium 147mg; Fibre 2.0g; Sodium 1.0g.

p331 Pink and Green Salad Energy 440Kcal/1843kJ; Protein 19g; Carbohydrate 44g, of which sugars 2g; Fat 22g, of which saturates 4g; Cholesterol 125mg; Calcium 74mg; Fibre 3.0g; Sodium 0.2g.

p332 Thai Shellfish Salad with Chilli Dressing and Frizzled Shallots Energy 297Kcal/1241kJ; Protein 17g; Carbohydrate 17g, of which sugars 15g; Fat 18g, of which saturates 3g; Cholesterol 158mg; Calcium 98mg; Fibre 3.3g; Sodium 1.1g.

p334 Scallop Conchiglie Energy 528Kcal/2223kJ; Protein 27g; Carbohydrate 62g, of which sugars 4g; Fat 21g, of which saturates 5g; Cholesterol 43mg; Calcium 49mg; Fibre 2.6g; Sodium 0.3g.

p335 Spicy Squid Salad Energy 152Kcal/637kJ; Protein 19g; Carbohydrate 6g, of which sugars 4g; Fat 6g, of which saturates 1g; Cholesterol 253mg; Calcium 37mg; Fibre 1.0g; Sodium 0.3g.

p336 Chilli Chicken Salad Energy 151Kcal/639kJ; Protein 26g; Carbohydrate 6g, of which sugars 1g; Fat 2g, of which saturates 1g; Cholesterol 101mg; Calcium 17mg; Fibre 0.2g; Sodium 0.4g.

p336 Thai Beef Salad Energy 202Kcal/845kJ; Protein 28g; Carbohydrate 5g, of which sugars 3g; Fat 8g, of which saturates 3g; Cholesterol 57mg; Calcium 27mg; Fibre 0.9g; Sodium 0.4g.

p338 Chicken, Vegetable and Chilli Salad Energy 205Kcal/855kJ; Protein 20g; Carbohydrate 8g, of which sugars 6g; Fat 10g, of which saturates 2g; Cholesterol 59mg; Calcium 69mg; Fibre 3.0g; Sodium 0.1g.

p339 Thai Beef and Mushroom Salad Energy 328Kcal/1370kJ; Protein 37g; Carbohydrate 9g, of which sugars 2g; Fat 16g, of which saturates 6g; Cholesterol 103mg; Calcium 16mg; Fibre 0.2g; Sodium 0.4g.

p342 Fresh Pineapple with Ginger Energy 167Kcal/704kJ; Protein 1g; Carbohydrate 31g, of which sugars 30g; Fat 3g, of which saturates 2g; Cholesterol 0mg; Calcium 27mg; Fibre 1.7g; Sodium 0.1g.

p343 Coconut and Nutmeg Ice Cream Energy 253Kcal/1065kJ; Protein 9g; Carbohydrate 34g, of which sugars 34g; Fat 10g, of which saturates 6g; Cholesterol 35mg; Calcium 305mg; Fibre 0g; Sodium 0.2g.

p344 Spicy Noodle Pudding Energy 681Kcal/2849kJ; Protein 20g; Carbohydrate 70g, of which sugars 34g; Fat 38g, of which saturates 19g; Cholesterol 197mg; Calcium 188mg; Fibre 1.9g; Sodium 0.5g.

p345 Spiced Nutty Bananas Energy 480Kcal/2011kJ; Protein 8g; Carbohydrate 60g, of which sugars 53g; Fat 20g, of which saturates 10g; Cholesterol 11mg; Calcium 34mg; Fibre 4.6g; Sodium 0.1g.

p346 Caramel Rice Pudding Energy 364Kcal/1534kJ; Protein 10g; Carbohydrate 59g, of which sugars 49g; Fat 11g, of which saturates 7g; Cholesterol 37mg; Calcium 336mg; Fibre 2.7g; Sodium 0.2g.

p346 Spiced Rice Pudding Energy 607Kcal/2251kJ; Protein 14g; Carbohydrate 103g, of which sugars 79g; Fat 19g, of which saturates 10g; Cholesterol 56mg; Calcium 418mg; Fibre 1.3g; Sodium 0.2g.

p348 Baklava Energy 1160Kcal/4879kJ; Protein 19g; Carbohydrate 153g, of which sugars 113g; Fat 56g, of which saturates 18g; Cholesterol 58mg; Calcium 77mg; Fibre 5.0g; Sodium 0.3g.

p349 Spiced Bread Pudding Energy 971Kcal/4045kJ; Protein 23g; Carbohydrate 73g, of which sugars 34g; Fat 66g, of which saturates 28g; Cholesterol 165mg; Calcium 313mg; Fibre 4.5g; Sodium 0.2g.

p350 Date and Nut Pastries Energy 178Kcal/747kJ; Protein 3g; Carbohydrate 18g, of which sugars 8g; Fat 11g, of which saturates 4g; Cholesterol 15mg; Calcium 36mg; Fibre 1.1g; Sodium 0.1g.

p351 Cinnamon Balls Energy 96Kcal/401kJ; Protein 3g; Carbohydrate 6g, of which sugars 6g; Fat 7g, of which saturates 1g; Cholesterol 0mg; Calcium 34mg; Fibre 0.9g; Sodium 0.1g.

p352 Apple and Cinnamon Crumble Cake Energy 6510Kcal/27296kJ; Protein 60g; Carbohydrate 838g, of which sugars 408g; Fat 348g, of which saturates 226g; Cholesterol 778mg; Calcium 1957mg; Fibre 363g; Sodium 3.9g.

p354 Banana Ginger Cake Energy 3210Kcal/13561kJ; Protein 50g; Carbohydrate 598g, of which sugars 326g; Fat 85g, of which saturates 15g; Cholesterol 233mg; Calcium 468mg; Fibre 19.7g; Sodium 3.3g.

p355 Spiced Date and Walnut Cake Energy 2624Kcal/11066kJ; Protein 61g; Carbohydrate 429g, of which sugars 243g; Fat 86g, of which saturates 10g; Cholesterol 8mg; Calcium 714mg; Fibre 34.8g; Sodium 0.2g.

p356 Mexican Bread Pudding Energy 513Kcal/2160kJ; Protein 8.8g; Carbohydrate 55g, of which sugars 28g; Fat 29g, of which saturates 15g; Cholesterol 8mg; Calcium 27mg; Fibre 4.6g; Sodium 0.3g.

p356 Drunken Plantain Energy 286Kcal/1212kJ; Protein 2.7g; Carbohydrate 36g, of which sugars 17g; Fat 13g, of which saturates 5.3g; Cholesterol 21mg; Calcium 37mg; Fibre 4.8g; Sodium 0.1g.

p358 Cinnamon Rolls Energy 96Kcal/403kJ; Protein 2g; Carbohydrate 16g, of which sugars 4g; Fat 2g, of which saturates 2g; Cholesterol 2mg; Calcium 27mg; Fibre 0.5g; Sodium 0.1g.

p359 Peach Kuchen Energy 522Kcal/2213kJ; Protein 7g; Carbohydrate 83g, of which sugars 51g; Fat 20g, of which saturates 12g; Cholesterol 108mg; Calcium 180mg; Fibre 2.5g; Sodium 0.2g.

p360 Caribbean Fruit and Rum Cake Energy 10186Kcal/42839kJ; Protein 147g; Carbohydrate 1510g, of which sugars 1175g; Fat 446g, of which saturates 254g; Cholesterol 3277mg; Calcium 3128mg; Fibre 49.8g; Sodium 6.0g.

p364 Spiced Mocha Drink Energy 289Kcal/1207kJ; Protein 5g; Carbohydrate 26g, of which sugars 26g; Fat 19g, of which saturates 12g; Cholesterol 27mg; Calcium 133mg; Fibre 0.4g; Sodium 0.1g.

p365 Mulled Wine Energy 131Kcal/550kJ; Protein 0g; Carbohydrate 14g, of which sugars 14g; Fat 0g, of which saturates 0g; Cholesterol 0mg; Calcium 22mg; Fibre 0.4g; Sodium 0.1g.

p366 Sangrita Energy 155Kcal/655kJ; Protein 1g; Carbohydrate 22g, of which sugars 22g; Fat 0g, of which saturates 0g; Cholesterol 0mg; Calcium 18mg; Fibre 0.8g; Sodium 0.3g.

p367 Sangria Energy 199Kcal/835kJ; Protein 0g; Carbohydrate 23g, of which sugars 23g; Fat 0g, of which saturates 0g; Cholesterol 0mg; Calcium 17mg; Fibre 0g; Sodium 0.1g.

p368 Bloody Maria Energy 129Kcal/545kJ; Protein 1g; Carbohydrate 18g, of which sugars 18g; Fat 0g, of which saturates 0g; Cholesterol 0mg; Calcium 12mg; Fibre 0.5g; Sodium 0.4g.

p369 Margarita Energy 194Kcal/815kJ; Protein 0g; Carbohydrate 25g, of which sugars 25g; Fat 0g, of which saturates 0g; Cholesterol 0mg; Calcium 2mg; Fibre 0g; Sodium 0.2g.

p370 Demerara Rum Punch Energy 234Kcal/984kJ; Protein 11g; Carbohydrate 26g, of which sugars 26g; Fat 0g, of which saturates 0g; Cholesterol 0mg; Calcium 33mg; Fibre 1.1g; Sodium 0.1g.

p371 Caribbean Cream Stout Punch Energy 483Kcal/2022kJ; Protein 17g; Carbohydrate 46g, of which sugars 46g; Fat 18g, of which saturates 11g; Cholesterol 65mg; Calcium 566mg; Fibre 0g; Sodium 0.4g.

INDEX